Contents

This book is accompanied by additional online material. To access these resources go
to www.koganpage.com/resources and under 'Academic Resources' click on either
'Student Resources' or 'Lecturer Resources' as appropriate.

Introduction

This handbook is designed to provide guidance on the approaches that can be adopted to the development and management of reward systems that will contribute to improving organizational, team and individual performance while respecting and catering for the needs of employees.

The book is evidence-based in that it makes use of the practical lessons learned from academic research projects but also refers to the considerable number of reward surveys and case studies produced over the last few years by e-reward together with surveys conducted by the Chartered Institute of Personnel and Development (CIPD).

The theme of the book is that reward delivers performance. This is especially the case when a total reward management philosophy is adopted: that is, an integrated approach to reward designed to enhance engagement by responding to individual as well as organizational needs and making appropriate use of both financial and non-financial rewards. It is in line with the main message of the new performance and reward professional map produced by the CIPD. This spells out that those involved in reward management are there to build a high-performance culture by delivering programmes that recognize and reward critical skills, capabilities, experience and performance, and ensure that reward systems are market based, equitable and cost effective.

Plan of the book

The book consists of the following parts:

Part I: Essentials of reward management

This provides an overview of what reward management is about and examines the three fundamental elements of reward management: the structure and elements of reward systems, the concept of total rewards, and the contribution made by strategic reward management processes. This part also covers the special features of international reward policy and practice.

Part II: Performance and reward

The aim of this part is to explore the relationship between performance and reward. It starts with an examination of how performance management functions as part of the reward system at individual, group and organizational levels and how it helps to create a performance culture. On the grounds that engagement and discretionary effort contribute significantly to high performance, Chapter 7 deals with how reward can enhance them. The following two chapters examine the features of financial and non-financial rewards to provide a conceptual framework for the next five chapters, which are concerned with describing contingent reward and recognition schemes and how they impact on performance.

Part III: Valuing and grading jobs

This part deals with the factors affecting pay levels and fundamental processes of valuing jobs and the characteristics of the grade and pay structures that are developed on the basis of the outcomes of job evaluation and market pricing. It also deals with equal pay issues.

Part IV: Rewarding special groups

Consideration is given in this part to the reward requirements of the special groups of people who are employed in organizations – directors, sales and customer service staff, knowledge workers and manual workers. Reward practices may differ between these groups and the result may be a degree of segmentation in the reward system.

Part V: Employee benefit and pension schemes

This part focuses on policies and practices in the provision of benefits and pensions and the flexible benefit schemes that allow an element of choice to employees.

Part VI: The practice of reward management

The practice of reward management is a complex business covering the development, management and evaluation of reward systems and the allocation of responsibility for reward.

Part I
Essentials of Reward Management

An Overview of Reward Management

Key concepts and terms

- Best fit
- Best practice
- Cognitive evaluation theory
- Content (needs) theory
- Discretionary effort
- Distributive justice
- Equity theory
- Evidence-based reward management
- Expectancy theory
- Goal theory
- Horizontal integration
- Human capital advantage
- Human capital management
- Human process advantage
- Incentive alignment
- Instrumentality theory
- Integrated reward management
- Internal integration
- Motivation
- Principal agent theory
- Procedural justice
- Process theory
- Psychological contract
- Resource-based view
- Reward management
- Reward system
- Segmentation
- Strategic integration
- Strategic reward
- Total reward
- Vertical integration

Learning outcomes

On completing this chapter you should be able to define these key concepts. You should also know about:

- The characteristics of reward management
- The reward management framework
- The aims of reward management
- The concepts of reward management

- Valuing people and jobs
- The contextual factors affecting reward
- Motivation theory

Introduction

The purpose of this introductory chapter is to set the scene for the rest of the book by explaining what is meant by reward management, setting out its aims, summarizing how they can be achieved and examining its underpinning concepts.

Reward management defined

Reward management is concerned with the strategies, policies and processes required to ensure that the value of people and the contribution they make to achieving organizational, departmental and team goals is recognized and rewarded. It is about the design, implementation and maintenance of reward systems (interrelated reward processes, practices and procedures) that aim to satisfy the needs of both the organization and its stakeholders and to operate fairly, equitably and consistently. These systems will include arrangements for assessing the value of jobs through job evaluation and market pricing, the design and management of grade and pay structures, performance management processes, schemes for rewarding and recognizing people according to their individual performance or contribution and/or team or organizational performance, and the provision of employee benefits. Reward systems are described in more detail in Chapter 2.

It should be emphasized that reward management is not just about financial rewards, pay and employee benefit. It is equally concerned with non-financial rewards such as recognition, learning and development opportunities and increased job responsibility.

Characteristics of reward management

Reward management is fundamentally about people. It is stakeholder orientated, integrated, strategic and evidence based.

Reward management and people

Reward management is concerned with people – especially the employees who are rewarded for their efforts, skills and contribution but also the directors, managers and reward specialists who plan, manage and administrate rewards. This is in accordance with the view expressed by Schneider (1987) that:

> *organizations are the people in them:... people make the place.* His point was that: *Attraction to an organization, selection by it, and attrition from it yield particular kinds of persons in an organization. These people determine organizational behaviour... Positive job attitudes for workers in an organization can be expected when the natural inclinations of the persons there are allowed to be reflected in their behaviours by the kinds of processes and structures that have evolved there.*

A stakeholder approach

The purpose of human resource management (HRM) is to meet the needs of all the stakeholders in the business – employees, customers, suppliers and the public at large as well as management and shareholders. Reward management shares that purpose. In doing so, it can make a significant contribution to meeting the varied needs of stakeholders successfully. It is accordingly concerned with improving business performance, shaping the behaviour of employees and developing a climate of trust. And reward management can best do this if it is evidence-based.

But there is also an ethical dimension. Reward management policies in association with HR policies can help to create a working environment that provides for the just, fair and ethical treatment of employees. These are policies about treating people properly and avoiding the creation of unacceptable reward practices that reflect badly on the organization. The bonus schemes for top management operated in the banks and elsewhere in the financial services sector are good examples of where reward policy and practice went wrong. They were against the interests of every stakeholder except the recipients of the huge sums of money involved.

Integrated reward management

Integrated reward management is an approach to reward management that provides for reward policies and practices to be treated as a coherent whole in which the parts contribute in conjunction with one another to ensure that the contribution people make to achieving organizational, departmental and team goals is recognized and rewarded. It consists of a related set of activities that impinge and impact on all aspects of the business and the HRM practices within it. As White (2005) points out, in an integrated approach 'each individual element of reward supports the other to reinforce organizational objectives.'

Integration takes three forms:

- Strategic integration: the vertical integration of reward strategy with business strategy.

- HRM integration: the horizontal integration of reward strategies with other HR strategies, especially those concerned with high performance, engagement, talent management and learning and development.

- Reward integration: the internal integration of reward to ensure that its various aspects cohere and that a total reward philosophy is adopted that means a full range of mutually supporting financial and non-financial rewards is used.

The integrated approach adopted by Aegon UK is:

- Reward: market driven, with overall performance dictating rate of progress of salaries within broad bands rather then existing grades.

- Recruitment: competency based, with multi-assessment processes as the basic approach.

- Performance management: not linked to pay, concentrated on personal development, objective setting and competency development.

- Training and development: targeted on key competencies and emphasizing self-development.

Strategic reward management

Strategic reward can be described as an attitude of mind – to be convinced of the virtue of systematically deciding what must be done and to believe in the need to plan ahead and make the plans happen. In the words of Duncan Brown (2001) strategic reward 'is ultimately a way of thinking that you can apply to any reward issue arising in your organization, to see how you can create value. Its aim is to create reward processes which are based on beliefs about what the organization values and wants to achieve. It does this by aligning reward practices with both business goals and employee values.' Strategic reward focuses on methods of achieving vertical, horizontal and internal integration.

Evidence-based reward management

Evidence-based reward management is the management of reward systems on the basis of fact rather than opinion, on understanding rather than assumptions, on grounded theory rather than dogma. This is in line with the views of the logical positivists (Ayer, 1959) that it is necessary to seek 'analytical truths' and that the fundamental question to ask when examining beliefs is: 'How do you know what you think you know?' It is also in accord with Quine's (1970) opinion that beliefs can only be expressed in statements that 'face the tribunal of experience'.

Use is made in evidence-based reward management of the extensive research conducted over the last 50 years into how reward systems work in organizations and what can be done to improve them. It subjects the theories derived from this research to critical evaluation on their relevance and application in the context of particular organizations. Someone once said that 'theory without practice is sterile, practice without theory is futile.' But it should be remembered that, as Douglas McGregor wrote in 1960, there is nothing as practical as a good theory: that is, one substantiated by rigorous research within organizations that tells you how it is and not how you think it is.

Importantly, evidence-based reward management also makes use of the information obtained from the detailed evaluation of the effectiveness and impact of existing reward practices and from systematic benchmarking. It is concerned with establishing what constitutes good practice, although it does not assume that good practice is necessarily 'best practice'. What works well elsewhere will not necessarily work as well within the organization. In general, best fit is more important than best practice.

The reward management framework

Reward management is a complex process with many interconnecting elements and underpinning concepts. The reward management framework expressed as a concept map is shown in Figure 1.1.

This model of reward is indeed complex but it can be analysed under the headings of aims, strategic reward, contextual factors and reward concepts.

Aims of reward management

In the words of Ghoshal and Bartlett (1995) the overall aim of reward management should be to 'add value to people'. It is not just about attaching value to them. More specifically, the aims are to:

- support the achievement of business goals through high performance;

- develop and support the organization's culture;

- define what is important in terms of behaviours and outcomes;

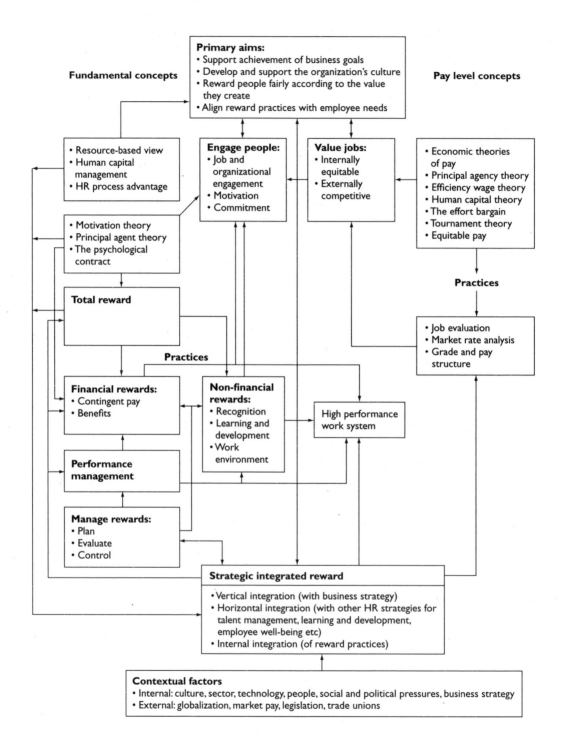

Figure 1.1 The reward management framework

- reward people according to the value they create;
- reward people according to what the organization values;
- align reward practices with employee needs;
- help to attract and retain the high-quality people the organization needs;
- win the engagement of people.

Overall and specific approaches to achieving these aims are described below.

Achieving the aims in general

The overall approach to achieving reward aims is based on a philosophy and takes into account factors related to distributive and procedural justice, fairness, equity, consistency and transparency. It is also concerned with achieving strategic alignment and cultural/contextual fit, developing a high-performance culture and segmentation.

Reward philosophy

Reward management is based on a well-articulated philosophy – a set of beliefs and guiding principles that are consistent with the values of the organization and help to enact them. The philosophy recognizes that if HRM is about investing in human capital from which a reasonable return is required, then it is proper to reward people differentially according to their contribution (ie the return on investment they generate).

The philosophy of reward management also recognizes that it must be strategic in the sense that it addresses longer-term issues relating to how people should be valued for what they do and what they achieve. Reward strategies and the processes that are required to implement them have to flow from the business strategy.

Reward management adopts a 'total rewards' approach that emphasizes the importance of considering all aspects of reward as a coherent whole that is linked to other HR initiatives designed to win the engagement of employees and further their development. This requires the integration of reward strategies with other HRM strategies, including talent management and human resource development. Reward management is an integral part of an HRM approach to managing people.

Distributive justice

As defined by Leventhal (1980), distributive justice refers to how rewards are provided to people. They will feel that they have been treated justly if they believe that the rewards have been distributed in accordance with the value of their contribution, that they receive what was promised to them and that they get what they need.

Procedural justice

Procedural justice refers to the ways in which managerial decisions are made and reward policies are put into practice. The five factors that affect perceptions of procedural justice as identified by Tyler and Bies (1990) are:

- The viewpoint of employees is given proper consideration.
- Personal bias towards employees is suppressed.
- The criteria for decisions are applied consistently to all employees.
- Employees are provided with early feedback about the outcome of decisions.
- Employees are provided with adequate explanations of why decisions have been made.

Fairness

A fair reward system is one that operates in accordance with the principles of distributive and procedural justice. It also conforms to the 'felt-fair' principle formulated by Eliot Jaques (1961). This states that pay systems will be fair if they are felt to be fair. The assumptions underpinning the theory are that:

- There is an unrecognized standard of fair payment for any level of work.
- Unconscious knowledge of the standard is shared among the population at work.
- Pay must match the level of work and the capacity of the individual to do it.
- People should not receive less pay than they deserve by comparison with their fellow workers.

This felt-fair principle has passed into the common language of those involved in reward management. It is sometimes used as the final arbiter of how a job should be graded (the so-called 'felt-fair' test), possibly overriding the conclusions reached by an analytical job evaluation exercise. Such tests are in danger of simply reproducing existing prejudices about relative job values.

Equity

Equity is achieved when people are rewarded appropriately in relation to others within the organization. Equitable reward processes ensure that relativities between jobs are measured as objectively as possible and that equal pay is provided for work of equal value.

Consistency

A consistent approach to reward management means that decisions on pay do not vary arbitrarily – without due cause – between different people or at different times. They do not deviate irrationally from what would generally be regarded as fair and equitable.

Transparency

Transparency exists when people understand how reward processes function and how they are affected by them. The reasons for pay decisions are explained at the time they are made. Employees have a voice in the development of reward policies and practices.

Strategic alignment

The strategic alignment of reward practices ensures that reward initiatives are planned by reference to the requirements of the business strategy and are designed to support the achievement of business goals.

Contextual and culture fit

The design of reward processes should be governed by the context (the characteristics of the organization, its business strategy and the type of employees) and the organization's culture (its values and behavioural norms). The design will be affected by the political and social factors present in the organization.

Account should be taken of good practice elsewhere, but this should not be regarded as best practice (ie universally applicable).

Performance and reward

Reward strategies, policies and practices focus on performance and contribute to the achievement of a high-performance culture. This is one in which people are aware of the need to perform well and behave accordingly in order to meet or exceed expectations. Employees will be engaged with their jobs and the organization and be prepared to exercise productive discretionary effort in getting their work done. Such a culture embraces a number of interrelated processes that together make an impact on the performance of the organization through its people in such areas as productivity, quality, levels of customer service, growth, profits and, ultimately, in profit-making firms, the delivery of increased shareholder value. In our more heavily service and knowledge-based economy, employees have become the most important determinant of organizational success. The subject of performance and reward is dealt with more thoroughly in Chapter 6.

Segmentation

Different segments of the workforce, and individuals at different stages in their career, will be motivated by different combinations of rewards. A total rewards package should be tailored to meet these different needs. Organizations may consider segmenting their package for different types of jobs, or to reflect the different types and levels of contribution people make, or to respond to different needs. For example, it is usually appropriate to have different reward packages for sales and customer services staff because the nature of the sales or service role is different from that of, say, administration.

Achieving the specific aims

Support the achievement of business goals and high performance

Reward management supports the achievement of business goals by helping to ensure that the organization has the talented and engaged people it needs. It contributes to the achievement of high performance by ensuring that the reward system recognizes and encourages it.

Support and develop the organization's culture

Reward management can support and help to change the organization's culture by:

- stressing the importance of high performance through contingent pay and performance management;
- reinforcing the behaviours required in a high-performance culture;
- emphasizing that upholding core values is a major criterion when assessing performance;
- linking rewards specifically to behaviour that is in line with core values;
- demonstrating that the organization cares about the well-being of employees through the provision of pensions and other benefits.

Define the right behaviours and outcomes

Reward management can define expectations through performance management and contingent pay schemes.

Reward people according to the value they create and what the organization values

People are assessed according to the contribution they make to achieving organizational goals and rewarded accordingly. Having defined expectations, reward management can provide for people to be rewarded in line with the degree to which people meet them. Managers should be aware of the results expected from people and the behaviour needed to achieve these results and to support the organization's values. The reward system should ensure that the results and behaviour are valued and recognized.

Align reward practices with employee needs

Employees need to be paid fairly for what they do, in line with the principles of distributive and procedural justice and equity as defined above. Their needs for recognition can be directly satisfied by the reward system and a total rewards approach will enable other needs such as those for growth, responsibility and autonomy to be met. Segmentation of rewards may be appropriate to reflect the different needs of employees.

Help to attract and retain high-quality people

Pay levels are important means of attracting people to organizations, although the employer's reputation and the opportunities it provides for career development and scope to use skills and abilities are also important. Decisions to remain with an organization are affected by expectations on pay growth, feelings about the fairness of the reward system and comparisons with what could be earned elsewhere. This is what labour economists call the 'sorting effect'.

Win the engagement of people

Employee engagement takes place when people are interested in and positive, even excited, about their jobs and are prepared to go the extra mile to get them done to the best of their ability. A total rewards system (see Chapter 3) can win the engagement of people through a mix of elements tailored to meet individual needs. These elements will include financial incentives but also other forms of non-financial rewards in the form of recognition, scope for growth and job design.

Factors influencing the achievement of the aims

The achievement of the aims is influenced by the context and the reward strategy as affected by the context. The aims of total reward management are also affected by the concepts of the resource-based view, human capital management, human process advantage and HR process advantage.

Contextual factors

Reward strategies and practices must take account of the internal and external context – the concept of 'best fit'.

Internal context

The characteristic features of the internal context are as follows.

The organization's culture

Organizational culture consists of shared values, norms and assumptions that influence the way people act and the way things get done. In reward management, the most important aspects of culture that need to be taken into account are the core values of the organization, which express beliefs on what sort of behaviour is desirable. Reward practices should fit in with and support the culture and they can help to reshape it.

The organization's business or sector

The business or sector of the organization, for example manufacturing, financial services, retail services, transport, media, public sector services, not-for-profit services or education – will govern its ethos and therefore its core values. It will influence the type of people it employs and the degree to which it is subject to turbulence and change. All these factors will contribute to the reward strategy.

Work environment

The ways in which work is organized, managed and carried out will influence pay structure and the use of contingent pay. The introduction of new technology may result in consider-able changes to systems and processes. Different skills are required, new methods of working and therefore reward are developed. The result may be an extension of the skills base of the organization and its employees, including multiskilling (ensuring that people have a range of skills that enable them to work flexibly on a variety of tasks, often within a teamworking environment). Traditional piecework pay systems in manufacturing industry have been replaced by higher fixed pay and rewards focused on quality and employee teamwork.

People

People's occupations may affect their wants and needs. Entrepreneurial directors or sales representatives may be more interested in financial incentives than, say, people engaged in charitable work. Reward strategies and policies should take account of the different needs of people and this may mean segmenting rewards to meet those individual needs.

Business strategy

Where the business is going – the business strategy – determines where reward should go – the reward strategy. Integrating reward and business strategies means combining them as a whole so they contribute effectively to achieving the mission or purpose of the organization.

Political and social climate

Organizational politics and social factors such as the way people interact will affect how the organization functions and therefore what approach to reward management it adopts.

External context

The following aspects of the external context may affect reward management policies.

Globalization

Globalization requires organizations to move people, ideas, products and information around the world to meet local needs. Traditionally, discussions of international reward strategies and practices have tended to focus on an elite of expatriate workers, sourced from headquarter locations and rewarded in isolation from local country staff. We are now seeing a more diverse and complex pattern emerging, requiring a much more strategic approach as described in Chapter 5.

Rates of pay in the market place

The external environment exerts a major influence on rates of pay and pay reviews within organizations. Market or going-rate levels and movements have to be taken into account by organizations if they want their pay to be competitive. Some organizations are affected by national agreements with trade unions.

The economy

The economy, whether it is in a boom or bust mode, will inevitably affect reward policy and practice. A recession such as the one that began in 2008 increases the attention organizations pay to getting value for money and reduces the amounts that can be distributed in the form of base and contingent pay and the scale of benefits provision.

Societal factors

Views about reward held in society at large may affect internal reward policies. For example, the opprobrium levelled in 2009 at 'fat cats' in boardrooms and the bonus culture in the City may possibly have some influence on members of remuneration committees. Again, it may not.

UK employment legislation

The following pieces of UK legislation directly or indirectly affect pay policies and practices:

- The Equal Pay Act 1970 and the Equal Pay (Amendment) Regulations 1983 provide that pay differences are allowable only if the reason for them is not related to the sex of the job holder. The Employment Act 2002 provides for the use of equal pay question-naires. Equal pay legislation is described in Chapter 17.

- The National Minimum Wage Act 1998 provides workers in the UK with a level of pay below which their wages must not fall – regardless of where they live or work or the sector or size of company in which they work. It is not a going rate. The government prescribes by regulation the minimum wage.

- The Working Time Regulations 1998 provide, inter alia, for a limit of 48 hours on average weekly working time, which an individual worker may voluntarily agree to exceed, and a minimum of four week's paid annual leave subject to a 13-week qualify-ing period.

- The Data Protection Act 1998 provides among other things that employees are entitled to make a formal request to access information on the personal data held on them and the uses to which this will be put.

- The Transfer of Undertakings (Protection of Employment) Regulations 1981 (TUPE) provide that when a business or part of a business is transferred, the workers in that business automatically transfer into the employment of the transferee together with their existing terms and conditions of employment (except for pensions) intact and with their accrued periods of continuous service.

- The Financial Services Act 1986 places restrictions on the provision of financial advice to employees. Only those who are directly authorized by one of the regulatory organizations or professional bodies are permitted to give detailed financial advice on investments.

The trade unions

Trade unions influence reward practices at national level through national pay negotiations, pronouncements on such issues as the pay of top executives, and exerting pressure to achieve equal pay. They produce policies and advice for their members on job evaluation (they are in favour of analytical schemes while emphasizing the need for involvement in their design), pay structures (they tend to be against broad-banded structures) and performance-related pay (they are generally hostile to it, preferring the traditional service-related incremental scales).

Fundamental concepts

The following fundamental concepts influence the aims of reward management, reward strategy and how people are valued.

The resource-based view

This is the view that it is the range of resources in an organization, including its human resources, that produces its unique character and creates competitive advantage. HRM delivers added value and helps to achieve sustainable competitive advantage through the strategic development of the organization's rare, hard to imitate and hard to substitute human resources. Boxall (1999) refers to the situation in which people are employed with competitively valuable knowledge and skills, as one that confers 'human capital advantage'.

The role of reward management is to contribute to the acquisition and retention of such people.

Human capital management

The concept of human capital is often associated with the resource-based view. Chatzkel (2004) observes that 'it is human capital that is the differentiator for organizations and the actual basis for competitive advantage'. Human capital management (HCM) is often described as being about measurement in the sense of obtaining, analysing and reporting on data relating to employees that inform HRM decisions. But it is sometimes defined more broadly without the emphasis on measurement. Chatzkel states that 'Human capital management is an integrated effort to manage and develop human capabilities to achieve significantly higher levels of performance.' And Kearns (2005) refers to HCM as 'The total development of human potential expressed as organizational value'. He believes that 'HCM is about creating value through people' and this is a prime purpose of reward management.

Human process advantage

Boxall (1999) notes that a distinction should be made between 'human process advantage' and 'human capital advantage'. The former results from the establishment of 'difficult to imitate, highly evolved processes within the firm', while the latter follows from employing people with competitively valuable knowledge and skills. This suggests that one of the roles of reward management is to differentiate from rather than imitate the 'best practices' of other firms.

Motivation theory

Motivation is the force that energizes, directs and sustains behaviour. Motivation theory explains how motivation works and the factors that determine its strength. It deals with how money and other types of rewards affect the motivation to work and levels of performance, what creates job satisfaction, and the link between job satisfaction and performance. It therefore influences decisions on how people should be valued, the choice and design of financial rewards and the use of non-financial rewards.

A distinction is made between extrinsic and intrinsic motivation. Extrinsic motivation occurs when things are done to or for people to motivate them. These include rewards, such as incentives, increased pay, praise, or promotion, and punishments, such as disciplinary action, withholding pay, or criticism. Intrinsic motivation is provided by the work itself.

There are four main categories of motivation theories as described below.

Instrumentality theory

'Instrumentality' is the belief that if we do one thing it will lead to another. In its crudest form, instrumentality theory states that people only work for money. It assumes that people will be motivated to work if rewards and penalties are tied directly to their performance; thus the awards are contingent upon effective performance. Instrumentality theory has its roots in the scientific management methods of Taylor (1911), who wrote: 'It is impossible, through any long period of time, to get workmen to work much harder than the average men around them unless they are assured a large and permanent increase in their pay.'

Content (needs) theory

This theory focuses on the content of motivation in the shape of needs. It provides guidance on what needs should be satisfied by the reward system if motivation is to occur. The basis of content theory is the belief that an unsatisfied need creates tension and a state of disequilibrium. To restore the balance a goal is identified that will satisfy the need, and a behaviour pathway is selected that will lead to the achievement of the goal and the satisfaction of the need. All behaviour is therefore motivated by unsatisfied needs. The main contributors to needs theory were Alderfer (1972), McClelland (1961) and Maslow (1954). Herzberg (1968) identified a number of 'satisfiers', which are in effect needs.

The main needs identified by these and other writers are those for achievement, recognition, responsibility, autonomy and the opportunity to develop and use skills. These have to be taken into account in deciding how people should be rewarded and also in achieving motivation through job design. But a note of caution is necessary. Content theories propose that to a large extent all people strive for the same fundamental goals. In fact, people are more varied and complex than this. Theories stating that there are strong similarities between people lead to the conclusion that there is 'one best way' to motivate and reward them, which is simply not true. Process theory as described below is based on more realistic, albeit more complex ideas.

Process theory

In process theory, the focus is on the psychological processes or forces that affect motivation, as well as on basic needs. The three main theories are:

- Expectancy theory (Vroom, 1964 and Porter and Lawler, 1968), which states that motivation will be high when people know what they have to do to get a reward, expect that they will be able to get the reward and expect that the reward will be worthwhile.

- Goal theory (Latham and Locke, 1979), which states that motivation and performance are higher when individuals are set specific goals, when goals are difficult but accepted, and when there is feedback on performance.

- Equity theory (Adams, 1965), which states that people will be better motivated if they are treated equitably, and demotivated if they are treated inequitably. There are two forms of equity: distributive equity or distributive justice, which is concerned with the fairness with which people feel they are rewarded in accordance with their contribution and in comparison with others; and procedural equity or procedural justice, which is concerned with the perceptions employees have about the fairness with which company procedures in such areas as performance management, promotion and discipline are being operated.

The main distinction between content and process theory is that the former provides guidance on what needs should be satisfied by a reward system while the latter indicates how they should be satisfied, especially in pay schemes that are contingent on performance, contribution or skill. In their case, process theory is the most important.

Cognitive evaluation theory

Cognitive evaluation theory (CET) as devised by Deci (1975) and Deci and Ryan (1985) argues that placing strong emphasis on monetary rewards decreases people's interest in the work itself, thus dampening a powerful alternative source of motivation. In other words, extrinsic rewards erode intrinsic interest.

Principal agent theory

Principal agent theory, sometimes known as agency theory, is based on the supposition that the separation between the owners (the principals) and the agents (the managers) means that the principals may not have complete control over their agents. The latter may therefore act in ways which conflict with what the principals want. So it is desirable to provide for 'incentive alignment', which means paying for measurable results deemed to be in the best interests of the owners.

The psychological contract

A psychological contract is a set of unwritten expectations that exist between individual employees and their employers. As Guest (2007) noted, it is concerned with: 'The perceptions of both parties to the employment relationship of the reciprocal promises and obligations implied in that relationship'. A psychological contract is a system of beliefs that encompasses the actions employees think are expected of them and what response they expect in return from their employer, and, reciprocally, the actions employers believe are expected of them and what response they expect in return from their employees.

The concept of the psychological contract highlights the fact that employee/employer expectations take the form of unarticulated assumptions. Disappointments on the part of management as well as employees may therefore be inevitable. These disappointments can, however, be alleviated if managements appreciate that one of their key roles is to manage expectations, which means clarifying what they believe employees should achieve, the competencies they should possess and the values they should uphold. All this can be done through reward and performance management.

Pay level concepts

There are a number of explanations of how levels of pay are determined and, therefore, the factors that need to be taken into account in deciding on the value of jobs and the design of grade and pay structures. Economic theories of pay and efficiency wage theory are perhaps the more influential ones but there are other concepts such as human capital, principal agent theory, tournament theory and the effort bargain. These are described in Chapter 15.

Effective reward management

The criteria for judging the effectiveness of a reward management system is the extent to which it:

- is fit for purpose – the contribution it makes to achieving organizational objectives and recognizing the needs and wants of stakeholders;
- is appropriate – fits the culture and context of the organization;
- is designed in accord with what is generally regarded as good practice in the particular context of the organization, subject to the requirement that it must be appropriate;
- functions in line with well-defined guiding principles, which include the need to achieve fairness, equity, consistency and transparency in operating the reward system;
- includes processes for valuing and grading jobs and rewarding people according to their performance or contribution that are properly conceived and function well;
- makes a significant impact on performance through performance management or contributions to high-performance working;
- has produced an attractive employee-value proposition;
- provides rewards that attract and retain people and enlist their engagement;
- maintains competitive and equitable rates of pay;
- incorporates successfully a total rewards approach;
- manages reward processes carefully and obtains value for money;
- provides for the evaluation of reward processes and taking corrective action as necessary;
- communicates to all concerned how the reward system operates and how it affects them;
- provides for the devolution of a reasonable degree of authority to line managers to make reward decisions, taking steps to ensure that they have the skills and support required and that their decisions are in line with reward policy guidelines.

Effective reward in the best performing firms

The best-performing firms as established by Watson Wyatt (2002) view their reward programmes differently from the lower-performing organizations:

- Top firms are more likely to use rewards as tools to engage people in improving business performance.

- These firms make greater efforts than others to communicate their plans and to measure reward plan effectiveness.

- They are more likely than the rest to link rewards to their organization's business strategies.

Reward management: six tips

- Reward people according to the value they create.
- Reward people according to what the organization values and wants to pay for.
- Take account of employee as well as business needs.
- Best fit is preferable to best practice.
- Strive to be different, even unique, when developing reward policy and practice.
- Adopt an evidence-based management approach that involves managing reward systems on the basis of fact rather than opinion, on understanding rather than assumptions, on grounded theory rather than dogma.

References

Adams, J S (1965) Injustice in social exchange, in *Advances in Experimental Psychology*, ed L Berkowitz, Academic Press, New York

Alderfer, C (1972) *Existence, Relatedness and Growth*, Free Press, New York

Ayer, A J (1959) *Logical Positivism*, Free Press, Glencoe, IL

Boxall, P (1999) Human resource strategy and competitive advantage: a longitudinal study of engineering consultancies, *Journal of Management Studies*, **36** (4), pp 443–63

Brown, D (2001) *Reward Strategies: From intent to impact*, CIPD, London

Chatzkel, J L (2004) Human capital: the rules of engagement are changing, *Lifelong Learning in Europe*, **9** (3), pp 139–45

Deci, E L (1975) *Intrinsic Motivation*, Plenum, New York

Deci, E L and Ryan, R M (1985) *Intrinsic Motivation and Self-determination in Human Behavior*, Plenum, New York

Ghoshal, S and Bartlett, C A (1995) Changing the role of top management: beyond structure to process, *Harvard Business Review*, January–February, pp 86–96

Guest, D (2007) HRM: Towards a new psychological contract, in *Oxford Handbook of Human Resource Management*, ed Peter Boxall, John Purcell and Patrick Wright, Oxford University Press, Oxford

Herzberg, F (1968) One more time: how do you motivate your employees? *Harvard Business Review*, January–February, pp 109–20

Jaques, E (1961) *Equitable Payment*, Heinemann, London

Kearns, P (2005) *Human Capital Management*, Reed Business Information, Sutton, Surrey

Latham, G and Locke, E A (1979) Goal setting: a motivational technique that works, *Organizational Dynamics*, Autumn, pp 68–80

Leventhal, G S (1980) What should be done with equity theory? in *Social Exchange: Advances in theory and research*, ed G K Gergen, M S Greenberg and R H Willis, Plenum, New York

Maslow, A (1954) *Motivation and Personality*, Harper & Row, New York

McClelland, D C (1961) *The Achieving Society*, Van Nostrand, New York

McGregor, D (1960) *The Human Side of Enterprise*, McGraw-Hill, New York

Porter, L W and Lawler, E E (1968) *Managerial Attitudes and Performance*, Irwin-Dorsey, Homewood, IL

Quine, W V (1970) *The Web of Belief*, Random House, New York

Schneider, B (1987) The people make the place, *Personnel Psychology*, **40** (2), pp 437–53

Taylor, F W (1911) *Principles of Scientific Management*, Harper, New York

Tyler, T R and Bies, R J (1990) Beyond formal procedures: the interpersonal context of procedural justice, in *Applied Social Psychology and Organizational Settings*, ed J S Carrol, Lawrence Earlbaum, Hillsdale, NJ

Vroom, V (1964) *Work and Motivation*, Wiley, New York

Watson Wyatt (2002) *Strategic Reward Survey*, Watson Wyatt, New York

White, R (2005) A strategic approach to building a consistent global rewards program, *Compensation & Benefits Review*, July/August, pp 23–40

2

The Reward System

- Base pay
- Broad-banded pay structure
- Broad-graded pay structure
- Career-family pay structure
- Combination approach
- Competency-related pay
- Contingent pay
- Contribution-related pay
- Employee benefits
- Flexible benefits
- Grade and pay structure
- Job-based pay
- Job evaluation
- Job family
- Job-family pay structure
- Market rate analysis
- Multi-graded pay structure

- Non-financial rewards
- Pay progression
- Pay spine
- Pension
- Performance management
- Person-based pay
- Reward policy
- Reward practices
- Reward procedures
- Reward processes
- Reward strategy
- Reward system
- Service-related pay
- Skills-based pay
- Spot rate
- Total remuneration
- Total reward

Introduction

A reward system consists of the interrelated processes and practices that combine to ensure that reward management is carried out effectively to the benefit of the organization and the people who work there. It operates in accordance with the principles of systems theory, which as Katz and Kahn (1966) wrote, 'is basically concerned with problems of relationship, of structure and of interdependence'. It has the characteristics of an open system as described by Miller and Rice (1967), who stated that organizations should be treated as such in that they are continually dependent upon and influenced by their environments.

This chapter starts with an analysis of how a reward system operates and continues with a description of the components of a system. Examples of actual systems are then given.

How a reward system operates

How a reward system operates is shown in Figure 2.1.

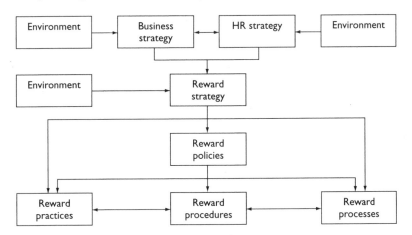

Figure 2.1   How a reward system operates

Reward systems are based on the reward strategy, which flows from the business strategy, for example to gain competitive advantage, and the HR strategy, which is influenced by the business strategy but also influences it. The HR strategy may, for example, focus on resourcing but it should also be concerned with satisfying people as well as business needs. All these aspects of strategy are affected by the environment. Reward strategies direct the development and operation of reward practices and processes and also form the basis of reward policies, which in turn affect reward practices, processes and procedures. These different aspects of a reward system are defined below.

Reward strategies

These set out what the organization intends to do in the longer term to develop and implement reward policies, practices, processes and procedures that will further the achievement of its business and HRM goals.

Reward policies

These set guidelines for decision making and action.

Reward practices

These comprise the schemes, structures and techniques used to implement reward strategy and policy: for example, the policy on pay levels will lead to the practice of collecting and analysing market rate data, and making pay adjustments that reflect market rates of increase.

Reward processes

These consist of the ways in which policies are implemented and practices carried out; for example, how the outcomes of surveys are applied and how managers manage the pay adjustment and review process.

Reward procedures

These are operated in order to maintain the system and to ensure that it functions efficiently and flexibly and provides value for money; an example is a procedure for conducting an annual pay review.

Components of a reward system

The components of a reward system and the interrelationships between them are shown in Figure 2.2. A brief description of each element follows.

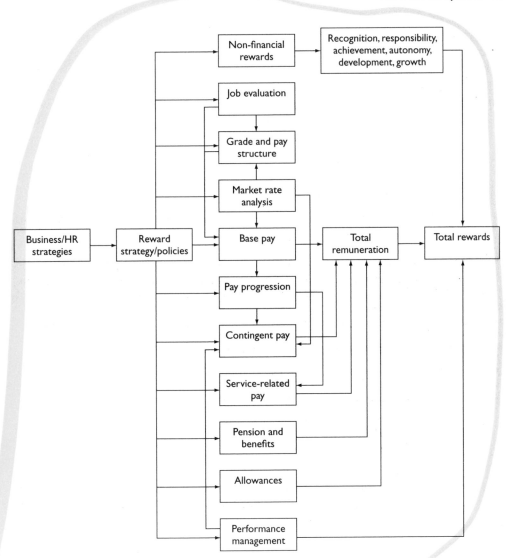

Figure 2.2   Reward system components and interrelationships

Business strategy

The starting point of the reward system is the business strategy of the organization. This identifies the business drivers and sets out the business goals. The drivers are unique to any organization but will often include items such as high performance, profitability, productivity, innovation, customer service, quality, price/cost leadership and the need to satisfy stakeholders – investors, shareholders, employees, elected representatives.

Reward strategy

The reward strategy flows from an analysis of the business drivers. The question is: 'How can these be supported by reward in order to achieve the goals of the business?' The strategy will define longer-term intentions in such areas as pay structures, contingent pay, employee benefits, steps to increase engagement and commitment and adopting a total reward approach.

Reward policy

Reward policy will cover such matters as:

- The level of rewards: this will be related to a view on how internal rates should compare with market rates, in other words, the organization's 'market stance'.

- External competitiveness versus internal equity: the balance between being 'market driven', whereby pay levels are governed by market rates, and being more concerned with the extent to which equal pay is provided for work of equal value.

- Transparency: how much information will be released about pay policies and levels.

- Pay decisions: fixing rates of pay on appointment or promotion.

- Assimilation: how employees will be assimilated into revised grade and pay structures.

- Protection: how employees whose pay is above the maximum for their grade should be protected from a reduction in salary.

Base or basic pay

The base rate is the amount of pay (the fixed salary or wage) that constitutes the rate for the job. It may be varied according to the grade of the job or, for shopfloor workers, the level of skill required.

Base pay will be influenced by internal and external relativities (going rates). The internal relativities may be measured by some form of job evaluation. External relativities are assessed by tracking market rates. Alternatively, levels of pay may be agreed through collective bargaining with trade unions or by reaching individual agreements. Base pay management is achieved through grade and pay structures.

Base pay may be expressed as an annual, weekly or hourly rate. The latter is sometimes called a time rate system of payment. The base rate may be adjusted to reflect increases in the cost of living or market rates by the organization unilaterally or by agreement with a trade union. Pay that is related entirely to the value of the job rather than the person is called job-based pay. Where the base rate can be enhanced by payments related to a person's level of competency or skill it is known as person-based pay. The latter term can be extended to include contingent pay, which rewards people for their performance or contribution.

Job evaluation

Job evaluation is a systematic process for defining the relative worth or size of jobs within an organization in order to establish internal relativities and provide the basis for designing an equitable grade structure, grading jobs in the structure and managing relativities. It does not determine the level of pay directly. Job evaluation can be analytical or non-analytical. It is based on the analysis of jobs or roles, which leads to the production of job descriptions or role profiles. Job evaluation is described in Chapter 16.

Market rate analysis

Market rate analysis is the process of identifying the rates of pay in the labour market for comparable jobs to inform decisions on levels of pay within the organization and on pay structures. A policy decision may be made on how internal rates of pay should compare with external rates – an organization's market stance. Market rate analysis is described in Chapter 18.

Grade and pay structure

This is a hierarchy of job grades, bands or levels into which groups of jobs that are broadly comparable in size are placed. Pay ranges are attached to grades that take account of market rates and provide scope for pay progression based on performance, contribution, competence or service. The main types of structures are:

- Multi-graded structure: one consisting of 10 or more job grades into which jobs of broadly equivalent value are placed. The pay span in each grade may be fairly small. Also known as a narrow-graded structure.

- Broad-banded structure: a pay structure with a small number (typically four or five) of wide bands.

- Broad-graded structures: grade and pay structures with six to nine grades.

- Job-family structure: a grade and pay structure consisting of a number of separate job families. Each family may constitute a market group in which rates of pay are related to market rates and may differ from that of equivalent jobs in other families. (A job family consists of a group of jobs in a function or occupation that are related through the activities carried out and the basic knowledge and skills required, but in which levels of responsibility, knowledge, skills and competency levels differ.)

- Career-family structure: a grade and pay structure consisting of a number of separate job families. It is distinguished from a job-family structure by having the same levels of pay for equivalent jobs in different families. As the name implies, the emphasis is on defining career paths or ladders as well as providing a grade and pay structure.

- Pay spine: a structure consisting of a series of fixed increments (incremental points) extending from the lowest to the highest-paid jobs covered by the structure. Progression is usually based on service but scope is sometimes given for it to be related to performance or contribution. The pay spine may be divided into grades.

- Spot rate: the rate for a job or an individual that is not fitted into a grade or band in a conventional grade structure and does not allow any scope for pay progression.

Pay progression

Pay progression takes place when base pay advances through pay brackets in a grade and pay structure or through promotions or upgradings. Progression through pay brackets may be determined formally through a contingent pay scheme or by means of fixed increments as described below. Informal progression takes place when there is no contingent or incremental pay scheme and increases are arbitrary. This is often the case when there is a spot rate system in the absence of a pay structure. As established by the CIPD 2009 reward survey, the most popular method of progressing someone along their pay scale (66 per cent of respondents) is to use a combination approach consisting of a number of factors such as individual performance, competency and length of service.

Contingent pay progression is typically but not inevitably governed by performance ratings, which are often made at the time of the performance management review but may be made separately in a special pay review. Some organizations do not base increases on formal ratings and instead rely on a general assessment of how much the pay of individuals should increase by reference to performance, potential, the pay levels of their peers and their 'market worth' (the rate of pay it is believed they could earn elsewhere).

The CIPD 2009 reward survey found that the most popular approach (66 per cent) to progressing someone along their pay scale is to use a number of factors (a combination approach), such as individual performance and length of service, while other employers use solely one factor, such as individual performance (13 per cent) or length of service (8 per cent).

Contingent pay for performance, contribution, competence or skill

Contingent pay is concerned with answering two fundamental reward management questions: 1) what do we value?, and 2) what are we prepared to pay for? Individual contingent pay schemes provide additional financial rewards related to levels of performance, contribution, competence or skill. Contingent pay may be related to team or organizational performance (profit sharing, gain sharing or employee share schemes).

Individual contingent scheme payments may be added to base pay (ie 'consolidated'). Alternatively or additionally they may be paid as cash bonuses. This is described as 'variable pay' and the payments are not consolidated. The main contingent pay schemes for individuals are:

- performance-related pay, which provides individuals with financial rewards in the form of increases to basic pay or cash bonuses that are linked to an assessment of performance, usually in relation to agreed objectives;

- contribution-related pay, which provides financial rewards related to both outputs (performance) and inputs (competence);

- competency-related pay, which rewards people by reference to the level of competence they demonstrate in carrying out their roles;

- skill-based pay, which provides employees with a direct link between their pay progression and the skills they have acquired and use effectively.

Service-related pay

Service-related pay provides fixed increments, which are usually paid annually to people on the basis of continued service either in a job or a grade in a pay spine structure. Increments may be withheld for unacceptable performance (although this is rare) and some structures have a 'merit bar' that limits increments unless a defined level of 'merit' has been achieved. This is the traditional form of contingent pay and is still common in the public and voluntary sectors and in education and the health service, although it has largely been abandoned in the private sector.

Service-related pay is supported by many unions because they perceive it as being fair – everyone is treated equally. It is felt that linking pay to time in the job rather than performance or competence avoids the partial and ill-informed judgements about people that managers are prone to make. Some people believe that the principle of rewarding people for loyalty through continued service is a good one. It is also easy to manage; in fact, it does not need to be managed at all.

The arguments against service-related pay are that:

- It is inequitable in the sense that an equal allocation of pay increases according to service does not recognize the fact that some people will be contributing more than others and should be rewarded accordingly.

- It does not encourage good performance; indeed, it rewards poor performance as much as good.

- It is based on the assumption that performance improves with experience, but this is not automatically the case.

- It can be expensive – everyone may drift to the top of the scale, especially in times of low staff turnover, but the cost of their pay is not justified by the added value they provide.

The arguments against service-related pay have convinced most businesses, although some are concerned about managing any other form of contingent-pay schemes. They may also have to face strong resistance from their unions and can be unsure of what exit strategy they should adopt if they want to change. They may therefore stick with the status quo.

Pensions and employee benefits

Pensions and employee benefits such as sick pay, insurance cover, company cars and a number of other 'perks' comprise elements of remuneration additional to the various forms of cash pay, and also include provisions for employees that are not strictly remuneration, such as annual holidays (see Chapters 24–26). 'Flexible' benefit schemes allow employees to decide on the make-up of their benefits package within certain limits.

Allowances

Allowances are paid in addition to basic pay for special circumstances (eg living in London) or features of employment (working unsocial hours). They may be determined unilaterally by the organization but they are often the subject of negotiation. The main types of allowances are location allowances, overtime payments, shift payments, working conditions allowances, and stand-by or call-out allowances (made to those who have to be available to come in to work when required).

Performance management

Performance management processes (see Chapter 6) define individual performance and contribution expectations, assess performance against those expectations, provide for regular constructive feedback, and result in agreed plans for performance improvement, learning and personal development. They are a means of providing non-financial motivation and may also inform contingent pay decisions.

Non-financial rewards

Non-financial rewards (see Chapter 9) do not involve any direct payments and often arise from the work itself, for example recognition, achievement, autonomy, scope to use and develop skills, training, career development opportunities and high-quality leadership.

Total remuneration

Total remuneration is the value of all cash payments (base pay, contingent pay and allowances, ie total earnings) plus the pensions and benefits received by employees.

Total rewards

Total rewards are the combination of financial and non-financial rewards available to employees (see Chapter 3).

Reward systems in action

Aegon UK

- The career-family structure contains four career families.

- Target rates are defined that support three performance zones, providing guidance on the pay range for different roles within the band.

- Pensionable, lump-sum bonus payments are awarded on a non-consolidated basis. An incentive scheme enables line managers to recognize and reward outstanding contribution by individuals or teams outside of the annual pay cycle.

- A variety of financial and non-financial awards are available to recognize personal development and ongoing contributions that employees make towards the overall effectiveness and efficiency of the company.

B&Q

- The 20,000 customer advisors are paid on one of six different spot rates in the upper quartile of similar jobs.

- Pay progression is based on the acquisition – and application on the shopfloor – of skills and knowledge. There are four additional spot rates beyond the established rate designed to reward 'excellence in the role'.

- There is a store team bonus, based on sales, shrinkage (resulting from losses such as theft and stocktaking errors) and customer service measures set at store level, and a formal recognition scheme.

BT

Job-family structure

- Pay structure of 250-plus roles in 18 different job families representing major work functions.

- Broad pay ranges attached to each role are determined by reference to market data.

- All roles are benchmarked against equivalent roles and salary ranges in the external market in order to gather competitive reward data.

- Published salary ranges are attached to each generic role.

- Hierarchical promotion from grade to grade is replaced by role change.

Benefits and bonus aligned with roles

- simplified benefits package and target bonus percentage defined for each role;

- based on benchmarking in external market;

- each role assigned to one of three benefit levels;

- three levels of bonus achievement linked to balanced scorecard.

Salary management

- Salary progression within a role range is predominantly via annual reviews based on individual performance, position in range and affordability.

- Other principal type of salary progression results from role change – a move between job families or within a job family.

Friends Provident

- There are five broad career bands for non-management staff. Three additional bands cover everyone below executive director.

- There are 18 job families with a small number of generic role profiles, based on key skills and competency levels, in each of the five career bands.

- Job-family salary ranges for each career band.

- An annual salary review, with individual reviews analysed by a range of criteria, such as gender, helps ensure fairness and equity across the company.

- Regional salary ranges reflect the influence of regional pay where appropriate.

- Performance management.

- A discretionary non-consolidated performance bonus.

GlaxoSmithKline (GSK)

- The pay structure has five bands. Each band is divided into a number of zones. The combination of band and zone produces the grade, and there are 29 grades in total. The grades determine bonus entitlement. The pay for each grade ranges approximately 25 per cent either side of the range mid-point.

- The main method of paying for performance each year is through the bonus scheme, but individuals are also able to progress through their grade range on the basis of performance, their 'behaviours', relativities with peers and their market value.

- There is a two-way performance and development planning process whereby individuals agree their objectives with their manager and identify development needs for the forthcoming year.

- The financial recognition scheme rewards effort above normal job requirements. There are four different levels of award.

Kent County Council

- Jobs are allocated to one of 35 generic job profiles organized into seven job families.

- Jobs are evaluated using the Hay system and placed into one of six pay grades.

- Summary band descriptions of the grades enable staff to understand why their job falls in a particular grade.

- The analytical points factor system ensures that staff are all evaluated on a fair and equal basis.

- Regular equal pay reviews are conducted.

- Total contribution pay (TCP) rewards the 'how' of someone's performance, as well as the results that they deliver.

- Managers can recognize the contribution of their staff on an ongoing basis with cash and non-cash awards.

- A total award approach is adopted.

Reward systems: six tips

- Ensure that the system is developed and operated in accordance with a clearly defined set of guiding principles.
- Provide for the system to be integrated – the separate parts are mutually supporting and contribute to achieving the overall aim of the system.
- Take account of the views of stakeholders on the design and operation of the system.
- Do not over-complicate the system as a whole or any part of it.
- Communicate regularly to employees on how the system functions and how it affects them.
- Review and evaluate the effectiveness of the system regularly.

References

CIPD (2009) *Reward Management Annual Survey Report*, CIPD, London

Katz, D and Kahn, R (1966) *The Social Psychology of Organizations*, John Wiley, New York

Miller, E and Rice, A (1967) *Systems of Organization*, Tavistock, London

3

Total Rewards

Key concepts and terms

- Bundling
- Employee value proposition
- Extrinsic rewards
- Financial rewards
- Intrinsic rewards
- Non-financial rewards

- Recognition scheme
- Relational rewards
- Total rewards
- Transactional rewards
- Work environment
- Work–life balance

Learning outcomes

On completing this chapter you should be able to define these key concepts. You should also know about:

- The overall concept of total rewards
- The underpinning concepts of total rewards
- The elements of total rewards

- The significance of total rewards
- The benefits of total rewards
- Total rewards models
- How to introduce total rewards

Introduction

The concept of total rewards describes an approach to reward management that emphasizes the need to consider all aspects of the work experience of value to employees, not just a few such as pay and employee benefits. It aims to blend the financial and non-financial elements of reward into a cohesive whole. The first person to refer in effect to total rewards was Adam Smith in 1776. He identified several components of what he called 'total net advantage' besides pay, namely: agreeableness or disagreeableness of work, difficulty and expense of learning it, job security, responsibility and the possibility of success or failure.

This chapter begins with a definition of the total rewards concept. Its importance is then explained and the various models and different components of total rewards are described. The chapter concludes with a description of how a total rewards approach to reward management can be developed, and a number of examples.

Total rewards defined

A total rewards approach links all aspects of reward together and treats them as an integrated and coherent whole. It means that when developing the reward system employers must consider all aspects of the work experience that employees value. One of the first people to write about total rewards after Adam Smith (O'Neal, 1998) commented that: 'Total reward embraces everything that employees value in the employment relationship.' As defined by Manus and Graham (2003), total rewards 'includes all types of rewards – indirect as well as direct, and intrinsic as well as extrinsic'. Kantor and Kao (2004) define total rewards as 'Everything an employee gets as a result of working for the company'.

An equally wide definition was offered by WorldatWork (2000), who stated that total rewards are 'all of the employer's available tools that may be used to attract, retain, motivate and satisfy employees'. Paul Thompson (2002) suggests that:

> *Definitions of total rewards typically encompass not only traditional, quantifiable elements like salary, variable pay and benefits, but also more intangible non-cash elements such as scope to achieve and exercise responsibility, career opportunities, learning and development, the intrinsic motivation provided by the work itself and the quality of working life provided by the organization.*

The total rewards approach recognizes that it is necessary to get financial rewards (pay and benefits) right. But it also appreciates the importance of providing people with rewarding experiences that arise from the work they do, their work environment, how they are managed and the opportunity to develop their skills and careers. It contributes to the production of an employee value proposition that provides a clear, compelling reason why talented people should work for a company.

It is a holistic view of reward that looks at the overall reward system in order to determine how its elements should be integrated so that they provide mutual support in contributing to the overall effectiveness of the system. Reliance is not placed on one or two reward mechanisms operating in isolation; instead, account is taken of every way in which people can be rewarded and obtain satisfaction through their work. The whole is greater than the sum of its parts. The aim is to maximize the combined impact of a wide range of reward initiatives on motivation, commitment and job engagement.

However, IDS (2008) commented that: 'While as a philosophy, total reward emphasizes the value of the non-financial aspects of the employee value proposition, pay remains the foundation upon which everything else is built.'

The notion of total rewards can be described as a perspective on reward management rather than reward management itself. It influences those aspects of reward management concerned with the nature and choice of rewards but does not specifically deal with the reward management functions of job evaluation, market rate analysis, grade and pay structure design and the administration of reward systems. The term total rewards rather than total reward is adopted in this book because it was the term used when the concept was first introduced in the United States in the 1990s and it conveys the basic principle that there are a number of ways of rewarding people besides pay.

Underpinning concepts

Two concepts underpin total rewards: intrinsic motivation and integration.

Intrinsic motivation

The philosophy of total rewards is strongly influenced by the concept of intrinsic motivation, which arises from the work itself and its impact on the self-generated factors that influence people's behaviour. Motivation theory spells out the difference between extrinsic and intrinsic motivation and indicates that high levels of motivation and performance are achieved by satisfying a variety of needs, only one of which is for money, and this is precisely what total rewards aims to do. Intrinsic motivation takes place when individuals feel that their work is important, interesting and challenging and provides them with a reasonable degree of autonomy (freedom to act), opportunities to achieve and advance, and scope to use and develop their skills and abilities. Deci and Ryan (1985) suggested that intrinsic motivation is based on the needs to be competent and self-determining (that is, to have a choice).

Integration

A total rewards strategy involves the horizontal integration of reward and other HR strategies to achieve greater impact and internal consistency. This is the process of 'bundling' – the development and implementation of several HR practices together so that they are interrelated and therefore complement and reinforce each other (also referred to as configuration or the use of 'complementarities'). MacDuffie (1995) explained the concept of bundling as follows:

> *Implicit in the notion of a 'bundle' is the idea that practices within bundles are interrelated and internally consistent, and that 'more is better' with respect to the impact on performance, because of the overlapping and mutually reinforcing effect of multiple practices.*

The elements of total rewards

The concept of total rewards combines the impact of the two major categories of reward as defined below and illustrated in Figure 3.1:

- Transactional rewards: tangible (financial) rewards arising from transactions between the employer and employees concerning pay and benefits. These are all extrinsic.

- Relational rewards: intangible (non-financial) rewards concerned with the work environment (quality of working life, the work itself, work–life balance), recognition, performance management and learning and development. The work environment provides intrinsic rewards, recognition is extrinsic, performance management is mainly extrinsic and learning and development is primarily intrinsic in so far as it provides opportunities for growth.

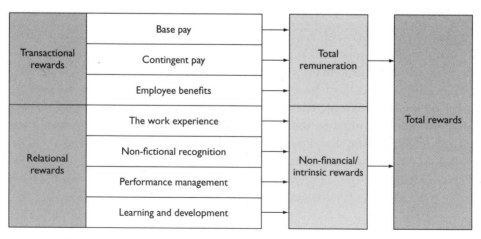

Figure 3.1 The elements of total rewards

The significance of total rewards

The basic premise of total rewards is that there is more to rewarding people than throwing money at them. As Giancola (2008) notes, 'It is effective because it focuses on the big picture.'

For Sandra O'Neal (1998), a total rewards strategy is critical to addressing the issues created by recruitment and retention as well as providing a means of influencing behaviour: 'It can help create a work experience that meets the needs of employees and encourages them to contribute extra effort, by developing a deal that addresses a broad range of issues and by spending reward dollars where they will be most effective in addressing workers' shifting values.'

A powerful argument for a total rewards approach was produced by Pfeffer (1998):

> *Creating a fun, challenging, and empowered work environment in which individuals are able to use their abilities to do meaningful jobs for which they are shown appreciation is likely to be a more certain way to enhance motivation and performance – even though creating such an environment may be more difficult and take more time than simply turning the reward lever.*

Benefits of total rewards

The benefits of a total rewards approach are:

- Greater impact: the combined effect of the different types of rewards will make a deeper and longer-lasting impact on the motivation and commitment of people.

- Enhancing the employment relationship: the employment relationship created by a total rewards approach makes the maximum use of relational as well as transactional rewards and will therefore appeal more to individuals.

- Flexibility to meet individual needs: as pointed out by Milkovich and Bloom (1998): 'Relational rewards may bind individuals more strongly to the organization because they can answer those special individual needs.' Kantor and Kao (2004) comment that: 'Companies today are managing a much more heterogeneous population. For the diverse workforce, no single component becomes a value driver. Employees have choices to make and a need for greater flexibility.'

- Attraction and retention: relational rewards help to deliver a positive psychological contract. The organization can become an 'employer of choice' and 'a great place to work', thus attracting and retaining the talented people it needs.

Models of total rewards

Many models of total rewards have been produced and a selection of the better-known ones is summarized below. The purpose of the models is to provide a framework for developing total rewards by identifying financial and non-financial elements and in some cases indicating how they relate to one another. They provide a basis for defining a total rewards policy and for communicating it to employees.

Towers Perrin

The Towers Perrin model shown in Figure 3.2 is a matrix with four quadrants. The upper two quadrants – pay and benefits – represent transactional or tangible rewards. These are financial in nature and are essential to recruit and retain staff but can be easily copied by competitors. By contrast, the relational or intangible non-financial rewards represented in the lower two quadrants cannot be imitated so readily and can therefore create both human capital and human process advantage, as defined in Chapter 1. They are essential to enhancing the value of the upper two quadrants. The real power, as Thompson (2002) states, comes when organizations combine relational and transactional rewards. The model also makes a useful distinction between individual and communal rewards, particularly in the latter case.

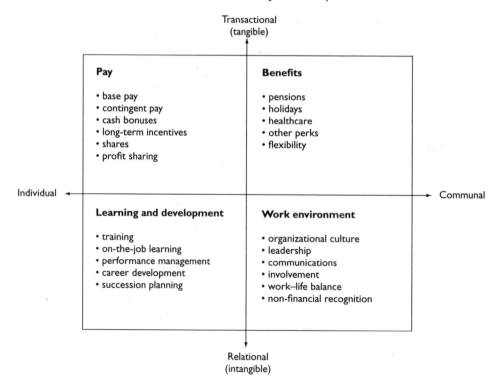

Figure 3.2   Model of total rewards: Towers Perrin

The current and required total rewards strategy in a public sector organization, developed with their top 50 managers working in groups and using the Towers Perrin model, is shown in Figure 3.3.

WorldatWork

WorldatWork, formerly the American Compensation Association, introduced the concept of total rewards in the 1990s. Their first model was produced in 2000 and revised in 2006 (Christopherson and King, 2006).

The five elements of total rewards in the 2006 model are compensation, benefits, work–life balance, performance and recognition, and development and career opportunities. These are influenced by the external environment, the work experience, organizational culture and the business and HR strategies. The combined five elements facilitate the attraction, motivation and retention of employees, which enhances their satisfaction and engagement and impacts on business performance and results.

Zingheim and Schuster

The total rewards model developed by Zingheim and Schuster (2000) expresses total rewards as four interlocked and directly related components as shown in Figure 3.4.

Pay	Benefits
Now • Secure • Below average • 'One size fits all'	*Now* • Family friendly • Paternalistic • Secure
Future • Aligned to business goals • Market rates • Flexible	*Future* • Individually tailored • Flexibility • Valued by employees
Learning	**Environment**
Now • Good learning opportunities • Spoon fed • Structures	*Now* • Comfortable • Family • Formal
Future • More targeted training • Focused on business goals • Good opportunities as before	*Future* • Challenging • Responsive • Enjoyable

Figure 3.3   Current and required reward strategy

Individual growth	Total pay
• Investment in people • Development and training • Performance management • Career enhancement	• Base pay • Variable pay (cash and stock) • Benefits or indirect pay • Recognition and celebration
Compelling future	**Positive workplace**
• Vision and values • Company growth and success • Company image and reputation • Stakeholdership • Win–win over time	• People focus • Leadership • Colleagues • Work itself • Involvement • Trust and commitment • Open communications

Figure 3.4   Model of total rewards: Zingheim and Schuster

Hay Group

The Hay Group's total rewards framework is illustrated in Figure 3.5.

IDS

IDS (2008) places pay and benefits at the heart of its total rewards model and, in increasing degrees of intangibility, adds personal development, career progression, work–life balance, environment and culture.

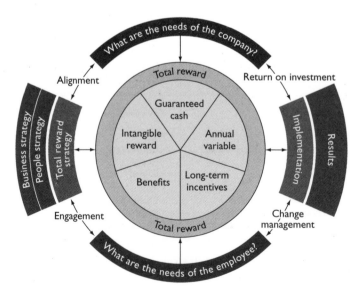

Figure 3.5   The Hay Group total rewards model

Models of total rewards produced by other consultants

- Mercer (2007):
    - compensation, including recognition;
    - benefits;
    - careers, including training and development.
- Sibson Consulting (2006):
    - direct financial;
    - indirect financial, including work arrangements;
    - career, including training and employee security;
    - work content;
    - affiliation, including work environment.
- Watson Wyatt (2006):
    - role-based rewards, including perquisites;
    - performance rewards, including recognition;
    - career and environmental rewards, including learning and development and work–life balance.

Summary of models

The elements included in the various models are summarized in Table 3.1.

Table 3.1   Summary of elements in total rewards models

	Hay	IDS	Mercer	Sibson	Towers Perrin	Watson Wyatt	World atWork	Zingheim and Schuster
Financial rewards (general)	*	*	*	*		*	*	
Base pay	*				*			*
Contingent pay	*				*	*		*
Benefits	*		*		*		*	*
Career development		*	*	*	*	*	*	
Compelling future								*
Involvement					*		*	*
Leadership					*			*
Learning and development		*	*		*	*		*
Organizational culture		*			*			
People focus								*
Performance management					*		*	*
Recognition			*			*	*	*
Work environment, including the work itself		*		*	*			
Work–life balance		*	*		*	*	*	
Intangible reward	*							

This summary shows, as might be expected, a common approach to financial rewards. There is a wider range of non-financial elements. The six most popular are:

- career development;
- recognition;
- work–life balance;
- performance management;
- involvement;
- work environment, including the work itself.

It is interesting to note the comments on the notion of the 'work itself' as an important intrinsic reward made by two consultancies following their research. Sibson Consulting (2006) noted that: 'Work content is always the largest motivator of good performance and most consistent driver of retention' and Towers Perrin (2007) observed that challenging and meaningful work is among the top 10 items for attracting and engaging employees.

Introducing total rewards

The steps required to introduce total rewards are set out in Figure 3.6.

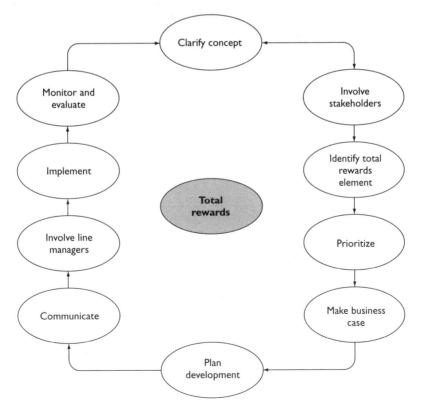

Figure 3.6   Introducing total rewards

These steps are discussed below.

Clarify the concept of total rewards

A programme for developing total rewards should start with a clarification of the meaning of the concept to the organization and a definition of its objectives, taking into account the circumstances and requirements of the business and the views and needs of its employees and other stakeholders. Statements of meaning and purpose provide the basis for further discussions with stakeholders, decisions on the elements of a total rewards programme and the preparation of a business case.

Involve stakeholders

Stakeholders should be involved as much as possible in developing total rewards. These include line managers, employees and employee representatives. Their commitment to the programme will be enhanced if they can contribute their ideas at the stages when the broad aims and features of the concept are defined and when the elements of total rewards are selected and their introduction prioritized.

As described by McCormick (2009), the method of involvement used by Camden Council in developing total rewards was to conduct focus groups with a cross-section of employees, carry out an employee total rewards attitude survey online and re-analyse a recent general staff survey.

Identify total rewards elements

In its basic form, a total rewards approach means simply getting the financial reward elements right and consciously doing whatever is possible progressively to enhance the elements that contribute to non-financial rewards. These include HR practices such as learning and development, career management, reward practices such as recognition schemes and flexible benefits, and HR policies such as work–life balance, leadership development programmes, job and work design and anything else that will improve the working environment. The only problem with this approach is that it could be unfocused. Something more specific based on one of the total rewards models may be better.

The core of any model will be pay and benefits, but there is a choice on what other non-financial elements should be included. An analysis of the non-financial elements contained in the various models listed earlier shows that there are plenty to choose from – 37 in all. The choice is made more difficult because while some elements such as recognition, performance management, work–life balance and, to a degree, learning and development are clear-cut, others such as the work environment and organizational culture are more diffuse. It is relatively easy to plan programmes for developing clear-cut elements. It is more difficult to deal with the diffuse elements. For example, culture change is a long-haul activity that is not susceptible to precise programming in order to achieve quick-fix results although, as noted in Chapter 1, there are a number of ways in which a reward system can reinforce and in the longer term help to change a culture.

There are three basic approaches that can be adopted:

- A deductive approach, as described by Peter Reilly of the Institute for Employment Studies (2009), which means taking one of the models and seeing how well it applies and then using the management perspective to see how well employees fit. It may involve selecting the most appealing consultant's model on the grounds that it contains a more attractive portfolio of elements and/or because of the reputation of the consultancy. The consultants can then be engaged to develop total rewards, as the Hay Group did for the Cabinet Office in the UK.

- An inductive approach, as described by Reilly, which means first collecting the views of employees and making sense of them, then interactively fitting these views with a model and finally establishing and dealing with any gap between the positions of employees and management.

- Distil the existing models, benchmark the total rewards experiences of other organizations and produce an individualized approach: for example pay, benefits, recognition, career development, work–life balance, performance management and work environment. These could all be defined and programmes produced for their development.

  Add recognition or another element to pay and benefits as a starting point, and bring in other elements as part of a longer-term strategic HR plan.

There is plenty of choice, and decisions on what elements should be included should be based on an assessment by all the stakeholders of the context and the requirements of the organization and its employees. Current arrangements should be analysed to determine the extent to which any element can be included or the amount of work required to introduce it as part of the model. The criteria for choice would be the extent to which the element is appropriate, will benefit the organization and its employees in specific ways, and can be implemented without too much difficulty.

Prioritize

It is best not to be too ambitious in introducing total rewards. Start by identifying 'win–win' initiatives – those that are likely to have a notable effect on employee engagement and can be developed without too much difficulty. If a comprehensive approach is envisaged, priorities will need to be established and the introduction of the less immediate elements phased. In a recent example of a local authority introducing total rewards, it was decided that some aspects of financial rewards, namely job evaluation and the pay structure, needed to be changed, while for non-financial rewards priority should be given to introducing a recognition scheme. Initiatives in other areas such as job design, leadership development and improvements in the performance management system were scheduled to follow.

Examples of possible developments are given below:

- Revise grade and pay structure, possibly instituting a career-family structure that defines career paths.

- Revise contingent pay scheme or develop new one. Include leadership and upholding core values as important factors in a contribution-related pay scheme.

- Introduce flexible benefits scheme.

- Issue total rewards statements that spell out to employees the value of all the benefits they receive in addition to pay.

- Introduce a non-financial recognition scheme.

- Improve performance management system, including leadership and upholding core values as important factors.

- Enhance learning and development, talent management and career development programmes.

- Focus management development programmes on improving the ability of line managers to play a major part in providing relational rewards.

- Take steps to improve work–life balance.

- Educate line managers in the principles of job design and provide guidance to them on developing roles that provide for intrinsic motivation.

Make the business case for total rewards

The business case for total rewards aims to demonstrate that an investment of time, effort and money in introducing total rewards will produce a return in the form of performance improvements resulting from higher levels of engagement. But this is not easy to do. As Giancola (2008) remarked: 'Total rewards is a very challenging concept when it includes the intrinsic work-environment' factors. He noted that in these circumstances a total rewards strategy can seem to equate to HR strategy. This is fine if it means that reward strategy is integrated with HR strategy but a lot of practitioners – and senior managers – may feel that there is nothing new in the concept. If the HR strategy of a company is to create a learning culture, implement leadership development programmes, pursue talent management initiatives, develop work–life balance policies, encourage and train line managers to pay attention to job design, and improve employee voice arrangements, it will probably seem that the notion of total rewards is superfluous. Not many companies do all these things all at once. Even if they only do some of them, it may be difficult to persuade management that a total rewards approach offers new insights, although it can provide impetus to developments on a broader HR front.

But there are a number of compelling points that can be made in a business case for total rewards. It can be argued that it can help to achieve one or more of the following:

- promote a culture that values, recognizes and rewards outstanding performance;
- achieve competitive advantage by offering levels of choice and personalization not provided by other employers competing for the same type of people;
- meet varied and changing employee needs by introducing more value, choice and flexibility;
- help to make the company an 'employer of choice' for people already employed there, as well as for potential recruits;
- enhance employees' engagement and therefore performance;
- ensure that the best use is made of all the possible ways of rewarding people, in combination as well as individually;
- avoid dependence on dubious and expensive financial incentives.

The arguments need to be supported by explanations related to the specific circumstances and needs of the organization of how any of these desirable results will be obtained with the help of total rewards.

Plan the development programme

Introducing total rewards in its fullest sense is not easy. WorldatWork (2000) commented that total rewards are 'simple in concept and, at best, complex in execution'. The transactional and tangible elements of total rewards (financial rewards) are quite clear-cut. It may not be easy to make them work well but, as explained in later chapters of this book, it is not too difficult to decide on what needs to be done. There are plenty of guidelines available to help in selecting the approach and to indicate the means available for the design and implementation of tangible reward processes. Recognition schemes, which may be financial or non-financial (or a combination of the two), can be included in this category.

Relational or non-financial rewards are more difficult. It is not a matter of implementing quick-fix programmes. The organization can contribute by communicating the values, giving employees a voice, setting up performance management processes, instituting formal recognition schemes and taking steps to improve work–life balance. A conscious effort can be made to 'bundle' reward and HR practices together, for example developing career-family structures where the emphasis is on mapping career paths rather than providing a pay structure. Importantly, the organization can ensure that line managers appreciate the importance of using relational rewards – exercising effective leadership, giving feedback, recognizing achievement and providing meaningful work. Ultimately, relational rewards are in the hands of line managers, and what the organization must do is to ensure as far as possible that they understand the significance of this aspect of their work and are given the training and guidance needed to acquire the skills to do it well.

Communicate

The nature of the total rewards concept – how it will be introduced and managed and how people will benefit – needs to be communicated. Models such as those used in the examples given later in this chapter can help. It is particularly important to communicate to line managers the importance of their role in implementing total rewards.

Total rewards statements, as discussed in Chapter 24, communicate to employees the value of the employee benefits such as pensions, holidays, company cars, free car parking and subsidized meals they receive in addition to their pay. They also describe any other rewards they get such as learning and development opportunities. The aim is to ensure that they appreciate the total value of their reward package.

Involve line managers

Line managers contribute to the management of total rewards in six important ways:

- They have considerable influence over the management of financial rewards, agreeing starting salaries and proposing pay increases and bonuses.

- The effectiveness of performance management as a reward process involving feedback and the initiation of individual learning and development programmes is mainly up to them.

- They are the most important elements in a recognition scheme – giving praise where praise is due, publicly acknowledging high performance and making recognition awards as provided for by the scheme.

- They strongly influence how jobs are designed and therefore the degree to which people are provided with intrinsic rewards from the work itself.

- They control the degree of work flexibility that can take place, and therefore work–life balance.

- It is their qualities of leadership that largely contribute to the creation of a rewarding work environment.

This is why their involvement in the development of total rewards is vital. Management development and training programmes that define their role and increase their total rewards management skills are also important.

Implement

The successful introduction of total rewards is well worthwhile. But while planning a total rewards programme may be hard, implementing it can be even more difficult. It is an exercise in change management, for employees generally when new reward practices are being introduced and for line managers in particular if they are expected to change their behaviour. Continuing communications and involvement of stakeholders are essential.

Monitor and evaluate

It is essential to monitor the implantation of total rewards carefully and then to evaluate how well each element has worked against the objectives set for it. This can lead to a re-clarification of the concept and amendments to reward practices as required.

Total rewards in practice

The CIPD 2009 reward management survey found that 20 per cent of respondents claimed that they had a total rewards strategy although it was not revealed what their strategies contained. More insight into total rewards practices is provided by looking at examples such as the 10 set out below.

Agon (formerly Norwich Union Insurance)

A model of the total rewards policy developed by Agon is shown in Figure 3.7.

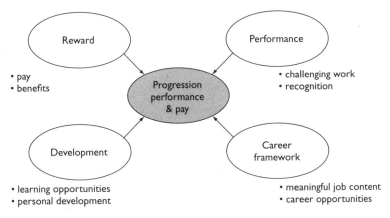

Figure 3.7   Model of total rewards at Agon

The commitment to total rewards made by senior management was to:

- recognize our best people through career opportunities and reward packages;
- develop all staff to their full potential;
- widen career opportunities for all;
- provide managers with the means to recognize and reward performance locally.

There is a notable emphasis on learning and development.

AstraZeneca

The total rewards strategy consists of three strands that are packaged as a single value proposition in the minds of employees and potential employees so that the collective value is enhanced beyond the individual value of the components.

Competitive and flexible reward

The first pillar of total rewards is the flexible benefits plan, entitled 'Advantage'. This allocates employees a sum equal to their previous salary and benefits package. They can take most of this fund in cash, apart from a small core of benefits – such as a minimum of 20 days' holiday entitlement – or choose to spend it on items from a large menu of new benefits.

Additionally, the compensation package includes a broad-banded salary structure and three employee share schemes – a performance-based share plan, an Inland Revenue-approved SAYE scheme, and a new-style share incentive plan, to be introduced shortly.

Excellent development opportunities

The second pillar of total rewards includes developing an 'active' performance management culture – in other words, not just an annual appraisal but a management style that coaches, challenges and develops people on the job. Staff are set stretch performance targets, and the opportunities for learning and progression are clear.

This component of the total rewards strategy also encompasses on-the-job learning, career development, mentoring, e-learning and further education.

Energized working environment

The third pillar of total rewards is made up of six elements that if executed right can create a working environment in which people feel motivated and excited. It involves establishing a consistent organization climate and values to which staff can align their personal beliefs and values. The elements are effective leadership, communications, the physical environment, recognition by peers as well as managers, and formalized work–life policies.

Cabinet Office

The total rewards approach adopted by the Cabinet Office in the form of a toolkit for government departments is derived from the Hay Engaged Performance model. As explained by the Cabinet Office it draws together all the financial and non-financial investments an employer makes in its workforce. It emphasizes all aspects of reward as an integrated and coherent whole, from pay and benefits through flexible working to learning and development and the quality and challenge of the work itself.

The Cabinet Office suggests that the benefits of the total rewards approach to public sector organizations are that it will help them to recruit, retain and win the engagement of high-quality staff, align their investment with employee expectations and needs and secure better value for money. For employees a properly developed total rewards strategy will respond to employee preferences and values to create an environment that brings out the best in them.

Centrica

The total rewards approach at Centrica concentrates overall on developing reward management as a strategic, innovative and integrative process that is designed to meet the evolving needs of the organization and the people it employs. It involves the use of both:

- Financial rewards: base pay, contingent or variable pay, share ownership and employee benefits.

- Non-financial rewards: the work environment, recognition, quality of working life, opportunity to develop and learn skills, and work–life policies.

Financial Services Authority (FSA)

The four elements of the FSA's total rewards model are:

- Pay: basic salary structured into five broad overlapping pay bands, allowing flexibility to reflect the external (financial services) market, plus variable pay in the form of a bonus worth up to 15 per cent of base salary.

- Benefits: a flexible benefits plan, covering pensions, health care, insurance, holidays, childcare, and a subsidized gym and restaurant on site.

- Learning and development: a career development and learning framework based on competencies, training and secondment opportunities, performance management, induction programmes, succession planning and study sponsorship – including time off and fees paid.

- Work environment: single-status climate with open-plan offices and first names for all, an open internal job market, an emphasis on leadership, flat structures and devolved decision making, a staff consultation committee and work–life balance.

GlaxoSmithKline (GSK)

Paying for performance is the ultimate goal at GSK, and this is championed at the highest level, by the chief executive. TotalReward, the name by which GSK refers to its approach to reward, consists of three elements:

- total cash (base salary and bonus), plus long-term incentives for managers and executives;
- lifestyle benefits (health care, employee assistance, family support, dental care;
- savings choices (pension plan, ShareSave, ShareReward).

The complete package, the concept of which is based on employees understanding the total value of all the rewards they receive, not just the individual elements, is designed to attract, retain, motivate and develop the best talent. The proposition for employees is that TotalReward gives them the opportunity to share in the company's success, makes it easier to balance home and working life, and helps them to take care of themselves and their families.

There is also a recognition scheme, which is seen as another and more immediate way to motivate staff and reward good performance rather than having to wait for the annual bonus. The scheme gives financial recognition to effort over and above the normal job requirements and there are four different levels of award – bronze, silver, gold and platinum – with taxable payouts ranging from £50 to £5,000.

Iris

A model of total rewards adopted in the software company Iris is shown in Figure 3.8.

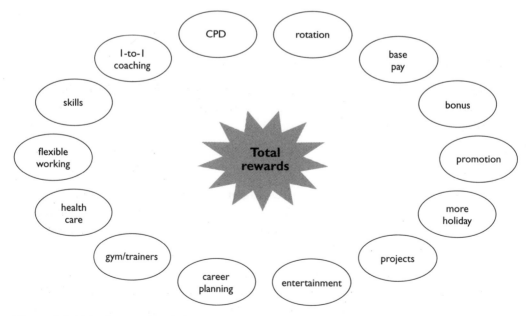

Figure 3.8   Total rewards at Iris

Lloyds TSB

The total rewards strategy at Lloyds TSB comprises four elements:

- performance and development;
- employee involvement;
- career management and resourcing;
- reward.

A basic tenet underpinning the concept of total rewards at Lloyds TSB is that managerial aims such as improving levels of engagement, encouraging better performance and generating a culture of innovation can rarely be achieved through cash alone.

Nationwide

Total rewards is defined at Nationwide as: 'A mixture of pay elements, with a defined cash value, benefits which have an intrinsic value, a positive and enjoyable work environment and opportunities for learning and development, all designed to make Nationwide an employer of choice'.

The Nationwide model of total rewards is shown in Figure 3.9.

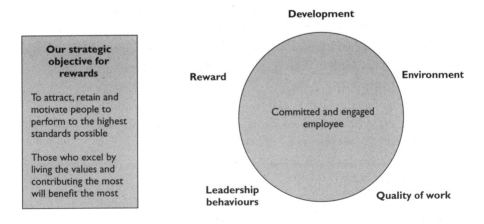

Figure 3.9 Model of total rewards at Nationwide

Unilever

Unilever believes that total rewards encompasses all the elements in 'what it means to come to work'. It supports the Towers Perrin model of total rewards covering pay, benefits, learning and development and the work environment, which for Unilever means that it is essential to create an environment worth working in. For managers, development has been at the heart of the company's employment offering.

Conclusion

The rhetoric of the total rewards concept is compelling. The reality of total rewards – making it work – is much more difficult. It requires a lot of effort on the part of top management and line managers, with the determined encouragement and guidance of HR.

Six tips for introducing total rewards

- Review the work environment and analyse current reward policies and practices.
- Research different approaches (models) and benchmark total rewards practices elsewhere, especially those to do with selecting and defining the elements of total rewards and methods of introduction.
- Involve stakeholders – senior management, line managers, employees and their representatives – both in developing the concept of total rewards and at later stages as appropriate.
- Select or develop the total rewards model to be adopted, prioritize the introduction of elements as necessary, integrate the total rewards strategy with the HR strategy, and plan and implement the programme.
- Ensure that line managers are equipped to play their part in the total rewards programme.
- Communicate throughout the programme about what is happening and how people will be affected.

References

Christopherson, J and King, B (2006) The 'it' factor: a new total rewards model leads the way, *WorldatWork Journal*, fourth quarter, pp 18–19, 22, 24, 26–27

CIPD (2009) *Reward Management Annual Survey Report*, CIPD, London

Deci, E L and Ryan, R M (1985) *Intrinsic Motivation and Self-determination in Human Behavior*, Plenum, New York

Giancola, F (2008) Total rewards; a current reassessment, *WorldatWork Journal*, fourth quarter, pp 50–61

IDS (2008) *Total Reward*, IDS Study 871, IDS, London

Kantor, R and Kao, T (2004) Total rewards: clarity from the confusion and chaos, *WorldatWork Journal*, third quarter, pp 7–15

MacDuffie, J P (1995) Human resource bundles and manufacturing performance, *Industrial Relations Review*, **48** (2), pp 199–221

Manus, T M and Graham, M D (2003) *Creating a Total Rewards Strategy*, American Management Association, New York

McCormick, L (2009) Introducing total reward in Camden Council, presentation at e-reward conference, 18 June, London

Mercer (2007) *Total Rewards: Mercer's approach*, Mercer HR Consulting, New York

Milkovich, G T and Bloom, M (1998) Rethinking international compensation, *Compensation and Benefits Review*, **30** (1), pp 15–23

Murlis, H (2009) Total reward: the holistic approach, *Hay Group News Letter*, **3**, pp 1–3

O'Neal, S (1998) The phenomenon of total rewards, *ACA Journal*, **7** (3), pp 8–14

Pfeffer, J (1998) *The Human equation: Building profits by putting people first*, Harvard Business School Press, Boston, MA

Reilly, P (2009) An approach to total reward, presentation at e-reward conference, 18 June, London

Sibson Consulting (2006) *Rewards of Work Study: Fifth report of 2006 results*, Sibson Consulting, New York

Thompson, P (2002) *Total Reward*, CIPD, London

Towers Perrin (2007) Adapting Total Rewards to Support a Changing Business Strategy, Towers Perrin, New York

Watson Wyatt (2006) Strategic Rewards and Pay Practices, Watson Wyatt, New York

WorldatWork (2000) *Total Rewards: From strategy to implementation*, WorldatWork, Scottsdale, AZ

Zingheim, P K and Schuster, J E (2000) *Pay People Right! Breakthrough strategies to create great companies*, Jossey-Bass, San Fransisco

Strategic Reward

Introduction

Strategic reward management is the process of planning the future development of reward practices through the development and implementation of reward strategies that are based on a reward philosophy and incorporate the concept of total rewards. This chapter starts with a definition of strategic reward and continues with an explanation of its rationale. It next deals with the philosophical basis of strategic reward as expressed in guiding principles and then examines how strategic reward functions through the development and implementation of reward strategies.

Strategic reward management defined

Strategic reward management is an approach to the development and implementation of reward strategies and the guiding principles that underpin them. As described by Armstrong and Brown (2006), it provides answers to two basic questions: first, where do we want our reward practices to be in a few years' time? And second, how do we intend to get there? It therefore deals with both ends and means. As an end it describes a vision of what reward processes will look like in the future. As a means, it shows how it is expected that the vision will be realized. Strategic reward can be described as an attitude of mind – a belief in the need to plan ahead and make the plans happen.

Strategic reward is based on beliefs about what the organization values and wants to achieve. It does this by aligning reward practices with both business goals and employee values. As Duncan Brown (2001) emphasizes, the 'alignment of your reward practices with employee values and needs is every bit as important as alignment with business goals, and critical to the realization of the latter.'

The rationale for strategic reward

In the words of Duncan Brown (2001), strategic reward 'is ultimately a way of thinking that you can apply to any reward issue arising in your organization, to see how you can create value from it'. More specifically, there are four arguments for adopting a strategic approach to reward management:

- You must have some idea where you are going, or how do you know how to get there, and how do you know that you have arrived (if you ever do)?

- As Cox and Purcell (1998) explain: 'The real benefit in reward strategies lies in complex linkages with other human resource management policies and practices.' Isn't this a good reason for developing a reward strategic framework that indicates how reward processes will be aligned to HR processes so that they are coherent and mutually supportive?

- There can be a positive relationship between rewards, in the broadest sense, and performance, so shouldn't we think about how we can strengthen that link?

- Pay costs in most organizations are by far the largest item of expense – they can be 60 per cent and often much more in labour-intensive organizations – so doesn't it make sense to think about how they should be managed and invested in the longer term?

The problem with the concept of strategic reward

To what extent can pay be strategic? This question was posed by Trevor (2009). He noted that pay is seen as 'a means of aligning a company's most strategic asset – their employees – to the strategic direction of the organization' and that strategic pay theory is predicated on the notion of strategic choice. But he claimed that rationalism is limited and pointed out that pay systems tend to be selected for their legitimacy (best practice as advocated by institutions such as the CIPD and by management consultants) rather than for purely economic reasons.

His research into the pay policies and practice of three large consumer goods organizations revealed a gap between intended and actual practice – intent does not necessarily lead to action. 'Irrespective of the strategic desire or the saliency of the design, ineffectual execution results in ineffectual pay practice which then reacts negatively upon the pay outcomes experienced as a result.' The main implications of the findings from this research were that: 'theory is out of step with reality and may represent a largely unattainable ideal in practice.' As Wright and Nishii (2004) commented: 'not all intended HR practices are actually implemented and, those that are, may often be implemented in ways that differ from the original intention.' The conclusion is that an 'alternative approach for the use of pay systems in support of strategy is required: one that acknowledges the relative limits on the ability of companies to manage pay strategically.'

A similar point was made by Armstrong and Brown (2006) when they described 'the new reality' of strategic reward management as follows:

> When mostly North American concepts of strategic HRM and reward first entered into management thinking and practice in the UK we were both some of their most ardent advocates, writing and advising individual employers on the benefits of aligning their reward systems so as to drive business performance. We helped to articulate strategic plans and visions, and to design the pay and reward changes that would secure better alignment and performance.
>
> Some 20 years later, we are a little older and a little wiser as a result of these experiences. We remain passionate proponents of a strategic approach to reward management. But in conducting and observing this work we have seen some of the risks as well as the opportunities in pursuing the reward strategy path: of an over-focus on planning at the expense of process and practice; on design rather than delivery; on the boardroom and the HR function rather than on first and front-line managers and employees; and on concept rather than communications.

At times there has been a tendency to over-ambition and optimism in terms of what could and couldn't be achieved by changing pay and reward arrangements, and how quickly real change could be delivered and business results secured. At times the focus on internal business fit led to narrow-minded reward determinism, and a lack of attention to the increasingly important external influences and constraints on reward, from the shifting tax and wider legislative, economic and social environment. And sometimes the focus on designs and desires meant that the requirements and skills of line and reward managers were insufficiently diagnosed and developed.

Characteristics of strategic reward

In the light of these comments it is best to regard strategic reward as an attitude of mind rather than a set of prescribed techniques. It is based on a belief in the need to be forward looking – to plan ahead and make the plans happen. It is visionary in the sense that it is concerned with creating and conceptualizing ideas of where the reward policies and processes of the organization should be going. But it is also empirical management that decides how in practice it is going to get there.

An important characteristic of strategic reward is that it is systematic in the sense that it is based on analyses of the organization's internal and external environment, its business needs and the needs of its stakeholders. It is conducted within a framework of articulated beliefs and values, and it is goal-orientated – the desired ends and the means of attaining them are clearly defined. It takes account of the business strategy and what can be done by reward to further its achievement. Importantly, it is a key instrument in achieving an integrated approach to reward management, one in which the various aspects of the reward system cohere and are linked to other HR practices so that they are mutually supportive. It focuses on implementation – it is about getting things done rather than just thinking about what needs to be done. Finally, strategic reward is based upon a philosophy expressed in the form of guiding principles.

Reward philosophy

Strategic reward management is based on a well-articulated philosophy – a set of beliefs expressed through guiding principles that are consistent with the values of the organization and help to enact them. These include beliefs in the need to operate in accordance with the principles of distributive and procedural justice. Reward strategies in the past have sometimes focused exclusively on business needs and alignment. Yet unless employees see and experience fairness and equity in their rewards, the strategy is unlikely to be delivered in practice.

The philosophy recognizes that reward management is a key factor in establishing a positive employment relationship, one in which there is mutuality – the state that exists when management and employees are interdependent and both benefit from this interdependency. Such a relationship provides a foundation for the development of a climate of trust.

Guiding principles

A reward philosophy can be expressed through a set of guiding principles that define the approach an organization takes to dealing with reward. They are the basis for reward policies and provide guidelines for the actions contained in the reward strategy. Importantly, they can be used to communicate to employees how the reward system operates and takes into account their interests as well as those of the business.

Reward guiding principles will be concerned with matters such as:

- operating the reward system justly, fairly, equitably and transparently in the interests of all stakeholders;
- developing reward policies and practices that support the achievement of business goals;
- rewarding people according to their contribution;
- recognizing the value of everyone who is making an effective contribution, not just the exceptional performers;
- creating an attractive employee value proposition;
- providing rewards that attract and retain people and enlist their engagement;
- helping to develop a high-performance culture;
- maintaining competitive rates of pay;
- maintaining equitable rates of pay;
- allowing a reasonable degree of flexibility in the operation of reward processes and in the choice of benefits by employees;
- devolving more responsibility for reward decisions to line managers.

Examples of guiding principles are given below.

Aegon UK

Aegon UK wishes to:

- establish an integrated approach to performance management development and the reward of all staff and ensure that this is aligned with the needs of the business;

- ensure that salaries and benefits remain competitive when compared with comparators within our industry sector, so that we can retain and attract staff of the highest quality;

- reduce the previous focus upon grades in favour of broader bands so that personal development can be encouraged;

- Aegon UK motivate staff sufficiently so that they will ensure the company remains successful, thereby allowing for continued competitive levels of reward for superior performance.

BT

The five key principles of the reward framework at BT are:

- Clarity: the reward framework brings transparency to the way people are rewarded for their contribution to the business. The same role profiles (within the same job families) now apply right across BT, and command the same published salary ranges. People know exactly where they stand.

- External focus: the way we reward and recognize people must conform to the market in which we operate. Under the new reward framework, salary ranges are now aligned with the going rate for equivalent jobs across a range of comparable organizations, geographies and skill sets. This will ensure we remain competitive, and are able to recruit and retain the people we need.

- Focus on roles: a person's place in the organization should be valued by the work they do – not by where they sit in a hierarchy. The new reward framework has replaced grades with job families, which represent a group of similar roles in a similar field of activity. A large number of operational managers from across the business have helped to define a structure that reflects the roles individuals actually do, not historical grades.

- Reward for performance: people who perform well will earn higher rewards than people who don't. Reward decisions are now based on capability in role and proven contributions through achievement of objectives. People should be clear about why they earn what they do.

- Choice: the framework offers an increased choice over the benefits people receive as part of their total reward package. This approach ensures that everyone knows exactly where he or she stands in relation to the market, and in relation to his or her performance.

British Airways

- Total reward is aligned to the business strategy. It engages and involves people in the achievement of business goals.

- Reward is aligned to company performance and supports a performance culture.

- Reward helps employees understand how their efforts contribute to company success.

- Rewards will be cost effective.

- Total reward is actively supported in the business.

- Individual value is recognized through base pay; delivery of results is linked to variable pay.

- Reward will take into account market forces and drivers.

- Total reward policy and practice will be well communicated and administered.

Colt Telecom

Colt's reward philosophy states that:

- Colt believes that talented and motivated people make a difference; talented people put us ahead of the competition and deliver the results on which the success of Colt is built. Colt seeks to offer a compensation and benefits package that rewards people for their contribution to the success of the company and ensures that external market competitiveness and internal relativities are taken into account.

- The reward mix is designed to promote a performance culture that underpins the company business strategy. Reward is geared to driving exceptional effort through the variable elements of the total package whilst maintaining flexibility, simplicity and equity within the guiding principles of driving discretionary effort, rewarding employee contribution and encouraging employees to behave like owners.

- The compensation package includes cash and non-cash payments as well as fixed and variable elements. The ability to have an impact on shareholder value influences the mix of the total reward package, with a greater emphasis on variable pay (bonus, share incentive and share ownership schemes) for those at the senior level within the company.

- Base salaries are benchmarked regularly across Europe against other telecommunication operators, the high-tech sector and other appropriate industries.

- The performance management system ensures that performance is assessed and used to differentiate achievement among employees at all levels, thus driving discretionary effort. The bonus scheme rewards individual performance against a mix of company and individual objectives and contribution to overall company performance.

- The company believes in encouraging an ownership mindset, so share option schemes offer employees a stake in the organization, which will allow them to share in the company's success over the medium and long term. Colt offers voluntary, all-employee share participation schemes in the countries where it is possible to do so. Management can participate in performance-related option schemes, and it is expected that those with greater opportunities to influence directly the success of the business will have a larger proportion of shareholding within their total reward package.

- Benefits are designed to be market competitive whilst protecting both employees and the company. They comply with local legislation, are tax effective and take into account social security benefits in all the countries within which Colt operates.

Diageo

Diageo's approach to recognition and reward is based around four key principles:

- Performance: rewards are developed that reflect team and individual achievements.

- Market: rewards reflect the market in which an employee is based, whether that be geographical or functional, and compare favourably with those of competitors.

- Communication: Diageo aims to explain to 'everyone the components and value of their reward package, the criteria that affect it, and how they can influence it'.

- Effectiveness: the company seeks 'best practice' and ensures its benefits programmes 'remain effective for the business and our employees'.

KPMG

The firm's reward philosophy is based on the overarching reward strategy of 'market-leading rewards for market-leading performance'. It contains six explicit principles that make the emphasis on rewarding performance very clear. They are:

- market-leading bonus for market-leading performance;
- performance-driven reward that is fair and equitable;
- a variable proportion of reward that increases with grade;
- market-competitive salaries;
- competitive benefits, with choice and flexibility;
- people management leaders empowered to make and communicate reward decisions.

Lloyds TSB

The guiding reward strategy principles at Lloyds TSB are:

- Basic pay is linked to the market.
- Benefits are market driven and individually focused.
- Pay decisions are devolved to line managers.
- Pay reflects individual contribution in a high-performance organization.
- Rewards comply with equal pay principles.
- Variable pay is linked to performance.
- Wealth creation and share ownership are encouraged.
- Reward and HR practices are managed in an integrated way.

Tesco

The guiding principles in Tesco are:

- We will provide an innovative reward package that is valued by our staff and communicated brilliantly to reinforce the benefits of working for Tesco.
- Reward investment will be linked to company performance so that staff share in the success they create and, by going the extra mile, receive above average reward compared to local competitors.
- All parts of the total reward investment will add value to the business and reinforce our core purpose, goals and values.

UK Civil Service

The principles applied in the UK Civil Service are summarized in Table 4.1.

Table 4.1   Reward principles for the UK Civil Service

---

1 Meet business need and be affordable

- Business, operational and workforce needs are the drivers for a reward strategy.
- Business cases outline benefits, risks and costs and justify investment.
- Reward arguments need to be sustainable.

2 Reflect nature of work

- Recognize and reflect workforce groups identified by function and skills utilized (eg operational, corporate or policy decisions).
- Organizations employing similar workforce groups in similar markets are encouraged to consider similar reward arrangements.

3 Recognize performance

- Reward reflects the continuing value and the sustained contribution of employees and their performance in given positions.
- Value and performance rewarded reflect how jobholders contribute to their organization, impact delivery and meet professional government (PSG) requirements.

4 Manage total reward

- Reward includes all aspects of the 'employee deal': tangible and intangible elements of what is offered.
- Total reward is tailored and promoted to attract, engage and retain the right talent as well as providing personal choice and flexibility.
- Employers/employees need to develop a full understanding and appreciation of the value of the total reward package.

5 Manage all cash

- Total cash comprises base pay and variable pay.
- Base pay reflects job challenge and individuals' competence in their jobs.
- Variable pay reflects performance delivered against agreed objectives.

6 Face the market

- Reward levels, generally and for specific skills, are aligned with agreed market positioning to attract, motivate and retain the right talent.
- Reward competitiveness covers each element of total reward (eg base pay, pensions, leave) and the overall deal.

Support Equal Pay

- Eliminate direct and indirect reward discrimination and reduce any unjustified gender pay gaps.
- Operate reward systems that are perceived by staff to be reasonable and transparent.
- Reward systems and structures evaluated and kept up to date to ensure that they continue to meet the requirements of legislation.

Reward strategy

The process of strategic reward is operationalized through overall or specific reward strategies. These provide business and people-focused descriptions of what the organization wants to do about reward in the next few years and how it intends to do it. They generally start with a review of the current reward arrangements and situation, then a definition of the desired future state, and the development of reward initiatives and activities to close the gap between the two.

Aim of reward strategy

The aim of reward strategy is to provide the organization with a sense of purpose and direction in delivering reward programmes that support the achievement of business goals and meet the needs of stakeholders. It defines pathways that link the needs of the business and its people with the reward policies and practices of the organization and thereby communicate and explain these practices.

Kantor and Kao (2004) elaborate on this description as follows: 'Reward strategies should have two primary aims: to articulate a distinctive value proposition that attracts and retains the right people for the business, and to provide a framework from which the company designs, administers and evaluates effective reward programmes.'

The content of reward strategy

As Helen Murlis (1996) pointed out: 'Reward strategy will be characterized by diversity and conditioned both by the legacy of the past and the realities of the future.' All reward strategies are different just as all organizations are different. Of course, similar aspects of reward will be covered in the strategies of different organizations but they will be treated differently in accordance with variations between organizations in their contexts, business strategies and cultures. But the reality of reward strategy is that it is not such a clear-cut process as some believe. It evolves, it changes and it has sometimes to be reactive rather than proactive.

Reward strategy often has to be a balancing act because of potentially conflicting goals. For example, it may be necessary to reconcile the competing claims of being externally competitive and internally equitable – paying a specialist more money to reflect market rate pressures may disrupt internal relativities. Or the belief that a universally applicable reward system is required may conflict with the perceived need to adopt a policy of segmentation, as described in Chapter 28.

There are two approaches: 1) a grand design involving the development of overall strategy, and 2) a focus on one or two specific strategies.

Overall strategy

An overall strategy may cover all aspects of rewards – valuing roles, the design of grade and pay structures, contingent pay, non-financial recognition, and pensions and benefits, including flexible benefits. The aim would be to develop a substantially revised reward system that would operate as a coherent whole. Alternatively, the strategy may be concerned only with implementing total rewards.

The following are some examples of an overall approach (further examples of total reward strategies are given in Chapter 3).

AstraZeneca

The reward goals of AstraZeneca are:

- everyone to benefit from a common reward programme with the same features;

- draw upon the widest possible pool of talent and to be the 'employer of choice' for people already employed within the company, as well as for potential new recruits;

- meet varied and changing employee needs by introducing more value, choice and flexibility;

- win the 'war for talent' by being the first in the industry to offer this level of choice and personalization;

- promote a culture that values, recognizes and rewards outstanding performance;

- enhance employees' commitment to AstraZeneca's objectives so that they deliver their personal best.

British Telecommunications

The reward strategy at British Telecommunications (BT) indicates the general direction in which it is thought reward management at BT should go, with an emphasis on adopting a more holistic, total reward approach: It states that it will:

Use the full range of rewards (salary, bonus, benefits and recognition) to recruit and retain the best people, and to encourage and reward achievement where actions and behaviours are consistent with the BT values.

Centrica

At Centrica, following the merger between British Gas and Enron, the aim of the reward strategy was to:

- establish a link between pay and performance;

- align pay with the market;
- boost teamworking and the creation of a single Centrica culture, rather than to have the two cultures of British Gas Trading and Enron;
- create a single Centrica Business Services employment contract instead of the two that then existed.

The Children's Society

The Children's Society defined its overarching reward strategy as follows: 'We intend to develop reward systems which will support our mission and corporate objectives. We will move towards processes which:

- recognize contribution;
- are transparent;
- are owned by line managers and staff;
- reinforce leadership, accountability, teamworking and innovation;
- are market sensitive but not market led;
- are flexible and fair.'

Colt Telecom

The reward strategy of Colt Telecom is expressed as follows:

- Base salaries should be determined generally by position against median market, but always taking account of personal performance and contribution to business success.
- At the senior level there will be greater emphasis on the variable portion of the total package including bonus potential and the opportunity to participate in share programmes.
- Internal equity is sought by working to ensure that the overall compensation package reflects the value and contribution of each job, in relation to other jobs in the organization across Europe through the introduction of Colt job levels.
- Increases to base salary and variable pay will always be related to the company's ability to pay. Compensation must be affordable by the business in relation to its business success and equitable to its employees, customers and shareholders.

Diageo

The overall objective of the reward strategy at Diageo is to 'release the potential of every employee to deliver Diageo's performance goals'. The role of the reward strategy comprises five key elements:

- Support and enable the talent agenda. 'Our role in reward is to help to provide the talent the business needs, at the right time, in the right place and for the right price,' said Nicki Demby, Diageo's former Performance and Reward Director. 'This means developing reward processes and plans that will hire the best talent, keep it and develop it. We simply can't buy all the talent that we need to take the organization into its future. We need to grow our own.'

- Provide clear principles to enable decision making in the business. By developing clear principles, Diageo hopes that when line managers are faced with choices, the right decisions will be more obvious. 'Less demand will be placed on reward "experts" in the business, who can spend more of their time on value creating enhancements to our processes.'

- Align the reward approach with Diageo business strategy. The success of the reward strategy depends heavily on developing appropriate performance measures in incentives, the cost-effective delivery of reward and consistent processes.

- Enable every employee to understand why they get paid what they get paid. 'We need to have a big push on communication,' admits Nicki Demby. 'People do not necessarily understand what they are paid and how we perform. The connection between performance and reward needs to become visceral. As a formal part of each business review, we are telling people the impact the performance of their business is likely to have on their pay. It helps people to make the connections between the business decisions that they make and the likely personal impact.'

- Have a customer service ethic that results in great execution. The reward team's ethic is now based on a much greater orientation towards the needs of employees – its internal customers. 'This demands great planning, great communication and great execution,' said Nicki Demby.

Friends Provident

The rationale behind the development of a reward strategy at Friends Provident was the need to:

- match salaries directly to the market;

- give line managers greater accountability for staff salaries and career progression;

- increase the flexibility of pay arrangements at business unit level;

- facilitate a real and fundamental top-down change in corporate culture;

- reward the best performers by paying salaries above the market rate;

- manage salary costs;

- encourage greater accountability by staff for development of their own competencies.

Kent County Council

The reward strategy is to:

- pay people a fair rate for the job and give additional reward for excellent contribution;

- ensure the pay structure is simple, fair, transparent and modern;

- offer a flexible package that meets the needs of a diverse workforce;

- recognize family commitments, provide opportunities for flexible working and promote personal fitness and a healthy work–life balance.

Lloyds TSB

The emphasis at Lloyds TSB is on creating a 'compelling employment offer' – one that is more individually focused, tailored to employees' needs and interests, and more in tune with the expectations of a diverse workforce.

Nationwide

At Nationwide the organizational redesign of their reward system emerged from the company's desire to:

- respond to occupational and labour market pressures;

- encourage more flexible working practices;

- streamline operations;

- improve customer service;

- increase skills.

Tesco

Tesco's overall reward strategy is to:

- be on the right side of the competition on total reward, with the reward package being above the median;

- focus on making reward investment deliver more rather than reducing the size of the pot;

- reinvest to ensure that every element of reward adds value to the business and is valued by staff;

- build a simplified, global pay and grading system that enables mobility and flexibility and supports the values that are critical to future business growth;

- ensure the affordability of the reward package is sustainable, and use Tesco's buying power to deliver as much unbeatable value to staff as to customers;

- focus on rewarding staff for their contribution in a way that enables them to benefit directly from the success they help to create;

- ensure more transparency so that the reward package offered by the company is fully understood and valued.

Specific reward strategies

Specific reward strategies are more closely focused on one issue, or two or three linked issues that can be dealt with in a single programme, often over a limited timescale to respond to pressing needs. Examples of such issues include:

- placing reward in a programme for developing a high-performance work system;

- introducing a substantially revised job evaluation scheme;

- conducting a systematic programme for ensuring that as far as possible equal pay for work of equal value is achieved;

- developing a new grade and pay structure such as a broad-banded, job-family or career-family structure;

- introducing or revising a contingent pay scheme;

- replacing a traditional performance appraisal scheme with performance management processes which emphasize development and motivation;

- introducing flexible benefits.

Examples of more closely focused reward strategies are given below.

The aims of the reward strategy devised by Airbus were to introduce performance pay for all employees, ensure that its rates were competitive with the external market and deal with anomalies caused by previous rigidities, such as grade drift brought about by people having to be promoted to a higher grade to receive additional pay.

The reward strategy at Comet concentrated on developing a comprehensive recognition scheme, defined as that part of total reward that is not 'promised' and is also typically non-cash. The aim was to recognize the accomplishment of 'extra mile' performance rather than everyday performance.

In the Corporation of London, a long-standing job evaluation scheme had decayed and grade drift (upgradings not justified by a real increase in responsibility) was common. The strategy was to develop an entirely new job evaluation scheme and use that to help in the design of a broad-banded job-family structure.

When Glaxo Wellcome and SmithKline Beecham merged to form GlaxoSmithKline (with 100,000 employees worldwide), the organization adopted a new approach to reward that embodied the new GSK 'spirit' of entrepreneurship, innovation and performance. This stressed pay for performance and increased the proportion of pay 'at risk'.

In the National Union of Teachers the strategy was to develop a new broad-graded pay structure. To do this it was necessary to design a new job evaluation scheme as a basis for the structure.

When Price Waterhouse merged with Coopers and Lybrand to form PriceWaterhouseCoopers, only the former had a flexible benefits plan. Flex had been successful in Price Waterhouse but the two approaches needed to be harmonized and staff formerly with Coopers and Lybrand made it clear that they also wanted flexibility, so Choices, its new flexible benefits plan, was developed for all 20,000 UK employees.

The Shaw Trust, a voluntary organization providing employment for people with disabilities, had a traditional public sector-type pay scheme – a spine with progression by fixed increments related to service. The pressure for the trust to function more like a business than a charity led to the trustees advocating performance pay. Following extensive analysis and discussion a strategy emerged to introduce contribution-related pay that, because it was concerned with both results and competency, was felt to be in tune with the culture of the organization.

The structure of reward strategy

Reward strategies are diverse and so is the structure used by different organizations to define and present them. Some reward strategies are more complex than others but in one form or other their structure may contain:

- A declaration of intent: the proposed reward developments.

- A rationale: the reasons why the proposals are being made. The rationale makes out the business case for the proposals, indicating how they will meet business needs and setting out the costs and the benefits. It also refers to any people issues that need to be addressed and how the strategy will deal with them. It includes a clear statement of the objectives of the strategy and the criteria for success.

- A definition of guiding principles: the values that it is believed should be adopted in formulating and implementing the strategy.

- A plan: how, when and by whom the reward initiatives will be implemented. The plan indicates what steps have to be taken and allows for resource constraints and the need for communications, involvement and training. The priorities attached to each element of the strategy are indicated and a timetable for implementation drawn up.

Criteria for an effective reward strategy

- It supports the achievement of business goals.

- It takes account of the needs of employees as well as those of the organization and its other stakeholders.

- It is founded on detailed analysis and study, not just wishful thinking.

- It has clearly defined and achievable objectives.

- It can be turned into actionable programmes that anticipate implementation requirements and problems.

- It is coherent and integrated, being composed of components that fit with and support each other.

- It provides a framework within which consistent reward decisions can be made.

Developing reward strategy

The formulation of reward strategy is best described as a process for developing a sense of direction, making the best use of resources and ensuring strategic fit. The considerations that should be taken into account when reviewing and rethinking existing rewards are discussed below.

Limitations of the formal approach to developing reward strategy

The development of reward strategy has often been described as a logical, step-by-step affair, the outcome of which is a formal written statement that provides a definitive guide to the organization's intentions. Many people still believe this and act as if it were the case, but it is a misrepresentation of reality. In practice the formulation of strategy can never be as rational and linear a process as some writers describe it or as some managers attempt to make it. There are limitations to the totally logical model of management that underpins the concept of strategic reward. In the words of Mabey *et al* (1998) this is 'a model of management which is more rational than is achievable in practice'. The temptation is to prescribe specific stages for the process, but this depends largely on political and social considerations, the organizational context and the scale and nature of the reward changes involved. Reward strategy is a complex process that does not and in many situations cannot take place in a sequence of predetermined steps.

It's about evolution not revolution

Reward professionals rarely start with a clean sheet. They have to take note, and keep taking note, of changes in organizational requirements that are happening all the time. They must track emerging trends and modify their views accordingly, as long as they do not leap too hastily on the latest bandwagon. They have to ensure that reward strategy can be implemented at a pace the organization can manage and people can deal with. The fundamental change in culture often inherent in such projects takes a lot of time – and trouble – to achieve.

It may be helpful to define reward strategy formally for the record and as a basis for planning and communication. But this should be regarded as no more than a piece of paper that can be modified when needs change – as they will – not as a tablet of stone. Reward strategy, like business strategy, is likely to be formulated and re-formulated as it is used. It may emerge over time in response to evolving situations to become, in the words of Mintzberg (1987), a 'pattern in a stream of activities'. An HR Director told Duncan Brown and Steven Perkins (2007) that: 'We deliberately didn't have a reward strategy, it would have been a nine-day wonder… we let it evolve, step-by-step.' Brown and Perkins also noted that: 'Truly strategic reward approaches are not about supposed best practice or quick fixes or quick wins.'

Focus on the context

Developing reward strategy is a matter of thinking about what is likely to work best for the organization within its context, rather than the 'next big thing'. Will Astill, Reward Manager of B&Q, explains the thinking behind their reward review:

> An overriding theme running through our review was on the desirability of adopting a strategic approach. It wasn't a case of 'let's follow the best practice', nor were we lured into adopting the latest fads and fashions. Taking what someone has done before will not push you ahead of rivals.

Tim Fevyer, when Senior Manager Compensation and Benefits at Lloyds TSB, had a similar message: 'We need to get away from adopting new initiative after new initiative and move away from a culture of "flavour of the month".'

Manage the balance

A reward strategy can include all sorts of things. But it is necessary to get the balance right, to pay attention to the initiatives that are most needed and are most likely to make a difference. It is also necessary to establish priorities, reflect realities and make the right strategic choices. If an attempt is made to do too much too soon, or go too far and too fast in one direction, trouble will ensue. For example, it is necessary to balance the often competing claims of pay flexibility against cost control, the devolution of reward responsibilities down the organization against consistency across it, internal equity against external competitiveness and individual incentives against teamwork.

Keep it simple

Over-complexity is the bane of reward management. It complicates implementation, puts off the people affected, hampers effective communication and makes the life of line managers difficult. The history of reward management is littered with examples of 'the light that failed' – over-engineered and ambitious plans that did not work.

Think implementation

No reward initiative should be planned without thinking about how it is going to be implemented, what problems might arise and how they will be dealt with. It is particularly important to consider the part that will be played by line managers in implementation and whether they are up to the task. It is also necessary to consider the reactions of people generally – the extent to which they might resist change and what can be done about it. Change management has to be planned; it won't work if it takes place on an ad hoc basis after the event.

Achieve vertical and horizontal integration

One of the most important characteristics of the strategic reward concept is the quest for vertical and horizontal integration as defined at the beginning of this chapter.

Vertical integration

The factors that can make the achievement of vertical integration difficult are:

- The business strategy may not be clearly defined. It could be in an emergent or evolutionary state, which would mean that there would be little or nothing with which to fit the reward strategy.

- Even if the business strategy is clear, it may be difficult to determine precisely how reward strategies could help in specific ways to support the achievement of particular business objectives. A good business case can only be made if it can be demonstrated that there will be a measurable link between the reward strategy and business performance in the area concerned.

- Even if there is a link, reward specialists have to possess the strategic capability to make the connection. They need to be able to see the big picture, understand the business drivers and appreciate how reward policies and practices can impact on them – and none of this is easy.

- Barriers exist between top management and the reward or HR function. The former may not be receptive because they don't believe this is necessary, and reward or HR specialists are not capable of persuading them that they should listen, or do not have access to them on strategic issues, or lack credibility with top management as a function that knows anything about the business or should even have anything to do with the business.

It is up to reward practitioners in their strategic role to overcome these problems by getting to know what the business is aiming to do and what drives it (this should be possible even when strategies are 'emergent'), understanding just how reward practices make an impact, and achieving access to strategic business decision making by demonstrating their credibility as an integral part of the management of the business.

Horizontal integration

The factors that inhibit the achievement of horizontal fit are difficulties in:

- deciding which bundles are likely to be best;
- actually linking practices together – it is always easier to deal with one practice at a time;
- managing the interdependencies between different parts of a bundle;
- convincing top management and line managers that bundling will benefit the organization and them.

These can be overcome by dedicated reward professionals but it is hard work.

Examples of vertical and horizontal integration

The following examples of vertical and horizontal integration are derived from case studies produced by e-reward (2003–2005).

B&Q summarized the alignment between their business and HR and reward strategies as shown in Figure 4.1.

In GlaxoSmithKline the business strategy is very different from that adopted by B&Q but, similarly, it is reinforced by the HR and reward strategies as shown in Figure 4.2.

The integration of strategy at Lands' End is shown in Figure 4.3.

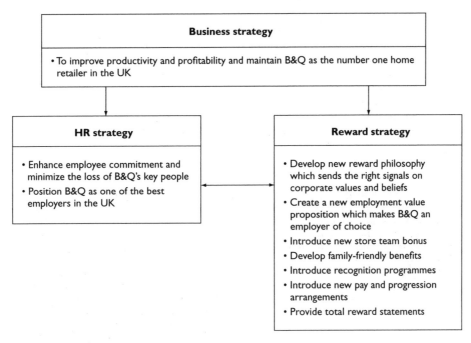

Figure 4.1 Integrated reward strategy at B&Q

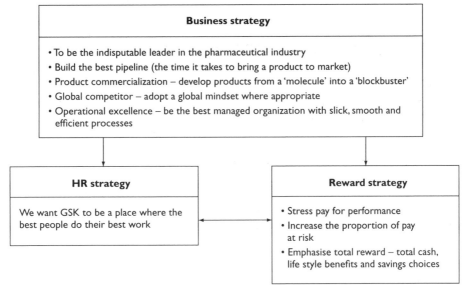

Figure 4.2 Integrated reward strategy at GlaxoSmithKline

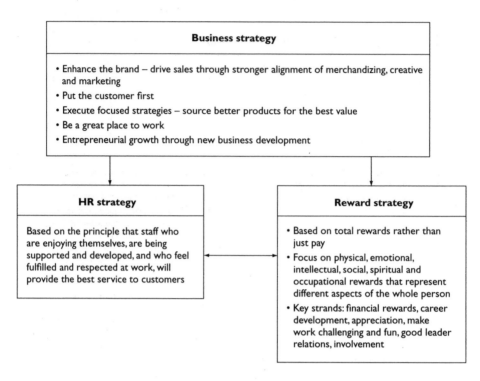

Figure 4.3   Integrated reward strategy at Lands' End

Implementing reward strategy

The aim of implementation is to make the reward strategy an operating reality by building the capacity of the organization to put into practice the proposals worked out in the development stage. It is always essential to design with implementation in mind.

Issues and problems of reward strategy implementation

A say–do gap in reward strategy often occurs when the reward strategy as conceived at the development stage is unrealistic and unduly complex, and implementation is hurried without adequate pilot testing or analysis of the likely consequences. Problems can be caused by poor project management, inadequate attention to managing change and neglecting to ensure that the supporting processes such as performance management are in place. Failure to achieve acceptance and understanding of the strategy and commitment to it, by involving line managers, staff and their representatives in the design and testing of processes and by communicating properly are common reasons for implementation problems. Underestimating the importance of providing guidance and training to line managers to ensure they are capable of playing their part in implementing and operating the strategy can also create difficulties.

Implementing worthwhile, realistic and achievable strategies

Strategy must be implementation orientated. Effective implementation is dependent on good design, and good design is always concerned with producing something worthwhile that will work. No initiative should be implemented without examining the return on investment. This is the foundation for a business case.

Six tips for implementing reward strategy

- Define what objectives are to be achieved by the strategy and how its impact will be measured.
- Create a project plan that sets out what needs to be done, when and by whom.
- Decide what supporting processes will be needed and how they can be made available.
- Ensure through communication, involvement and training that those involved know what they have to, know why they are expected to do it, believe that it is worthwhile and have the skills to do it.
- Establish a change management programme to ensure that the strategy is introduced smoothly and deal with the concerns of anyone who may react negatively to it.
- Identify any other likely implementation problems and decide how they will be dealt with.

References

Armstrong, M and Brown, D (2006) *Strategic Reward: Making it happen*, Kogan Page, London

Brown, D (2001) *Reward Strategies: From intent to impact*, CIPD, London

Brown, D and Perkins, S (2007) Reward strategy: the reality of making it happen, *WorldatWork Journal*, **16** (2), pp 82–93

Cox, A and Purcell, J (1998) Searching for leverage: pay systems, trust, motivation and commitment in SMEs, in *Trust, Motivation and Commitment*, ed SJ Perkins and St John Sandringham, Strategic Remuneration Centre, Faringdon

e-reward (2003–2005) Reward case studies, e-reward, Stockport

Kantor, R and Kao, T (2004) Total rewards: clarity from the confusion and chaos, *WorldatWork Journal*, third quarter, pp 7–15

Mabey, C, Salaman, G and Storey, J (1998) *Human Resource Management: A strategic introduction*, 2nd edn, Blackwell, Oxford

Mintzberg, H (1987) Crafting strategy, *Harvard Business Review*, July–August, pp 66–74

Murlis, H (1996) *Pay at the Crossroads*, IPD, London

Trevor, J (2009) Can pay be strategic? In *Rethinking Reward*, ed S Corby, S Palmer and E Lindop, Palgrave Macmillan, Basingstoke

Wright, P M and Nishii, L H (2004) Strategic HRM and organizational behaviour: integrating multiple levels of analysis, Erasmus University Conference 'HRM: What's Next'

International Reward

Key concepts and terms

- Convergence
- Divergence
- Globalization
- Home-based pay

- Host-based pay
- International firms
- Multinational firms

Learning outcomes

On completing this chapter you should be able to define these key concepts. You should also know about:

- The international scene
- International reward strategy
- Convergent or divergent reward policies and practices

- Guiding principles for international reward
- Expatriate pay and allowances

Introduction

International reward management is the process of rewarding people in international or multinational organizations. It can involve the worldwide management of rewards, not just the management of expatriates. This chapter starts with a review of the international scene, including definitions of what is meant by international and multinational firms and globalization. It continues with a review of international reward strategy before dealing in more detail with the management of rewards for expatriates.

The international scene

The international scene is composed of international and multinational firms working in the context of globalization.

International firms are those in which operations take place in subsidiaries overseas that rely on the business expertise or manufacturing capacity of the parent company. They offer products or services that are rationalized and standardized to enable production or provision to be carried out locally in a cost-efficient way. Perkins and Hendry (1999) state that international firms seem to be polarizing around two organizational approaches: a) regionalization, where local customer service is important, or b) global business streams that involve setting up centrally controlled business segments that deal with a related range of products worldwide.

Multinational firms are those in which a number of businesses in different countries are managed as a whole from the centre. The degree of autonomy they have will vary and the subsidiaries are not subject to rigid control except over the quality and presentation of the product or service. They rely on the technical know-how of the parent company but usually carry out their own manufacturing, service delivery or distribution activities.

The international scene is linked to the notion of globalization, that is, international economic integration in worldwide markets. This is defined by the International Monetary Fund (1997) as 'the growing economic interdependence of countries worldwide through increasing volume and variety of cross-border transactions in goods and services, freer international capital flows, and more rapid and widespread diffusion of technology'. Globalization is associated with easily transferable technology and reductions in international trade barriers. As Ulrich (1997) has pointed out, it requires organizations to move people, ideas, products and information around the world to meet local needs. New and important ingredients must be added to the mix when making business strategy: volatile political situations, contentious global trade issues, fluctuating exchange rates and unfamiliar cultures.

Firms are being forced to react to these issues in their international resourcing and reward approaches. A survey by Cendant Mobility (2002) showed that a majority of international organizations were planning to move more staff between locations to meet their increasingly global businesses' needs and to transfer relevant knowledge and skills. Yet a growing number also reported increasing difficulty in actually achieving this, with factors such as the growth of dual-career couples and political instability contributing to an apparent greater reluctance to move overseas. All these impact on reward strategy.

Traditionally, discussions of international reward strategies and practices have tended to focus on an elite of expatriate workers, sourced from headquarter locations and rewarded in isolation from local country staff. Today a diverse and complex pattern is emerging, requiring a more strategic approach than simply copying the near-universal practice of other multinationals.

Stephen Perkins (2006) explains that achieving an appropriate 'global/local' balance in international staffing and rewards has therefore become a much more strategic and challenging issue for HR and reward managers to address. Major organizations such as BP and The World Bank have overhauled their policies in recent years to achieve their key strategic reward goals of mobility and affordability in this more demanding global context.

International reward strategy

International reward strategy is concerned with the development of an integrated approach to building reward policies and practices across international boundaries. It should be integrated in the sense that it takes into account the business goals and drivers of the parent company while at the same time fitting the strategy to the different contexts and cultures across the globe. The issue of the extent to which the reward strategy should be centralized or decentralized (convergence or divergence) needs to be addressed. The strategy should be based on guiding principles and should cover all aspects of reward management.

Integration

As White (2005) points out, 'Best practice tells us that global rewards must not be considered piecemeal'. He also emphasizes that:

> The development of any reward programme calls for an integrated approach whereby each individual element of reward supports the others to reinforce organizational objectives. A global rewards philosophy and total rewards approach can facilitate alignment of an organization's rewards with business strategy, focus employees on the business goals, and reinforce consistent pay practices.

But he also comments that 'different local market practices, regulations and culture are indicators that a one size fits all system will not be truly effective.'

Convergence or divergence: general considerations

An issue facing all international firms is the extent to which their HR policies, including reward, should either 'converge' worldwide to be basically the same in each location, or 'diverge' to be differentiated in response to local requirements. There is a natural tendency for managerial traditions in the parent company to shape the nature of key decisions, but there are strong arguments for giving as much local autonomy as possible in order to ensure that local requirements are sufficiently taken into account. These arguments are often expressed in the phrase: 'Think globally but act locally.'

As noted by Adler and Ghader (1990) organizations have to follow very different HR policies and practices according to the relevant stage of their international corporate evolution: domestic, international, multinational and global. Harris and Brewster (1999) refer to this as 'the global/local dilemma', the issue being the extent to which operating units across the world are to be differentiated and at the same time integrated, controlled and coordinated. They suggest that the alternative strategies are the global approach in which the company's culture predominates and HRM is centralized and relatively standardized (an 'ethnocentric' policy), or the decentralized approach in which HRM responsibility is devolved to subsidiaries. They state that the factors affecting this choice are:

- the extent to which there are well-defined local norms;

- the degree to which an operating unit is embedded in the local environment;

- the strength of the flow of resources – finance, information and people – between the parent and the subsidiary;

- the orientation of the parent to control;

- the nature of the industry – the extent to which it is primarily a domestic industry at local level;

- the specific organizational competences including HRM that are critical for achieving competitive advantage in a global environment.

Chris Brewster (2004) believes that convergence may be increasing as a result of the power of the markets, the importance of cost, quality and productivity pressures, the emergence of transaction cost economies and the development of like-minded international cadres. The widespread practice of benchmarking 'best practice' may have contributed to convergence.

However, Brewster considers that European firms at least are so locked into their respective national institutional settings that no common model is likely to emerge in the foreseeable future. Since HR systems reflect national institutional contexts and cultures, they do not respond readily to the imperatives of technology or the market. Managers in each country operate within a national institutional context and share a set of cultural assumptions. Neither institutions nor cultures change quickly, and they rarely change in ways that are the same as those of other countries. As Hofstede (1980) emphasizes, it follows that managers in one country behave in a way that is noticeably different from those in other countries.

Laurent (1986) proposes that a truly international approach to human resource management would require the following steps:

1. An explicit recognition by the parent organization that its own peculiar ways of managing human resources reflect some of the assumptions and values of its home culture.

2. An explicit recognition by the parent organization that its peculiar ways are neither universally better or worse than others but are different and likely to exhibit strengths and weaknesses, particularly abroad.

3. An explicit recognition by the parent organization that its foreign subsidiaries may have other preferred ways of managing people that are neither intrinsically better nor worse but could possibly be more effective locally.

4. A willingness from headquarters not only to acknowledge cultural differences, but also to take active steps in order to make them discussable and therefore useable.

5. The building of a genuine belief by all parties that more creative and effective ways of managing people could be developed as a result of cross-cultural learning.

These principles apply equally well to reward management and are useful criteria to apply when deciding on the degree of centralization (convergence) or decentralization (divergence) that should be adopted.

Convergence or divergence in reward policy and practice

The reward strategy should clarify the extent to which reward policy and practice should converge or diverge internationally. There are four levels, as set out in Table 5.1.

Table 5.1   Levels of convergence and divergence of reward policies and practices

Level 1: Total convergence	Central reward policies and practices have to be followed by each operating unit. These may include a standard job evaluation scheme, uniform grade and pay structure (with scope for local market differentiation), a common approach to incentives and a common set of benefits.
Level 2: Partial convergence	Central reward policies are applied in some but not all aspects of reward management. Centralization may be limited to senior management or international staff (expatriates or nationals from countries other than the parent company working in the local country – third country nationals). Reward policies and practices for local nationals are decentralized.
Level 3: Partial divergence	Corporate job evaluation schemes and grade structures are recommended but modification is permitted to fit local conditions. However, all locations are expected to comply with the international guiding principles for reward. There may still be centralized policies for senior managers, expatriates, and third country nationals, and some benefits may be standardized. But pay levels and pay progression and incentive arrangements are determined locally.
Level 4: Total divergence	Local companies have complete freedom to develop and apply their own reward policies and practices, although they may be made aware of the international guiding principles.

Guiding principles for international reward

Guiding principles for international reward can be set out under the following policy headings:

- the importance attached to a total rewards approach;

- the use of job evaluation to provide for internal equity;

- the relationship between levels of pay in the local company and local market rates;

- the degree of flexibility present in grade and pay structures;

- the scope for pay progression;

- the importance attached to paying for contributions;

- the use of variable pay – short, medium and long-term incentives;

- the use of forms of recognition other than pay;

- the use of flexible benefits;

- the basis upon which expatriates and third country nationals should be paid.

The content of international reward strategy

International reward strategy may cover the areas included in the guiding principles, namely: total reward, job evaluation, market pricing grade and pay structures, contingent pay, benefits and remuneration of expatriates and third-country nationals.

Rewards for expatriates

As businesses expand globally, they tend to send an increasing number of staff abroad as expatriates. The assignment may be a short-term attachment to provide guidance and expertise, or it may be a secondment to an overseas location that lasts two or three years. Managing expatriates presents a number of problems: for example persuading people to work in possibly unpleasant or even dangerous countries, convincing them that an overseas assignment is a good career move, dealing with the issues raised by the partners of employees who do not want their career or life at home disrupted, and coping with the fact that on returning to their home country, expatriates often find that their real earnings have fallen. A particularly difficult problem is that of remuneration (pay, benefits and allowances) and the approaches available to solving it are considered below.

Expatriate remuneration policies

Expatriate remuneration policies may be based on the following propositions:

- Expatriates should not be worse off as a result of working abroad, neither should they be significantly better off for doing essentially the same job although they may be compensated for the extra demands made overseas or for the living and working conditions there.

- Home country living standards should be maintained as far as possible.

- Higher responsibility should be reflected in the salary paid (this may be a notional home salary).

- The remuneration package should be competitive.

- In developing the remuneration package, particular care has to be taken to giving proper consideration to the conditions under which the employee will be working abroad.

- Account should be taken of the need to maintain equity as far as possible in remuneration between expatriates, some of whom will be from different countries.

- Account also has to be taken of the problems that may arise when expatriates are paid more than nationals in the country in which they are working who are in similar jobs.

- The package should be cost effective; in other words, the contribution made by expatriates should justify the total cost of maintaining them abroad – assignment costs can total three or four times the equivalent package in the home country.

Expatriate pay

There are four approaches to calculating expatriate pay: home country, host country, selected country and hybrid.

Home-country basis

The home based method (sometimes called the balance sheet approach) 'builds up' the salary to be paid to the expatriate in the following steps:

1. Determine the salary that would be paid for the expatriate's job in the home country, net of income tax and National Insurance contributions.

2. Calculate the 'home country spendable' or 'net disposable' income. This is the portion of income used for day-to-day expenditure at home.

3. Apply a cost of living index to the 'host country expendable income' to give the equivalent buying power in the host country. This is used as a measure of expenditure levels in the

host country and is an important yardstick that is used to ensure that the expatriate will be no worse off abroad than at home.

4. Add extra allowances for working abroad (see below).

This is the most popular approach.

Host-country basis

This involves paying the market rate for the job in the host country. Allowances may be paid for the expenditure incurred by expatriates because they are living abroad, such as second home costs and children's education.

Selected-country basis

The salary structure in a selected country (often where the company's headquarters are sited) provides the base and this is built up as in the home country method.

Hybrid basis

This approach divides the expatriate's salary into two components. One – the local component – is the same for all expatriates working in jobs at the same level irrespective of their country of origin. The other local component is based on a calculation of the spendable income in the host country required to maintain a UK standard of living.

Choice of approach

The choice is often between the two most popular approaches – the home and host-based methods. Their advantages and disadvantages are set out in Table 5.2.

The choice will depend upon the organization's convergence or divergence strategy. To a large extent it also depends on how important it is to encourage people to work overseas for limited duration assignments, and how much importance is attached to ensuring the motivation and commitment of the host country staff.

Allowances

Companies add a number of allowances, as described below, to the expatriate's salary to calculate the total expatriate remuneration package. They are designed to compensate for disruption and to make the assignment attractive to the employee. Most are applied to the notional home salary but one of them, the cost-of-living allowance, is based on spendable income.

Table 5.2 Advantages and disadvantages of the home and host-based methods of paying expatriates

Method	Advantages	Disadvantages
Home-based	• Ensures that expatriates do not lose out by working abroad. • Easy to communicate to expatriates. • Easier to slot back into home country salary on return. • Particularly appropriate for shorter assignments after which the employee will return home.	• Expatriates may be paid significantly more than local nationals doing the same jobs, thereby causing dissatisfaction and possible friction. • In effect there will be two reward systems in the same country, which can cause confusion.
Host-based	• Avoids the possible dissatisfaction and friction which can arise when expatriates are paid significantly more than local nationals doing the same jobs. • Enables one coherent pay system to be maintained.	• Expatriates might lose out, making it more difficult to persuade people to work abroad. • May be harder to assimilate expatriates back into their own country's pay systems.

- Cost-of-living-allowance: the cost-of-living allowance is reached by applying an index to the home country spendable income. The index measures the relative cost, in the host country, of purchasing conventional 'shopping basket' items such as food and clothing.

- Incentive premium: this offers the expatriate a financial inducement to accept the assignment. It may be intended to compensate for disruption to family life. But companies are tending to reduce this premium or do away with it altogether, particularly for intra-European assignments. They are questioning why an employee should receive 10–15 per cent of gross salary for simply moving from one culturally similar country to another when no such allowance would be payable in the case of a relocation within the UK.

- Hardship allowance: this compensates for discomfort and difficulty in the host country such as an unpleasant climate, health hazards, poor communications, isolation, language difficulties, risk and poor amenities.

- Separation allowance: this may be paid if expatriates cannot take their family abroad.

- Clothing allowance: a payment for special clothing and accessories that expatriates need to buy.

- Relocation allowance: this covers the cost of expenses arising when moving from one country to another.

- Housing/utilities: any additional costs of accommodation or utilities.

Benefits

The benefits provided to expatriates include cars, the costs of educating children, home leave, rest and recuperation leave if the expatriate is working in a high hardship territory.

International reward: six tips

- Decide on the extent to which you want international reward policies to be uniformly based on those in headquarters or varied in different countries (a convergence or divergence policy).

- If the policy is inclined to convergence, decide what elements of corporate reward policy and practice you want to be applied internationally.

- If the policy is inclined to divergence, decide what guiding principles, if any, you wish to be adopted in overseas territories.

- Take steps to ensure that managements in overseas territories are capable of applying the central policies or following the guidelines, and monitor how these policies and guidelines are implemented.

- Evaluate the advantages and disadvantages of each method of rewarding expatriates in different countries and decide on the most appropriate method.

- Remember that important aspects of the total reward package for expatriates will be their working environment, the existence of family-friendly policies, career opportunities abroad and when they return and the existence of satisfactory re-entry policies (job placement and career choice).

References

Adler, N J and Ghader, F (1990) Strategic human resource management: a global perspective, in *International Human Resource Management*, ed R Pieper, W De Gruyter, Berlin/New York

Brewster, C (2004) European perspectives of human resource management, *Human Resource Management Review*, **14** (4), pp 365–82

Cendant Mobility (2002) *Worldwide Benchmark Study: New approaches to global mobility*, Cendant Mobility, Danbury, Conn

Harris, H and Brewster, C (1999) International human resource management: the European contribution, in *International HRM: Contemporary issues in Europe*, ed C Brewster and H Harris, Routledge, London

Hofstede, G (1980) *Cultural Consequences: International differences in work-related values*, Sage, Beverley Hills, CA

International Monetary Fund (1997) *World Economic Outlook*, IMF, Washington DC

Laurent, A (1986) The cross-cultural puzzle in international human resource management, *Human Resource Management*, **21**, pp 91–102

Perkins, S (2006) *Guide to International Reward and Recognition*, CIPD, London

Perkins, S and Hendry, C (1999) *The IPD Guide on International Reward and Recognition*, IPD, London

Ulrich, D (1997) *Human Resource Champions*, Harvard Business School Press, Boston

White, R (2005) A strategic approach to building a consistent global rewards program, *Compensation & Benefits Review*, July/August, pp 23–40

Part II
Performance and Reward

Performance Management and Reward

Introduction

Performance management can be defined broadly as the process of taking systematic action to improve organizational, team and individual performance. It enables performance expectations to be defined and creates the basis for developing organizational and individual capability. For individuals and teams, performance management is associated with both financial and non-financial rewards.

Organizations exist to meet the needs of their stakeholders. They do this in five ways: first by delivering high-quality goods and services, second by acting ethically (exercising social responsibility) with regard to their employees and the public at large, third by rewarding their employees equitably according to their contribution, fourth, in the private sector, rewarding shareholders by increasing the value of their holdings, as long as this is consistent with the requirement to meet the needs of other stakeholders, and fifth, ensuring that the organization has the capability required to guarantee continuing success.

Performance is the key and reward can make a significant contribution to achieving high performance by enhancing engagement, as described in Chapter 7. As Nicki Demby, formerly Diageo's performance and reward director, told the e-reward researcher (e-reward, 2003a): 'Great incentives should be used to drive great business performance. Great performers will always perform. Great reward programmes can help the whole organization to perform.'

Performance also depends on organizational capability – the capacity of an organization to perform effectively in order to achieve desired results. These could include sustained competitive advantage and increased shareholder-value in the private sector or high-quality and cost-effective services in the public and not-for-profit sectors.

The questions that will be answered in this chapter are: What is meant by performance? What are the factors that influence performance? How can high performance be achieved? How do rewards help to achieve high performance? What can be done to manage organizational, team and individual performance?

All these questions relate to the definition in the CIPD's HR Profession Map of what an HR professional needs to do and know about performance and reward, which is as follows:

> Builds a high-performance culture by delivering programmes that recognize and reward critical skills, capabilities, experience and performance.

The meaning of performance

The Oxford English Dictionary defines performance as: 'The accomplishment, execution, carrying out, working out of anything ordered or undertaken.' This refers to outputs/outcomes (accomplishment) but also states that performance is about doing the work as well as about the results achieved.

Performance is indeed often regarded as simply the outcomes achieved: a record of a person's accomplishments. Kane (1996) argues that performance 'is something that the person leaves behind and that exists apart from the purpose'. Bernardin *et al* (1995) believe that: 'Performance should be defined as the outcomes of work because they provide the strongest linkage to the strategic goals of the organization, customer satisfaction, and economic contributions.'

Borman and Motowidlo (1993) put forward the notion of contextual performance, which covers non-job specific behaviours such as cooperation, dedication, enthusiasm and persistence and is differentiated from task performance covering job-specific behaviours. As Fletcher (2001) mentions, contextual performance deals with attributes that go beyond task competence and that foster behaviours that enhance the climate and effectiveness of the organization.

Performance could therefore be regarded as behaviour – the way in which organizations, teams and individuals get work done. Campbell (1990) states that: 'Performance is behaviour and should be distinguished from the outcomes because they can be contaminated by systems factors.'

A more comprehensive view of performance is achieved if it is defined as embracing both behaviour and outcomes. This was well put by Brumbach (1988) as follows: 'Performance means both behaviours and results. Behaviours emanate from the performer and transform performance from abstraction to action. Not just the instruments for results, behaviours are also outcomes in their own right – the product of mental and physical effort applied to tasks – and can be judged apart from results.'

Performance is a complicated notion. As Bates and Holton (1995) emphasize, 'Performance is a multi-dimensional construct.' It has been pointed out by Campbell *et al* (1993) that the components of performance are: 1) job-specific task proficiency, 2) non-job-specific proficiency (eg organizational citizenship behaviour), 3) written and oral communication proficiency, 4) demonstration of effort, 5) maintenance of personal discipline, 6) facilitation of peer and team performance, 7) supervision/leadership, and 8) management/administration.

This concept of performance leads to the conclusion that when managing the performance of teams and individuals a number of factors have to be considered, including both inputs (behaviour) and outputs (results).

Influences on performance

The performance of individuals depends on a number of factors as reviewed below, their level of engagement as covered in Chapter 7, their levels of competency and skill, which can be developed with the help of a performance management system as considered later in this chapter, and, importantly, the work system and the quality of leadership they experience as discussed at the end of this section.

Influences on individual performance

Vroom (1964) suggested that performance is a function of ability and motivation as depicted in the formula: Performance = f (Ability x Motivation). The effects of ability and motivation on performance are not additive but multiplicative. People need both ability and motivation to perform well and if either ability or motivation is zero there will be no effective performance.

A formula for performance was originated by Blumberg and Pringle (1982). Their equation was: Performance = Individual Attributes × Work Effort × Organizational Support. By including organizational support in the formula they brought in the organizational context as a factor affecting performance.

Research carried out by Bailey *et al* (2001) in 45 establishments focused on another factor affecting performance – the opportunity to participate. They noted that 'organizing the work process so that non-managerial employees have the opportunity to contribute discretionary effort is the central feature of a high-performance work system.' (This was one of the earlier uses of the term discretionary effort.)

The 'AMO' formula put forward by Boxall and Purcell (2003) is a combination of the Vroom's and Bailey, Berg and Sandy's ideas This model posits that performance is a function of Ability + Motivation + Opportunity to Participate (note that the relationship is additive not multiplicative).

The work system

All these formulas are concerned with individual performance, but this is influenced by systems as well as person factors. These include the support people get from the organization and the leadership and support they get from their managers, and other contextual factors outside the control of individuals. Jones (1995) makes the radical proposal that the aim should be to 'manage context not performance' and goes on to explain that:

> *In this equation, the role of management focuses on clear, coherent support for employees by providing information about organization goals, resources, technology, structure, and policy, thus creating a context that has multiplicative impact on the employees, their individual attributes (competency to perform), and their work effort (willingness to perform). In short, managing context is entirely about helping people understand; it is about turning on the lights.*

It was emphasized by Deming (1986) that differences in performance are largely due to systems variations. Coens and Jenkins (2002) were even more adamant. They wrote:

An organizational system is composed of the people who do the work but far more than that. It also includes the organization's methods, structure, support, materials, equipment, customers, work culture, internal and external environments (such as markets, the community, governments), and the interaction of these components. Each part of the system has its own purpose but at the same time is dependent on the other parts... Because of the interdependency of the parts, improvement strategies aimed at the parts, such as appraisal, do little or nothing to improve the system.

Leadership

Leadership as provided by line managers is a key factor in improving performance. The consulting firm Hay McBer, as reported by Goleman (2000), found in a study of 3,871 executives, selected from a database of more than 20,000 executives worldwide, that leadership had a direct impact on organizational climate, and that climate in turn accounted for nearly one-third of the financial results of organizations. Research by Northouse (2006) into 167 US firms in 13 industries established that over a 20-year period, leadership accounted for more variations in performance than any other variable.

Leadership can be defined as the process of getting people to do their best to achieve a desired result. This is the job of line managers, who play a crucial role in providing non-financial rewards (positive feedback, recognition, opportunity to develop and scope to exercise responsibility). They also, of course, have considerable influence on financial reward decisions – pay reviews and fixing rates of pay. Importantly, it is they who are largely responsible for operating the performance management system, job design and on-the-job coaching and development. All these activities impact directly on the performance of their teams and the individuals in them.

Taking action

All these activities are concerned with developing a high-performance culture, as discussed later in this chapter. Such a culture depends on adopting the right approach to improving organizational, team and individual performance and getting the work system and leadership right. This is the responsibility of senior leaders but they can benefit from the advice, guidance and support of HR in developing performance and reward systems.

How does reward impact on performance?

Reward makes an overall positive impact on performance when it contributes to the development of a high-performance culture, one in which the values, norms and HR practices of an organization combine to create a climate in which the achievement of high levels of performance is a way of life. Such a culture can be manifested in a high-performance work system. Within the high-performance culture and work system, reward impacts on individual and organizational performance by:

- focusing attention on the values of the organization for high performance and the behaviours required to achieve it;

- ensuring that performance expectations are defined and understood;

- providing the means to encourage and recognize high performance;

- enhancing engagement and promoting positive discretionary effort;

- persuading talented people to join and stay with the organization.

The next four sections of this chapter examine in more detail the concept of a high-performance culture, the features of a high-performance work system, and the impact of reward on individual and organizational performance. These sections provide the background to the final three sections of the chapter, which deal with approaches to developing organizational, team and individual performance.

High-performance cultures

A high-performance culture is one in which people are aware of the need to perform well and behave accordingly in order to meet or exceed expectations. Such a culture embraces a number of interrelated processes that together make an impact on the performance of the organization through its people in such areas as productivity, quality, levels of customer service, growth, profits, and ultimately, in profit-making firms, the delivery of increased shareholder value. In our more heavily service and knowledge-based economy, employees have become the most important determinant of organizational success.

Characteristics of a high-performance culture

The following characteristics of a high-performance culture were defined by Lloyds TSB (source: e-reward, 2003b):

- People know what's expected of them – they are clear about their goals and accountabilities.

- They have the skills and competencies to achieve their goals.

- High performance is recognized and rewarded accordingly.

- People feel that their job is worth doing, and that there's a strong fit between the job and their capabilities.

- Managers act as supportive leaders and coaches, providing regular feedback, performance reviews and development.

- A pool of talent ensures, a continuous supply of high performers in key roles.

- There's a climate of trust and teamwork, aimed at delivering a distinctive service to the customer.

Another important characteristic is the encouragement of discretionary behaviour.

Discretionary behaviour

Discretionary behaviour takes place when employees exercise an element of choice about the amount of effort, care, innovation and productive conduct they display and how they do their job. On the basis of their longitudinal research Purcell *et al* (2003) suggested that the following conditions were required to achieve this:

- Discretionary behaviour is more likely to occur when individuals have commitment to their organization and/or when they feel motivated to do so and/or when they gain high levels of job satisfaction.

- Commitment, motivation and job satisfaction, either together or separately, will be higher when people positively experience the application of HR policies concerned with creating an able workforce, motivating valued behaviours and providing opportunities to participate.

- This positive experience will be higher if the wide range of HR policies necessary to develop ability, motivation and opportunity are both in place and mutually reinforcing.

- The way HR and reward policies and practices are implemented by front-line managers and the way top-level-espoused values and organizational cultures are enacted by them will enhance or weaken the effect of HR policies in triggering discretionary behaviour by influencing attitudes.

- The experience of success seen in performance outcomes helps reinforce positive attitudes.

Developing a high-performance culture

The above prescriptions by John Purcell and his colleagues for encouraging discretionary behaviour can be applied to the development of a high-performance culture. They are mainly concerned with general HR policies and approaches to managing people. Overall, there are three development approaches that can be adopted: 1) the implementation of high-performance working through a high-performance work system, 2) the use of rewards, and 3) the use of systematic methods of managing performance, including performance management systems. These are discussed in the remaining sections of this chapter.

High-performance work systems

A high-performance work system (HPWS) is described by Becker and Huselid (1998) as: 'An internally consistent and coherent HRM system that is focused on solving operational problems and implementing the firm's competitive strategy'. They suggest that such a system 'is the key to the acquisition, motivation and development of the underlying intellectual assets that can be a source of sustained competitive advantage'. This is because it has the following characteristics:

- It links the firm's selection and promotion decisions to validated competency models.

- It is the basis for developing strategies that provide timely and effective support for the skills demanded to implant the firm's strategies.

- It enacts compensation and performance management policies that attract, retain and motivate high-performance employees.

High-performance work systems provide the means for creating a performance culture. They embody ways of thinking about performance in organizations and how it can be improved. They are concerned with developing and implementing bundles of complementary practices that as an integrated whole will make a much more powerful impact on performance than if they were dealt with as separate entities.

Becker, Huselid and Ulrich (2001) have stated that the aim of such systems is to develop a 'high-performance perspective in which HR and other executives view HR as a system embedded within the larger system of the firm's strategy implementation'. As Nadler (1989) commented, they are deliberately introduced in order to improve organizational, financial and operational performance. Nadler and Gerstein (1992) have characterized an HPWS as a way of thinking about organizations. It can play an important role in strategic human resource management by helping to achieve a 'fit' between information, technology, people and work.

In their seminal work *Manufacturing Advantage: Why high-performance work systems pay off*, Appelbaum *et al* (2000) stated that high-performance work systems facilitate employee involvement, skill enhancement and motivation. An HPWS is 'generally associated with workshop practices that raise the levels of trust within workplaces and increase workers' intrinsic reward from work, and thereby enhance organizational commitment'. They define high performance as a way of organizing work so that front-line workers participate in decisions that have a real impact on their jobs and the wider organization.

It is sometimes believed that high-performance work systems are just about HR policies and initiatives. But as Godard (2004) suggested, they are based on both alternative work practices and high-commitment employment practices. He called this the high-performance paradigm and described it as follows.

Alternative work practices that have been identified include: 1) alternative job design practices, including work teams (autonomous or non-autonomous), job enrichment, job rotation and related reforms; and 2) formal participatory practices, including quality circles or problem-solving groups, town hall meetings, team briefings and joint steering committees. Of these practices, work teams and quality circles can be considered as most central to the high-performance paradigm. High-commitment employment practices that have been identified include: 1) sophisticated selection and training, emphasizing values and human relations skills as well as knowledge skills; 2) behaviour-based appraisal and advancement criteria; 3) single status policies; 4) contingent pay systems, especially pay-for-knowledge, group bonuses, and profit sharing; 5) job security; 6) above-market pay and benefits; 7) grievance systems; and others.

High-performance work systems are also known as high-performance work practices (Sung and Ashton, 2005). Thompson and Heron (2005) referred to them as high-performance work organizations that 'invest in the skills and abilities of employees, design work in ways that enable employee collaboration in problem-solving, and provide incentives to motivate workers to use their discretionary effort'. The terms high-performance system, high-commitment system and high-involvement system sometimes seem to be used interchangeably. There is indeed much common ground between the practices included in them although, following Godard (2004), there may be more emphasis in a high-performance work system on alternative work practices. Sung and Ashton (2005) noted that:

> *In some cases high-performance work practices are called 'high commitment practices' (Walton, 1985) or 'high involvement management' (Lawler, 1986). More recently they have been termed 'high-performance organizations' (Lawler et al, 1998; Ashton and Sung, 2002) or 'high-involvement' work practices (Wood et al, 2001). Whilst these studies are referring to the same general phenomena the use of different 'labels' has undoubtedly added to the confusion.*

The term high-performance work system (HPWS) is the one most commonly used in both academic and practitioner circles and it is therefore adopted in this chapter. But it is recognized that high commitment and high involvement are both important factors in the pursuit of high performance. The notions incorporated in these practices therefore need to be incorporated in any programme for improving organizational capability wherever they add to the basic concepts of a high-performance work system.

Components of an HPWS

There is no generally accepted definition of an HPWS and there is no standard list of the features or components of such a system. Appelbaum and Batt (1994) identified six models: American lean production, American team production, German diversified quality production, Italian flexible specialization, Japanese lean production and Swedish socio-technical systems. These systems vary in the degree of autonomy they give the workforce, the nature of the supporting human resource practices, and the extent to which the gains from the systems are shared.

In spite of this problem of definition, an attempt to define the basic components of an HPWS was made by Shih *et al* (2005) as follows:

- Job infrastructure: workplace arrangements that equip workers with the proper abilities to do their jobs, provide them with the means to do their jobs, and give them the motivation to do their jobs. These practices must be combined to produce their proper effects.

- Training programmes to enhance employee skills: investment in increasing employee skills, knowledge and ability.

- Information sharing and worker involvement mechanisms: to understand the available alternatives and make correct decisions.

- Compensation and promotion opportunities that provide motivation: to encourage skilled employees to engage in effective discretionary decision making in a variety of environmental contingencies.

Developing a high-performance work system

A high-performance work system has to be based on a high-performance strategy that sets out intentions and plans for how a high-performance culture can be created and maintained. The strategy has to be aligned to the context of the organization and to its business strategy. Every organization will therefore develop a different strategy, as is illustrated by the case study examples set out in Table 6.1.

The approach to developing an HPWS is based on an understanding of what the goals and performance drivers of the business are, what work arrangements are appropriate to the attainment of those goals and how people can contribute to their achievement. This leads to an assessment of what type of performance culture is required and what approach to reward is appropriate for the different segments of the workforce.

The development programme requires strong leadership from the top. Stakeholders – line managers, team leaders, employees and their representatives – should be involved as much as possible through surveys, focus groups and workshops.

A high-performance work system is the basis for developing a performance culture and provides the framework for managing performance. This is sometimes assumed to be simply concerned with managing individual performance through performance management systems. But it is also very much about managing organizational and team performance as described

Table 6.1 Examples of high-performance working ingredients

Organization	High-performance working ingredients
Halo Foods	• A strategy that maintains competitiveness by increasing added value through the efforts and enhanced capability of all staff. • The integration of technical advance with people development. • Continuing reliance on teamworking and effective leadership, with innovation and self and team management skills.
Land Registry	• Organizational changes to streamline processes, raise skill levels and release talents. • Managers who could see that the problems were as much cultural as organizational. • Recruitment of people whose attitudes and aptitudes match the needs of high performance work practices.
Meritor Heavy Vehicle Braking Systems	• Skill enhancement, particularly of management and self management skills using competence frameworks. • Teamworking skills and experience used on improvement projects. • Linking learning, involvement and performance management.
Orangebox	• A strategy that relies on constant reinvention of operational capability. • Engagement and development of existing talent and initiative in productivity improvement. • Increasing use of cross-departmental projects to tackle wider opportunities.
Perkinelmer	• A vision and values worked through by managers and supervisors. • Engagement of everyone in the organization and establishment of a continuous improvement culture. • Learning as a basis for change.
United Welsh Housing Association	• Linking of better employment relations with better performance. • Using staff experience to improve customer service. • Focusing management development on the cascading of a partnership culture.

(Source: Stevens, 2005)

below. This, quite rightly, extends the study of reward management into the field of organizational management where, as an element in a coherent bundle of HR policies and practices, it should be.

Impact of reward on individual performance

Extrinsic rewards can be used as motivators to improve performance, although they are not necessarily effective in this role. They can also convey the message that performance is important and help to focus on specific aspects of performance that need to be improved. There is plenty of evidence, as quoted in Chapter 8, that in the right circumstances incentives can make a considerable impact on performance (a total of 190 studies covered individually or in meta-analyses). Although, as mentioned in that chapter, it is generally accepted that while extrinsic rewards can have an immediate and, in the right circumstances, a powerful effect on motivation and performance, intrinsic rewards can have a deeper and longer-lasting effect.

People can be motivated to achieve certain goals and will be satisfied if they achieve these goals through improved performance. They may be even more satisfied if they are then rewarded by extrinsic recognition or an intrinsic sense of achievement. This suggests that performance improvements can be achieved by giving people the opportunity to perform through job and work-system design and leadership, ensuring that they have the knowledge and skill required to perform, and rewarding them by financial or non-financial means when they do perform.

Impact of reward on organizational performance

The assumption is that improvements in organizational performance will follow improvements in individual performance. This sounds reasonable but it is difficult to prove, although some research has attempted to do this.

The findings of the research conducted by Allen and Helms (2001) were that reward practices were significant predictors of performance and explained nearly 41 per cent of the variance in organizational performance. A relatively small number of reward practices explained the bulk of variability in organizational performance; these were: employee share option plans (ESOPs), individual-based performance systems, regular expressions of appreciation, and customer-satisfaction monitoring tied to rewards. Team-based pay, flexible benefits and increased job autonomy were not significant predictors of firm performance.

A study by Brown *et al* (2003) explored the relationship between pay policy as indicated by pay levels and pay structure on organizational performance in 333 general hospitals in the State of California. The findings were:

- Pay-level practices and pay structures interact to affect resource efficiency, patient care outcomes and financial performance.
- Higher pay levels are associated with greater efficiency.
- There are diminishing returns for pay's effects on employee performance.

- No single theory can fully explain how compensation relates to organizational performance, but the results show support for efficiency theory (the belief that high levels of pay will contribute to increases in productivity).

- Higher wages can compensate for the negative effects of inequitable pay systems.

Data on pay satisfaction and organizational level outcomes was collected by Curral *et al* (2005) from 6,394 public school teachers and 117 public school districts. The findings were that pay satisfaction was positively related to school district level academic performance and negatively related to intention to quit.

Research carried out by McAdams and Hawks (1994) supported the premise that performance reward plans are instrumental in performance improvements, often with calculable returns. Just under half the companies in the study were able to attach a financial value to their plans. For these organizations, the value of the performance improvement translated into a 134 per cent net return on what was paid out to employees (excluding the costs associated with training, communications and consulting).

Managing organizational performance

The management of organizational performance takes place on a number of dimensions. It is a strategic approach that has to take account of the needs of multiple stakeholders. It is the prime responsibility of top management who plan, organize, monitor and control activities and provide leadership to achieve strategic objectives and satisfy the needs and requirements of stakeholders.

As Gheorghe and Hack (2007) observe: 'Actively managing performance is simply running a business – running the entire business as one entity. It's a continuous cycle of planning, executing, measuring results and planning the next actions. In the context of a larger strategic initiative, that means continuous improvement.'

Organizational capability

The aim of managing organizational performance is to increase organizational capability, the capacity of an organization to function effectively. It is about the ability of an organization to guarantee high levels of performance, achieve its purpose (sustained competitive advantage in a commercial business), deliver results and, importantly, meet the needs of its stakeholders. It is concerned with the organization as a system and is in line with the belief expressed by Coens and Jenkins (2002) that to 'focus on the overall "system" of the organization yields better results than trying to get individual employees to improve their performance'.

The aim is to increase organizational effectiveness by obtaining better performance from people, getting them to work well together, improving organizational processes such as the formulation and implementation of strategy, the achievement of high quality and levels of customer service, and facilitating the management of change.

This has to take place in a context in which organizations are increasingly embracing a new management culture based on inclusion, involvement and participation, rather than on the traditional command, control and compliance paradigm, which Flaherty (1999) claims 'cannot bring about the conditions and competence necessary to successfully meet the challenges of endless innovation; relentless downsizing, re-engineering, and multicultural working holistically'. This new management paradigm requires the development of a high-performance work environment through management practices that value and support achievement, growth and learning. It also calls for facilitative behaviours that focus on employee empowerment, learning and development. In other words, it needs performance management.

The dimensions of managing organizational performance

Sink and Tuttle (1990) stated that managing organizational performance includes five dimensions:

- creating visions for the future;

- planning: determining the present organizational state, and developing strategies to improve that state;

- designing, developing and implementing improvement interventions;

- designing, redesigning, developing, and implementing measurement and evaluation systems;

- putting cultural support systems in place to reward and reinforce progress.

A strategic approach to managing organizational performance means taking a broad and long-term view of where the business is going and managing performance in ways that ensure that this strategic thrust is maintained. The objective is to provide a sense of direction in an often turbulent environment, so that the business needs of the organization and the individual and collective needs of its employees can be met by the development and implementation of integrated systems for managing and developing performance.

Implementing organizational performance management

Organizational performance management systems are strategic in the sense that they are aligned to the business strategy of the organization and support the achievement of its strategic goals. They will focus on developing work systems and the working environment as well as developing individuals. To develop the systems and make them function effectively it is necessary to ensure that the strategy is understood, including, as Kaplan and Norton (2000) put it: 'The crucial but perplexing processes by which intangible assets will be converted into tangible outcomes'. The notion of mapping strategy was originated by them as a development of their concept of the balanced scorecard. Strategy maps show the cause-and-effect links by which specific improvements create desired outcomes. They are means of describing the elements of the organization's systems and their interrelationships. They therefore provide a route map for systems improvement, leading to performance improvement. In addition, they give employees a clear line of sight into how their jobs are linked to the overall objectives of the organization and provide a visual representation of a company's critical objectives and the relationships between them that drive organizational performance. Bourne *et al* (2003) call them 'success maps' which they describe as diagrams that show the logic of how the objectives of the organization interact to deliver overall performance. An example of a strategy map is given in Figure 6.1.

Figure 6.1   A strategy map

This map shows an overall objective to improve profitability as measured by return on capital employed. In the next line the map indicates that the main contributors to increased profitability are increases to the gross margin (the difference between the value of sales and the cost of sales), improvements to operational capability and better cost management. At the next level down the objective is to increase sales turnover in order to increase the gross margin. How this is to be achieved is set out in the next group of objectives and their interconnections, comprising increases in customer satisfaction and sales force effectiveness, innovations in product/market development and marketing, and improvements in customer service and quality levels. The key objective of improving operational capability is underpinned by developments in high-performance working and the contribution of the organization's human capital. The latter is supported by human resource management objectives in the fields of performance management, reward management, talent management, levels of employee engagement, and learning and development.

The overall objective of increasing profitability in this example addresses the concerns of only one section of the stakeholders of an organization, namely the investors. This need would probably be given precedence by many quoted companies. But there are other objectives that they could and should have that relate to their other stakeholders, for example those related to corporate social responsibility. These could be catered for in separate strategy maps. Better still, they could be linked to their commercial objectives. Public and voluntary sector organizations will certainly have objectives that relate to all their stakeholders as well as their overall purpose. A stakeholder approach to strategic performance management is required.

The performance prism

A multiple stakeholder framework for organizational performance management – the performance prism – has been formulated by Neely *et al* (2002). This framework is based on the proposition that organizations exist to satisfy their stakeholders, and their wants and needs should be considered first. Neely *et al* contend that companies in particular must assume a broader role than simply delivering value to their shareholders. To be successful over time, even for and on behalf of shareholders, businesses must address multiple stakeholders. If companies do not give each of these the right level of focus, both their corporate reputation and their market capitalization – and therefore shareholder value – are likely to suffer in one way or another. They suggest that the performance prism can facilitate or structure the analysis of multiple stakeholders in preparation for applying performance measurement criteria.

They explain the term 'performance prism' as follows: 'A prism refracts light. It illustrates the hidden complexity of something as apparently simple as white light. So it is with the Performance Prism. It illustrates the true complexity of performance measurement and management. It is a thinking aid which seeks to integrate five related perspectives and provide a structure that allows executives to think through the answers to five fundamental questions:

1. Stakeholder Satisfaction: Who are our stakeholders and what do they want and need?

2. Stakeholder Contribution: What do we want and need from our stakeholders?

3. Strategies: What strategies do we need to put in place to satisfy these wants and needs?

4. Processes: What processes do we need to put in place to satisfy these wants and needs?

5. Capabilities: What capabilities – people, practices, technology and infrastructure – do we need to put in place to allow us to operate our processes more effectively and efficiently?'

Managing team performance

As Purcell *et al* (1998) pointed out, teams supply the 'elusive bridge between the aims of the individual employee and the objectives of the organization... teams can provide the medium for linking employee performance targets to the factors critical to the success of the business.'

Managing team performance involves the key activities of setting work and process objectives, and conducting team reviews and individual reviews, which are described below.

Setting work objectives

Work objectives for teams should be based on an analysis of the purpose of the team and its accountabilities for achieving results. Targets and standards of performance should be discussed and agreed by the team as a whole. These may specify what individual members are expected to contribute. Project teams will agree project plans that define what has to be done, who does it, the standards expected and the timescale.

Setting process objectives

Process objectives are defined by the team getting together and agreeing how the members should conduct themselves as a team under headings related to team competencies including:

- interpersonal relationships;
- the quality of participation and collaborative effort and decision making;
- the team's relationships with internal and external customers;
- the capacity of the team to plan and control its activities;
- the ability of the team and its members to adapt to new demands and situations;
- the flexibility with which the team operates;
- the effectiveness with which individual skills are used;

- the quality of communications within the team and between the team and other teams or individuals.

Team performance reviews

Team performance review meetings analyse and assess feedback and control information on their joint achievements against objectives and project plans. The agenda for such meetings could be as follows:

- General feedback review:
  - progress of the team as a whole;
  - problems encountered by the team that have caused difficulties or hampered progress;
  - helps and hindrances to the operation of the team.
- Work reviews:
  - how well the team has functioned;
  - review of the individual contribution made by each team member – ie peer review (see below);
  - discussion of any new problems encountered by individual team members.
- Group problem solving:
  - analysis of reasons for any shortfalls or other problems;
  - agreement of what needs to be done to solve them and prevent their re-occurrence.
- Update objectives:
  - review of new requirements, opportunities or threats;
  - amendment and updating of objectives and project plans.

Managing individual performance

Individual performance is developed through performance management systems, which play an important part in performance and reward management. They provide the framework for improving performance through the agreement of performance expectations and the formulation of performance development plans. As vehicles for feedback and recognition they have a major role in a performance and reward system. They inform contingent pay decisions.

This section starts with definitions of performance management strategy and the purpose and principles of performance management. Summaries of the processes involved follow. It ends with descriptions of how performance management functions as a rewarding process, how it relates to pay and the use of ratings.

Performance management strategy

Performance management strategy is based on the resource-based view that it is the strategic development of the organization's rare, hard to imitate and hard to substitute human resources that produces its unique character and creates competitive advantage. The strategic goal will be to 'create firms which are more intelligent and flexible than their competitors' (Boxall, 1996) by developing more talented staff and by extending their skills base, and this is exactly what performance management aims to do.

The purpose of performance management

The purpose of performance management is to get better results from the organization, teams and individuals by understanding and managing performance within an agreed framework of planned goals, standards and competency requirements. It is a process for establishing shared understanding about what is to be achieved, and an approach to managing and developing people in a way that increases the probability that it will be achieved in the short and longer term. It is owned and driven by line management. Performance management enhances the engagement of people by providing the foundation upon which many non-financial motivation approaches can be built.

Principles of performance management

The extensive research conducted by the CIPD (Armstrong and Baron, 1998, 2004) identified 10 principles of performance management as stated by practitioners:

- 'A management tool which helps managers to manage.'
- 'Driven by corporate purpose and values.'
- 'To obtain solutions that work.'
- 'Only interested in things you can do something about and get a visible improvement.'
- 'Focus on changing behaviour rather than paperwork.'
- 'It's about how we manage people – it's not a system.'
- 'Performance management is what managers do: a natural process of management.'
- 'Based on accepted principle but operates flexibly.'

- 'Focus on development not pay.'

- 'Success depends on what the organization is and needs to be in its performance culture.'

The performance management cycle

Performance management is a natural process of management. It is not an HRM technique or tool. As a natural process of management, the performance management cycle as shown in Figure 6.2 corresponds with William Deming's (1986) Plan–Do–Check–Act model.

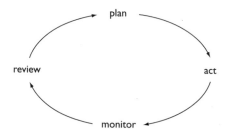

Figure 6.2   The performance management cycle

The performance management processes taking place in this cycle are:

- Plan: agreeing objectives and competence requirements; identifying the required behaviours; producing plans expressed in performance agreements for meeting objectives and improving performance; preparing personal development plans to enhance knowledge, skills and competence and reinforce the desired behaviours.

- Act: carrying out the work required to achieve objectives by reference to the plans and in response to new demands.

- Monitor: checking on progress in achieving objectives and responding to new demands; treating performance management as a continuous process – 'managing performance all the year round' – rather than an annual appraisal event.

- Review: a 'stocktaking' discussion of progress and achievements, held in a review meeting and identifying where action is required to develop performance as a basis for completing the cycle by continuing into the planning stage.

Key features of performance management

The key features of performance management are that:

- At every stage the aim is to obtain agreement between managers and individuals on how well the latter are doing and what can be done jointly to develop strengths and deal with any weaknesses.

- Discussions between managers and individuals take the form of a dialogue; managers should not attempt to dominate the process and it should not be perceived as an alternative method of control.

- Performance management is largely about managing expectations; both managers and individuals understand and agree what they expect of one another, thus developing a more positive psychological contract.

- Positive feedback is used to motivate people by recognizing their achievements and potential.

- The process is forward looking: it does not dwell on the past and the dialogue is about what can be done in the future to develop performance and give individuals the opportunity to grow (this is an important means of motivation).

- Performance management is a continuous process, not an annual event; managers and individuals are there to manage performance throughout the year.

Performance management as a rewarding process

Performance management, if carried out properly, can reward people by recognition through feedback, opportunities to achieve, the scope to develop skills, and guidance on career paths. All these are non-financial rewards that can encourage job and organizational engagement and make a longer-lasting and more powerful impact than financial rewards such as performance-related pay.

Performance management is, of course, also associated with pay by generating the information required to decide on pay increases or bonuses related to performance, competence or contribution. In some organizations this is its main purpose, but performance management is, or should be, much more about developing people and rewarding them in the broadest sense.

Performance management and pay

Performance management is not inevitably linked to pay, although this is often assumed to be the case. Only 42 per cent of respondents to the CIPD 2003/04 survey (Armstrong and Baron, 2004) with performance management had contingent pay. The proportion in public sector organizations was even less – 29 per cent.

However, those who use contingent pay must have a means of deciding on increases, which has to be based on some form of assessment. The most typical approach is performance appraisal, which generates ratings to inform contingent pay decisions, often through a formula (a pay matrix as described in Chapter 28). This may conflict with the developmental purposes of performance management – the performance review meeting is in danger of focusing on the ratings that emerge from it and how much money will be forthcoming. Issues concerning development and the non-financial reward approaches discussed earlier will be subordinated to this preoccupation with pay. Many organizations attempt to get over this problem by holding development and pay review meetings on separate dates, often several months apart (decoupling). Some try to do without formulaic approaches (ratings and pay matrices) altogether, although it is impossible to dissociate contingent pay completely from some form of assessment.

Rating performance

Traditional performance appraisal schemes almost always included some form of overall rating of performance, and 80 per cent of the respondents to the 2009 e-reward survey of contingent pay schemes with performance management used ratings. As set out in Table 6.2 there are arguments for the use of rating as a summary of the assessment and to inform performance-related or contribution-related pay decisions; but there are also powerful arguments against.

Table 6.2   Arguments for and against rating

Arguments for rating	Arguments against rating
• Ratings let people know where they stand. • It is necessary to sum up judgements about people. • Ratings give people something to strive for. • They provide a basis for assessing potential. • They are needed to inform performance or contribution pay decisions.	• Ratings are likely to be subjective and inconsistent. • To sum the overall performance of a person with a single rating is a gross over-simplification of what may be a complex set of factors affecting that performance. • It is hard to rate qualitative aspects of performance. • To label people as 'average' or 'below average' or whatever equivalent terms are used is both demeaning and demotivating. • Line managers tend not to differentiate between ratings. • The use of ratings to inform decisions on performance pay or inclusion in a talent management programme will dominate performance reviews and prejudice the real purpose of such reviews, which is to provide the basis for developing skills and improving performance.

The most common number of rating levels among the respondents to the 2003/4 CIPD survey who used them was five (47 per cent of respondents) followed by four (28 per cent of respondents). Traditionally, five-level scales have been used on the grounds that raters prefer this degree of fineness in performance definition and can easily recognize the middle grade and distinguish those who fall into higher or lower categories. Four-level scales are used when it is believed that they avoid the problem inherent in five-level scales of taking the easy route of rating in the middle of the scale. Three examples of a five-level scale and two of a four-level scale are given in Table 6.3 below.

Table 6.3   Examples of rating scales

CEMEX	• Significantly above target = 5 • Above target = 4 • On target = 3 • Below target = 2 • Unsatisfactory = 1
DHL	• Far exceeds: Consistently demonstrating the competency behaviours effectively, role model. • Exceeds: Demonstrates the competency behaviours beyond what is expected. • Fully meets: Behaviours fully correspond with what is expected in the current role. • Partially meets: Demonstrates minor deficiencies (coachable) in the behaviour. • Does not meet: Does not demonstrate behaviours expected in the current role.
Ladbrokes	1 Did not meet performance criteria. 2 Met more than half performance criteria, most of the time. 3 Met all performance criteria, most of the time. 4 Met all performance criteria, all the time and above the standard. 5 Met all performance criteria, all the time and did more than was expected.
Agon (Norwich Union)	*Outperforming* – overall contribution exceeds all aspects of the relevant skills, knowledge and behaviours model and is demonstrated through superior delivery of individual accountabilities of the role. *Performing* – overall contribution fulfils all aspects of the relevant skills, knowledge and behaviours model and is demonstrated through the competent delivery of individual accountabilities of the role. *Developing* – overall contribution does not currently fulfil all relevant aspects of the skills, knowledge and behaviours model and is demonstrated through progress towards delivery of individual accountabilities of the role. *Underperforming* – overall contribution failing to demonstrate the skills, knowledge and behaviours model relevant to the role.
Hitachi	'O' Failed to meet objectives. 'S' After assessing performance against objectives has met some of the objectives. 'M' Meets expectations and has completed all objectives. 'M*' Achieved significantly more than the agreed objectives so performance was exceptional.

Developing a high-performance culture through reward: six tips

- Identify the performance drivers and key performance indicators in the organization.
- Use rewards generally to draw attention to the importance of performance.
- Decide on which aspects of the performance drivers should be focused on.
- Use rewards specifically to draw attention to these aspects.
- Use performance management systems to identify performance development needs.
- Incorporate performance and reward processes as key elements in a high-performance work system.

References

Allen, R S and Helms, M H (2001) Reward practices and organizational performance, *Compensation & Benefits Review*, July/August, pp 74–80

Appelbaum, E, Bailey, T, Berg, P and Kalleberg, A L (2000) *Manufacturing Advantage: Why high performance work systems pay off*, ILR Press, Ithaca, NY

Appelbaum, E, and Batt, R (1994) *The New American Workplace*, Cornell University Press, Ithaca, NY

Armstrong, M and Baron, A (1998) *Performance Management: The new realities*, CIPD, London

Armstrong, M and Baron, A (2004) *Managing Performance: Performance management in action*, CIPD, London

Ashton, D and Sung, J (2002) *Supporting Workplace Learning for High performance*, ILO, Geneva

Bailey, T, Berg, P and Sandy, C (2001) The effect of high performance work practices on employee earnings in the steel, apparel and medical electronics and imaging industries, *Industrial and Labor Relations Review*, **54** (2A), pp 525–43

Bates, R A and Holton, E F (1995) Computerized performance monitoring: a review of human resource issues, *Human Resource Management Review*, Winter, pp 267–88

Becker, B E and Huselid, M A (1998) High performance work systems and firm performance: a synthesis of research and managerial implications, *Research on Personnel and Human Resource Management*, 16, pp 53–101

Becker, B E, Huselid, M A and Ulrich, D (2001) *The HR Score card: Linking people, strategy, and performance*, Harvard Business School Press, Boston, MA

Bernardin, H J, Hagan, C and Kane, J (1995) The effects of a 360 degree appraisal system on managerial performance, Proceedings at the 10th annual conference of the Society for Industrial and Organizational Psychology, Orlando, FL

Blumberg, M and Pringle, C (1982) The missing opportunity in organizational research: some implications for a theory of work performance, *Academy of Management Review*, **7** (4), pp 560–69

Borman, W C and Motowidlo, S J (1993) Expanding the criterion domain to include elements of contextual performance, in *Personnel Selection in Organizations*, ed N Schmitt and W C Borman, Jossey-Bass, San Francisco

Bourne, M, Franco, M and Wilkes, J (2003) Corporate performance management, *Measuring Business Excellence*, **7** (3), pp 15–21

Boxall, P F (1996) The strategic HRM debate and the resource-based view of the firm, *Human Resource Management Journal*, **6** (3), pp 59–75

Boxall, P F and Purcell, J (2003) *Strategy and Human Resource Management*, Palgrave Macmillan, Basingstoke

Brown, M P, Sturman, M C and Simmering, M J (2003) Compensation policy and organizational performance: the efficiency, operational and financial implications of pay levels and pay structure, *Academy of Management Journal*, **46** (6), pp 752–82

Brumbach, G B (1988) Some ideas, issues and predictions about performance management, *Public Personnel Management*, Winter, pp 387–402

Campbell, J P (1990) Modeling the performance prediction problem in industrial and organizational psychology, in *Handbook of Industrial and Organizational Psychology*, ed MP Dunnette and LM Hugh, Blackwell, Cambridge, MA

Campbell, J P, McCloy, R A, Oppler, S H and Sager, C E (1993) A theory of performance, in *Personnel Selection in Organizations*, ed N Schmitt and W Borman, Jossey-Bass, San Francisco

Coens, T and Jenkins, M (2002) *Abolishing Performance Appraisals: Why they backfire and what to do instead*, Berrett-Koehler, San Francisco

Curral, S C, Towler, A J, Judge, T A and Kohn, L (2005) Pay satisfaction and organizational outcomes, *Personnel Psychology*, **58** (3), pp 613–40

Deming, W E (1986) *Out of the Crisis*, Massachusetts Institute of Technology Centre for Advanced Engineering Studies, Boston, MA

e-reward (2003a) *Research Report no 15, Strategic reward at Diageo*, e-reward, Stockport

e-reward (2003b) *Research Report no 17, Pay in a high performance organization: a case study of Lloyds TSB*, e-reward, Stockport

e-reward (2009) *Contingent Pay Survey*, e-reward, Stockport

Flaherty, J (1999) *Coaching: Evoking excellence in others*, Butterworth-Heinemann, Burlington, MA

Fletcher, C (2001) Performance appraisal and management: the developing research agenda, *Journal of Occupational and Organizational Psychology*, **74**, (4), pp 473–87

Gheorghe, C and Hack, J (2007) Unified performance management: how one company can tame its many processes, *Business Performance Management*, November, pp 17–19

Godard, J (2004) A critical assessment of the high-performance paradigm, *British Journal of Industrial Relations*, **42** (2), pp 349–78

Goleman, D (2000) Leadership that gets results, *Harvard Business Review*, March–April, pp 78–90

Jones, T W (1995) Performance management in a changing context, *Human Resource Management*, **34** (3), pp 425–42

Kane, J S (1996) The conceptualization and representation of total performance effectiveness, *Human Resource Management Review*, Summer, pp 123–45

Kaplan, R S and Norton, D P (2000) Having trouble with your strategy? Then map it, *Harvard Business Review*, September–October, pp 167–76

Lawler, E E (1986) *High Involvement Management*, Jossey-Bass, San Francisco

Lawler, E E, Mohrman, S and Ledford, G (1998) *Strategies for High Performance Organizations: Employee involvement, TQM, and re-engineering programs in Fortune 1000*, Jossey-Bass, San Francisco

McAdams, J and Hawks, E J (1994) *Organizational Performance and Rewards*, American Compensation Association, Scottsdale, AZ

Nadler, D A (1989) Organizational architecture for the corporation of the future, *Benchmark*, Fall, 12–13

Nadler, D A and Gerstein, M S (1992) Designing high-performance work systems: organizing people, technology, work and information, *Organizational Architecture*, Summer, pp 195–208

Neely, A, Adams, C and Kennerley, M (2002) *The Performance Prism: The Scorecard for measuring and managing business success*, Pearson Education, Harlow

Northouse, P G (2006) *Leadership: Theory and practice*, 4th edn, Sage, Thousand Oaks, CA

Purcell, J, Hutchinson, S and Kinnie, N (1998) *The Lean Organization*, IPD, London

Purcell, J, Kinnie, K, Hutchinson, S, Rayton, B and Swart, J (2003) *People and Performance: How people management impacts on organizational performance*, CIPD, London

Shih, H-A, Chiang, Y-H and Hsu, C-C (2005) Can high performance work systems really lead to better performance? Academy of Management Conference Paper, pp 1–6

Sink, D S and Tuttle, T C (1990) The performance management question in the organization of the future, *Industrial Management*, **32** (1), pp 4–12

Stevens, J (2005) *High Performance Wales: Real experiences, real success*, Wales Management Council, Cardiff

Sung, J and Ashton, D (2005) *High Performance Work Practices: Linking strategy and skills to performance outcomes*, DTI, London

Thompson, M and Heron, P (2005) Management capability and high performance work organization, *The International Journal of Human Resource Management*, **16** (6), pp 1029–48

Vroom, V (1964) *Work and Motivation*, Wiley, New York

Walton, R E (1985) Towards a strategy of eliciting employee commitment based on principles of mutuality, in *HRM Trends and Challenges*, ed R E Walton and P R Lawrence, Harvard Business School Press, Boston, MA

Wood, S, de Menezes, L M and Lasaosa, A (2001) High involvement management and performance, paper delivered at the Centre for Labour Market Studies, University of Leicester, May

Engagement and Reward

Introduction

The concept of 'engagement' has become very popular. The term is sometimes used loosely as a powerful notion that embraces pretty well everything the organization is seeking with regard to the contribution and behaviour of its employees in terms of levels of job performance, willingness to do that much more by exercising discretionary effort, motivation and identification with the organization. It is also used in a more specific way to describe what takes place when people are interested in and positive, even excited, about their jobs and motivated to achieve high levels of performance. This specific idea of 'job engagement' is distinguished from organizational commitment or engagement, which focuses on attachment to the organization as a whole rather than to a job.

Reilly and Brown (2008) noted that the terms job satisfaction, motivation and commitment are generally being replaced now in business by engagement because it appears to have more descriptive force and face validity. As Emmott (2006) commented: 'Employee engagement has become a new management mantra – and it's not difficult to see why. Engaged employees – those who feel positive about their jobs – perform better for their employers and can promote their organization as "an employer of choice".' In this chapter consideration is given to the meaning of employee engagement (there are different definitions) and the relationship between reward and employee engagement.

The meaning of employee engagement

The concept of engagement was defined by Gallup (2009) as: 'The individual's involvement and satisfaction with as well as enthusiasm for work'. Balain and Sparrow (2009) noted that a number of other well-known applied research and consultancy organizations have defined engagement on similar lines, often emphasizing the importance of discretionary effort as the key outcome or distinguishing feature of an engaged employee. An academic definition based on research by Maslach *et al* (2001) referred to engagement as: 'A positive, fulfilling, work-related state of mind that is characterized by vigour, dedication, and absorption'.

The Institute for Employment Studies (IES) (Robinson *et al*, 2004) defined employee engagement as follows:

> *Engagement is a positive attitude held by the employee towards the organisation and its values. An engaged employee is aware of business context, and works with colleagues to improve performance within the job for the benefit of the organisation. The organisation must work to nurture, maintain and grow engagement, which requires a two-way relationship between employer and employee.*

The IES model of engagement is shown in Figure 7.1.

Motivation can be defined as goal-directed behaviour, commitment as the relative strength of the individual's identification with and involvement in an organization, and organizational citizenship behaviour as 'innovative and spontaneous activity directed toward achievement of organizational objectives, but which goes beyond role requirements' (Katz and Kahn, 1966).

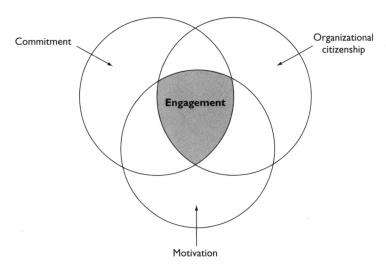

Figure 7.1 IES model of employee engagement

Other definitions place more emphasis on job engagement as distinct from organizational engagement or commitment. An engaged employee was defined by Bevan *et al* (1997) as someone 'who is aware of business context, and works closely with colleagues to improve performance within the job for the benefit of the organization'. Murlis and Watson (2001) defined 'engaged performance' as: 'A result that is achieved by stimulating employees' enthusiasm for their work and directing it towards organizational success. This result can only be achieved when employers offer an implied contract to their employees that elicits specific positive behaviours aligned with the organization's goals.'

A comprehensive analysis of the concept of engagement was made by Balain and Sparrow (2009). They distinguished between job engagement and organizational engagement and concluded that:

> To understand what really causes engagement, and what it causes in turn, we need to embed the idea in a well-founded theory. The one that is considered most appropriate is social exchange theory, which sees feelings of loyalty, commitment, discretionary effort as all being forms of social reciprocation by employees to a good employer. This work separates out job engagement from organizational engagement.

Anther perspective on engagement is provided by the Hay Group employee effectiveness model, which shows how employee engagement and 'employee enablement' combine to produce employee effectiveness, as shown in Figure 7.2.

Employee Effectiveness Model

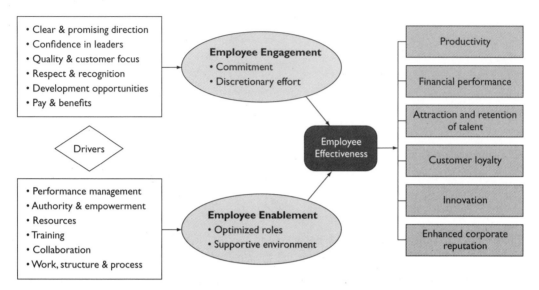

Figure 7.2   The Hay Group model of employee effectiveness
(Reproduced with permission)

Why engagement is important

However it is defined, employee engagement is important to employers because a considerable amount of research indicates that high levels of engagement that result in behaviours such as maximizing discretionary effort, taking initiative, wanting to develop, or aligning actions with organizational needs deliver a range of organizational benefits; for example:

● Higher productivity/performance: engaged employees perform 20 per cent better than the average (Conference Board, 2006).

● Lower staff turnover: engaged employees are 87 per cent less likely to leave (Corporate Leadership Council, 2004).

● Better attendance: engaged employees have lower sick leave levels (CIPD, 2007).

● Improved safety (Vance, 2006).

The factors that influence engagement

Research cited by IDS (2007) has identified two key elements that have to be present if genuine engagement in its broadest sense is to exist. The first is the rational aspect, which relates to employees' understanding of their role, where it fits in the wider organization, and how it aligns with business objectives. The second is the emotional aspect, which has to do with how people feel about the organization, whether their work gives them a sense of personal accomplishment and how they relate to their managers.

Engagement will be affected by work and job design, the quality of life provided by the working environment and the quality of leadership. A detailed explanation of the antecedents, types and consequences of engagement by Balain and Sparrow (2009) based on their research is shown in Table 7.1.

Table 7.1   Antecedents, types and consequences of engagement

Antecedents of engagement	Types of employee engagement	Consequences
• Enriched and challenging jobs (job characteristics). • Quality of the employee–organization relationship (perceived organizational support). • Quality of the employee–supervisor relationship (perceived supervisor support). • Rewards and recognition. • Fairness in the processes that allocate resources or resolve disputes (procedural justice). • What is considered just or right in the allocation of goods in a society (distributive justice).	• Job engagement. • Organizational engagement.	• Job satisfaction. • Organizational commitment. • Level of intention to quit. • Organizational citizenship behaviour.

(Source: Balain and Sparrow, 2009)

Enhancing engagement

Financial incentives may increase engagement for some people in the short run, but the greatest impact on engagement is made by non-financial rewards, especially when they generate intrinsic motivation through the work itself and the work environment, and when they are provided by line managers.

Intrinsic motivation

Intrinsic motivation depends on the way in which work or jobs are designed. Three characteristics have been distinguished by Lawler (1969) as being required in jobs if they are to be intrinsically motivating:

- Feedback: individuals must receive meaningful feedback about their performance, preferably by evaluating their own performance and defining the feedback. This implies that they should ideally work on a complete product/process/service, or a significant part of it that can be seen as a whole.

- Use of abilities: the job must be perceived by individuals as requiring them to use abilities they value in order to perform the job effectively.

- Self-control (autonomy): individuals must feel that they have a high degree of self-control over setting their own goals and over defining the paths to these goals.

The approaches to motivation through job design suggested by Robertson and Smith (1985) are to influence: 1) skill variety, by providing opportunities for people to do several tasks and combining tasks; 2) task identity, by combining tasks and forming natural work units; 3) task significance, by informing people of the importance of their work; 4) autonomy, by giving people responsibility for determining their own working systems; and 5) feedback, by establishing good relationships and opening feedback channels.

These approaches may be used when setting up new work systems or jobs, and the intrinsic motivation strategy should include provision for guidance and advice along these lines to those responsible for such developments. But the greatest impact on the design of work systems or jobs is made by line managers on a day-to-day basis. The strategy should therefore include arrangements as part of a leadership development programme for educating them in the importance of good work and job design and what they can do to improve intrinsic motivation. Performance management, with its emphasis on agreeing role expectations, is a useful means of doing this.

The work environment

A strategy for increasing engagement through the work environment will be generally concerned with developing a culture that encourages positive attitudes to work, promoting interest and excitement in the jobs people do, and reducing stress. Lands' End believes that staff who are enjoying themselves, who are being supported and developed and who feel fulfilled and respected at work will provide the best service to customers. The thinking behind the company's wish to inspire staff is straightforward – employees' willingness to do that little bit extra arises from their sense of pride in what the organization stands for: quality, service and value. It makes the difference between a good experience for customers and a poor one.

The strategy also needs to consider particular aspects of the work environment, especially communications, involvement, work–life balance and working conditions. It can include the formulation and application of 'talent relationship management' policies that are concerned with building effective relationships with people in their roles, treating individual employees fairly, recognizing their value, giving them a voice and providing opportunities for growth.

Line managers

Line managers play a vital and immediate part in increasing levels of engagement through leadership. They need help to understand what they are expected to do and to develop the skills they need. This help can be given through blended learning programmes, which may include formal training (especially for potential managers or those in their first leadership role), e-learning, coaching and mentoring.

Performance management can provide line managers with a useful framework in which they can deploy their skills in improving performance through increased engagement. This applies particularly to the performance management activities of role definition, performance improvement planning, joint involvement in monitoring performance and feedback.

Developing engagement policies through reward

Reilly and Brown (2008) contend that appropriate reward practices and processes, both financial and non-financial and managed in combination, can help to build and improve employee engagement , and that badly designed or executed rewards can hinder it. Their model based on research into how reward policies influence performance through engagement is shown in Figure 7.3.

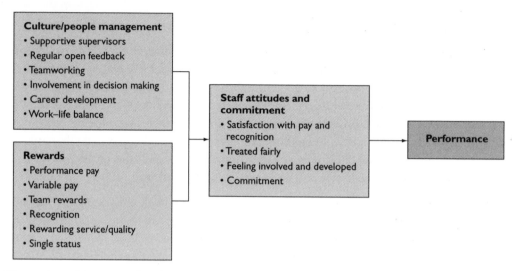

Figure 7.3 How reward policies influence performance through engagement

---

Enhancing engagement through reward: six tips (Reilly and Brown, 2008)

- Analyse the existing performance culture of the organization and develop an engagement model that describes what brings people to work, what keeps them with the organization and what motivates them to perform whilst there.

- Define the drivers of engagement (and disengagement) for different categories of employees.

- Assess and define the reward elements that affect engagement for the different groups of employees and develop reward programmes that will enhance these different aspects of engagement.

- Introduce a total rewards approach that brings together all the reward elements (pay and non-pay) that engage staff.

- Segment total reward to take account of key employee differences.

- Implement the total rewards approach and measure and evaluate its impact and success.

References

Balain, S and Sparrow, P (2009) *Engaged to Perform: A new perspective on employee engagement*, Lancaster University Management School, Lancaster

Bevan, S, Barber, L and Robinson, D (1997) *Keeping the Best: A practical guide to retaining key employees*, Institute for Employment Studies, Brighton

CIPD (2007) *Working Life: Employee attitudes and engagement*, CIPD, London

Conference Board (2006) *Employee Engagement: A review of current research and its implications*, Conference Board, New York

Corporate Leadership Council (2004) *Driving Performance and Retention through Employee Engagement*, Corporate Executive Board, Washington DC

Emmott, M (2006) Hear me now, *People Management*, 23 November, pp 38–40

Gallup (2009) *Workplace Audit*, Gallup Inc, Washington DC

IDS (2007) *Building an Engaged Workforce*, HR Studies Update, IDS London

Katz, D and Kahn, R (1966) *The Social Psychology of Organizations*, John Wiley, New York

Lawler, E E (1969) Job design and employee motivation, *Personnel Psychology*, 22, pp 426–35

Maslach, C, Schaufeli, W B and Leiter, M P (2001) Job burnout, *Annual Review of Psychology*, **52**, pp 397–422

Murlis, H and Watson, S (2001) Creating employee engagement – transforming the employment deal, *Benefits and Compensation International*, **30** (8), pp 6–17

Reilly, P and Brown, D (2008) Employee engagement: future focus or fashionable fad for reward management? *WorldatWork Journal*, **17** (4), pp 37–49

Robertson, IT and Smith, M (1985) *Motivation and Job Design*, IPM, London

Robinson, D, Perryman, S and Hayday, S (2004) *The Drivers of Employee Engagement*, Institute for Employment Studies, Brighton

Vance, R J (2006) *Effective Practice guidelines: employee engagement and commitment*, SHRM Foundation, Alexandria, VA

8

Financial Rewards

Introduction

Financial rewards comprise all rewards that have a monetary value and add up to total remuneration – base pay, pay contingent on performance, contribution, competency or skill, pay related to service, financial recognition schemes, and benefits such as pensions, sick pay and health insurance. As explained in Chapter 3 they are the core elements in total rewards.

The management of a reward system requires decisions on levels of pay, how jobs should be valued, the design and operation of grade and pay structures and the choice of benefits. Such decisions can be complex and difficult, but the problems pale by comparison with the issues surrounding the use of financial rewards contingent on performance, contribution, competence or skill.

Labour economists distinguish between the incentive effect of financial rewards (generating more engagement and effort) and the sorting effect (attracting better-quality employees). The fundamental issue is the extent to which financial rewards provide an incentive effect. The sorting effect is important but creates less controversy, perhaps because it is more difficult to pin down.

A vociferous chorus of disapproval has been heard on the incentive effect. One of the best-known and most influential voices is that of Alfie Kohn (1993) who stated in the *Harvard Business Review* that 'bribes in the workplace simply can't work.' He asserted that: 'Rewards, like punishment, may actually undermine the intrinsic motivation that results in optimal performance. The more a manager stresses what an employee can earn for good work, the less interested that employee will be in the work itself.' He also claimed that: 'At least two dozen studies over the last three decades have conclusively shown that people who expect to receive a reward for completing a task or for doing that task successfully simply do not perform as well as those who expect no reward at all.' He did not identify these studies. He returned to the fray in 1998 when he wrote that: 'Offering workers the equivalent of a doggie biscuit for whatever we demand is never going to be successful in any meaningful sense.'

Jeffrey Pfeffer (1998) concluded in his equally influential *Harvard Business Review* article 'Six dangerous myths about pay' that: 'Most merit-pay systems share two attributes: they absorb vast amounts of management time and make everybody unhappy.'

More recently, Adrian Furnham (2006) asserted that: 'The idea that better paid people are more productive and happy is naïve and essentially evidence free.' And Simon Caulkin (2009) wrote in his *Observer* column that: 'Evidence to show monetary incentives improve performance is simply non-existent.'

On the other hand there is the less audible chorus of those who have collected evidence that financial incentives do improve performance (seemingly unknown to commentators such as those mentioned above) and have questioned some of the findings and theories of the researchers who have cast doubts on the effectiveness of financial incentives.

Gerhart and Rynes (2003) in their comprehensive review of compensation research noted that managers may well be confused by the fact that: 'Researchers often disagree on many of the most central questions surrounding pay, depending on their disciplinary training, ideological beliefs and other factors.' Amongst the disagreements they instanced was whether or not pay is a strong motivator of performance.

The aim of this chapter is to present the evidence on the role and effectiveness of financial incentives so as to inform decisions on what can usefully be done about them by means of contingent pay schemes (as described in Chapter 10) or, if financial incentives are not favoured, other non-financial methods of rewarding people (as considered in Chapter 9). The chapter starts with a review of the motivation theories and research that have influenced views about how incentives work or don't work. To understand the use of financial rewards it is necessary to know about the role of money and the extent to which it matters to people, and to appreciate the factors that affect satisfaction with pay, as discussed in the next section of the chapter. Decisions on financial rewards also need to take account of the many research projects that have studied their effectiveness, and the following section of the chapter summarizes the major negative and positive research findings. The next section lists the advantages and disadvantages of financial rewards in the shape of contingent pay, and the final section sets out criteria for their use. First, however, it is necessary to consider the difference between incentives and rewards.

Incentives and rewards

There is a strong body of opinion, at least in academic circles, that financial rewards are bad – because they don't work and indeed are harmful – while non-financial rewards are good, at least when they provide intrinsic motivation. But the critics quoted at the beginning of this chapter and later on are mainly referring to financial incentives. They do not appear to recognize that incentives are not the same as rewards. They can be distinguished as follows:

- Rewards offer tangible recognition to people for their achievements and contribution. Financial rewards consist of job-based pay, which provides base pay related to the value of the job, and person-based pay, which provides rewards that recognize the individual's contribution, competence or skill. Rewards can also be non-financial, for example recognition. If rewards are worth having and attainable and people know how they can attain them, they can act as motivators.

- Incentives are intended to encourage people to work harder and achieve more. They are supposed to provide direct motivation: 'Do this and we will make it worth your while.' Incentives are generally financial but they can take the form of non-financial rewards such as promotion or a particularly interesting assignment.

If this distinction is not made it may be assumed that financial rewards only exist to provide an incentive. They may do this or, as the nay-sayers contend, they may not. But financial rewards can act as rewards in the sense referred to above and may be justified because they are a form of tangible recognition – they are a means of informing people that they have done well, and accord with the reasonable belief that people who do better should be valued more and rewarded accordingly.

Of course the opponents of financial rewards say that there are better ways of recognizing people than throwing money at them. They emphasize the power of intrinsic rewards, assert that extrinsic rewards erode intrinsic interest, claim that money is not so important to people as the supporters of financial rewards believe and suggest that job satisfaction is not dominated by feelings about pay. These issues are discussed in the next two sections of this chapter, in the first of which the theories that have influenced the opinions of those dubious about financial rewards are summarized and in the second the role of money and the relationship between pay and job satisfaction are considered. These are followed by a review of the research evidence on the effectiveness of financial incentives, which leads to final sections in which conclusions are reached on the case for or against financial rewards, and the factors that lead to success in the contingent pay schemes that are devised to provide such rewards are analysed.

The theoretical framework

The theoretical framework is based on the concepts of extrinsic and intrinsic motivation. Extrinsic motivation arises when something is done to or for people to motivate them. Extrinsic rewards include pay, praise and promotion. Intrinsic motivation as originally defined by Deci (1975) is provided by the self-generated factors that influence people to behave in a particular way or to move in a particular direction. Intrinsic rewards include responsibility (feeling that the work is important and having control over one's resources), freedom to act, scope to use and develop skills and abilities, interesting and challenging work and opportunities for advancement and growth. In the phrase coined by Herzberg (1968), intrinsic rewards arise from the work itself. It is generally accepted that while extrinsic rewards can have an immediate and, in the right circumstances, a powerful effect on motivation and performance, intrinsic rewards can have a deeper and longer-lasting effect.

Financial rewards are, of course, extrinsic rewards and the doubts about them expressed by commentators such as those quoted at the beginning of this chapter are mainly based on three motivation theories: Maslow's (1954) hierarchy of human needs, Herzberg's (1957, 1968) motivation-hygiene theory, and Deci and Ryan's (1985) cognitive evaluation theory. All these theories downgrade the role of money or extrinsic rewards as motivators. They have been very influential, especially Maslow and Herzberg, but in some circles the contribution of Deci and Ryan appears to have had the most powerful effect on, for example, Kohn, Furnham and Pfeffer.

Maslow's hierarchy of human needs

Maslow's theory is based on the proposition that human needs are arranged in a hierarchy of significance. At the bottom of the hierarchy are physiological and safety needs that are best satisfied by money. Once these basic needs are satisfied individuals progress to 'higher' needs not associated with money – social needs, esteem and, ultimately, self-fulfilment, which is achieved by being engaged in meaningful work.

The problem with this theory is that it was based on interviews with highly creative individuals and has not been verified by empirical research.

Herzberg's motivation-hygiene theory

Herzberg's theory concentrates on identifying the factors that contribute to satisfaction or dissatisfaction at work. He explained that: 'The factors involved in producing job satisfaction (and motivation) are separate and distinct from the factors that lead to job dissatisfaction.' He called the latter 'hygiene factors', using hygiene in the medical sense as being preventative, because they can cause dissatisfaction and need to be stopped from doing so. But they cannot produce lasting satisfaction, which means that while financial incentives may motivate in the short term the effect quickly wears off. In contrast the 'satisfiers' associated with the work itself (achievement, responsibility, recognition and advancement) have a deeper and longer-lasting effect on motivation.

Herzberg's two-factor theory has been criticized by Opsahl and Dunnette (1966) who stated that the data on feelings about pay 'seem inconsistent with the interpretations and lend no substantial support to hypotheses of a so-called differential role for money in leading to job satisfaction or job dissatisfaction'. They contended that Herzberg's research methodology was flawed because no attempt was made to measure the relationship between satisfaction and performance and they suggested that the two-factor nature of the theory is an inevitable result of the questioning method used by the interviewers. Gerhart and Rynes (2003) noted from Herzberg's (1968) summary of his research that pay was mentioned as a satisfier nearly as often as it was listed as a dissatisfier It has also been suggested (Schwab and Cummings, 1970; Kanfer, 1990) that wide and unwarranted inferences have been drawn from small and specialized samples and that there is no evidence to indicate that 'satisfiers' act as motivators – it has been argued by both Maslow (1954) and Adams (1965) that a satisfied need is no longer a motivator.

In spite of these criticisms the Herzberg two-factor theory continues to thrive; partly because it is easy to understand and seems to be based on 'real-life' rather than academic abstractions, and partly because it convincingly emphasizes the positive value of the intrinsic motivating factors. It is also in accord with a fundamental belief in the dignity of labour and the Protestant ethic – that work is good in itself. As a result, Herzberg had immense influence on the job enrichment movement, which sought to design jobs in a way that would maximize the opportunities to obtain intrinsic satisfaction from work and thus improve the quality of working life. His emphasis on non-financial motivators is also reflected in the concept of total rewards. As Dunham (1984) commented: 'Herzberg is living proof that a theory need not be perfect to make a valuable contribution.' The same applies to Maslow.

Cognitive evaluation theory

Deci (1975) defined intrinsically motivated behaviours as 'those in which there is no apparent reward except with the activity itself'. Deci and Ryan (1985) explained that: 'Intrinsic motivation is non-drive-based motivation. It is based on the needs to be competent and self-determining (that is, to have a choice). It means that a person carries out an activity in the absence of a reward contingency or control.' They analysed evidence from over 100 studies (possibly those referred to by Alfie Kohn and Jeffrey Pfeffer), which they claimed showed that when subjects received monetary rewards their intrinsic motivation for rewarded activity declined because it reduced their self-determination through the shift from internal to external control. This led to the development of their cognitive evaluation theory (CET).

They pointed out that 'Rewards, like feedback, when used to convey to people a sense of appreciation for work well done, will tend to be experienced informationally and will maintain or enhance intrinsic motivation. But when they are used to motivate people, they will be experienced controllingly and will undermine intrinsic motivation.' In other words, they were making the distinction between rewards and incentives referred to earlier in this chapter.

Deci et al (1999) followed up this research by carrying out a meta-analysis of 128 experiments on rewards and intrinsic motivation to establish the extent to which intrinsic motivation was undermined by rewards. Meta-analysis is a technique for combining the results of a large number of conceptually related studies to reach generalizations based on statistical criteria. What is called a 'between-groups design' is used, in which a rewarded group is compared to a control group (a non-rewarded group) on a common dependent measure (intrinsic motivation). The aim is to establish the relation between the independent and dependent variables of rewards and intrinsic motivation and to determine what factors moderate the size of the relation (eg type of reward and the basis upon which the reward is given). Relevant studies are identified and the results of each study are transformed into a measure called an effect size, which indicates the extent to which the experimental rewarded group and the control non-rewarded group differ in terms of intrinsic motivation (interest in the task and continuing to carry it out after the rewards have been removed).

The meta-analysis study conducted by Deci *et al* focused on the overall effects of rewards on intrinsic motivation for tasks of initial high interest only, on the grounds that in low-interest tasks there was little or no intrinsic motivation to undermine. The results of the study indicated that for high-interest tasks, rewards had significant negative effects on what the researchers called 'free-choice measures', which included the time spent on the task after the reward was removed.

As noted by Gerhart and Rynes (2003): 'The vast majority of research on this theory has been performed in school rather than work settings, often with elementary school-aged children.' But that did not stop other commentators assuming that the results were equally significant for working adults. It is interesting to note that research in industry conducted by Ryan, Mimms and Koestner (1983), while it found that financial incentives did decrease intrinsic motivation in high-control organizational cultures, also established that in organizations with the opposite high-involvement culture, both intrinsic and extrinsic motivation was increased by monetary incentives. Context is all-important.

Moreover, the outcomes of the Deci *et al* study were challenged by another meta-analysis of 145 studies conducted by Cameron *et al* (2001). This concluded that tangible rewards can be used to produce both negative and positive effects on measures of intrinsic motivation. As they commented:

Our results suggest that in general, rewards are not harmful to motivation to perform a task. Rewards given for low-interest tasks enhance free-choice intrinsic motivation. On high-interest tasks, verbal rewards produce positive effects on free-choice motivation and self-reported task interest. Negative effects are found on high-interest tasks when the rewards are tangible, expected (offered beforehand), and loosely tied to level of performance. When rewards are linked to level of performance, measures of intrinsic motivation increase or do not differ from a non-rewarded control group.

They quoted a number of studies including Dickinson and Taylor (1989), Mawhinney *et al* (1989) and Skaggs *et al* (1992), which showed that rewards do not inevitably have pervasive negative effects on intrinsic motivation.

Conclusions on the theory

As Gerhart and Rynes (2003) commented:

> *Although the ideas developed by Maslow, Herzberg and Deci have had considerable appeal to many people, the prevailing view in the academic literature is that the specific predictions of these theories is not supported by empirical evidence. On the other hand it would be a mistake to underestimate the influence that these theories have had on research and practice. Pfeffer, Kohn and others continue to base their argument regarding the ineffectiveness of money as a motivator on such theories.*

Steers (2001) contended that: 'Motivation theories that were discredited long ago still permeate current textbooks.' He was referring mainly to Maslow and Herzberg.

The role of money

Commentators who question the usefulness of financial rewards often contend that money is much less important than many people think. As Pfeffer (1998) wrote: 'People do work for money – but they work even more for meaning in their lives. In fact, they work to have fun. Companies that ignore this fact are essentially bribing their employees and will pay the price in a lack of loyalty and commitment.' Furnham (2006) stated that: 'Money is not everything. Many would be happy with more time off, or more job security, than more money. People are prepared to trade-off things for money once they have enough or grow weary of the game.'

Views about the importance of pay

Many surveys have been carried out to assess the relative importance of pay in relation to other factors affecting motivation. Typically, pay is somewhere down the list after job interest, achievement, recognition and development opportunities. As Kohn (1998) stated: 'Numerous studies have shown that when people are asked what is most important to them about work, money ranks well behind such factors as interesting work or good people to work with.' For example, 1,355 managers and other professionals surveyed by Ritchie and Martin (1999) placed money and tangible rewards ninth in a list of 12 'motivational drivers'.

In an earlier study, Jurgensen (1978) assessed the relative importance of job characteristics (including pay) to 50,000 job applicants over a 30-year period. Pay was the fifth most important characteristic to men and the seventh most important to women. However, when asked to rate the importance of the same 10 attributes to 'someone just like yourself – same age, education, gender and so on', pay jumped to being the most important factor among both men and women. In other words, people seemed to believe that pay was the main motivator to everyone except themselves.

As Slovic and Lichtenstein (1971) commented, people tend to give lower ratings to factors that are regarded as socially less acceptable than others. They overrate the socially desirable importance of job challenge and opportunities for learning, and underrate the importance of 'low-level motivators such as pay'. Such ranking exercises, as Lawler (1971) pointed out, produce results that vary according to the methodology used and can therefore be misleading. They do not prove that pay is perceived to be relatively unimportant. Studies such as those conducted by McDougall (1973) and Blackburn and Mann (1979) have indicated that the opposite is the case.

Money and motivation

It is reasonable to assume that people need money and therefore want money but the question is: How well does it perform as a motivator? It has been suggested by Wallace and Szilagyi (1982) that money can serve the following reward functions:

- It can act as a goal that people generally strive for, although to different degrees.
- It can act as an instrument that provides valued outcomes.
- It can be a symbol that indicates the recipient's value to the organization.
- It can act as a general reinforcer because it is associated with valued rewards and therefore takes on reward value itself.

Money can motivate because it is linked directly or indirectly with the satisfaction of many needs. It satisfies the basic need for survival and security, if income is regular. It can also satisfy the need for self-esteem (it is a visible mark of appreciation) and status – money can set you in a grade apart from your fellows and can buy you things they cannot afford. Money satisfies the less desirable but nevertheless prevalent drives of acquisitiveness and cupidity. So money may in itself have no intrinsic meaning, but it acquires motivating power because it comes to symbolize so many intangible goals. It acts as a symbol in different ways for different people, and for the same person at different times. Pay is often a dominant factor in the choice of employer and is an important consideration when people are deciding whether or not to stay with an organization. Money can indeed motivate but it is not the only motivator. As Gerhart and Rynes (2003) comment: 'Although we see little evidence to support the notion that money is of secondary importance as a motivator, there is nevertheless ample evidence that money is not the only reward that motivates.'

However, according to Herzberg (1968) money does not result in lasting satisfaction. People may feel good when they get an increase as, apart from the extra money, it is a way of making people feel they are valued. But the feeling of euphoria can die away and it must be re-emphasized that different people have different needs. Some will be much more motivated by money than others. What cannot be assumed is that money motivates everyone in the same way and to the same extent.

To believe that financial incentives will always motivate people to perform better is as simplistic as to assume, like Kohn, that they never motivate people to perform better. Some people will be more motivated by money that others and, if handled properly, an incentive scheme in the right context can encourage them to perform more effectively as long as they can link their effort to the reward and the reward is worth having. But others may be less interested in money and will respond more to intrinsic or non-financial rewards. It can be argued in accordance with total rewards philosophy that most people are likely to react positively to a judicious mix of both financial and non-financial rewards.

What is clear is that simplistic assumptions about the power of money to motivate can lead organizations into developing simplistic performance-related pay schemes or other forms of incentives. And we can be sure that a multiplicity of interdependent factors are involved in motivating people. Money is only one of those factors that may work for some people in some circumstances, but may not work for other people in other circumstances.

It should also be remembered that while an increase in pay arising from a contingent pay scheme may motivate people who get it, for a limited period perhaps, it may well demotivate those who don't get it or feel that they are not getting enough compared with other people. The number of people demotivated in this way could be larger than the number who have been motivated. Paradoxically, therefore, contingent pay schemes are in danger of increasing the amount of demotivation existing in the organization rather than enhancing motivation.

Factors affecting satisfaction with pay

As Lawler (1990) points out, people's feelings about the adequacy of their pay are based upon comparisons they make between their own and others'. External market comparisons are the most critical because they are the ones that strongly influence whether individuals want to stay with the organization. Many people, however, are unlikely to leave for pay reasons alone unless the increase they expect from a move is substantial, say 10 per cent.

Lawler also comments: 'Sometimes it seems that individuals are never satisfied with the pay.' One of the reasons suggested by Lawler for low pay satisfaction seems to be that individuals seek out unfavourable comparisons. First they look externally: if comparisons there are favourable, they focus on internal comparisons. Only if these are favourable as well are they likely to be satisfied. He states that: 'A finding that employees are dissatisfied with pay is, in effect, a non-finding. It is to be expected. The key thing that the organization needs to focus on is whether its employees are more dissatisfied with their pay than are employees in other organizations.'

Reactions to reward policies and practices will depend largely on the values and needs of individuals and on their employment conditions. It is therefore dangerous to generalize about the causes of satisfaction or dissatisfaction. However, it seems reasonable to believe that, as mentioned above, feelings about external and internal equity (the 'felt fair' principle as defined by Jaques, 1961) will strongly influence most people. Research by Porter and Lawler (1968) has also shown that higher-paid employees are likely to be more satisfied with their rewards but the satisfaction resulting from a large pay increase may be short-lived. People tend to want more of the same. In this respect, at least, the views of Maslow and Herzberg have been supported by research.

Other factors which may affect satisfaction or dissatisfaction with pay include the degree to which:

- individuals feel their rate of pay or increase has been determined fairly (the principle of procedural justice);

- rewards are commensurate with the perceptions of individuals about their ability, contribution and value to the organization founded on information or beliefs about what other people, inside and outside the organization, are paid (the principle of distributive justice);

- individuals are satisfied with other aspects of their employment – for example, the quality of working life, work–life balance, their status, promotion prospects, opportunity to use and develop skills, and relations with their managers and colleagues.

Job satisfaction and performance

Pay may increase job satisfaction but does job satisfaction improve performance? It is a commonly held and a seemingly not unreasonable belief that it does. But research has not established any strongly positive connection between satisfaction and performance. A review of the extensive literature on this subject by Brayfield and Crockett (1955) concluded that there was little evidence of any simple or appreciable relationship between employee satisfaction and performance. An updated review of their analysis by Vroom (1964) covered 20 studies, in each of which one or more measures of job satisfaction or employee attitudes was correlated with one or more criteria of performance. The median correlation of all these studies was 0.14, which is not high enough to suggest a marked relationship between satisfaction and performance

It can be argued that it is not job satisfaction that produces high performance but high performance that produces job satisfaction, and that a satisfied worker is not necessarily a productive worker and a high producer is not necessarily a satisfied worker. People are motivated to achieve certain goals and will be satisfied if they achieve these goals through improved performance. They may be even more satisfied if they are then rewarded by extrinsic recognition or an intrinsic sense of achievement. It can also be argued that some people may be complacently satisfied with their job and will not be inspired to work harder or better. They may find other ways to satisfy their needs.

Research on the effectiveness of financial rewards

Much research has been conducted on the effectiveness of financial rewards in terms of their impact on people and performance. A number of UK projects in the early 1990s produced negative results on the impact of performance-related pay (PRP) on people, and these have influenced views about PRP ever since. But four more recent studies in the UK and many studies in the United States over the years have established a positive relationship between incentive pay and performance. A selection of these negative and positive projects are summarized below.

Research projects producing mainly negative results
Kessler and Purcell (1992)

Research into individual performance-related pay (PRP) was conducted over a three-year period in nine private and public sector organizations of varying sizes and operating in different product and labour markets. Material was also gained from interviews with over 60 senior and management figures.

The main findings and conclusions were that:

- PRP was seen as a means of targeting pay to those who most deserve it and thus provides better value for money than inflexible, less discriminatory increases related to cost of living or service.

- Managements often experienced difficulties in operating the scheme because of the lack of formal supporting systems, absence of prior management training and the highly subjective nature of assessments.

- The potential for distorting the system is perhaps at its greatest at the assessment stage.

- PRP depends on 'sending messages' to individual members of staff but this entails the risk of sending the wrong messages.

At the crudest of levels, PRP schemes are informed by the view that employees will be motivated if they perceive a direct relationship between effort and reward. Such a view is simplistic for a number of reasons. First, as a means of explaining employee behaviour it clearly has limited value, with a whole body of research stressing the importance of employee expectations and need in understanding motivation. Second, it is highly questionable whether employee expectations of the performance–reward link underlying this motivational approach can remain undistorted by ongoing social, political and economic workplace pressures influencing the operation of this pay system. Third, and perhaps most significant, it misses the point because many senior managers are sceptical of such a link themselves and do not necessarily claim any major impact in this particular respect.

- The amount of money available may be too small to make any impact.

- The sophisticated procedures and systems needed and their application by managers present a range of difficulties to the achievement of recruitment, retention and motivation.

- 'There are major difficulties in finding measures of PRP effectiveness. The bottom line measure of effectiveness for any payment system is arguably an improvement in overall organizational performance, assumed to flow from improved employee performance. It is, however, clear that the complex range of factors interacting to determine organizational performance make it difficult to isolate the impact of a payment system alone.'

Thompson (1992a)

Marc Thompson, then with the IMS (now the Institute for Employment Studies), investigated the employer's experience of individual performance-related pay (IPRP) in 20 organizations in the public and private sectors. He found that:

- Employers did not know if their scheme was effective in raising productivity for the simple reason that they did not monitor schemes on this basis.

- Many companies did not think through the introduction of IPRP in a coherent manner.

- There was some indication that line managers were neither totally aware nor convinced of the appropriateness of IPRP – it was this issue that led to some of the most difficult problems in practice.

- There are two main problems with the operation of IPRP schemes: 1) the values of employers may conflict with the values of employees, and 2) tensions may arise from employers' beliefs about employee motivation and behaviour.

- One employer commented: 'It's an act of faith really… we think things would be worse if we weren't using it.'

- One of the few employers who had conducted a survey on perceptions of IPRP found that when it was first introduced, less than 20 per cent felt it motivated; changes in the scheme's administration had seen this rise to over 60 per cent (just over 80 per cent felt that they were rated fairly).

- One of the most consistent problems encountered in studying the effects of performance pay is that of causality – attributing increases or decreases in productivity to the payment system rather than to other factors such as technology, changes in working practices or changes in the product market.

- The theoretical framework most used to support IPRP is expectancy theory, but this is based exclusively on the motivating effects of extrinsic rewards and ignores intrinsic rewards – it implies that 'money is the central incentive in terms of human motivation.'

- There is no best approach to the introduction of IPRP and employers are advised to tread carefully when considering its implementation.

Thompson (1992b)

A survey was conducted of nearly 1,000 employees in three organizations to obtain their views about performance-related pay. The findings were as follows:

- There was little evidence that PRP had served to motivate employees.

- 'It is possible that performance pay may be more successful in demotivating the very employees it needs to stimulate most – the average performers – and may , in practice, contribute to a downward spiral of motivation among such employees.'

- In only one of the three cases was PRP associated with the retention of high performers.

- Poor performers were as likely to stay as high performers.

- The relationship between the subordinate and the line manager was the most important in influencing employee perceptions about PRP.

- Achieving distributive and procedural justice was important.

- 'Informing staff, training them in appraisal and involving them in the design of the scheme from the outset is key to gaining employee trust in and winning commitment to PRP.'

- 'Unfortunately none of the three organizations undertook all three interventions and very few had either informed or trained their staff.'

- The lack of these interventions 'may explain the widespread distrust of the fairness and equity of the schemes'.

- 'Across the three case study organizations there was a surprising consensus in the perceived poor management of the appraisal and merit pay process by line managers.'

- 'Given that performance management is a policy intervention to be owned by the line there is a need to equip managers to take on this responsibility.'

- 'There is evidence that participative processes may be important in ensuring the greater success of PRP among employees.'

Marsden and Richardson (1994)

The results of a survey of 2,000 Inland Revenue staff indicated that the system had only a small positive motivational effect on staff. The researchers concluded that: 'If motivation was not improved at all significantly, or had deteriorated, it is hard to see why performance should have been changed for the better. Why should performance pay have had so little general effect on motivation when 57 per cent of the staff reported being in favour of the principle of PRP? First, and most importantly, it was widely judged to be unfair in its operation.'

Research projects producing mainly positive results

Evidence is available from a number of academic studies that indicate that performance pay improves performance:

- Abowd (1990) showed that bonus payments based on economic or market measures could contribute to a strong economic return.

- Booth and Frank (1999) found through their analysis of UK data provided by the British Household Panel Survey that jobs with performance-related pay attracted workers of higher ability and induced workers to provide greater effort.

- Gupta and Shaw (1998) conducted a meta-analysis of 39 rigorously designed studies examining the effects of financial incentives on performance. A strong positive effect was found on performance quantity. Only six studies examined performance quality separately and a consistent relationship between incentives and quality was not found.

- Guzzo et al (1985) found through a meta-analysis that, when applied in the right way and in the right situations, incentives can have strongly positive effects on productivity.

- Heneman (1992) reviewed five studies that established a positive link between a merit-pay system and performance.

- Jenkins et al (1998) said of their study that it 'underscores the generalizable positive relationship between financial incentives and performance'.

- Lazear (1999) found that the productivity of operatives in a factory increased by 44 per cent following the introduction of a piece-rate incentive plan.

- Locke et al (1980) reviewed 44 studies on the adoption of incentive systems that showed in almost all cases a substantial improvement in performance.

- Marsden (2004) conducted a series of attitude surveys across a range of UK public services on employee and line manager judgements on the effects of performance pay. Performance pay was the instrument of a major renegotiation of performance norms, and this rather than motivation was the principal dynamic. Goal-setting and appraisal by line managers played a key role in this process.

- Prendergast (1999) reviewed the effect of incentives in both private and public sectors, leading to the conclusion that workers do respond to them.

- Prentice *et al* (2007) found that research indicated strong evidence that UK civil servants do respond to financial incentives.

- Stajkovic and Luthans (2001) showed that routine pay for performance increased performance over its baseline level by 11 per cent, while performance pay applied through the systematic procedures of the organizational behaviour model increased performance by 31.7 per cent.

- Sturman *et al* (2003) used utility analysis techniques to assess the costs and benefits of a contingent pay strategy. The conclusion was that the four-year benefit of linking pay to performance was substantial.

- Thompson (1998) in a study of 400 companies in the British aerospace industry established that the high-value-added and low-value-added companies were clearly differentiated in terms of their pay practices, with virtually double the number of high-value-added companies applying individual performance-related pay schemes to more than two-thirds of their staff.

- West *et al* (2005) conducted research in 15 customer service organizations into methods of rewarding customer service, and found that in the five organizations superior to others in terms of customer service, 60 per cent had performance pay while in the other 10 only 29 per cent had performance pay.

Implications

A recurring theme in the negative UK studies was that the problems arose because of the ways in which schemes were introduced and operated within particular contexts rather than because of the principles upon which they were based. An example was the incorrect assumption that schemes that worked well in the private sector would work equally well in the public sector.

This was confirmed in research conducted for the Department of Employment by Bowey and Thorpe (1982). This showed that performance pay design bore no correlation with successful outcomes, which were more dependent on the effectiveness of communication and support systems. The quality and communication of scheme objectives linked to business strategy and goals was found to be a key differentiator between successful and unsuccessful performance. It was noted that the essential requirement is to tailor pay schemes to suit the particular organization and environment.

Arguments for and against financial rewards

The concept of financial rewards in the shape of contingent pay has aroused strong feelings amongst those who support and those who oppose them. The arguments for and against are set out below.

Arguments for

The most powerful argument advanced for financial rewards is that those who contribute more should be paid more. It is right and proper to recognize achievement with a financial and therefore tangible reward. This is in accordance with the principle of distributive justice, which, while it states that rewards should be provided equitably, does not require them to be equal except when the value of contribution is equal.

Arguments against

The main arguments against financial rewards are that:

- The extent to which contingent pay schemes motivate is questionable – the amounts available for distribution are usually so small that they cannot act as an incentive.

- The requirements for success are exacting and difficult to achieve.

- Money by itself it will not result in sustained motivation; intrinsic motivation provided by the work itself goes deeper and lasts longer.

- People react in widely different ways to any form of motivation – it cannot be assumed that money will motivate all people equally, yet that is the premise on which contingent pay schemes are based.

- Financial rewards may possibly motivate those who receive them but they can demotivate those that don't, and the numbers who are demotivated could be much higher than those who are motivated.

- Contingent pay schemes can create more dissatisfaction than satisfaction if they are perceived to be unfair, inadequate or badly managed.

- Employees can be suspicious of schemes because they fear that performance bars will be continuously raised; a scheme may therefore only operate successfully for a limited period.

- Schemes depend on the existence of accurate and reliable methods of measuring performance, contribution, competence or skill, which might not exist.

- Individuals are encouraged to emphasize only those aspects of performance that are rewarded.

- Contingent pay decisions depend on the judgement of managers, which in the absence of reliable criteria can be partial, prejudiced, inconsistent or ill-informed.

- The concept of contingent pay is based on the assumption that performance is completely under the control of individuals when in fact it is affected by the system in which they work.

- Contingent pay, especially performance-related pay, can militate against quality and teamwork.

Another powerful argument against contingent pay is that it has proved difficult to manage. Organizations, including the Civil Service, rushed into performance-related pay in the 1980s without really understanding how to make it work. Inevitably problems of implementation arose. Studies such as those mentioned earlier have all revealed these difficulties. Failures may arise because insufficient attention has been given to fitting schemes to the context and culture of the organization; instead they are often rooted in implementation and operating processes, especially those concerned with performance management, the need for effective communication and involvement, and line management capability.

The last factor is crucial. As Thompson (1992a, 1992b) explained, the success of contingent pay rests largely in the hands of line managers. They have to believe in it as something that will help them as well as the organization. They must also be good at practising the crucial skills of agreeing targets, measuring performance fairly and consistently, and providing feedback to their staff on the outcome of performance management and its impact on pay. Line managers can make or break contingent pay schemes. Vicky Wright (1991) summed it up: 'Even the most ardent supporters of performance-related pay recognize that it is difficult to manage well,' and Oliver (1996) made the point that 'performance pay is beautiful in theory but difficult in practice.'

There is also the problem of moral hazard inherent in financial incentives. The concept of moral hazard originated in insurance, where it describes the phenomenon of people who because they are insulated from risk by being insured proceed to take unnecessary risks. The term was extended to incentives by Prendergast (1999), who pointed out that: 'Contracts offering incentives can give rise to dysfunctional behaviour whereby agents emphasize only those objects of performance that are rewarded... Compensation on any sub-set of tasks will result in reallocation of activities towards those that are directly compensated and away from the uncompensated activities.' A 'moral hazard' exists when incentive schemes encourage undesirable behaviour in which people strive to obtain higher rewards by manipulating results, hiding or even falsifying poor figures, focusing on easy short-term gains rather than the tougher long-term demands or going for one result and neglecting another important outcome, as when they pursue output increases at the expense of quality. These problems can be difficult to spot, especially if everyone's attention is focused on headline figures and not what lies beneath them. As Lawler (1971) warned: 'It is quite difficult to establish criteria that are both measurable quantitatively and inclusive of all the important job behaviours.'

Criteria for effectiveness

The effectiveness of financial rewards in the shape of contingent pay depends on the following factors:

- There must be accurate, consistent and fair assessment of performance or contribution.

- Pay differences can be related to performance or contribution differences and can be seen to be related.

- The principles of procedural and distributive justice are upheld.

- There is a climate of trust in the organization – as Thompson (1992b) commented: 'Where there is trust, involvement and a commitment to fairness, the (PRP) schemes work.'

- Performance management systems function well.

- Line managers have the necessary skills and commitment.

- Stakeholders, including line managers, employees and employee representatives, have been involved in the design of the scheme.

- The scheme is appropriate to the context and culture of the organization.

- The scheme is not unduly complex.

- The purpose, methodology and effect of the scheme have been communicated and understood.

- There is a clear line of sight between effort and reward.

- Rewards are attainable and worth attaining.

Summaries of the factors that have been found in various research projects to relate to the success of financial rewards in the shape of contingent pay plans are shown in Table 8.1.

Gupta and Shaw (1998) summed up the dos and don'ts of financial incentives admirably, as set out in Table 8.2.

Table 8.1 Factors relating to the success of financial rewards

Study	Factors affecting the success of contingent pay
Bowey and Thorpe (1982)	• Staff involvement in design • Amount of consultation • Supervisory skills • Fit to context and culture
Bullock and Tubbs (1990)	• Staff involvement in design • Favourable attitude of employees • Participative management style • Productivity rather than profit orientation
De Matteo *et al* (1997)	• Communication and understanding of schemes • Clarification of team goals • Team independence
Towers Perrin (1997)	• Senior management commitment • Employee involvement • Employee support • Emphasis on communications • Related HR activities, eg training

Table 8.2 The dos and don'ts of financial incentives

• Do tie financial incentives to *valued* behaviours. • Do have good measurement systems. • Do have good communications. • Do make the system complete, ie cover all relevant and valued aspects of performance. • Do use financial incentives to supplement other rewards. • Do make meaningful differentiations. • Do set realistic goals. • Do provide relevant skills and resources. • Do emphasize long-term as well as short-term success. • Do accept reality – use incentives that *do* work rather than those that *should* work.	• Don't give in to hope and fad. • Don't equate rewards and punishments. • Don't rely on invalid behaviour measurement tools. • Don't keep things secret. • Don't violate employee expectations.

(Source: Gupta and Shaw, 1998)

Conclusions

A comprehensive study by Brown and Armstrong (1999) into the effectiveness of contingent pay as revealed by a number of research projects produced two overall conclusions: 1) contingent pay cannot be endorsed or rejected universally as a principle, and 2) no type of contingent pay is universally successful or unsuccessful. They concluded their analysis of the research findings by stating that 'the research does show that the effectiveness of pay-for-performance schemes is highly context and situation-specific; and it has highlighted the practical problems which many companies have experienced with these schemes.'

Six tips for using financial rewards

- Provide for the accurate, consistent and fair assessment of performance or contribution.
- Fit the scheme to the context and culture of the organization.
- Keep it simple.
- Involve stakeholders, including line managers, employees and employee representatives, in the design of the scheme.
- Communicate the purpose, methodology and effect of the scheme.
- Ensure that there is a clear line of sight between effort and reward and that the rewards provided by the scheme are attainable and worth attaining.

References

Abowd, J M (1990) Does performance-based managerial compensation affect corporate performance? *Industrial and Labor Relations Review*, **43** (3), pp 52–73

Adams, J S (1965) Injustice in social exchange, in *Advances in Experimental Psychology*, ed L Berkowitz, Academic Press, New York

Armstrong, M and Baron, A (2004) *Performance Management: Action and impact*, CIPD London

Blackburn, R M and Mann, R (1979) *The Working Class in the Labour Market*, Macmillan, London

Booth, A L and Frank, J (1999) Earnings, productivity and performance related pay, *Journal of Labor Economics*, **17** (3), pp 447–63

Bowey, A and Thorpe, R (1982) *The Effects of Incentive Pay Systems*, Department of Employment, London

Brayfield, A H and Crockett, W H (1955) Employee attitudes and employee performance, *Psychological Bulletin*, **52**, pp 346–424

Brown, D and Armstrong, M (1999) *Paying for Contribution*, Kogan Page, London

Brumbach, G B (1988) Some ideas, issues and predictions about performance management, *Public Personnel Management*, Winter, pp 387–402

Bullock, R J and Tubbs, M E (1990) A case meta-analysis of gainsharing plans as organizational development interventions, *Journal of Applied Behavioural Science*, **26** (3), pp 383–406

Cameron, J, Banko, K M and Pierce, W D (2001) Pervasive negative effects of rewards on intrinsic motivation: the myth continues, *The Behavior Analyst*, **24** (1), pp 1–44

Caulkin, S (2009) We can't afford to give bosses a blank cheque, *The Observer*, 9 February, p 7

Deci, E L (1975) *Intrinsic Motivation*, Plenum Press, New York

Deci, E L and Ryan, R M (1985) *Intrinsic Motivation and Self-determination in Human Behavior*, Plenum Press, New York

Deci, E L, Koestner, R and Ryan, R M (1999) A meta-analytical review of experiments examining the effects of extrinsic rewards on intrinsic motivation, *Psychological Bulletin*, **25**, pp 627–68

De Matteo, J S, Rush, M C, Sundstorm, E and Eby, L T (1997) Factors relating to the successful implementation of team-based reward, *ACA Journal*, Winter, pp 16–28

Dickinson, A M and Taylor, L A (1989) The detrimental effects of extrinsic reinforcement on 'intrinsic motivation', *The Behavior Analyst*, **12**, pp 1–15

Dunham, R B (1984) *Organizational Behaviour*, Irwin, Homewood IL

Furnham, A (2006) Pouring money down the drain? *British Journal of Administrative Management*, June/July, pp 26–27

Gerhart, B and Rynes, S L (2003) *Compensation: Theory, evidence and strategic implications*, Sage, Thousand Oaks, CA

Gupta, N and Shaw, J D (1998) Financial incentives, *Compensation & Benefits Review*, March/April, pp 26, 28–32

Guzzo, R A, Jette, R D and Katzell, R A (1985) The effects of psychologically based intervention programs on worker productivity: a meta-analysis, *Personnel Psychology*, **38** (2), pp 275–91

Heneman, R L (1992) *Merit Pay: Linking pay increases to performance ratings*, Addison-Wesley, Reading MA

Herzberg, F (1968) One more time: how do you motivate employees? *Harvard Business Review*, January–February, pp 109–20

Herzberg, F W, Mausner, B and Snyderman, B (1957) *The Motivation to Work*, Wiley, New York

Jaques, E (1961) *Equitable Payment*, Heinemann, London

Jenkins, D G, Mitra, A, Gupta, N and Shaw, J D (1998) Are financial incentives related to performance? A meta-analytic review of empirical research, *Journal of Applied Psychology*, **3**, pp 777–87

Jurgensen, C E (1978) Job preferences (what makes a job good or bad?), *Journal of Applied Psychology*, **63**, pp 267–76

Kanfer, R (1990) Motivation theory and industrial and organizational psychology, in *Handbook of Industrial and Organizational Psychology*, ed M D Dunnette and L M Hough, Consulting Psychologists Press, Palo Alto CA

Kessler, I and Purcell, J (1992) Performance-related pay: objectives and application, *Human Resource Management Journal*, **2** (3), pp 16–33

Kohn, A (1993) Why incentive plans cannot work, *Harvard Business Review*, September–October, pp 54–63

Kohn, A (1998) Challenging behaviorist myths about money and motivation, *Compensation & Benefits Review*, March/April, pp 27, 33–37

Kohn, A (2000) *Punished by Rewards, The trouble with gold stars, incentive plans, A's, praise and other bribes*, Houghton Mifflin, Boston MA

Lawler, E E (1971) *Pay and Organizational Effectiveness*, McGraw-Hill, New York

Lawler, E E (1988) Pay for performance: making it work, *Personnel*, October, pp 68–71

Lawler, E E (1990) *Strategic Pay*, Jossey-Bass, San Francisco

Lawler, E E (1993) Who uses skill-based pay, and why, *Compensation & Benefits Review*, March/April, pp 22–26

Lazear, E P (1999) Performance pay and productivity, *American Economic Review*, **90**, pp 1346–61

Locke, E A, Feren, D B, McCaleb, V M, Shaw, K N and Denny, A T (1980) The relative effectiveness of four methods of motivating employee performance, in *Changes in Work, Changes in Working Life*, ed K D Duncan, M M Gruneberg and D Wallis, Wiley, New York

Marsden, D (2004) The role of performance-related pay in renegotiating the 'effort bargain': the case of the British public service, *Industrial and Labor Relations Review*, **57** (3), pp 350–70

Marsden, D and Richardson, R (1994) Performing for pay? The effects of 'merit pay' on motivation in a public service, *British Journal of Industrial Relations*, **32** (2), pp 243–61

Maslow, A (1954) Motivation and Personality, Harper & Row, New York

Mawhinney, T C, Dickinson, A M and Taylor, L A (1989) The use of concurrent schedules to evaluate the effects of extrinsic rewards on 'intrinsic motivation', *Journal of Organizational Behavior Management*, **10**, pp 109–29

McDougall, C (1973) How well do you reward your managers? *Personnel Management*, March, pp 12–14

McNabb, R and Whitfield, K (2004) Does pay-for-performance pay? Incentive pay, employee participation and earnings, Working Papers in Human Resource Management No 3, International Industrial Relations Association Human Resource Management Study Group, Manchester

Murlis, H (2009) Total reward –the holistic approach, *Hay Group News Letter*, **3**, pp 1–3

Oliver, J (1996) Cash on delivery, *Management Today*, August, pp 52–55

Opsahl, R C and Dunnette, M D (1966) The role of financial compensation in individual motivation, *Psychological Bulletin*, **56**, pp 94–118

Pfeffer, J (1998) Six dangerous myths about pay, *Harvard Business Review*, May–June, pp 109–19

Prendergast, C (1999) The provision of financial incentives in firms, *Journal of Economic Literature*, **37**, pp 7–63

Prentice, G, Burgess, S and Propper, C (2007) *Performance Pay in the Public Sector: A review of the issues and evidence*, Office of Manpower Economics, London

Porter, L W and Lawler, E E (1968) *Managerial Attitudes and Performance*, Irwin-Dorsey, Homewood IL

Ritchie, S and Martin, P (1999) *Motivation Management*, Gower, Aldershot

Ryan, R M, Mimms, V and Koestner, R (1983) The relation of reward contingency and interpersonal context to intrinsic motivation: a review and test using cognitive evaluation theory, *Journal of Personality and Social Psychology*, **45** (4), pp 736–50

Schwab, D P and Cummings, L L (1970) Theories of performance and satisfaction: a review, *Industrial Relations*, **9**, pp 408–30

Skaggs, K J, Dickinson, A M and O'Connor, K A (1992) The use of concurrent schedules to evaluate the effects of extrinsic rewards on intrinsic motivation: a replication, *Journal of Organizational Behavior Management*, **12**, pp 45–83

Slovic, P and Lichtenstein, S (1971) Comparison of Bayesian and regression approaches to the study of information processing in judgment, *Organizational Behavior and Human Performance*, **6**, pp 649–744

Sparrow, P A (1996) Too good to be true, *People Management*, 5 December, pp 22–27

Stajkovic, A D and Luthans, F (2001) Differential effects of incentive motivators on work performance, *Academy of Management Journal*, **4** (3), pp 580–90

Steers, R M (2001) Call for papers: the future of work motivation theory, *Academy of Management Review*, **26** (4), pp 686–87

Sturman, M C, Trevor, C O, Boudreau, J W and Gerhart, B (2003) Is it worth it to win the talent war? Evaluating the utility of performance-based pay, *Personnel Psychology*, **56** (4), pp 997–1035

Thompson, M (1992a) *Pay and Performance: The employer experience*, IMS, Brighton

Thompson, M (1992b) *Pay and Performance: The employee experience*, IMS, Brighton

Thompson, M (1998) HR and the bottom line, *People Management*, 16 April, pp 38–41

Towers Perrin (1997) *Learning from the Past: Changing for the future*, Towers Perrin, London

Vroom, V (1964) *Work and Motivation*, Wiley, New York

Wallace, M J and Szilagyi, A D (1982) *Managing Behaviour in Organizations*, Scott, Glenview IL

West, M, Fisher, G, Carter, M, Gould, V and Scully, J (2005) *Rewarding Customer Service? Using reward and recognition to deliver your customer service strategy*, CIPD, London

Wright, V (1991) Performance related pay, in *The Performance Management Handbook*, ed E Neale, IPM, London

9

Non-financial Rewards

Key concepts and terms

- Autonomy
- Concierge services
- Core values
- Employee well-being
- Extrinsic rewards
- Intrinsic motivation
- Intrinsic rewards

- Recognition
- Recognition scheme
- Responsibility
- Sorting effect
- Voluntary benefits
- Work–life balance

Learning outcomes

On completing this chapter you should be able to define these key concepts. You should also know about:

- The significance of non-financial rewards
- Extrinsic non-financial rewards

- Intrinsic non-financial rewards
- Using non-financial rewards

Introduction

Non-financial rewards are those that focus on the needs people have to varying degrees for recognition, achievement, responsibility, autonomy, influence and personal growth. They incorporate the notion of relational rewards, which are the intangible rewards concerned with the work environment (quality of working life, the work itself, work–life balance), recognition, performance management, and learning and development.

Non-financial rewards can be extrinsic, such as praise or recognition, or intrinsic, arising from the work itself associated with job challenge and interest and feelings that the work is worthwhile.

This chapter starts with an exploration of the significance of non-financial rewards. It then deals with each of the major aspects of non-financial rewards and ends with a discussion on how they can be developed as an important part of a total rewards approach.

The significance of non-financial rewards

Latham and Locke (1979) noted that: 'Money is obviously the primary incentive' but they went on to say that 'money alone is not enough to motivate high performance.' Money may be an important factor in attracting and retaining people (the sorting effect). It can produce satisfaction, but this may be short-lived. And if the principles of distributive and procedural justice are not followed, it can cause lasting dissatisfaction.

It can be said that money will motivate some of the people all of the time and, perhaps, all of the people some of the time. But it cannot be relied on to motivate all of the people all of the time. To rely on it as the sole motivator is misguided. Money has to be reinforced by non-financial rewards, especially those that provide intrinsic motivation. When motivation is achieved by such means it can have a more powerful and longer-lasting effect on people, and financial and non-financial rewards can be mutually reinforcing.

Reward systems should therefore be designed and managed in such a way as to provide the best mix of all kinds of motivators according to the needs of the organization and its members.

Types of non-financial rewards

Non-financial rewards can be classified as follows:

- individual extrinsic rewards: non-financial recognition, praise, feedback;
- individual intrinsic rewards: fulfilling work, opportunity to grow;

- collective extrinsic rewards: work–life balance policies, employee well-being services, concierge services, voluntary benefits, learning and development and talent management programmes;

- collective intrinsic rewards: work environment enhancement, work system design.

Individual extrinsic rewards

Non-financial recognition

Recognition is one of the most powerful methods of rewarding people. They need to know not only how well they have achieved their objectives or carried out their work but also that their achievements are appreciated. Recognition needs are linked to the esteem needs in Maslow's (1954) hierarchy of needs. They are defined by Maslow as the need to have a stable, firmly based, high evaluation of oneself (self-esteem) and to have the respect of others (prestige). These needs are classified into two subsidiary sets: first, 'the desire for achievement, for adequacy, for confidence in the face of the world, and for independence and freedom', and second, 'the desire for reputation or status defined as respect or esteem from other people, and manifested by recognition, attention, importance or appreciation'.

Belief in the motivational value of recognition is supported by Herzberg's (1957, 1968) research, which identified recognition as an important 'satisfier'. Although the methodology he used has been heavily criticized, the proposition that recognizing people for what they achieve makes them feel good and therefore helps to enlist their engagement rings true.

Recognition is a form of feedback that lets people know that they have done well and therefore provides positive reinforcement. Research by Brand et al (1982) found that a feedback programme in a US government agency that involved public recognition brought about an increase in productivity of 26 to 149 per cent in different sections. A meta-analysis by DeNisi and Kluger (2000) of 131 empirical studies that had tested how well feedback interventions worked indicated a modest but positive effect of feedback on performance overall.

Recognition can be provided by positive and immediate feedback from managers and colleagues that acknowledges individual contributions, and by managers who listen to and act upon the suggestions of their team members. Other actions that provide recognition include allocation to a high-profile project and enrichment of the job to provide scope for more interesting and rewarding work.

There are other forms of recognition such as public 'applause', status symbols of one kind or another, sabbaticals, treats, trips abroad and long-service awards, all of which can function as rewards. But they must be used with care. One person's recognition implies an element of non-recognition to others and the consequences of having winners and losers need to be carefully managed. Recognition schemes are examined more thoroughly in Chapter 14.

Praise

Praise is, of course, a form of recognition. It can be given privately during the course of work or in a performance review meeting. Public praise can be even more rewarding. But the praise must be genuine and saved for real achievements. It should not be fulsome.

Feedback

Feedback is another form of recognition. If done properly it can increase self-belief and provide the basis for self-directed learning.

Individual intrinsic rewards

Fulfilling work

Work can be fulfilling and therefore motivating when individuals feel that what they do is worthwhile and adds value. This implies that they should ideally work on a complete process or product, or a significant part of it that can be seen as a whole. Work is also fulfilling when it requires people to use abilities they value to perform it effectively and scope is provided for achievement, responsibility, autonomy and influence.

Use of abilities

Fulfilling work enables people to use and develop their abilities. This is particularly the case when people are stretched, but not too hard, to achieve more than they expected they could achieve.

Achievement

The need to achieve applies in varying degrees to all people in all jobs, although the level at which it operates will depend on the orientation of the individual and the scope provided by the work to fulfil a need for achievement. People feel rewarded and motivated if they have the scope to achieve as well as being recognized for the achievement.

Responsibility

Individuals can be motivated by being given more responsibility for their work. People are in positions of responsibility when they are held to account for what they do. They are in charge of their work and the resources required to do it. Being given more responsibility can satisfy needs for achievement and increase self-esteem. It is also a form of recognition.

Autonomy

Autonomy exists when an individual has freedom to make decisions and act independently without reference to higher authority. It enhances self-belief, gives people more opportunity to achieve and provides an opportunity to develop skills.

Influence

Jobs are more fulfilling if people can influence what they do or exert wider influence on policy and operational decisions.

Opportunity to grow

Alderfer (1972) emphasized the importance of providing people with opportunities for personal growth as a means of rewarding and therefore motivating them. He believed that satisfaction of growth needs takes place when individuals have the opportunity to be what they are most fully and to become what they can. Most learning and development opportunities take place in the course of everyday work, and the organization can encourage this through coaching, mentoring and support in the implementation of personal development plans created as part of the performance management process.

Collective extrinsic rewards

Collective extrinsic rewards are provided by the organization in the shape of policies, procedures, services and programmes such as the following:

- Work–life balance policies reward people by recognizing their needs outside work by, for example, adopting family-friendly policies, including the provision of more flexible working arrangements.

- Employee well-being services can be provided for individuals to help them deal with their problems. This may involve counselling or personal casework where the aim is as far as possible to get individuals to help themselves.

- Concierge services provide employees with help by undertaking mundane personal tasks such as getting their car serviced, home repairs or waiting at home for deliveries.

- Voluntary benefit schemes provide opportunities for employees to buy goods or services at discounted prices. The employer negotiates deals with the suppliers.

- Learning and development programmes give employees the chance to develop their skills and careers.

Collective intrinsic rewards

Collective intrinsic rewards are provided mainly through the work environment. They relate to the quality of working life provided and the organization's core values.

Quality of working life

The quality of working life refers to the feelings of satisfaction and well-being arising from the work itself and the way people are treated. On the basis of their longitudinal research in 12 companies Purcell *et al* (2003) concluded that:

> What seems to be happening is that successful firms are able to meet peoples' needs both for a good job and to work 'in a great place'. They create good work and a conducive working environment. In this way they become an 'employer of choice'. People will want to work there because their individual needs are met – for a good job with prospects linked to training, appraisal and working with a good boss who listens and gives some autonomy but helps with coaching and guidance.

Specifically, the quality of working life depends on having a system of work that enables jobs to be designed that provide for intrinsic motivation, on good working conditions and on the leadership qualities of line managers and team leaders.

Core values

The significance of the core values of an organization as a basis for creating a rewarding work environment was identified by the research conducted by John Purcell and his colleagues referred to above. The most successful companies had what the researchers called 'the big idea'. They had a clear vision and a set of integrated values that were embedded, enduring, collective, measured and managed. They were concerned with sustaining performance and flexibility. Clear connections existed between positive attitudes towards HR policies and practices, levels of satisfaction, motivation and commitment, and operational performance.

Using non-financial rewards: six tips

- Develop the use of non-financial rewards as part of a total rewards policy.
- Introduce employment practices designed to ensure the fair and ethical treatment of employees.
- Involve employees as stakeholders in drawing up a set of core values associated with the employment relationship and in planning and implementing the steps required to ensure that everyone concerned 'lives the values'.
- Review the features of the work environment and introduce changes that will improve the quality of working life and deal with any issues that may affect it.
- Examine ways in which the design of the work system and jobs can be improved to make them more rewarding. Ensure that all those involved in work or job design (which means line managers) know what they can do and why and how they should do it.
- Develop and implement specific policies and practices in such areas as recognition, work–life balance, well-being programmes, concierge services, voluntary benefits, performance management, learning and development and talent management.

References

Alderfer, C (1972) *Existence, Relatedness and Growth*, New York, The Free Press

Brand, D D, Staelin, J R, O'Brien, R M and Dickinson, A M (1982) Improving white collar productivity at HUD, in *Industrial Behavior Modification*, ed R M O'Brien, A M Dickinson and M P Rosow, Pergamon, New York

DeNisi, A S and Kluger, A N (2000) Feedback effectiveness: can 360-degree appraisals be improved? *Academy of Management Executive*, 14 (1) pp 129–39

Herzberg, F (1968) One more time: how do you motivate employees? *Harvard Business Review*, January–February, pp 109–20

Herzberg, F W, Mausner, B and Snyderman, B (1957) *The Motivation to Work*, Wiley, New York

Latham, G and Locke, R (1979) Goal setting: a motivational technique that works, *Organizational Dynamics*, Autumn, pp 68–80

Maslow, A (1954) *Motivation and Personality*, Harper & Row, New York

Purcell, J, Kinnie, K, Hutchinson, S, Rayton, B and Swart, J (2003) *People and Performance: How people management impacts on organizational performance*, CIPD, London

10

Contingent Pay Schemes

Key concepts and terms

- Bonus
- Competency-related pay
- Contingent pay
- Contribution-related pay
- Expectancy theory
- Incentives
- Line of sight
- Performance-related pay
- Rewards
- Skills-based pay
- Variable pay

Learning outcomes

On completing this chapter you should be able to define these key concepts. You should also know about:

- Objectives of contingent pay
- Criteria for success
- Types of individual contingent pay

Introduction

Contingent pay is concerned with answering two fundamental reward management questions: 1) What do we value? and 2) What are we prepared to pay for? Contingent pay schemes are based on measurements or assessments. These may be expressed as ratings that are converted by means of a formula to a payment. Alternatively, there may be no formal ratings and pay decisions may be based on broad assessments rather than a formula.

This chapter deals only with schemes that provide payments to individuals in addition to their base rate, related to their performance, contribution, competency, or skill. Bonus schemes, which pay non-consolidated lump sums based on performance (variable pay), are covered in Chapter 11. Pay schemes rewarding for team or organizational performance are described in Chapters 12 and 13 respectively. In addition, rewards can be provided by recognition schemes as discussed in Chapter 14.

The e-reward 2009 survey of contingent pay established that contingent pay schemes were used by the 107 respondents in the proportions shown in Table 10.1.

Table 10.1   Incidence of contingent pay

Type of scheme	%
Performance-related pay	84
Contribution-related pay	57
Competency-related pay	33
Skills-based pay	21

Objectives of contingent pay

The main objectives for using contingent pay given by respondents to the e-reward 2009 survey are set out in Table 10.2.

Criteria for success

The following are the five criteria for effective contingent pay:

- Individuals have a clear line of sight between what they do and what they will get for doing it. A line of sight model adapted from Lawler (1988) is shown in Figure 10.1. The concept expresses the essence of expectancy theory: that motivation only takes place when people expect that their effort and contribution will be rewarded. The reward should be clearly and closely linked to accomplishment or effort – people know what they will get if they achieve defined and agreed targets or standards, and can track their performance against them.

Table 10.2 Objectives of performance pay

Objective	%
Recognize and reward better performance	88
Improve organizational performance	50
Attract and retain high-quality people	42
Focus attention on key results and values	29
Motivate people	26
Deliver a message about the importance of performance	25
Influence behaviour	22
Support cultural change	12

Figure 10.1 Line of sight model

- Rewards are worth having.

- Fair and consistent means are available for measuring or assessing performance, competence, contribution or skill.

- People are able to influence their performance by changing their behaviour and developing their competencies and skills.

- The reward follows as closely as possible the accomplishment that generated it.

These are demanding requirements and few schemes meet them in full. That is why contingent pay arrangements can often promise more than they deliver.

The various forms of contingent pay are described in the following sections of this chapter.

Performance-related pay

Performance-related pay (PRP) is the most popular contingent pay scheme. It is also controversial, largely because, especially in its early days, it was introduced and managed badly and the high expectations of its impact on performance and its ability to change cultures were not fulfilled. The assumptions governing the use of PRP and its method of operation are discussed below.

PRP assumptions

Performance-related pay rests heavily on three assumptions:

- that individual differences in performance can be accurately and fairly measured;
- that pay differences can be fairly related to performance differences and can be seen to be related;
- that individuals will increase their efforts to gain more rewards, resulting in increased performance.

These assumptions are difficult to justify. Fair measurement is hard in any situation where outcomes cannot be quantified, and this is the most typical situation. Relating pay fairly to performance can be subject to partiality or prejudice. The success of PRP largely depends on the line managers who make pay recommendations, and they are not necessarily equipped with the skills or the powers of judgement required to do so fairly and consistently.

In addition, the effectiveness of PRP as an incentive is highly questionable. As normally operated it fails to meet the requirements of expectancy theory in three critical ways: 1) people are too often unclear about what they have to do to get a reward, 2) people do not necessarily expect that they will get a reward, and 3) they do not expect that the reward will be worthwhile (the amounts available for distribution, typically around 3 per cent of pay, are far too small to act as an incentive). PRP schemes also fail the fifth criteria for contingent pay listed above, in that the reward is usually made annually and therefore fails to follow as closely as possible the accomplishment that generated it. Moreover, they usually rely on potentially subjective and inaccurate ratings. As Murphy and Cleveland (1995) concluded following their extensive review of performance appraisal: 'It is surprisingly difficult to determine whether or not performance ratings provide valid and accurate indications of individuals' performance.' And research carried out by Viswesvaran et al (1996) established the mean inter-rater reliability of supervisory ratings of overall job performance was only .52.

Methods of operating PRP

Methods of operating PRP vary considerably but its typical main features are modelled in Figure 10.2 and described below.

The basis of the scheme is that pay increases are related to the achievement of agreed results defined as targets or outcomes. Scope is provided for consolidated pay progression within pay brackets attached to grades or levels in a graded or career/job-family structure or zones in a broad-banded structure. Such increases are permanent.

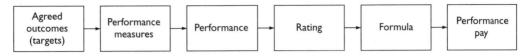

Figure 10.2 Performance-related pay model

A formula in the shape of a pay matrix as illustrated in Figure 10.3 is often used to decide on the size of increases. This indicates the percentage increase payable for different performance ratings according to the position of the individual's pay in the pay range. This is sometimes referred to as an individual 'compa-ratio' (short for comparison ratio) and expresses pay as a percentage of the mid-point in a range. A compa-ratio of 100 per cent means that the salary would be at the mid-point.

Pay progression in a graded structure is typically planned to decelerate through the grade for two reasons. First, it is argued in line with learning curve theory that pay increases should be higher during the earlier period in a job when learning is at its highest rate. Second, it may be assumed that the central or reference point in a grade represents the market value of fully competent people. Depending on the pay policy of the organization, this may be at or higher than the median. Especially in the latter case, it may be believed that employees should progress quite quickly to that level but, because beyond it they are already being paid well, their pay need not increase so rapidly. This notion is reasonable but it can be difficult to explain to people why they get smaller percentage increases when they are performing well at the upper end of their scale.

Alternatively or additionally, high levels of performance or special achievements may be rewarded by cash bonuses that are not consolidated and have to be re-earned. Individuals may be eligible for such bonuses when they have reached the top of the pay bracket for their grade, or when they are assessed as being fully competent, having completely progressed along their learning curve. The rate of pay for someone who reaches the required level of competence can be aligned to market rates according to the organization's pay policy.

	Percentage pay increase according to performance rating and position in pay range (compa-ratio)			
Rating	**Position in pay range**			
	80–90%	91–100%	101–110%	111–120%
Excellent	12%	10%	8%	6%
Very effective	10%	8%	6%	4%
Effective	6%	4%	3%	0
Developing	4%	3%	0	0
Ineligible	0	0	0	0

Figure 10.3 PRP pay matrix

Another approach is to define performance zones in a pay range as in the following examples.

XANSA

Salary ranges are divided into three levels:

- Entry level typically represents employees who are new to the job, meeting some objectives and demonstrating some of the skills and competencies at the required level.

- Market average typically represents employees who either consistently meet their objectives and demonstrate many of the skills and competencies at the required level, or who meet most but not all objectives and consistently demonstrate all of the skills and competencies at the required level.

- High level typically represents employees who meet all objectives and exceed some, and who demonstrate all of the skills and competencies at the required level and some at a higher level.

Nationwide

The majority of ranges consist of a target rate (100 per cent of the median market rate), a minimum (80 per cent), and a maximum (120 per cent). People tend to enter the range at the minimum. Progression thereafter is solely by means of performance. Each year, pay scales are uplifted by the percentage paid to 'good' performers. The percentage increases paid to individuals are applied to the target, rather than their own salaries, ensuring that everyone on a particular range with the same performance rating receives the same amount of money; that is, the same effort is guaranteed the same reward.

Employees who start on the minimum of a range are guaranteed progression to the target in three years if they receive consistently 'good' performance ratings. Those rated higher receive enhanced progression. Once the target has been reached, employees get the percentage increase resulting from their performance rating based on their target salary. This means that 'good' performers will stay at the target, since this (and the rest of the scales) is uprated by the percentage given to good performers, while better performers will move beyond the target towards the maximum.

Conclusions on PRP

PRP has all the advantages and disadvantages listed in Chapter 8 for any form of financial reward. Many people feel the latter outweigh the former. It has attracted a lot of adverse comment, primarily because of the difficulties organizations have met in managing it but also because it is uni-dimensional in that it is only concerned with results and not how the results are achieved. Contribution-related pay schemes, which aim to overcome the latter problem, are becoming more popular.

Contribution-related pay

Contribution-related pay as modelled in Figures 10.4 and 10.5 provides a basis for making pay decisions that are related to assessments of both the outcomes of the work carried out by individuals and their inputs in terms of the levels of competency that have influenced these outcomes. It focuses on what people in organizations are there to do: that is, to contribute by their skill and efforts to the achievement of the purpose of their organization or team. In some schemes the rewards are related to contributions both to achieving results and to upholding corporate core values.

Contribution-related pay is a holistic process that takes into account all aspects of a person's performance in accordance with Brumbach's (1988) view that performance means both behaviours and results.

The case for contribution-related pay was made by Brown and Armstrong (1999) as follows:

> *Contribution captures the full scope of what people do, the level of skill and competence they apply and the results they achieve, which all contribute to the organization achieving its long-term goals. Contribution pay works by applying the mixed model of performance management: assessing inputs and outputs and coming to a conclusion on the level of pay for people in their roles and their work; both in the organization and in the market; taking into account both past performance and future potential.*

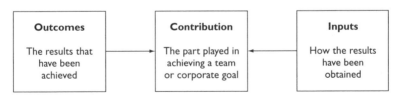

Figure 10.4 Contribution pay model (1)

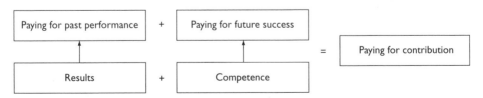

Figure 10.5 Contribution pay model (2)

However, there is the difficulty of measurement. It is hard enough to measure performance when outputs cannot be quantified, and it is even more difficult objectively to measure the level of competency. This is the problem of purely relating pay to competency as discussed later.

Main features

The main features of contribution-related pay are modelled in Figure 10.6.

An example of a pay for contribution scheme based on a balanced score card in a UK bank is shown in Figure 10.7.

Methods of deciding contribution awards

There are six basic approaches as described below.

Matrix formula

Pay awards are governed by assessments of performance and competency, and the amount is determined by a pay matrix such as the one illustrated in Figure 10.8.

This approach is rather mechanistic.

Figure 10.6 Contribution-related pay model (3)

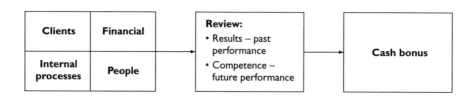

Figure 10.7 Paying for contribution in a UK bank

Performance Rating	Percentage pay increase according to performance rating and competence assessment		
	Competence assessment		
	Developing – does not yet meet all competence standards	Fully competent – meets all competence standards	Highly competent – exceeds most competence standards
Excellent	—	8%	10%
Very effective	—	6%	7%
Effective	—	4%	5%
Developing	3%	—	—
Ineligible	0	—	—

Figure 10.8   Contribution pay matrix

Separate consolidated increases and bonuses

Output is the only factor that governs cash bonuses but competency is the major component in determining base pay, on the grounds that the latter is paid for what people are capable of doing while the former rewards them for what they have already achieved.

Relate consolidated increases to competence up to a reference point and then pay cash bonuses for exceptional performance

This is a development of the second approach. Its main features are:

- A 'reference point' rate of pay is determined within each grade, band or level, which includes jobs of broadly equal size.

- The reference point is defined as the rate of pay for a person in a job who is highly competent, ie fully competent in all aspects of the job and therefore achieving high levels of performance.

- The reference point takes account of both internal relativities and market rates.

- The level of comparison for market rates is in accordance with the pay policy of the organization – this might be to set at above the median, eg at the upper quartile, to ensure that the high quality of staff required can be attracted and retained.

- The reference point is the maximum level of consolidated pay a high performer can expect to attain.

- A minimum level of pay for each grade is determined and progression to the reference point depends upon achieving defined levels of competence – there may be three or four levels.

- There is scope to reward those who perform exceptionally well with a re-earnable cash bonus, which could be consolidated if the level of exceptional performance is sustained over two to three years up to a maximum level defined for the grade.

A version of this contribution scheme developed for the Shaw Trust is modelled in Figure 10.9.

Rewards as either consolidated increases or bonuses

In this approach, as illustrated in Figure 10.10, performers can earn a mix of base pay increase and bonus that varies according to their position in the pay range. However, in this example, all outstanding performers receive a payment of 10 per cent of their base pay. Line managers would therefore not have to pass on the difficult message to outstanding individuals who are high in their pay range that they would be getting a smaller increase in spite of their contribution (this would be the case in a scheme using a typical PRP matrix as illustrated in Figure 10.3). Here, the higher up the range individuals are, the greater the proportion of their increase that is payable as a bonus. So those high in the range who are assessed as outstanding get 8 per cent as bonus and 2 per cent addition to their base pay, while outstanding individuals low in their range and below their market rates would get an 8 per cent addition to their base pay and a 2 per cent bonus.

Threshold payments

This method can be used to provide a measure of contingent pay related to contribution in a pay spine with progression based on fixed increments. A threshold is built into the pay range, as illustrated in Figure 10.11 for an incremental payment scheme. To cross the threshold into a higher part of the range individuals must meet contribution criteria that will define the level of competence required and indicate any performance (outcome) criteria that may be relevant.

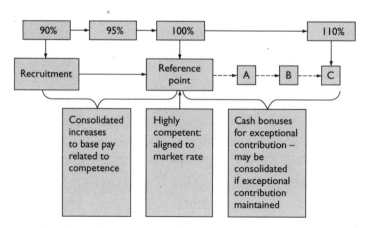

Figure 10.9   Contribution-related pay model: The Shaw Trust

Position in range			U	S	G	E	O
High – expert	Bonus	0%	2%	3%	6%	8%
	Base pay	0%	1%	2%	2%	2%
Mid-competent market rate	Bonus	0%	1%	2%	4%	6%
	Base pay	0%	2%	3%	4%	4%
Low – learning	Bonus	0%	0%	0%	1%	2%
	Base pay	0%	3%	6%	7%	8%
Competency assessment*		U	S	G	E	O

U = unsatisfactory S = satisfactory G = Good
E = excellent O = outstanding

Figure 10.10   Contribution matrix for base pay increases and bonuses

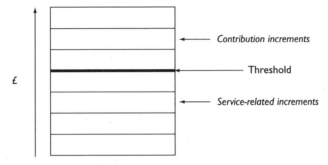

Figure 10.11   Contribution thresholds in a pay spine

Threshold systems may be particularly relevant where there is a large pay span in a grade, as in some incremental scales, and it is felt that progression needs to be controlled. They could be regarded as a halfway house to a full contribution pay scheme and, because they do not rely on a suspect formula and contain defined and transparent criteria, they may be more acceptable to staff and trade unions. However, their effectiveness depends on the definition of clear and assessable criteria and the willingness of all those concerned to assess contribution on the basis of evidence about the extent to which individuals meet the criteria. Judgements are still involved and the system depends on the ability of managers to exercise them fairly and consistently and to be prepared to make hard decisions on the basis of objective evidence that may mean that staff do not progress through the threshold. There is a real danger that if managers do not have the courage of their convictions, staff will more or less automatically progress through the thresholds as happened in the time of 'merit bars', although the criteria for crossing those bars were seldom defined explicitly.

Holistic assessment

A holistic approach can be adopted to assessing the level of contribution and therefore possible awards in the shape of base pay increases or bonuses. This approach leads to a decision on the level of pay appropriate for individuals in relation to the comparative levels of contribution of their peers and their own market worth, which will include consideration of their potential and the need to retain them.

Consideration is given both to what individuals have contributed to the success of their team and to the level of competence they have achieved and deployed. Team members who are contributing at the expected level will be paid at or around the reference point for the grade or zone, and this reference point will be aligned to market rates in accordance with the organization's market pay policies. If, in the judgement of the line manager, individuals are achieving this level of contribution but are paid below their peers at the reference point, the pay of those individuals would be brought up to the level of their peers, or towards that level if it is felt that the increase should be phased. Individuals may be paid above the reference point if they are making a particularly strong contribution or if their market worth is higher.

The policy guideline would be that the average pay of those in the grade should broadly be in line with the reference point (a compa-ratio of 100) unless there are special market rate considerations that justify a higher rate. Those at or above the reference point who are contributing well could be eligible for a cash bonus. A 'pay pot' would be made available for distribution, with guidelines on how it should be used.

This approach depends largely on the judgement of line managers, although they would be guided and helped in the exercise of that judgement by HR. Its acceptability to staff as a fair process depends on precise communications generally on how it operates and equally precise communications individually on why decisions have been made. The assessment of contribution should be a joint one as part of performance management, and the link between that assessment and the pay decision should be clear.

Other characteristics

The other characteristics of contribution pay are that:

- It is concerned with people as team members contributing to team performance, not acting as individuals.

- It can operate flexibly – approaches may be varied between different groups of people.

- It is tailored to suit the business and HR strategy of the organization.

- There is a clear business-related rationale that serves stated HR and reward purposes – individual and team contribution expectations are defined on the basis of the corporate and team business goals to be achieved and are measured accordingly.

- It operates transparently – everyone understands how the scheme operates and how it affects them, and staff and their representatives will have contributed to the design of the system and will take part in regular reviews of its effectiveness, leading to modifications when required.

Example: paying for contribution at Kent County Council

Kent County Council is unusual amongst local authorities in implementing for its staff an approach to pay review and progression that rewards high performance, in line with its stated goal, to improve the delivery of Kent County Council services. The approach is called Total Contribution Pay (TCP) and was developed and implemented in 2005/06 on a phased basis. The use of the word 'contribution' and avoidance of performance-related pay terminology was deliberate, and not just because Kent County Council was one of those authorities that experimented with and abandoned PRP in the 1990s.

The approach aims to 'maximize the contribution, skills and capability of all our employees', that is to reward the 'how' of someone's performance, as well as the results that they deliver. It focuses on 'the day-to-day actions and behaviours' of individuals to improve their performance, with the flexibility to appropriately reward those who achieve and contribute most.

Total contribution is assessed through an annual appraisal process that considers four elements: the delivery of agreed objectives and accountabilities, how the job is done by incorporating a behavioural competency framework, achievement relative to a personal development plan, and wider job contribution, which encapsulates everything else outside of the job description.

As part of the process, staff receive a rating on a five-point scale. On the basis of this rating, they can achieve faster incremental progression through their pay scale. There is a strong emphasis on fairness and consistency in ratings, and senior management review and moderate the initial rating distributions produced.

Conclusions on contribution pay

Contribution-related pay provides a broader basis for pay decisions than performance-related pay, and the concept of contribution is an attractive one in that it refers to the fundamental reason why people are employed in organizations – to make a contribution to organizational success. But contribution pay decisions depend on the measurement of both performance and competency. Measuring performance is bad enough. Measuring competency is even worse. The requirements for success are demanding and it is essential to ensure that the organization is ready for contribution pay and to plan its introduction with great care, including ample consultation and involvement. Organizations should never rush into contribution pay – more time than is usually thought necessary is needed to plan and implement it.

Competency-related pay

The main features of competency-related pay schemes are illustrated in Figure 10.12 and described below.

Method of operation

People receive financial rewards in the shape of increases to their base pay by reference to the level of competency they demonstrate in carrying out their roles. It is a method of paying people for the ability to perform now and in the future. As in the case of PRP, scope is provided for consolidated pay progression within pay brackets attached to grades or levels in a narrow graded or career-family structure, or zones in a broad-banded structure (competence pay is often regarded as a feature of such structures). The rate and limits of progression through the pay brackets can be based on ratings of competence using a PRP type matrix, but they may be governed by more general assessments of competence development.

Conclusions on competency-related pay

Competency-related pay is attractive in theory because it can be part of an integrated competency-based approach to HRM. It fits with the concept of human capital management, which emphasizes the skills and competencies people bring with them to the workplace. It is all about 'paying for the person'. As Brown and Armstrong (1999) comment: 'Increasingly, organizations are finding that success depends on a competent workforce. Paying for competency means that an organization is looking forward, not back.' Pay based on competency avoids the overemphasis in PRP schemes on quantitative and often unrealistic targets. It is appealing because it rewards people for what they are capable of doing, not for results over which they might have little control. However, as the 2009 e-reward survey showed, it is much less popular than performance or contribution pay.

There are three reasons for this. First, there is the problem of measurement. As Sparrow (1996) suggested, difficulties arise because of deciding the performance criteria on which competencies are based, the complex nature of what is being measured and the relevance of the results to the organization. He concluded that 'we should avoid over-egging our ability to test, measure and reward competencies.' Second, there is the problem raised by Sparrow of answering the question 'what are we paying for?' Are we paying for behavioural competencies, ie

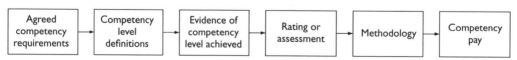

Figure 10.12   Competency-related pay

how people behave, or technical competencies (competences), ie what people have to know and be able to do to perform well? If we are just rewarding behaviour (competencies) then this increases the measurement difficulties. The third reason was explained by Lawler (1993). He expresses concern about schemes that pay for an individual's personality traits and emphasizes that such plans work best 'when they are tied to the ability of an individual to perform a particular task and when there are valid measures available of how well an individual can perform a task'. He also points out that 'generic competencies are not only hard to measure, they are not necessarily related to successful task performance in a particular work assignment or work role.'

This raises another question: 'Are we paying for the possession of competency or the use of competency?' Clearly it must be the latter. But we can only assess the effective use of competency by reference to performance. The focus is therefore on results and if that is the case, competency-related pay begins to look suspiciously like performance-related pay. Perhaps the difference between the two is all 'smoke and mirrors'. Competency-related pay could be regarded as no more than a more acceptable name for PRP.

It has also been noted by Zingheim and Schuster (2002) that pay systems built round competencies are:

- complex and over-designed;

- vague and ambiguous;

- laborious and time consuming;

- disconnected from the labour market;

- tentatively championed and communicated.

There may be a case for rewarding the possession of competency but there is an even stronger one for linking the reward to outcomes (performance) as well as inputs (competency). This is the basis of the notion of contribution-related pay as described above and provides the explanation for the growing popularity of that approach compared with the more rarefied notion of competency-related pay.

Skill-based pay

Skill-based pay provides employees with a direct link between their pay progression and the skills they have acquired and can use effectively. It focuses on what skills the business wants to pay for and what employees must do to demonstrate them. It is therefore a people-based rather than a job-based approach to pay. Rewards are related to the employee's ability to apply a wider range or a higher level of skills to different jobs or tasks. It is not linked simply with the scope of a defined job or a prescribed set of tasks.

A skill may be defined broadly as a learned ability that improves with practice in time. For skill-based pay purposes the skills must be relevant to the work. Skill-based pay is also known as knowledge-based pay, but the terms are used interchangeably, knowledge being regarded loosely as the understanding of how to do a job or certain tasks.

Skill-based pay was originally applied mainly to operatives in manufacturing firms, but it has been extended to technicians and workers in retailing, distribution, catering and other service industries. The broad equivalent of skill-based pay for managerial, professional and adminis-trative staff and knowledge workers is competency-related pay, which refers to expected behaviour as well as often to knowledge and skill requirements. There is clearly a strong family resemblance between skill and competency-related pay – they are both person-based pay schemes. But they can be distinguished both by the way in which they are applied, as described below and by the criteria used.

Method of operation

Skill-based pay works as follows:

- Skill blocks or modules are defined. These incorporate individual skills or clusters of skills that workers need to use and that will be rewarded by extra pay when they have been acquired and the employee has demonstrated the ability to use them effectively.

- The skill blocks are arranged in a hierarchy, with natural break points between clearly definable different levels of skills.

- The successful completion of a skill module or skill block will result in an increment in pay. This will define how the pay of individuals can progress as they gain extra skills.

- Methods of verifying that employees have acquired and can use the skills at defined levels are established.

- Arrangements for 'cross-training' are made. These will include learning modules and training programmes for each skill block.

Conclusions on skill-based pay

Skill-based pay systems are expensive to introduce and maintain. They require a considerable investment in skill analysis, training and testing. Although in theory a skill-based scheme will pay only for necessary skills, in practice individuals will not be using them all at the same time and some may be used infrequently, if at all. Inevitably, therefore, payroll costs will rise. If this increase is added to the cost of training and certification, the additional costs may be consider-able. The advocates of skill-based pay claim that their schemes are self-financing because of the resulting increases in productivity and operational efficiency, but there is little evidence that such is the case. For this reason, skill-base schemes have never been as popular as the other forms of contingent pay in the UK.

Overall conclusions on contingent pay

There are strong arguments against contingent pay, especially those referring to the problems of measurement and assessment and therefore perceived fairness that exist in all the varieties described in this chapter. Steps can be taken to reduce the problems through extensive consultation and communications, effective performance management processes, providing training and guidance to line managers, and monitoring the operation and impact of the contingent pay scheme carefully. However, it is very difficult to overcome them completely.

But what is the alternative? One answer is to rely more on non-financial motivators, although it is still necessary to consider what should be done about pay. The traditional alternative is service-related pay. This certainly treats everyone equally (and therefore appeals to trade unions) but pays people simply for being there and this could be regarded as inequitable in that rewards take no account of relative levels of contribution. Two other alternatives are team-based pay and pay based on organizational performance. But the former still has measurement difficulties and other problems, as described in Chapter 12, and has never become really popular, while the rewards provided by the latter, although they may increase commitment to the organization, are too remote from the day-to-day activities of most employees to make any real impact on performance.

Another alternative is a spot rate job-based system. Most people, however, want and expect a range of base pay progression or some other method of payment for results such as cash bonuses.

It is because none of these alternatives adequately satisfies the natural inclination of people to believe that individuals who contribute more should be paid more that contingent pay schemes are common in the private sector (according to the CIPD 2009 survey, 89 per cent of private sector service organizations and 85 per cent of manufacturing organizations have them), although they are used less in the public and voluntary sectors (33 and 30 per cent respectively).

Contingent pay schemes, whatever their faults, are here to stay. What is evident is that they are difficult to manage and considerable care and effort is therefore required when designing and operating them.

Summary of individual contingent pay schemes

The features, advantages and disadvantages and the appropriateness of individual contingent pay schemes and service-related pay are set out in Table 10.3.

Table 10.3 Summary of contingent pay schemes

Type of scheme	Main features	Advantages	Disadvantages	When appropriate
Performance-related pay	Increases to basic pay or bonuses are related to assessment of performance.	• May motivate (but this is uncertain). • Links rewards to objectives. • Meets the need to be rewarded for achievement. • Delivers message that good perform-ance is impor-tant and will be rewarded.	• May *not* motivate. • Relies on judgements of performance which may be subjective. • Prejudicial to teamwork. • Focuses on outputs, not quality. • Relies on good performance management processes. • Difficult to manage well.	• For people who are likely to be moti-vated by money. • In organiza-tions with a performance-orientated culture. • When per-formance can be measured objectively.
Competency-related pay	Pay increases are related to the level of competence.	• Focuses attention on need to achieve higher levels of competence. • Encourages competence development. • Can be integrated with other applica-tions of competency-based HR management.	• Assessment of competence levels may be difficult. • Ignores outputs – danger of paying for competences that will not be used. • Relies on well-trained and commit-ted line managers.	• As part of an integrated approach to HRM where competencies are used across a number of activities. • Where compe-tence is a key factor and it may be inappropriate or hard to measure outputs. • Where well-established competency frameworks exist.

Table 10.3 *continued*

Type of scheme	Main features	Advantages	Disadvantages	When appropriate
Contribution-related pay	Increases in pay or bonuses are related both to inputs (competence) and outputs (perform-ance).	Rewards people not only for what they do but how they do it.	As for both PRP and competence-related pay – it may be hard to measure contri-bution and it is difficult to manage well.	When it is believed that a well-rounded approach cover-ing both inputs and outputs is appropriate.
Skill-based pay	Increments related to the acquisition of skills.	Encourages and rewards the acquisition of skills.	Can be expensive when people are paid for skills they don't use.	On the shopfloor or in retail organizations.

Developing contingent pay schemes: six tips

- Define objectives and success criteria.
- Check on readiness for contingent pay – stakeholders' views, effective performance management, competent line managers.
- Identify alternatives – performance, contribution or competency pay – and evaluate them in terms of relevance to objectives and context.
- Involve stakeholders in scheme design (keep it simple and relevant).
- Pilot test scheme.
- Communicate details of scheme to all concerned.

References

Brown, D and Armstrong, M (1999) *Paying for Contribution*, Kogan Page, London

Brumbach, G B (1988) Some ideas, issues and predictions about performance management, *Public Personnel Management*, Winter, p 387–402

CIPD (2009) *Annual Reward Survey*, CIPD, London

e-reward (2009) *Survey of Contingent Pay*, e-reward.co.uk, Stockport

Lawler, E E (1988) Pay for performance: making it work, *Personnel*, October, pp 25–29

Lawler, E E (1993) Who uses skill-based pay, and why? *Compensation & Benefits Review*, March/April, pp 9–14

Murphy, K R and Cleveland, J N (1995) *Understanding Performance Appraisal*, Sage, Thousand Oaks CA

Sparrow, P A (1996) Too good to be true, *People Management*, December, pp 22–29

Viswesvaran, C, Ones, D S and Schmidt, F L (1996) Comparative analysis of the reliability of job performance ratings, *Journal of Applied Psychology*, **81**, pp 557–74

Zingheim, P K and Schuster, J R (2002) Pay changes going forward, *Compensation & Benefits Review*, **34** (4), pp 48–53

11

Bonus Schemes

Key concepts and terms

- At risk pay
- Bonus scheme
- Combination bonus plans
- Gain-sharing

- Moral hazard
- Profit sharing
- Variable pay

Learning outcomes

On completing this chapter you should be able to define these key concepts. You should also know about:

- The nature and aims of bonus schemes and their rationale
- The criteria for a bonus scheme
- The main types of bonus scheme

- Who benefits from bonus schemes
- How they should be designed and introduced

Introduction

Bonuses in the form of cash payments are an increasingly important part of the remuneration package. They received a very bad press during the banking crisis of 2008–09 due to what was perceived to be excessively high rewards for failure and to the belief that the attraction of astronomic bonuses led to excessive risk taking with other people's money. Clearly, bonus schemes can go wrong, especially when the 'moral hazard' is present of striving to obtain higher rewards by manipulating results or focusing on easy short-term gains rather than the tougher long-term goals. However, the worst excesses have applied to directors and senior executives as discussed in Chapter 20 rather than other staff. There is a case for bonus payments to the latter if the scheme is properly based and well administered. Certainly, bonus schemes are popular. The CIPD 2009 reward survey found that 61 per cent of respondents had schemes rewarding individual results, 56 per cent had schemes driven by business results and 41 per cent had combination schemes rewarding both individual and business results.

This chapter starts with definitions of what bonus schemes aim to achieve and their justification. It continues with a list of the criteria for bonus schemes, which leads to an analysis of the different types of bonus schemes and who can be covered by them. The chapter ends with a summary of how they can be designed and introduced.

Bonus schemes defined

Bonus schemes provide cash payments to employees that are related to the performance of their organization, their team or themselves, or a combination of two or more of these. Bonuses are often referred to as 'variable pay' or 'pay-at-risk'.

A defining characteristic of a bonus is that it has to be re-earned, unlike increases arising from contingent pay schemes such as performance or contribution-related pay or pay related to service, which are consolidated into base pay. Such payments can be described as annuities or 'gifts that go on giving'.

Cash bonuses may be the sole method of providing people with rewards in addition to their base pay, or they may be paid on top of individual contingent pay.

Aims of bonus schemes

The aims of bonus schemes may differ, but typically, they include one or more of the following:

- to enable people to share in the success of the organization and therefore increase their commitment to it;

- to provide rewards related to business performance so as to increase motivation, commitment and engagement;

- to provide a reward that recognizes past performance or achievements and encourages individuals and teams to perform well in the future;

- to provide a direct incentive that increases motivation and engagement and generates higher future levels of individual and team performance;

- to ensure that pay levels are competitive and will attract and retain good-quality people.

Rationale for bonus schemes

Bonuses can provide a reward for a special achievement and be used to provide financial recognition to people who are at the top of the salary range for their grade and are continuing to perform. Lump-sum payments can sometimes make a bigger impact on people (they can go out and spend them) than incremental increases spread thinly out over a year. Overall they contribute to the creation of a high-performance culture and make a positive impact on bottom-line results.

The business cases made by a number of respondents to the 2006 e-reward survey of bonus schemes are given below:

- 'The bonus structures are such that they are self-financing when people are over the 100 per cent to target levels. As the 100 per cent target level is set at the budget level, everything over this is of added benefit. The structure of the schemes also has a higher weighting of the products with more margin, which again helps to self-finance the schemes.'

- 'The industry is driven by margins and total operating profit at branch and regional levels, so the bonus schemes reflect this requirement to deliver. The schemes are rigorously enforced and tested by finance.'

- 'We have a pay-for-performance culture and in turn recognize and award high achievers. This is a key driver in motivating employees and organizational performance.'

- 'The bonus scheme is a key to attaining scorecard performance at levels necessary to achieve the flexibility to manage costs finely in line with varying volumes of production and the lowest margin products to ensure that the site can make a positive profit before tax contribution.'

When considering the rationale it is necessary to evaluate the case for having a bonus scheme either as an alternative to a more conventional individual contingent pay scheme (ie only providing cash bonuses), or as an addition to contingent pay (ie providing both cash bonuses and the opportunity to earn contingent pay that is consolidated in base pay). The advantages and disadvantages of these alternatives are summarized in Table 11.1.

Table 11.1   Advantages and disadvantages of alternative bonus arrangements

Approach	Advantages	Disadvantages
Bonus only	• Has to be re-earned. • Can be related to corporate or team performance as well as individual performance, thereby increasing commitment and enhancing teamwork. • Cash sums, as long as they are sizeable, can have a more immediate impact on motivation and engagement.	• May be perceived as arbitrary. • May not be pensionable. • Many people may prefer the opportunity to increase their base pay rather than rely on potentially unpredictable bonus payments. • If unconsolidated, the payment will not be pensionable.
Bonus and contingent pay	• Get best of both worlds – consolidated increases and cash payments.	• Potentially complex. • The impact made by either bonuses or consolidated payments might be dissipated, especially when the sums available are divided into two parts.

Criteria for a bonus scheme

An effective bonus scheme must:

- be based on realistic, significant and measurable key performance indicators;
- not create a moral hazard, ie an incentive to act inappropriately in pursuit of a high bonus;
- not encourage the pursuit of short-term gains or engagement in unduly risky enterprises at the expense of longer-term and sustained success;
- never reward failure;
- only pay out if a demanding threshold of performance is achieved;
- provide a clear line of sight between effort or contribution and the reward;
- operate fairly, equitably, consistently and transparently;
- be appropriate for the type of people to whom it applies;

- contain arrangements to restrict (cap) the maximum payment to an acceptable sum;
- provide for review at regular intervals to decide whether the scheme needs to be amended, replaced or cancelled;
- provide scope to moderate corporate bonuses by reference to personal performance.

Types of scheme

Table 11.2 summarizes the features of the different types of bonus schemes and their advantages and disadvantages.

Table 11.2 Features and advantages and disadvantages of different bonus schemes

Type of scheme	Main features	Advantages	Disadvantages
Business performance schemes	Bonus payments related to the performance of the whole business or a major function such as a division, store or site. Performance is measured by key performance indicators (KPIs), eg profit, contribution, shareholder value, earnings per share or economic value added.	• Enable employees to share in the organization's success, thus increasing commitment. • Can focus on a range of key factors affecting organizational performance. • Can readily be added to other forms of contingent pay to recognize collective as distinct from individual effort.	• Do not provide an individual incentive.
Individual bonus or incentive plans	Bonus payments related to individual performance.	• Provide a direct reward related to individual performance. • Cash, if sufficiently high, can make an immediate impact on motivation and engagement.	• May not be pensionable. • Some people may prefer consolidated increases to their base pay rather than rely on possibly unpredictable bonus payments which may be perceived as arbitrary.

Table 11.2 *continued*

Type of scheme	Main features	Advantages	Disadvantages
Team pay*	Payments to members of a formally established team are linked to the performance of that team. The rewards are shared among the members of the team in accordance with a published formula or on an ad hoc basis in the case of exceptional achievements.	• Encourage teamworking. • Enhance flexible working and multiskilling. • Clarify team goals. • Encourage less effective performance to improve by meeting team standards.	• May be difficult to identify well-defined teams with clear and measurable goals. • Individuals may resent the fact that their own performance is not recognized.
Combination plans	Bonuses are related to a combination of plans measuring performance across several levels, for example: corporate and individual performance; business, team and individual; team and individual.	• Combine the advantages of different types of bonus arrangements, eg business and individual (the most common form of combination scheme).	• May be over-complex. • Could disperse the impact of either the collective or the individual elements.
Cash-based profit sharing**	The payment of sums in cash related to the profits of the business. Such schemes operate on a corporate basis and usually make profit shares available to all employees, except possibly directors or senior managers. They do not require Inland Revenue approval and are fully liable for income tax and national insurance.	• Increases identification with the firm. • Recognizes that everyone contributes to creating profit.	• Does not provide an individual incentive. • Amounts distributed are taken for granted.

Table 11.2 *continued*

Type of scheme	Main features	Advantages	Disadvantages
Gain-sharing**	A formula-based company or factory-wide bonus plan which provides for employees to share in the financial gains made by a company as a result of its improved perform-ance as measured, for example, by added value.	• Recognizes that everyone working in a plant contributes to creating added value and should benefit accordingly. • Provides a platform for the joint analysis of methods of improving productivity.	• Does not provide an individual incentive. • Can be complex. • Ineffective if too high a proportion of added value is retained by the company.

Notes: * See Chapter 12.
         ** See Chapter 13.

Bonuses based on organizational performance may be made available to all staff to provide a general reward and encourage identification with the business. Such bonuses can be in addition to contingent pay. They are sometimes provided in organizations that have team pay for certain categories of staff, for example branch staff in a financial services company, but are unable to extend team payments to other categories of staff who do not work in such well-defined teams. Combination plans may also be applied to all staff, although they are sometimes restricted to senior managers. Bonuses based on individual performance may also be paid to all categories of staff or restricted to certain categories, such as directors or sales staff.

Designing a bonus scheme

The considerations affecting the design of a bonus scheme are set out below.

Formula

Every bonus scheme is different. In an individual scheme a single criterion such as profit before tax may be used for directors, with a threshold performance level to generate a bonus and a sliding scale up to a maximum that determines the size of the bonus. Alternatively, in a scheme applying to all staff, ratings may be used that determine the size of the bonus for individuals or teams by reference to the extent to which objectives have been achieved.

The formula for a combined scheme may be more complex:

- Individual or team payments may only be made if a threshold level of organizational performance is reached.

- The level of bonus related to organizational performance may be modified in accordance with the level of individual performance achieved.

- There are many variations on the split between corporate and individual bonuses, although a 50/50 division is quite common.

- The split may vary at different levels, providing a greater proportion of bonus for corporate performance at higher levels.

Examples of the formulae used by the e-reward survey respondents are given in Table 11.3.

Table 11.3 Bonus scheme formulae

Business performance	Earnings per share, revenue growth and R&D re-investment.
	Budgeted profit.
	Target set for financial performance: earnings before interest, tax, depreciation and amortisation. If first target is not met, no pool is generated. Three further targets are set, each generating a higher level of bonus.
	Key performance indicators and profit.
	Customer satisfaction levels, unique customer interactions and low-cost interventions.
Individual performance	Determined by performance rating indicator – the top three performance ratings receive a bonus.
	Individual performance is judged against pre-agreed objectives.
	Balanced scorecard – typically sales, customer service, call-handling time and a development objective for call handling.
	Individual criteria linked to the area of responsibility – eg to achieve budget target, a particular level of growth etc.
	Demonstrable achievement over and above normal performance in one of six core competencies.
Combined	50% business performance, 50% individual performance.
	20% company-wide performance, 30% business performance, 50% individual performance.
	30% business performance, 70% individual performance.
	Group-wide business performance. Individual element 'flexes' the maximum business performance downward for bad performance – eg if rating '1' to '3', get the full bonus; rating '4', the business performance bonus is reduced by 25%; a '5' rating by 50%; a '6' rating gets zero award.
	Business performance creates a bonus opportunity for an individual, which is then flexed according to a personal performance factor.

Introducing a bonus scheme

The actions required when introducing a scheme are:

- Consult with those concerned on the purpose and features of the scheme.

- Define responsibilities for introducing, maintaining and evaluating the scheme.

- Pilot test it if at all possible in a department or division or a representative sample of employees to obtain information on how well the formula works, the appropriateness of the measures, the cost of the scheme, its impact, the effectiveness of the process of making decisions on bonuses (eg the application of performance management) and the reactions of staff.

- Make amendments as necessary in the light of the test.

- Prepare a description for communication to staff of the purpose of the scheme, how it works and how staff will be affected.

- Ensure that the scheme is bedded down in the organization's day-to-day operating processes, including management reports and performance reviews.

- Draw up a budget for the costs of the scheme.

- Define operating and control processes including responsibilities, the achievement of fairness and consistency and cost control.

- Prepare a plan for introducing the scheme, covering the agreement of performance indicators and targets, methods of reviewing performance, the process of deciding on bonus payments and communications.

Bonus schemes: six tips

- Base the scheme on realistic, significant and measurable key performance indicators.
- Do not create a moral hazard, ie an incentive to act inappropriately in pursuit of a high bonus.
- Do not encourage the pursuit of short-term gains or engage in unduly risky enterprises at the expense of longer-term and sustained success.
- Never reward failure.
- Only pay out if a demanding threshold of performance is achieved.
- Provide a clear line of sight between effort or contribution and the reward.

References

CIPD (2009) *Annual Reward Survey*, CIPD, London

e-reward (2006) *Survey of Bonus Schemes*, e-reward, Stockport

Key concepts and terms

- Bonus formula
- Team

- Team pay

Learning outcomes

On completing this chapter you should be able to define these key concepts. You should also know about:

- The nature of team pay
- The nature of a team
- The aim of team pay
- The rationale for team pay

- How team pay works
- Advantages and disadvantages
- Developing team pay

Introduction

Two factors have combined to create interest in rewarding teams rather than individuals. The first is the significance attached to good teamwork and the belief that team pay would enhance it, and the second is dissatisfaction with the individual nature of performance-related pay, which is believed to be prejudicial to teamwork. The notion of team pay appeals to many people but the number of organizations who use it is relatively small. The e-reward 2009 survey of contingent pay found that only 11 per cent of respondents had team pay.

Team pay is an attractive idea but one difficult to put into practice The reason for the limited number of schemes may be that organizations find it hard to meet the quite exacting conditions for team pay set out later in this chapter. Others may believe that they have to focus their incentive schemes on individual rather than group effort.

This chapter starts with a definition of team pay and its aims and rationale, and continues with a description of how team pay works, an analysis of the arguments for and against team pay and suggestions on how team pay can be introduced. It ends with a summary of the outcomes of research into a team project in the NHS with mixed results that illustrates some of the difficulties with team rewards.

Team pay defined

Team pay links payments to members of a formally established team to the performance of that team. The rewards are shared among the members of the team in accordance with a published formula or on an ad hoc basis in the case of exceptional achievements. Rewards for individuals may also be influenced by assessments of their contribution to team results. To appreciate how team pay works it is necessary to understand the nature of a team and the various types of teams to which it can apply.

The nature of a team

A team has been defined by Katzenbach and Smith (1993) as 'A small number of people with complementary skills who are committed to a common purpose, performance goals and approach for which they hold themselves mutually accountable'.

Types of teams

There are four types of teams as described below.

Organizational teams

These consist of individuals who are linked together organizationally as members of, for example, the 'top management team', departmental heads in an operational or research division, section heads or team leaders in a department, or even people carrying out distinct and often separate functions, as long as they are all contributing to the achievement of the objectives of their department or section.

Members of organizational teams can be related to one another by the requirement to achieve an overall objective, but this may be loosely defined and the degree to which they act in consort will vary considerably. In a sense, organizations are entirely constructed of such 'teams', but team reward processes may be inappropriate unless their members are strongly united by a common purpose and are clearly interdependent. If such is not the case, some form of bonus related to organizational performance might be preferable.

Work teams

These are self-contained and permanent teams whose members work closely together to achieve results in terms of output, the development of products or processes, or the delivery of services to customers. This type of team will be focused on a common purpose and its members will be interdependent – results are a function of the degree to which they can work well together. It is for this type of team that continuing team pay reward schemes may be appropriate as long as team targets can be established and team performance can be measured accurately and fairly.

Project teams

These consist of people brought together from different functions to complete a task lasting several months to several years. When the project is completed the team disbands. Examples include product development teams or a team formed to open a new plant. Project teams may be rewarded with cash bonuses payable on satisfactory completion of the project to specification, on time and within the cost budget. Interim 'milestone' payments may be made as predetermined stages of the project are completed satisfactorily.

Ad hoc teams

These are functional or cross-functional teams set up to deal with an immediate problem. They are usually short-lived and operate as a task force. It is unusual to pay bonuses to such teams unless they deliver exceptional results.

Aim of team pay

The aim of team pay is to encourage and reinforce the sort of behaviour that leads to and sustains effective team performance by:

- providing incentives and other means of recognizing team achievements;
- clarifying what teams are expected to achieve by relating rewards to the attainment of predetermined and agreed targets and standards of performance, or to the satisfactory completion of a project or a stage of a project;
- conveying the message that one of the organization's core values is effective teamwork.

Rationale for team pay

There are four reasons for team pay:

- Teams are the natural unit in organizations and it is appropriate to reward them as such.

- Team pay encourages good teamwork while performance pay that encourages individual effort militates against it.

- Team performance measures are often the only ones available; measuring output at an individual level can be difficult, especially in the public sector.

- As noted by Prentice *et al* (2007) on the basis of their research, team incentives can help to promote peer monitoring in smaller teams, particularly when team members are mutually dependent on each other to achieve results.

How team pay works

The most common method of providing team pay is to distribute a cash sum related to team performance amongst team members. There are a number of formulas and ways of distributing team pay as described below.

The team pay formula

This establishes the relationship between team performance, as measured or assessed in quantitative or qualitative terms, and the reward. It also fixes the size of the bonus pool or fund earned by the team to be distributed among its members, or the scale of payments made to team members, in relation to team performance with regard to certain criteria. Bonuses may be related to performance in such specific areas as sales, throughput, achievement of targets in the form of the delivery of results for a project, levels of service or an index of customer satisfaction. Targets are agreed and performance is measured against the targets.

Alternatively bonuses may be related to an overall criterion, which can be a more subjective assessment of the contribution of the team to organizational performance.

Method of distributing bonuses

Bonuses can be distributed to team members in the form of either a percentage of base salary or the same sum for each member, usually based on a scale of payments. Payment of bonus as a percentage of base salary is the most popular method. The assumption behind it is that base salary reflects the value of the individual's contribution to the team. The correctness of this assumption clearly depends on the extent to which base salary truly indicates the level of performance of individuals as team members.

Team pay and individual pay

Some organizations pay team bonuses only. A minority pay individual bonuses as well, which are often related to an assessment of the competence of the person thus, it is thought, providing encouragement to develop skills and rewarding individuals for their particular contribution.

Dealing with high and low individual performance in a team

It is sometimes assumed by advocates of team pay that all members of a team contribute equally and should therefore be rewarded equally. In practice the contribution of individual team members will vary and if this is the case, for example, in shopfloor groups, team pressure may be forcing everyone to work at the same rate so as to avoid 'rate busting'. This is an example of how a highly cohesive team can work against the interests of the organization.

When designing a team pay scheme, decisions have to be made on the likelihood that some people will perform better or worse than others. It may be decided that, even if this happens, it would be invidious and detrimental to single anyone out for different treatment. It could, however, be considered that 'special achievement' or 'sustained high-performance' bonuses should be payable to individuals who make an exceptional contribution, while poor performers should receive a lower bonus or no bonus at all.

Project team bonuses

The design considerations described above apply to permanent work teams. Different arrangements are required for project teams specially set up to achieve a task and, usually, disbanded after the task has been completed. Project team bonuses should, wherever possible, be self-financing – they should be related to increases in income or productivity or cost savings arising from the project. Project teams can be set targets and their bonuses can be linked with achieving or surpassing targeted results. Alternatively, a fixed bonus can be promised if the project is on time, meets the specification and does not exceed the cost budget. The bonus could be increased for early completion or to reflect cost savings. For lengthy projects, interim payments may be made at defined 'milestones'.

Ad hoc bonuses

Where there are no predetermined arrangements for paying bonuses to teams, a retrospective bonus can be paid to a project or ad hoc team in recognition of exceptional achievement.

Requirements for team pay

Team pay works best if teams:

- stand alone as performing units for which clear targets and standards can be agreed and outputs measured;

- have a considerable degree of autonomy: team pay is likely to be most effective in self-managed teams;

- are composed of people whose work is interdependent: it is acknowledged by members that the team will deliver the expected results only if they work well together and share the responsibility for success;

- are stable: members are used to working with one another, know what is expected of them by fellow team members and know where they stand in the regard of those members;

- are mature: teams are well established, used to working flexibly to meet targets and deadlines, and capable of making good use of the complementary skills of their members.

These are exacting requirements. If they can be met there may be a good case for team pay.

Advantages and disadvantages of team pay

Team pay can:

- encourage teamworking and co-operative behaviour;

- enhance flexible working within teams and encourage multiskilling, clarify team goals and priorities and provide for the integration of organizational and team objectives;

- encourage less effective performers to improve in order to meet team standards;

- serve as a means of developing self-managed or self-directed teams.

But:

- The effectiveness of team pay depends on the existence of well-defined and mature teams, and they may be difficult to identify. Even if they can be identified, do they need to be motivated by a purely financial reward?

- Team pay may seem unfair to individuals who could feel that their own efforts are unrewarded.

- Pressure to conform, which is accentuated by team pay, could result in the team maintaining its output at lowest common denominator levels – sufficient to gain what is thought collectively to be a reasonable reward but no more.

- It can be difficult to develop performance measures and methods of rating team performance that are seen to be fair. Team pay formulae may well be based on arbitrary assumptions about the correct relationship between effort and reward.

- There may be pressure from employees to migrate from poorly performing teams to high-performing teams. If this is allowed, it could cause disruption and stigmatize the teams from which individuals transfer, while if it is refused, it could leave dissatisfied employees in the inadequate teams, making them even worse.

For many organizations, the disadvantages outweigh the advantages.

Developing team pay

If, in spite of the problems that may beset team pay, it is decided to introduce it, the development steps are as follows:

1. Initial analysis

    This should identify whether there are teams that satisfy the requirements set out above.

2. Select teams

    Decide on which teams will be eligible for team pay.

3. Scheme design

    Decide the team bonus formula (the criteria to be used in judging performance, the amount available for team pay and the method of distributing team pay).

4. Scheme introduction.

Team pay is likely to be unfamiliar and should therefore be introduced with care, especially if it is replacing an existing system of individual PRP. The process will be easier if employees have been involved in developing the scheme, but it is still essential to communicate in detail to all employees the reasons for introducing team pay, how it will work and how it will affect them.

It is easier to introduce team pay into mature teams whose members are used to working together, trust one another and can recognize that team pay will work to their mutual advantage. Although it may seem an attractive proposition to use team pay as a means of welding new work teams together, there are dangers in forcing people who are already having to adapt to a different situation to accept a radical change in their method of remuneration. It should be remembered that it may not be easy to get people in work teams to think of their performance in terms of how it impacts on others. It can take time for employees to adapt to a system in which a proportion of their pay is based on team achievement.

When it comes to launching team pay it may be advisable to pilot it initially in one or two well-established teams. Experience gained from the pilot scheme can then be used to modify the scheme before it is extended elsewhere. If the pilot scheme teams think it has been a success, other teams may be more willing to convert to team pay.

NHS case study

As reported by Reilly *et al* (2005), the UK Department of Health decided to trial team pay in NHS trusts. The 17 teams in the trial were based at a number of sites and were given targets aimed at improving the patient experience through faster response, better service or an improved environment. The team reward was a cash payment: money put into an 'improvement fund' for staff to spend on staff facilities/development or a mixture of the two.

Many positive results were achieved by the trials. These included improvements in the management of the trusts and benefits to patients and staff. The end-of-pilot survey results generally elicited positive responses to questions relating to the operation of team-based pay. But as the researchers involved in the survey observed: 'So far so good, but there are still question marks over the success of the scheme. First, not all sites met their targets… and not every participant was as keen about the benefits of the scheme. Second, even at the better performing sites, did team-based pay drive service improvement, even if the staff thought it did?'

In the opinion of the researchers, the causes of relative failure in some trusts can be attributed to the following three factors:

- Team structure: some people were excluded from teams, which they resented, and the teams sometimes cut across natural groupings. But the size of the team and the degree to which it was well established did not make much difference.

- Targets: there were a number of difficulties with targets. Some administrators found it hard to specify output, let alone outcome measures. They felt happier with input metrics. It was confirmed that the poorer the 'line of sight' between work actions and the target, the less likely there was to be employee engagement and thereby effort to deliver. In particular, when targets were externally imposed, failure was more probable. The degree of stretch in the targets varied greatly, but it did not always seem easy at the outset to predict what would be hard to achieve and what would be easier.

- Matters outside the team's control: these genuinely affected the teams' ability to deliver, producing understandable criticism.

The main conclusions reached by the researchers were that:

- Success depends on having a clear purpose, effective leadership, the trust of staff in the integrity and competence of management, good communications and efficient project management.

- The 'right' size of team depends on the objectives of the exercise; for example, bigger teams may be necessary to cope with complex processes and multiple targets.

- Targets need to be clear and simple, easy to communicate and evaluate, relate to the work people do and seen as achievable and within the team's control.

- As with all schemes, team-based pay will only operate successfully for a limited period, because employees fear that the performance bar will be continuously raised and the discretionary effort that schemes tap into may not always be there to exploit.

Team pay: six tips

- Be clear about the objectives of team pay.
- Ensure that there are clearly defined teams in the organization for which the results achieved by the joint efforts of team members can be measured.
- Involve team leaders and team members in developing the team pay scheme, including methods of setting targets and measuring and monitoring performance, and the formula used for calculating team pay.
- Provide training in team building and operating the scheme.
- Pilot test the scheme.
- Get teams involved in setting their own targets and monitoring their own performance.

References

e-reward (2009) *Survey of Contingent Pay*, e-reward, Stockport

Katzenbach, J and Smith, D (1993) *The Magic of Teams*, Harvard Business School Press, Boston, MA

Prentice, G, Burgess, S and Propper, C (2007) *Performance Pay in the Public Sector: A review of the issues and evidence*, Office of Manpower Economics, London

Reilly, P, Phillipson, J and Smith, P (2005) Team-based pay in the United Kingdom, *Compensation & Benefits Review*, July/August, pp 54–60

13

Rewarding for Business Performance

Key concepts and terms

- Employee share option plans (ESOPS)
- Gain-sharing
- Profit sharing
- Save-as-you-earn plans (SAYE)

Learning outcomes

On completing this chapter you should be able to define these key concepts. You should also know about:

- Aims of rewarding for business performance
- How profit-sharing schemes work
- How share ownership schemes work
- How gain-sharing schemes work

Introduction

Many organizations believe that their financial reward systems should extend beyond individual contingent pay, which does not recognize collective effort, or team pay, which is difficult. They believe that their system should help to enhance engagement and commitment and convince employees that they have a stake in the business as well as providing them with additional pay. The response to this belief is to offer financial rewards that are related to business or organizational performance (sometimes known as company-wide or factory-wide schemes). This is a popular form of reward – the 2009 e-reward reward survey found that 59 per cent of respondents had such schemes.

Types of schemes

The three types of formal business performance schemes are:

- Profit-sharing: the payment of sums in cash or shares related to the profits of the business.

- Share ownership schemes: employees are given the opportunity to purchase shares in the company; 29 per cent of the respondents to the 2009 CIPD survey had such schemes.

- Gain-sharing: the payment of cash sums to employees related to the financial gains made by the company because of its improved performance; only 3 per cent of the CIPD 2009 respondents had such schemes.

Less formally, managements can make decisions on the amount to be paid out in the form of individual performance or contribution-related increments or individual/team cash bonuses. These decisions are made on the basis of what they believe the organization can afford. This creates what is sometimes called a 'pot' from which payments are funded. The assessment of affordability (a potent word for many managements) can determine pay review budgets on the proportion of the pay roll, eg 3 per cent, that can be allocated for increments or bonuses.

Aims

The aims of relating rewards to business performance are to:

- increase the commitment of employees to the organization;

- enable employees to share in the success of the organization;

- stimulate more interest in the affairs of the organization;

- focus employees' attention on what they can contribute to organizational success and bring areas for improvement to their attention;

- obtain tax advantages for employees through approved share schemes – such 'tax-efficient' schemes enable the business to get better value for money from its expenditure on employee remuneration.

Perhaps the two most important reasons for organizational schemes are the beliefs that they increase the identification of employees with the company and that the company is morally bound to share its success with its employee stakeholders – those who collectively make a major contribution to it. However, it is generally recognized that they do not provide a direct incentive because the links between individual effort and the collective reward are too remote.

Profit-sharing

Profit-sharing is a plan under which an employer pays to eligible employees, as an addition to their normal remuneration, special sums related to the profits of the business. The amount shared is either determined by an established formula or entirely at the discretion of management. As a percentage of pay, the value of profit shares varies considerably between companies, and within companies from year to year. Between 2 per cent and 5 per cent is a fairly typical range of payments but it can be 20 per cent or more. It is unlikely that profit distributions of less than 5 per cent will make much impact on commitment, never mind motivation. Employees tend to take the smallish sums they receive for granted.

Profits can be distributed in the form of cash or shares, usually share options. The arrangements for profit-sharing are concerned with eligibility, the basis for calculating profit shares and the method of distribution. They vary considerably between companies.

Eligibility

In most schemes all employees except directors are eligible. A period of time, often one year's service, is usually required before profit shares can be received.

Basis of calculation

There are three approaches to calculating profit shares:

- A predetermined formula: a fixed percentage of profits is distributed. This clarifies the relationship of pay-out to profits and demonstrates the good faith of management, but it lacks flexibility and the amount available may fluctuate widely.

- No predetermined formula: the board determines profit shares entirely at its own discretion in accordance with the directors' assessment of what the company can afford. This gives them complete control over the amount distributed but, because of the secrecy involved, is at odds with the principle of getting employees more involved with the organization. This is the most typical approach.

- A threshold formula: a profit threshold is set below which no profits will be distributed and a maximum limit is defined. Between these, the board exercises discretion on the amount to be distributed.

Methods of distributing profit shares

There are four methods of distribution:

- Percentage of pay with no allowance for service: this is a fairly common method that recognizes that profit shares should be related to the employee's basic contribution as measured by their level of pay, which takes into account service.

- Percentage of pay with an allowance for service: this approach is also frequently used on the grounds that it rewards loyalty.

- Percentage of pay with an allowance for individual performance: this method is fairly rare below board level because of the difficulty of measuring the relationship between individual performance and profit.

- As a fixed sum irrespective of earnings, service or performance: this is an egalitarian approach but is fairly rare.

Share ownership schemes

There are two main forms of share ownership plans: share incentive plans and save-as-you-earn (SAYE) schemes. These can be Inland Revenue and Customs approved, and if so produce tax advantages as well as linking financial rewards in the longer term to the prosperity of the company.

Share incentive plans

Share incentive plans must be Inland Revenue and Customs approved. They provide employees with a tax-efficient way of purchasing shares in their organization, to which the employer can add 'free', 'partnership' or 'matching' shares. There is a limit to the amount of free shares that can be provided. Employees can use up a sum determined by the Inland Revenue and Customs out of pre-tax and pre-National Insurance Contributions pay to buy partnership shares, and employers can give matching shares at a ratio of up to two matching shares for each partnership share.

Save-as-you-earn schemes

SAYE schemes must be Inland Revenue and Customs approved. They provide employees with the option to buy shares in the company in three, five or seven years' time at today's price or at a discount of up to 20 per cent of that price. Purchases are made from a savings account from which the employee pays an agreed sum each month. The monthly savings must be between £5 and £250. Income tax is not chargeable when the option is granted.

Impact of share schemes

A study by Oxera (2007) examined the impact of tax-advantaged employee share schemes on company performance. The key findings were that the tax advantages of such schemes were not sufficient on their own to increase productivity. Other factors were important: namely, having non-tax-advantaged schemes, company size (only firms in the upper quartile experienced a statistically significant productivity effect) and being a listed company. In these circumstances productivity does increase; for example, companies with both tax-advantaged and non-tax-advantaged schemes achieved increases in productivity of around 5.2 per cent in the long run.

Gain-sharing

Gain-sharing is a formula-based company or factory-wide bonus plan that provides for employees to share in the financial gains made by a company as a result of its improved performance. The formula determines the share by reference to a performance indicator such as added value or some other measure of productivity. In some schemes the formula also incorporates performance measures relating to quality, customer service, delivery or cost reduction.

The most popular performance indicator is value added, which is calculated by deducting expenditure on materials and other purchased services from the income derived from sales of the product. It is, in effect, the wealth created by the people in the business. A manufacturing business 'adds value' by the process of production as carried out by the combined contribution of management and employees.

Gain-sharing differs from profit-sharing in that the latter is based on more than improved productivity. A number of factors outside the individual employee's control contribute to profit, such as depreciation procedures, bad debt expenses, taxation and economic changes. Gain-sharing aims to relate its pay-outs more specifically to productivity and performance improvements within the control of employees.

Although the financial element is obviously a key feature of gain-sharing, its strength as a means of improving performance lies equally in its other important features – ownership, involvement and communication. The success of a gain-sharing plan depends on creating a feeling of ownership that first applies to the plan and then extends to the operation. When implementing gain-sharing, companies enlist the support of employees in order to increase their commitment to the plan. The involvement aspect of gain-sharing means that information generated on the company's results is used as a basis for enabling employees to make suggestions on ways of improving performance, and for giving them scope to make decisions concerning their implementation.

However, gain-sharing has never been popular in the UK, perhaps because its use is mainly limited to the manufacturing sector and it takes time to plan and operate if it is to work well. Conventional profit-sharing and share ownership schemes are much easier to manage.

Rewarding for business performance: six tips

- Produce a case for the scheme; this could be a business case but it could also be a case based on the moral obligation of employers to share their prosperity with employees.
- Ensure that you get the maximum benefit in terms of engagement and commitment from whatever scheme you adopt.
- Ensure that the scheme is given full publicity (as long, of course, as it is paying out).
- Remember that a scheme may enhance engagement but will not directly motivate people.
- Make the most of any opportunities the scheme presents to involve employees in discussing their contribution to the firm's prosperity.
- Consider how a scheme could complement an individual or team bonus plan.

References

CIPD (2009) *Annual Reward Survey*, CIPD, London

e-reward (2009) *Survey of Contingent Pay*, e-reward, Stockport

Oxera (2007) *Tax-advantaged Employee Share Schemes: Analysis of productivity effects*, HM Revenue & Customs, Report 37, London

14

Recognition Schemes

Learning outcomes

On completing this chapter you should know about:

- The nature of recognition schemes
- Principles of recognition
- The different types of non-cash recognition awards
- How to design a scheme

You will also be able to learn from a number of examples.

Introduction

Recognition schemes acknowledge success. They can form an important part of a total reward approach, as described in Chapter 3. They complement direct financial rewards and can therefore enhance the reward system. As discussed in Chapter 9, recognition schemes are based on the belief that taking steps to ensure that people's achievements and contribution are recognized is an effective way of motivating them.

Recognition schemes defined

Recognition schemes enable appreciation to be shown to individuals for their achievements either informally on a day-to day basis or through formal recognition arrangements. They can take place quietly between managers and individuals in their teams or be visible celebrations of success.

A recognition scheme can be formal and organization wide, providing scope to recognize achievements by gifts or treats or public applause. Typically, the awards are non-financial but some organizations provide cash awards. Importantly, recognition is also given less formally when managers simply say 'well done', 'thank you' or 'congratulations' face to face or in a brief note of appreciation.

Benefits of recognition schemes

Recognition schemes can:

- enable people's achievements and contributions to be publicly acknowledged and provide an effective way of motivating them;
- complement and reinforce financial rewards as part of a total reward process;
- increase engagement by demonstrating that the organization values its employees;
- provide rewards for the average performers who are the core contributors in a business and may not benefit much if at all from performance pay;
- provide ways of rewarding teams as well as individual effort and contribution;
- give line managers the means to provide their people with instant rewards for achievement or contribution rather than making them wait until the end of the year for a possible performance pay increase.

Principles of recognition

The principles that need to be borne in mind when developing recognition schemes are that recognition:

- should be given for specially valued behaviours and exceptional effort as well as for special achievements;
- should be personalized so that people appreciate that it applies to them;
- needs to be applied equitably, fairly and consistently throughout the organization;
- must be genuine, not used as a mechanistic motivating device;
- should not be given formally as part of a scheme if the achievement has been rewarded under another arrangement, for example a bonus scheme;
- needs to be given as soon as possible after the achievement;
- should be available to all – there should be no limits on the numbers who can be recognized;

- should not be predicated on the belief that such schemes are just about rewarding winners;
- should be available for teams as well as individuals to reward collective effort;
- should not be based on an over-elaborate scheme.

It is also necessary to bear in mind that awards above £100 are subject to income tax in the UK.

Types of recognition

Day-to-day recognition

The most effective form of recognition is that provided by managers to their staff on a day-to-day basis. This is an aspect of good management practice in the same way as getting to know people, monitoring performance (without being oppressive) and providing positive feedback. It is provided orally on the spot or in a short note (preferably handwritten) of appreciation, and should take place soon after the event (not delayed until an annual performance review). It must be genuine – people can easily spot insincerity, or someone simply going through the motions.

This type of recognition should be a natural part of the daily routine. The organization should aim to develop a recognition culture that is nurtured by the management style of senior managers and permeates the organization through each level of management so that it becomes 'the way we do things around here'. Managers can be encouraged to adopt this style, but this should be more by example than by precept, not the subject of a scheme, process or system.

Public recognition

Recognition for particular achievements or continuing effective contributions can be provided by public 'applause' through an 'employee of the month scheme' or some other announcement using an intranet, the house journal or notice boards.

Formal recognition

Formal recognition schemes provide individuals (and importantly, through them, their partners) with tangible forms of recognition such as gifts, vouchers, holidays or trips in the UK or abroad, days or weekends away at hotels or health spas, or meals out. Some schemes also provide cash awards. Team awards may be through outings, parties and meals. Such schemes may be centrally driven, with formal award ceremonies. Managers and employees can nominate individuals for awards. If the awards are substantial, organizations can set up a recognition committee with employee representatives to agree on who should be eligible, thus ensuring that decisions are transparent.

Formal schemes can provide for different levels of recognition and rewards, as illustrated in the schedule, shown in Table 14.1, which was developed for a large local authority. This provides for a graduated series of awards that can be made by managers within a budget. At the lowest level, managers may be given quite a lot of autonomy to make immediate small recognition awards. The next higher level of rewards would have to be approved by a senior manager and the highest level would be reviewed by a recognition committee for final approval by top management.

Table 14.1   Levels of recognition

Level	Examples
1: Below £25	<ul><li>Volunteering to help others when the workload is heavy.</li><li>Providing extra help to a customer.</li><li>Working late or at weekends without extra pay to meet an important deadline.</li><li>Taking on a temporary extra task that is not part of normal duties.</li><li>Demonstrating valued behaviours.</li></ul>
2: £25 to £150	<ul><li>Identifying improved work practices.</li><li>Providing a sustained level of customer service.</li><li>Making or recommending cost savings when not part of role.</li><li>Demonstrating valued behaviours that make a significant short-term impact.</li></ul>
3: £500 to £1,000	<ul><li>Generating significant extra revenue when not part of role.</li><li>Reducing costs significantly when not part of role.</li><li>Successfully completing a major project that is not part of normal role.</li><li>Demonstrating valued behaviours that make a significant long-term impact.</li></ul>

Examples of non-cash awards

Some ideas for non-cash awards include:

- basket of fruit;
- books;
- bottle of champagne (with a personalized label);
- cinema or theatre vouchers;
- dinner out for two (include a taxi and a babysitter);
- experience days (eg hot air balloon ride, or a day at a health and beauty spa);
- flowers (delivered to the workplace or at home);
- food hamper;
- Fridays off for a month;
- gift certificates;
- jewellery;
- personal letter from the chairman or chief executive;
- plaques or certificates;
- points-based catalogue gifts;
- retail shopping vouchers;
- tickets to a concert, theatre or sports event;
- trip for two to Amsterdam, Barcelona or Paris;
- trophy (passed from one person to another);
- weekend in a hotel for two.

Designing a recognition scheme

The principles set out earlier in this chapter should be borne in mind when designing and implementing a recognition scheme. Line managers and employees should be consulted, guidelines prepared and explained to managers, and the details of the scheme publicized.

The implementation of the scheme should be monitored and steps taken to maintain the impetus – managers can lose interest. Progress reports should be made to employees so that they know that the scheme is working well.

Examples of recognition schemes

British Gas

Recognition awards at British Gas are focused more on behaviours than financial results, say, which should be recognized by the bonus scheme. There are several levels of recognition, none of which involve cash awards. These are:

- everyday recognition from the line manager who says 'thank you', either by means of a personal note or at a team meeting;
- site/directorate level;
- British Gas-wide and Centrica-wide recognition.

It is intended that a minimum of 20 per cent of staff should be recognized by their line manager; current rates are around 40 per cent. Three-hour workshops are being run to help line managers understand the benefits of recognition and how to do it.

Camelot

The company believes that it is important to reward staff as near to the event of exceptional performance as possible, so it has put in place a recognition scheme to provide instant rewards. Managers and the staff consultative forum were involved in designing the scheme.

The recognition scheme, called Above and Beyond, rewards 'one off, exceptional, performance that is not part of the normal job'. Managers make their nominations online and they are approved almost immediately. The employee is then informed and can spend the reward, in the form of points, straight away. Awards average £50, but range from £10 to £200. The company's recognition budget is £25 per quarter per employee, so there is an expectation that most staff will get at least one award each year.

Staff can 'spend' their awards on goods or retail vouchers or add them to their own money to buy big items such as holidays. Rather than train all the managers, the company used 'champions' to roll out the scheme. These could be employees at any level, who were trained and briefed to explain the scheme to everyone else.

Comet

The company distinguishes between 'recognition' and 'reward'. For Comet, recognition is that part of total reward that is not 'promised' and is also typically non-cash, although some of its recognition programmes use cash. It recognizes the accomplishment of 'extra mile' performance rather than everyday behaviour.

The recognition principles are as follows:

- Our schemes should recognize exceptional behaviours, ultimately building greater 'trust' at Comet.

- Recognition should drive the individual needs/success criteria of the business area.

- We should provide some corporate direction on recognition to drive consistency, but aim to retain the essence of spontaneous, local-led recognition.

- Our aim is to have a recognition solution across each business area and at each level – that is, colleague-led, manager-led and company-led.

- The reward team oversees all recognition initiatives to ensure branding, consistency and the achievement of principles without seeking to control and push responsibility to line managers.

Recognition is tied to Comet's four key behaviours. An internal company document states:

> *When you see a demonstration of great individual attitude, care for every detail, deep knowledge, or a colleague with a passion for service, make sure the behaviours are recognized. Your recognition initiatives could be linked to encouraging the behaviours and our core value of being trustworthy. Remember that colleagues living our values of being trustworthy make a difference to our business.*

Glenmorangie

Glenmorangie's scheme is called Heroes, which stands for Honouring Excellence and Rewarding Outstanding and Extended Service. It recognizes continuing professional development, improvement suggestions, long service and 'making a difference' – going the extra mile to get the job done. The scheme was developed by a working party consisting of a cross-section of Glenmorangie employees. There are no cash awards; instead, there are certificates and gifts chosen from a catalogue, which are presented by the manager at a team meeting.

Lands' End

Lands' End prefers the term appreciation to recognition, since it thinks the latter suggests something tangible. It prefers to look for any and every opportunity to demonstrate its real appreciation of what staff do, and comments that when managers focus on how they can show their appreciation it improves their own motivation as much as that of the people they recognize.

London & Quadrant Housing Association

There are two schemes:

- *The Outstanding achiever awards.* These annual awards are designed to recognize and celebrate exceptional achievements that demonstrate the organization's values. They are awarded to around 5 per cent of staff, who each receive a lump sum payment worth 2.5 per cent of salary. The process is fairly formal. Anyone with at least one year's service can be put forward, by a fellow employee, customer or supplier, but the formal nomination must come from the responsible group director. The group director of human resources then checks attendance records, since 'exemplary attendance' is expected from an outstanding achiever. The chief executive considers all the recommendations and decides who is to get the awards.

- *Our people: individual awards.* Nominations for this scheme can come from fellow employees, customers and suppliers, and must also be for behaviour that reflects the values of the organization. This scheme is less formal than the Outstanding achiever scheme and rewards less exceptional but nonetheless praiseworthy behaviour. Nominations are considered by the individual's manager, and awards are made to staff who meet the criteria. These can take the form of chocolates, flowers, vouchers, or a meal or evening or day out for the family.

Recognition schemes: six tips

- Whatever scheme you choose, make sure you can apply it fairly and consistently. Apply it to those who really deserve it, and remember to look for a 'well done' or a 'thank you' for everyone.

- For recognition to have any real value it must be genuine. Ensure that it is real, spontaneous and appropriate to what someone has done.

- Involve everyone in recognition; empower the whole management team to recognize people formally, and encourage all colleagues to recognize each other.

- Recognizing great behaviour as soon as it happens is the most powerful approach. Shout about great achievements and great behaviours.

- Public recognition can let others in the business know what has been done, and make a colleague feel proud. Award schemes, newsletters and notice boards are all great ways to publicly recognize achievement. But remember that not everyone likes public recognition.

- A lot of genuine recognition is simple and costs nothing, such as a thank you, a letter, or a photo on the wall. But sometimes spending wisely to treat the team to a meal or a day out can go a long way.

Part III
Valuing and Grading Jobs

15

Pay Levels

Key concepts and terms

- Agency costs
- Agency theory
- Annuity approach
- Clearing wage
- Efficiency wage theory
- Effort bargain
- Employment relationship
- Equalizing differences theory
- External labour market
- Fixed increment
- Going rate
- Incentive alignment
- Internal labour market
- Internal relativities
- Intrinsic value
- Job evaluation

- Market clearing or equilibrium wage
- Market driven
- Market pricing
- Market stance
- Market worth
- Pay dispersion
- Pay policy
- Pay progression
- Pay structure
- Pay system
- Resource dependence theory
- Spot rate
- Sticky wage
- Total net advantage
- Tournament theory

Learning outcomes

On completing this chapter you should be able to define these key concepts. You should also know about:

- Classical economic pay level theory
- The labour theory of value
- The nature of the external and internal labour market
- Human capital theory and pay levels
- Efficiency wage theory
- Agency theory
- The effort bargain
- The factors affecting pay levels within organizations
- Pay dispersion
- Tournament theory
- Significant points for practitioners

Introduction

Perhaps the most significant decisions that have to be made by those concerned with reward management are about levels of pay. In making these decisions it is necessary to be aware of the various factors that influence pay levels, including the key economic theories that explain those factors. The practical value of such awareness is that the parts to be played by job evaluation, market rate analysis and trade union negotiations in developing grade and pay structures, fixing pay levels and relativities and using recruitment premia will be understood and applied to produce equitable and competitive pay systems.

This chapter summarizes the main theoretical concepts and then deals with the factors influencing job values within organizations. Finally, conclusions are drawn on what these concepts and factors mean to practitioners.

Determinants of pay

The following theories and concepts provide guidance on the factors that affect pay levels:

- the nature of the external and internal labour market;
- classical economic theory (the economic 'laws' of supply and demand);
- the labour theory of value;
- human capital theory;

- efficiency wage theory;
- agency theory;
- the effort bargain.

The labour market

Markets consist of buyers and sellers of goods. Having too many buyers for a limited number of goods forces prices up, and a surplus of goods beyond what buyers want forces prices down. The labour market is a market like any other; it has buyers (employers) and sellers (employees). The price of labour is the rate of pay required to attract and retain people in organizations.

The efforts of these buyers and sellers to transact and establish an employment relationship constitute a labour market. An external market may be local, national or international. It may be related to specific occupations, sectors or industries in any of these areas. It is within these markets that the economic determinants of pay levels operate, which include not only supply and demand factors (see below) but also the impact of inflationary pressures.

In any sizeable organization there is also an internal labour market. This is the market that exists when firms fill their vacancies from the ranks of existing employees. Pay levels and relativities in the internal market may differ significantly between firms in spite of general external market pressures. These arise particularly when long-term relationships are usual, even though these are becoming less common. Pay in the internal market will be affected by views on the intrinsic value of jobs and what individuals are worth on the basis of their expertise and contribution, irrespective of the market rate for their job. Pay progression related to length of service and an 'annuity' approach to pay increments (ie pay which goes up but does not come down, what economists call 'the sticky wage') may lead to higher internal rates. But the relationship between internal and external rates will also depend on policy decisions within the firm about its levels of pay generally compared with the 'going rate' in the external market.

Classical economic theory

The first theory of wages was advanced by Adam Smith (1776) when he wrote that: 'The whole of the advantages and disadvantages of different employments and stock must, in the same neighborhood, be either perfectly equal or continually tending to equality.' He suggested that workers seek to maximize total utility, not just wages, with total utility (and thus job choice) being a function of the total net advantage of various jobs. Anticipating the concept of total rewards by over 200 years, Adam Smith specifically identified several components of total net advantage besides pay, namely: agreeableness or disagreeableness of work, difficulty and expense of learning it, job security, responsibility and the possibility of success or failure. A higher wage or 'compensating wage differential' was required for jobs without some or all of the benefits these conferred. Conversely, jobs with them could be paid less and still offer the same net advantages as those that pay more but lack the other advantages. Workers seek to maximize this net advantage or 'total utility', not just wages.

Later classical and neo-classical theory in the 19th century treated wages as the price of labour and therefore subject to the laws of supply and demand. This meant adopting the questionable assumption that all non-pecuniary aspects of jobs are equal. They focused on the external labour market, which is a market like any other market, as noted at the beginning of this section. Classical wages theory states that the external labour market has buyers (employers) and sellers (employees). If the supply of labour exceeds the demand, pay levels go down; if there is a scarcity of labour and demand exceeds the supply, pay goes up. Pay stabilizes when demand equals supply at the 'market clearing' or 'market equilibrium' wage. This is sometimes known as the theory of equalizing differences. According to the classical labour economists, the price of labour is the rate of pay required to attract and retain people in organizations.

As Elliott (1991) noted: 'Competitive theory predicts that the forces of supply in the market as a whole will determine the rates of pay within each firm. The relative pay of any two occupations in a single firm will be the mirror image of the relative pay of the same two occupations in the market as a whole.'

However, classical economic theory is based on the premises that 'other things are equal' and that a 'perfect market' for labour exists. In the real world, of course, other things are never equal and there is no such thing as a universally perfect market: that is, one in which everyone knows what the going rate is, there is free movement of labour within the market and there are no monopolistic or other forces interfering with the normal processes of supply and demand. Imperfections in the market exist because of poor information, lack of opportunity and immobility. They also arise when employers or trade unions exert pressures on pay levels, or when governments intervene in normal pay determination processes.

Human capital theory as discussed later also explains why individual rates of pay may be influenced by other forces besides supply and demand.

The labour theory of value

In 1865 Karl Marx wrote in *Das Kapital* that the value of goods and services is determined by the amount of labour that goes into them. It is not the marketplace that sets prices. Thus the content of labour determines the price of labour. Mainstream economists have never accepted this concept, and assert the primacy of supply and demand in the marketplace in setting prices of goods and services. However, as pointed out by Nielsen (2002), conventional job evaluation schemes are based on the labour theory of value, in that they are only concerned with job content and ignore market rate pressures. They make no attempt to price jobs directly.

Human capital theory

Levels of pay are influenced by the value of human capital in terms of the skills and expertise people possess. Workers invest in education and training to increase their value as human capital and so enhance their future earnings because this will influence their levels of pay. As explained in more detail by Ehrenberg and Smith (1994) human capital theory: 'conceptualizes workers as embodying a set of skills which can be 'rented out' to employers. The knowledge and skills a worker has – which comes from education and training, including the training that experience brings – generate a certain stock of productive capital.'

For the employee, the expected returns on human capital investments are a higher level of earnings, greater job satisfaction and, at one time but less so now, a belief that security in employment is assured. For the employer, the return on investment in human capital is expected to be improvements in performance, productivity, flexibility and the capacity to innovate that should result from enlarging the skill base and increasing levels of competence.

Efficiency wages theory

Efficiency wages theory proposes that firms will pay more than the market rate because they believe that high levels of pay will contribute to increases in productivity. This can happen in two ways: an incentive effect (generating greater effort among current employees) and a sorting effect (attracting higher-quality employees in the first place). This theory is also known as 'the economy of high wages'. Organizations are using efficiency wages theory (although they will not call it that) when they formulate pay policies that place them as market leaders or at least above the average.

Resource dependence theory (Pfeffer and Davis-Blake, 1987) is associated with efficiency wage theory but focuses on the idea of paying more to attract and retain high-quality employees in critical positions.

Agency theory

Agency theory, also known as principal agent theory, states that in most firms there is a separation between the owners (the principals) and the agents (the managers). Because the principals may not have complete control over their agents, the latter may act in ways that may not be in accordance with the wishes of those principals and are not revealed to them. This generates what economists call agency costs. These consist of the extent to which the amount earned for the company by the managers as agents to the owners or principals is more than what might have been earned if the principals had been the managers.

Agency theory as described above can be extended to the concept of the employment relationship, which may be regarded as a contract between a principal (the employer) and an agent (the employee). The payment aspect of the contract is the method used by the principal to motivate the agent to perform work to the satisfaction of the employer. But according to this theory, the problem of ensuring that agents do what they are told remains. It is necessary to clear up ambiguities by setting targets and monitoring performance to ensure that those objectives are achieved.

Agency theory also indicates that it is desirable to operate a system of incentives to motivate and reward acceptable behaviour. This process of 'incentive alignment' consists of paying for measurable results that are deemed to be in the best interests of the owners. Such incentive systems track outcomes in the shape of quantifiable indices of the firm's performance such as earnings per share, rather than being concerned with the behaviour that led up to them. Agency theory is used to justify executive bonuses in accordance with the belief that if incentives schemes are designed properly, top managers will out of self-interest closely monitor performance throughout the organization.

Agency theory was criticized by Bruce *et al* (2005), who suggested that it cannot be used to explain executive pay because some researchers adopting an agency theory perspective have failed to find a strong empirical link between executive pay and firm performance. A riposte to this from Gomez-Mejia *et al* (2005) claimed that agency theory does not make any reference to pay performance sensitivity, and that the failure of this research can be attributable to a variety of problems with the methodologies used.

The basic proposition of the theory is that the only way in which principals can get loyalty from their agents is by paying them more. As Perkins and Hendry (2005) comment: 'Agency theory takes an essentially negative view of the relationship between principal and agents.'

The effort bargain

The concept of the effort bargain is referred to less frequently nowadays but it has its uses as a further means of describing the employment relationship on pay matters. The concept states that the task of management is to assess what level and type of inducements it has to offer in return for the contribution it requires from its workforce.

The aim of workers is to strike a bargain about the relationship between what they regard as a reasonable contribution and what their employer is prepared to offer to elicit that contribution. This is termed the 'effort bargain' and is, in effect, an agreement that lays down the amount of work to be done for a rate of pay or wage rate, not just the hours to be worked. Explicitly or implicitly, all employees are in a bargaining situation with regard to pay. A system will not be accepted as effective and workable until it is recognized as fair and equitable by both parties and unless it is applied consistently.

Pay levels within organizations

Pay levels within organizations and the rates of pay for individual jobs are affected by all the economic factors described earlier in this chapter. There will be policies and practices on the range or 'dispersion' of pay between different levels, which are affected by an implicit belief in efficiency wage theory – that higher rates of pay attract good candidates (the sorting effect), increase productivity (the incentive effect) and help to retain employees.

The other factors affecting rates of pay are beliefs about the value of the job and the person, internal relativities, financial considerations (the ability to pay), the influence of trade unions and the minimum wage.

Value of the job

The intrinsic value of a job is a measure of what a job (not a person) is worth in terms of what it contributes to achieving the purpose of the organization. An intrinsic value is attached to jobs because of the impact they make on organizational results and by reference to the levels of responsibility and skill required to perform them. Increases in impact and these levels lead to higher rates of pay. This concept is in line with the labour theory of value and provides the theoretical base for job evaluation. However, as an explanation of the value attached to jobs it is limited because it ignores external relativities.

Value of the person

Individuals are valued by organizations for three main reasons: 1) the contribution they make to organizational success, 2) their skills and competences, and 3) the experience they bring to their jobs. People also have their own value in the market place – their 'market worth', which has to be taken into account by employers in setting their rates of pay.

Internal relativities

It can be argued that the value of anything, including jobs, is always relative to something else, that is, other jobs. Views on job values within organizations are based on perceptions of the worth of one job compared with others. This is the concept of internal equity, which is achieved when people are rewarded appropriately in relation to others according to the value of their contribution. The case for equal pay for work of equal value is based on the imperative to achieve internal equity.

Financial circumstances of the organization

'Affordability' is an important concept in reward management. Pay systems cannot cost more than the organization can afford, and this will influence the level of pay that can be offered to employees.

Trade union influence

Pay levels may be determined through collective bargaining with trade unions. They will want their members' pay to keep ahead of inflation, to match market rates and to reflect any increases in the prosperity of the business. The amount of pressure they can exert on pay levels will depend on the relative bargaining strengths of the employer and the union.

The minimum wage

Minimum wage legislation in the UK sets minimum rates of pay. The amount is increased from time to time.

Pay systems

Pay systems within organizations cover the ways in which pay is structured and the methods used to determine the value of jobs and the relativities between them. They create pay dispersion, which is explained by tournament theory, as discussed below.

Pay structures

Within most organizations there are defined or generally understood pay levels for jobs. These are usually set out in the form of a pay structure, which may cover the whole organization or groups of related occupations (job families). There may be different structures at various levels, for example senior management, other staff, manual workers. However, in some mainly smaller organizations, the pay system is highly flexible and relatively unstructured. It may, for example, simply consist of individual rates for the various jobs (spot rates) that bear no apparent logical relationship to one another and are determined by management intuitively. Structures for manual workers may also consist of spot rates that are based on negotiations and custom and practice.

Pay determination

Where there are formal structures, pay levels and ranges may be determined by the processes of job evaluation, which assesses the relative internal worth of jobs (internal relativities), and market pricing, which assesses external relativities. The type of processes used and the degree to which they are formal and analytical or informal and intuitive will vary widely. Rates of pay can also be determined by agreements with trade unions.

Individual rates of pay may be governed by the structure in the form of a fixed rate for the job or by movement in the form of fixed increments up a scale (a fixed increment is a predetermined addition to an individual's rate of pay that is related to service in the job). These may take place within a pay bracket with fixed minima and maxima in a graded structure, or by progression through defined pay ranges in a pay spine (a series of incremental pay points extending from the lowest to the highest jobs covered by the structure within which pay ranges for the jobs in the hierarchy are established). Alternatively, pay progression within brackets or bands or within job-family structures may vary according to individual performance, competence or contribution.

Pay dispersion

Pay dispersion takes place when the differentials between successive levels in a grade and pay hierarchy widen progressively. A dispersed pay structure is steeper than average with differentials increasing steadily. A compressed structure is flatter with relatively small differentials. The term can be used to describe the pay differential between the highest-paid executive and the lowest-paid worker, although this is usually expressed as a ratio.

Tournament theory

Tournament theory (Lazear and Rosen, 1981) explains the basis of pay dispersion. The tournament model, as its name suggests, describes a process of increasing the motivation of high-quality staff by offering lucrative 'prizes' (ie pay) for a small number of people who are promoted to higher-level jobs, with the highest prize of all given to the person who wins the tournament by getting the top job. Pay growth is larger at higher levels because the scope for further promotions is lower. The relationship between pay level and organizational level is therefore convex. The theory indicates that this arrangement will encourage managers to outperform other managers and thereby gain the prize of advancing up the pay structure. Winners stay on to compete again for even larger pay increases. Losers, however, are eliminated from further competitions and are expected to leave their organization, since their only alternative is to accept inferior pay and limited career expectations. Thus, according to the theory, dispersed pay structures help to retain the star managers in a firm and encourage poor-quality managers to leave. And people at the highest levels do not need to be worth the amount of the prize for the scheme to be efficient, because efficiency is a result of the incentive effects that these larger prizes have on people lower down in the hierarchy. Resource dependence theory, as mentioned earlier, focuses on the level of pay required to attract and retain staff in critical positions rather than the differentials between those at the higher levels.

Research on management pay hierarchies by Conyon *et al* (2001), using data on 500 executives from the top three levels of 100 UK firms, found not only the predicted convex relationship between executive pay and organizational level but also that higher chief executive differentials were associated with larger numbers of executives in the levels just below the top. For each added executive in the next two levels below the chief executive, the difference between the latter's pay and that of the rest of the executive team increased by 3.5 per cent.

Other research has questioned some of the claimed beneficial effects of the tournament model. The results of a study by Bloom (1999) indicated that greater dispersion in pay within an organization is associated with lower individual and group performance, at least where work interdependencies are important. Research by Bloom and Michel (2002) established that organizations with greater dispersion in their pay structures had managers with lower tenures and higher probabilities of turnover.

Factors affecting pay levels

The factors affecting individual pay levels are summarized in Figure 15.1.

An example of a policy on pay levels is provided by Aegon UK where the reward system is designed to recognize three core factors that affect the level of pay individuals should receive for their 'personal commitment and consistent contribution within their roles'. These are:

● Internal job value: the bigger the job, the higher the reward.

● External job value: the level of reward will be influenced by external market rates and the degree to which market forces affect the salaries required to attract and retain quality staff.

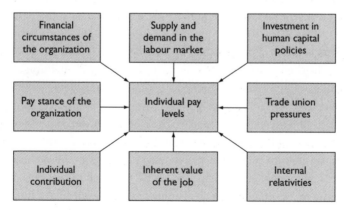

Figure 15.1 Factors affecting pay levels

- Value of the person: individual employees may be rewarded at a higher level because they are making a greater contribution, are performing better, meeting objectives and have achieved a higher level of skill or competence than their colleagues (measured through the performance management process).

As an internal policy statement explains: 'Whilst the first two factors are the primary responsibility of the compensation and benefits in group personnel, line managers are best placed to manage the third factor for all staff within their reporting teams.'

Pay level theory: six significant points for practitioners

- Labour market theory explains how pay levels are determined in external and internal labour markets.

- Classical economic theory focuses attention on external pressures and the perceived need for 'competitive pay': pay that matches or exceeds market rates. It can be used as a justification for 'market' pricing rather than job evaluation, concentrating on external competitiveness at the expense of internal equity.

- Human capital theory encourages a 'pay for the person' approach involving contribution or competency-related pay. It also underpins the concept of individual market worth. This indicates that individuals have their own value in the market place, which they acquire and increase through investments by their employer and themselves in gaining extra skills and expertise through training, development and experience.

- Efficiency wages theory can be used to justify paying more than the market rate because it is believed that high levels of pay will contribute to increases in productivity.

- Agency theory can be used to justify a policy of incentives related to firm performance, including share ownership, which will align the interests of managers with those of the shareholders.

- Tournament theory can provide a justification for widening pay differentials progressively up the hierarchy.

References

Bloom, M (1999) The performance effects of pay dispersion on individuals and organizations, *Academy of Management Journal*, **42** (1), pp 25–40

Bloom, M and Michel, J G (2002) The relationships among organizational context, pay dispersion, and managerial turnover, *Academy of Management Journal*, **45** (1), pp 33–47

Bruce, A, Buck, T and Main, B G (2005) Top executive remuneration: a view from Europe, *Journal of Management Studies*, **42** (7), pp 1493–1506

Conyon, M J, Beck, S I and Sadler, G V (2001) Corporate tournaments and executive compensation: evidence from the UK, *Strategic Management Journal*, **22** (8), pp 805–15

Ehrenberg, R G and Smith, R S (1994) *Modern Labor Economics*, Harper Collins, New York

Elliott, R F (1991) *Labor Economics*, McGraw-Hill, Maidenhead

Gomez-Mejia, L, Wiseman, R M and Dykes, B J (2005) Agency problems in diverse contexts: a global perspective, *Journal of Management Studies*, **42** (7), pp 1507–17

Lazear, E P and Rosen, S (1981) Rank order tournaments as an optimum labor contract, *Journal of Political Economy*, **89**, pp 841–64

Nielsen, N H (2002) Job content evaluation techniques based on Marxian economics, *WorldatWork Journal*, **11** (2), pp 52–62

Perkins, S J and Hendry, C (2005) Ordering top pay: interpreting the signals, *Journal of Management Studies*, **42** (7), pp 1443–68

Pfeffer, J and Davis-Blake, A (1987) Understanding organizational wages structures: a resource dependence approach, *Academy of Management Journal*, **30**, pp 437–55

Smith, Adam (1776) *The Wealth of Nations*, published by Penguin Books, Harmondsworth, 1986

16

Job Evaluation Schemes

Key concepts and terms

- Analytical job evaluation
- Analytical job matching
- Benchmark job
- Computer-aided job evaluation
- Explicit weighting
- Extreme market pricing
- Factor (job evaluation)
- Factor comparison
- Factor level
- Factor plan
- Going rates
- Implicit weighting
- Internal benchmarking
- Internal relativities
- Job classification
- Job evaluation

- Job ranking
- Job size
- Job slotting
- Job worth
- Levelling
- Market driven
- Market pricing
- Market rates
- Non-analytical job evaluation
- Paired comparison ranking
- Point-factor job evaluation
- Proprietary brand
- Tailor-made job evaluation scheme
- Time span of discretion
- Weighting

Learning outcomes

On completing this chapter you should be able to define these key concepts. You should also know about:

- The purposes of job evaluation
- Approaches to achieving the purposes
- Analytical job evaluation schemes
- Non-analytical job evaluation schemes
- Market pricing
- Levelling
- Job and role analysis
- Computer-aided job evaluation
- Choice of approach
- Designing a point-factor scheme

Introduction

Decisions about what jobs are worth take place all the time. The decisions may be made informally, based on assumptions about the value of a job in the market place or by comparison with other jobs in the organization. Or there may be a formal approach, either some type of job evaluation or 'levelling', as described in this chapter, or a systematic comparison with market rates. It has been stated by Gupta and Jenkins (1991) that the basic premise of job evaluation is that certain jobs 'contribute more to organizational effectiveness and success than others, are worth more than others and should be paid more than others'.

Evaluating 'worth' leads directly or indirectly to where a job is placed in a level or grade within a hierarchy and can therefore determine how much someone is paid. The performance of individuals also affects their pay, but this is not a matter for job evaluation, which is concerned with valuing the jobs people carry out, not how well they perform their jobs.

This chapter contains a definition of job evaluation and a description of the different types of analytical and non-analytical formal schemes and the processes of market pricing and levelling. This is followed by a description of job and role analysis techniques as these provide the factual basis for all formal evaluations. Finally, consideration is given to the use of computers as an aid to evaluation.

The purposes of job evaluation

Job evaluation is a systematic process for defining the relative worth or size of jobs within an organization in order to establish internal relativities. As described by Armstrong and Cummins (2008) there are three purposes of job evaluation:

- to generate the information required to develop and maintain an internally equitable grade and pay structure, by establishing the relative value of roles or jobs within the organization (internal relativities) based on fair, sound and consistent judgements;

- to provide the data required to ensure that pay levels in the organization are externally competitive, by making valid market comparisons with jobs or roles of equivalent complexity and size;

- to ensure transparency so that the basis upon which grades are defined, jobs graded and rates of pay determined is clear to all concerned.

The first aim was elaborated on by The Equal Opportunities Commission in its Good Practice Guide on *Job Evaluation Schemes Free of Sex Bias* (2003) where it was stated that: 'Non-discriminatory job evaluation should lead to a payment system which is transparent and within which work of equal value receives equal pay regardless of sex.'

Achieving the purposes

Approaches to achieving these purposes can either use a formal analytical or non-analytical job evaluation scheme or value jobs informally. In the former case the basis of the job evaluation is a detailed analysis of the job or role, which leads to the production of a job description or role profile. Informal evaluation is based on assumptions about what the job contains but may possibly refer to an existing job description that is probably inaccurate and out of date.

Formal job evaluation

Formal approaches use standardized methods to evaluate jobs, which can be analytical or non-analytical. Such schemes deal with internal relativities and the associated process of establishing and defining job grades or levels in an organization. Schemes may be used to evaluate all jobs or they may focus on 'benchmark' jobs that are typical of the different occupations and levels of work in an organization that are used as points of reference with which other jobs can be compared and evaluated.

An alternative approach is 'extreme market pricing', in which formal pay structures and individual rates of pay are entirely based on systematically collected and analysed information on market rates and no use is made of job evaluation to establish internal relativities. Extreme market pricing should be distinguished from the process of collecting and analysing market rate data used to establish external relativities after internal relativities have been determined through formal job evaluation.

In the 1980s and 1990s formal job evaluation fell into disrepute because it was alleged to be bureaucratic, time consuming and irrelevant in a market economy where market rates dictate internal rates of pay and relativities. However, job evaluation is still practised widely (60 per cent of the respondents to the 2007 e-reward job evaluation survey had a formal scheme) and, indeed, its use is increasing, not least because of the pressures to achieve equal pay. Although formal job evaluation may work systematically it should not be treated as a rigid, monolithic and bureaucratic system. It should instead be regarded as an approach that may be applied flexibly. Process – the way job evaluation is used – can be more important than the system itself when it comes to producing reliable and valid results.

Informal job evaluation

Informal approaches price jobs either on the basis of assumptions about internal and external relativities or simply by reference to going or market rates when recruiting people unsupported by any systematic analysis. There are, however, degrees of informality. A semi-formal approach might require some firm evidence to support a market pricing decision, and the use of role profiles to provide greater accuracy to the matching process.

Analytical job evaluation schemes

Analytical job evaluation is based on a methodology of breaking whole jobs down into a number of defined elements or factors such as responsibility, decisions and the knowledge and skill required. These are assumed to be present in all the jobs to be evaluated. In point-factor and fully analytical matching schemes, jobs are then compared factor by factor, either with a graduated scale of points attached to a set of factors or with grade or role profiles analysed under the same factor headings.

The advantages of an analytical approach are that, first, evaluators have to consider each of the characteristics of the job separately before forming a conclusion about its relative value, and second, they are provided with defined yardsticks or guidelines that help to increase the objectivity and consistency of judgements. It can also provide a defence in the UK against an equal pay claim. The main analytical schemes as described below are point-factor rating, analytical matching and factor comparison.

Point-factor rating

Point-factor schemes are the most common forms of analytical job evaluation. They were used by 70 per cent of the respondents to the e-reward 2007 job evaluation survey who had job evaluation schemes. The basic methodology is to break down jobs into factors. These are the elements in a job such as the level of responsibility, knowledge and skill or decision making that represent the demands made by the job on job holders. For job evaluation purposes it is assumed that each of the factors will contribute to the value of the job and is an aspect of all the jobs to be evaluated, but to different degrees. The 2007 e-reward job evaluation survey established that the respondents' schemes had between 3 and 14 factors, the average number being five.

Each factor is divided into a hierarchy of levels, typically five or six. Definitions of these levels are produced to provide guidance on deciding the degree to which the factor applies in the job to be evaluated. A maximum points score is allocated to each factor. The scores available may vary between different factors in accordance with beliefs about their relative significance. This is termed explicit weighting. If the number of levels varies between factors this means that they are implicitly weighted, because the range of scores available will be greater in the factors with more levels.

The total score for a factor is divided between the levels to produce the numerical factor scale. Progression may be arithmetic, eg 50, 100, 150, 200, or geometric, eg 40, 90, 150, 220. In the latter case, more scope is given to recognize senior jobs with higher scores.

The complete scheme consists of the factor and level definitions and the scoring system (the total score available for each factor and distributed to the factor levels). This comprises the 'factor plan'.

Jobs are 'scored' (ie allocated points) under each factor heading on the basis of the level of the factor in the job. This is done by comparing the features of the job with regard to that factor with the factor level definitions to find out which definition provides the best fit. The separate factor scores are then added together to give a total score that indicates the relative value for each job and can be used to place the jobs in rank order.

Evaluators, often formed into a panel consisting of management and staff representatives, have to interpret the definitions when comparing them with the job. But there are limits to the precision with which levels can be defined and the extent to which information about the job indicates which level is appropriate. Judgement is therefore required in making a 'best fit' decision and this is why point-factor evaluation, like any other form of valuing jobs, can never be wholly objective.

The members of a job evaluation panel often disagree initially about an evaluation and consensus may only be obtained after a prolonged discussion. The role of the panel facilitator is crucial in obtaining agreement without too many compromises. However, as evaluators become more experienced, possibly during the development and testing phases of a scheme, they become more skilled at interpreting the factor plan and the job information. They establish 'conventions' that, on the basis of past decisions and precedents, expand and clarify the meaning of level definitions and indicate how the information about a job can be interpreted in order to make a judgement.

A weighted factor plan is illustrated in Figure 16.1. In this example, the evaluations are asterisked and the total score would be 450 points. Examples of factor level definitions are given in Figure 16.2.

Knowledge and skills	20	50	90*	140	200
Interpersonal skills	15	40	70*	110	160
Planning and organizing	15	40	70*	110	160
Judgement and decision making	15	40	70	110*	160
Complexity	15	40	70*	110	160
Responsibility for resources	15	40*	70	110	160

* evaluations

Figure 16.1 Outline weighted factor plan

	Judgement and decision making: The requirement to exercise judgement in making decisions and solving problems, including the degree to which the work involves choice of action or creativity.
1	The work is well defined and relatively few new situations are encountered. The causes of problems are readily identifiable and can be dealt with easily.
2	Evaluation of information is required to deal with occasional new problems and situations and to decide on a course of action from known alternatives. Occasionally required to participate in the modification of existing procedures and practices.
3	Exercises discriminating judgement in dealing with relatively new or unusual problems where a wide range of information has to be considered and the courses of action are not obvious. May fairly often be involved in devising new solutions.
4	Frequently exercises independent judgement when faced with unusual problems and situations where no policy guidelines or precedents are available. May also frequently be responsible for devising new strategies and approaches that require the use of imagination and ingenuity.
5	Deals with widely differing problems calling for extreme clarity of thought in assessing conflicting information and balancing the risks associated with possible solutions. Additionally, one of the main requirements of the role may be to develop fundamentally new strategies and approaches.

Figure 16.2 Example of factor level definitions

A point-factor scheme can be operated manually – a 'paper' scheme – or computers can be used to aid the evaluation process. Methods of designing a scheme are described at the end of the chapter.

Analytical job matching

Like point-factor job evaluation, analytical job matching is based on the analysis of a number of defined factors. There are two forms of analytical matching. One matches role profile to grade/level profile; the other matches role profile to benchmark role profile.

Role-to-grade analytical matching

Profiles of roles to be evaluated that have been analysed and described in terms of a number of job evaluation factors are compared with grade, band or level profiles that have been analysed and described in terms of the same job evaluation factors. The role profiles are then 'matched' with the range of grade or level profiles to establish the best fit and thus grade the job.

Role-to-role analytical matching

Role profiles for jobs to be evaluated, analysed and described in terms of a number of job evaluation factors are matched analytically with benchmark role profiles that have been defined under the same factor headings. A benchmark job is one that has already been graded as a result of an initial job evaluation exercise. It is a typical job that represents the different occupations and levels of work in an organization and is used as a point of reference with which other jobs can be compared and evaluated. If there is a good fit between a role to be evaluated and a benchmark role that has already been graded, then the role being evaluated will be placed in that grade. Generic role profiles, that is those covering a number of like roles, will be used for any class or cluster of roles with essentially the same range of responsibilities, such as team leaders or personal assistants. Role-to-role matching may be combined with role-to-grade matching.

Use of analytical matching

Analytical matching can be used to grade jobs or place them in levels following the initial evaluation of a sufficiently large sample of benchmark jobs: representative jobs that can provide a valid basis for comparisons. This can happen in big organizations when it is believed that it is not necessary to go through the whole process of point-factor evaluation for every job, especially where 'generic' roles are concerned. When this follows a large job evaluation exercise such as in the NHS, the factors used in analytical matching may be the same as those in the point-factor job evaluation scheme that underpins the analytical matching process and can be invoked to deal with difficult cases or appeals. In some matching schemes the number of factors may be simplified; for example, the HERA scheme for higher education institutions clusters related factors together, reducing the number of factors from seven to four.

However, analytical matching may not necessarily be underpinned by a point-factor evaluation scheme, and this can save a lot of time in the design stage as well as when rolling out the scheme.

Factor comparison

The original factor comparison method compared jobs factor by factor, using a scale of money values to provide a direct indication of the rate for the job. It was developed in the United States but is not used in the UK. The Hay Guide Chart Profile method (a 'proprietary brand' of job evaluation) is described by the Hay Group as a factor comparison scheme but, apart from this, the only form of factor comparison now in use is graduated factor comparison, which compares jobs factor by factor with a graduated scale. The scale may have only three value levels – for example lower, equal, higher – and no factor scores are used. This is a method often used by the independent experts engaged by employment tribunals to advise on an equal pay claim. Their job is simply to compare one job with one or two others, not to review internal relativities over the whole spectrum of jobs in order to produce a rank order.

Tailor-made, ready-made and hybrid schemes

Any of the schemes referred to above can be 'tailor-made' or 'home-grown' in the sense that they are developed specifically by or for an organization, a group of organizations or a sector, such as further education establishments. The 2007 e-reward survey showed that only 20 per cent of the schemes were tailor-made. A number of management consultants offer their own 'ready-made' schemes or 'proprietary brands'. Consultants' schemes tend to be analytical (point-factor, factor comparison or matching) and may be linked to a market rate database. They often provide for computer aid. As many as 60 per cent of the respondents to the e-reward survey used these schemes.

Hybrid schemes are consultants' schemes that have been modified to fit the particular needs of an organization; 20 per cent of the e-reward respondents had such schemes. Typically, the modification consists of amendments to the factor plan or, in the case of Hay, to the Hay Guide Chart.

Non-analytical schemes

Non-analytical job evaluation schemes enable whole jobs to be compared in order to place them in a grade or a rank order – they are not analysed by reference to their elements or factors. They can stand alone or be used to help in the development of an analytical scheme. For example, the paired comparison technique described later can produce a rank order of jobs that can be used to test the outcomes of an evaluation using an analytical scheme. It is therefore helpful to know how non-analytical schemes function even if they are not used as the main scheme.

Non-analytical schemes can operate on a job-to-job basis in which one job is compared with another to decide whether it should be valued more, or less, or the same (ranking and 'internal benchmarking' processes). Alternatively, they may function on a job-to-grade basis in which judgements are made by comparing a whole job with a defined hierarchy of job grades (job classification) – this involves matching a job description to a grade description. They are distinguished from analytical matching schemes, which are based on the analysis and comparison of jobs on a factor-by-factor basis rather than the 'whole-job' comparisons used in non-analytical schemes. The e-reward 2007 survey showed that only 14 per cent of respondents' schemes were non-analytical.

Non-analytical schemes are relatively simple but rely on more subjective judgements than analytical schemes. Such judgements will not be guided by a factor plan and do not take account of the complexity of jobs. There is a danger therefore of leaping to conclusions about job values based on a priori assumptions that could be prejudiced. For this reason, non-analytical schemes do not provide a defence in a UK equal pay case.

There are four main types of non-analytical schemes: job classification, job ranking, paired comparison (a statistical version of ranking) and internal benchmarking.

Job classification

This approach is based on a definition of the number and characteristics of the levels or grades in a grade and pay structure into which jobs will be placed. The grade definitions may refer to such job characteristics as skill, decision making and responsibility but these are not analysed separately. Evaluation takes place by a process of non-analytical matching or 'job slotting'. This involves comparing a 'whole' job description (ie one not analysed into factors), with the grade definitions to establish the grade with which the job most closely corresponds. The difference between job classification and role-to-grade analytical matching as described above is that in the latter case the grade profiles are defined analytically, that is in terms of job evaluation factors, and analytically defined role profiles are matched with them factor by factor. However, the distinction between analytical and non-analytical matching can be blurred when the comparison is made between formal job descriptions or role profiles that have been prepared in a standard format that includes common headings for such aspects of jobs as levels of responsibility or knowledge and skill requirements. These 'factors' may not be compared specifically but will be taken into account when forming a judgement. But this may not satisfy the UK legal requirement that a scheme must be analytical to provide a defence in an equal pay claim.

Job ranking

Whole-job ranking is the most primitive form of job evaluation. The process involves comparing whole jobs with one another and arranging them in order of their perceived value to the organization. In a sense, all evaluation schemes are ranking exercises because they place jobs in a hierarchy. The difference between simple ranking and analytical methods such as point-factor rating is that job ranking does not attempt to quantify judgements. Instead, whole jobs are compared – they are not broken down into factors or elements although, explicitly or implicitly, the comparison may be based on some generalized concept such as the level of responsibility. Job ranking or paired comparison ranking as described below is sometimes used as a check on the rank order obtained by point-factor rating.

Paired comparison ranking

Paired comparison ranking is a statistical technique that is used to provide a more sophisticated method of whole-job ranking. It is based on the assumption that it is always easier to compare one job with another than to consider a number of jobs and attempt to build up a rank order by multiple comparisons.

The technique requires the comparison of each job as a whole separately with every other job. If a job is considered to be of a higher value than the one with which it is being compared, it receives two points; if it is thought to be equally important, it receives one point; if it is regarded as less important, no points are awarded. The scores are added for each job and a rank order is obtained.

Paired comparisons can be done factor by factor and in this case can be classified as analytical. A simplified example of a paired comparison ranking is shown in Figure 16.3.

The advantage of paired comparison ranking over normal ranking is that it is easier to compare one job with another rather than having to make multi-comparisons. But it cannot overcome the fundamental objections to any form of whole-job ranking – that no defined standards for judging relative worth are provided and it is not an acceptable method of assessing equal value or comparable worth. There is also a limit to the number of jobs that can be compared using this method – to evaluate 50 jobs requires 1,225 comparisons. Paired comparisons are occasionally used analytically to compare jobs on a factor-by-factor basis.

Job reference	a	b	c	d	e	f	Total score	Ranking
A	–	0	I	0	I	0	2	5=
B	2	–	2	2	2	0	8	2
C	I	0	–	I	I	0	3	4
D	2	0	I	–	2	0	5	3
E	I	0	I	0	–	0	2	5=
F	2	2	2	2	2	–	16	I

Figure 16.3 A paired comparison

Internal benchmarking

Internal benchmarking means comparing the job under review with any internal job that is believed to be properly graded and paid (a benchmark job) and placing the job under consideration into the same grade as that job. It is what people often do intuitively when they are deciding on the value of jobs, although it is not usually dignified in job evaluation circles as a formal method of job evaluation. The comparison is made on a whole-job basis without analysing the jobs factor by factor. It can be classified as a formal method if there are specific procedures for preparing and setting out role profiles and for comparing profiles for the role to be evaluated with standard benchmark role profiles.

Market pricing

Market pricing is the process of obtaining information on market rates (market rate analysis) to inform decisions on pay structures and individual rates of pay. It is called 'extreme market pricing' when market rates are the sole means of deciding on internal rates of pay and relativities, and conventional job evaluation is not used. An organization that adopts this method is said to be 'market driven'. Techniques of collecting and analysing market rate data are described in Chapter 18. This approach has been widely adopted in the United States. It is associated with a belief that 'the market rules, OK', disillusionment with what was regarded as bureaucratic job evaluation, and the enthusiasm for broad-banded pay structures (structures with a limited number of grades or bands, as described in Chapter 19). It is a method that often has appeal at board level because of the focus on the need to compete in the market place for talent.

Market rate analysis, as distinct from extreme market pricing, may be associated with formal job evaluation. The latter establishes internal relativities and the grade structure, and market pricing is used to develop the pay structure – the pay ranges attached to grades. Information on market rates may lead to the introduction of market supplements for individual jobs or the creation of separate pay structures (market groups) to cater for particular market rate pressures.

The acceptability of either form of market pricing is dependent on the availability of robust market data (not always easy) and, when looking at external rates, the quality of the job-to-job matching process (ie comparing like with like). It can therefore vary from analysis of data by job titles to detailed matched analysis collected through bespoke surveys focused on real market equivalence. Extreme market pricing can provide guidance on internal relativities even if these are market driven. But it can lead to pay discrimination against women where the market has traditionally been discriminatory and it does not satisfy UK equal pay legislation. To avoid a successful equal pay claim in the UK, any difference in pay between men and women carrying out work of equal value based on market rate considerations has to be 'objectively justified'; in other words, the employment tribunal will need to be convinced that this was not simply a matter of opinion and that adequate evidence from a number of sources was available. In such cases, the tribunal will also require proof that there is a business case for the market premium to the effect that the recruitment and retention of essential people for the organization was difficult because pay levels were uncompetitive.

Levelling

Levelling is an approach to job evaluation that focuses on defining the levels of work in an organization and fitting jobs into those levels. The levels may be defined in terms of one factor such as decision making. It may serve as the basis for a pay structure but, increasingly, levelling contributes to organizational analysis, provides guidance on career mapping and the development and description of international organization structures, and acts as a link to an information technology system such as PeopleSoft or SAP.

The levelling concept

The concept of defining levels of work was a feature of the work of Elliott Jaques (1956) on the measurement of responsibility. His research at Glacier Metal led to the conclusion that: 'It appeared as though there existed in people's minds a pattern of rates expected for levels of work done, and that this pattern was made manifest by stating level of work in maximum time-span terms.' This was his concept of the time span of discretion, which he defined as 'The maximum period of time that would elapse under the particular conditions of review, during which the member was authorized and expected to exercise discretion on his own account to discharge the responsibilities allocated to him'. He proposed that levels of work should be defined in terms of time span. This had some appeal as seemingly providing a single significant criterion for measuring responsibility, but it has not been widely adopted because of measurement difficulties, especially at higher levels. One example of a firm using time span as the main criterion is Nationwide, as illustrated in Figure 16.4.

An alternative criterion for defining levels of work, called the decision band method (DBM), was evolved by Paterson (1974). He observed that there are six levels or bands of decision making in organizations. They range from simple defined decisions 'made within the limits of a prescribed operation', to corporate policy-making decisions that 'determine the scope, direction and goal of the whole enterprise'. These definitions are used as the basis for assigning jobs to levels. The DBM method was adopted extensively in Africa but did not take hold in the UK.

A later approach that acknowledged the influence of Jaques but not Paterson was developed at Unilever. As described by Dive (2004) the notion of broad-banding was rejected and a 'work level' structure was introduced. The process was called 'the decision-making accountability

Job-family level	Level title	Nature of jobs
Level 1	Service and support	This level contains those roles in which decision making extends over a few days or weeks and the work is fairly well patterned, involving people working individually.
Level 2	Advice and team leading	For technical and professional employees where work cannot always be specified in advance. Decision making tends to involve tasks with a time span of between three months and one year.
Level 3	Senior management	Decision making tends to involve tasks with a time span of between one and two years. These managers are often responsible for other managers and may include senior specialists who refine professional practices.
Level 4	Executive management	This level contains general managers whose work involves designing and developing new systems, services and products with strategic direction and turning corporate strategies into action. The decision making would tend to involve tasks with a time span of between two and five years.
Level 5	Director	Decision making tends to involve tasks with a time span of between one and five years.

Figure 16.4   Nationwide's five job-family levels

solution set' (DMA). There are eight work levels, each defined in terms of seven separate elements, namely: expected work, resources, problem solving, change, lateral teams, environment and task horizon. As Dive explained, DMA 'concentrates on the added value of decisions taken'. Its key premise is that: 'Job holders must take decisions that cannot be taken at a lower level and which need not be taken at a higher level.' He emphasized that using DMA is a way of developing a healthy organization. It is not just a method of grading jobs.

Applications of levelling

When it is used simply as a means of defining pay structures, 'levelling' could be regarded as no more than another name for job evaluation. But it is more meaningful when the focus is on the organizational, career mapping and IT applications mentioned above. Defining an organization structure in levels may express the philosophy of a business about how it should be organized and the career steps that are available to its people.

In practice, levelling uses established job evaluation techniques such as analytical matching or job classification and may be underpinned by point-factor rating. It makes a decision on the number of levels required, which could be based on a ranking exercise using either point-factor scheme scores or whole-job ranking. Alternatively, an a priori decision may be made on the number of levels needed by a study of the organization structure, which may be supported by a role profiling exercise. This decision may be amended later after the level structure has been tested.

Levels may be defined in terms of job evaluation factors or a selection of them. Sometimes only a single descriptor is used. In cases where the focus is on career mapping as well as or instead of pay determination, the level definitions or profiles may be defined in ways that clearly establish the career ladder, often in a job family (ie a group of jobs in which the nature of the work will be similar but it is carried out at different levels). The definition may express what people are expected to know and be able to do at each level (technical competencies) and may refer to behavioural competencies. The aim is to produce a clear hierarchy of levels that will ease the process of allocating roles to levels and define career progression steps in and between families.

Job analysis for job evaluation

The reliability and validity of job evaluation depends largely on the quality of the analysis of jobs that provides the factual information in the form of job descriptions upon which the evaluation is based.

Existing job descriptions are seldom any use for job evaluation because they are generally limited simply to listing tasks or duties and do not cover the demands made on people in their roles. Further analysis is almost always necessary and there is a choice of methods as described below, namely: written questionnaires, structured interviews or computer-aided interviews. When developing a scheme, it may be worth trialling more than one method.

Written questionnaires

Embarking on a complete re-write of the organization's job descriptions could be a formidable and time-consuming task. Instead a questionnaire may be used, with a commitment to review the design of job descriptions or role profiles on completion of the job evaluation project, using the information drawn from the questionnaires.

Questionnaires ask for narrative responses to questions that relate to each factor in the scheme. They may be given to employees for completion on the basis that they know best how the job is done, or to the line manager, or, ideally, to both as a shared task.

Structured interviews

Alternatively, questionnaires can be used as the basis for a structured interview with job holders – either directly sharing the questionnaire with the job holders, or using an interview guide based on the questionnaire, administered by job analysts. The results of the interview are then written up in full after the interview. Sharing a questionnaire with job holders can increase the transparency of the process if it is given to job holders either before or during the interview.

Computer-aided analysis

Interactive computer-aided systems, as described later, use a set of online questions. The answers are converted into a job profile.

Job descriptions

The job descriptions resulting from the analysis contain information about the job's place in the organization structure followed by a definition of its overall purpose, a list of key result areas and an analysis of the job demands in terms of each of the factors in the scheme. An example is given in Figure 16.5.

Computer-aided job evaluation

Computer-aided job evaluation uses computer software to convert information about jobs into a job evaluation score or grade. It is generally underpinned by a conventional point-factor scheme. The 'proprietary brands' offered by consultants are often computer-aided. Computers may be used simply to maintain a database that records evaluations and their rationale. In the design stage they can provide guidance on weighting factors through multiple regression analysis, although this technique has been largely discredited and is little used now.

Methodology

The software used in a fully computer-aided scheme essentially replicates in digital form the thought processes followed by evaluators when conducting a 'manual' evaluation. It is based on defined evaluation decision rules built into the system shell. The software typically provides a facility for consistency checks by, for example, highlighting scoring differences between the job being evaluated and other benchmark jobs.

The two types of computer-aided evaluation are:

- Schemes in which the job analysis data is either entered direct into the computer or transferred to it from a paper questionnaire. The computer software applies predetermined rules to convert the data into scores for each factor and produce a total score. This is the most common approach.

Job title	Office Manager
Responsible to	HR Director
Responsible to job holder	• Administrative assistant • Receptionist • Security guards (2) • Maintenance fitter
Overall purpose of job	To ensure that the office building is maintained as a cost-effective, safe and secure environment, and provide office services.
Key results areas	1. Conduct or arrange for the periodic inspection and maintenance of offices. 2. Negotiate agreements with building, office equipment maintenance and cleaning contractors, and monitor their performance. 3. Maintain reception and security procedures. 4. Conduct or arrange for health and safety inspections. 5. Liaise with fire service on fire precautions. 6. Purchase office equipment and stationery and other office supplies. 7. Provide petty cash facilities.
Factor analysis	Knowledge and skills (general)	• Knowledge of maintenance methods. • Knowledge of health, safety and fire precautions. • Knowledge of office systems. • Maintenance skills.

Factor analysis	Sub-factor	Description
	Knowledge and skills (general)	• Knowledge of maintenance methods. • Knowledge of health, safety and fire precautions. • Knowledge of office systems. • Maintenance skills.
	Planning and organizing	• Plans fairly complex maintenance schedules. • Organizes teams of internal and external staff to carry out cleaning and maintenance work.
	Interpersonal skills	• Negotiating skills. • Keeping internal customers satisfied.
	Judgement and decision making	• Within budget, negotiates standard terms with contractors and suppliers. • Obtains approval for the engagement of new contractors and suppliers, or for major variations in contractual terms. • Deals with health, safety, fire and security issues on own initiative.
	Complexity	• The work is diverse, involving many different elements, often unconnected.
	Responsibility for resources	• Five staff. • Controls a large budget for maintenance and purchasing. • Controls petty cash float.

Figure 16.5 Example of job description prepared for job evaluation

- Interactive computer-aided schemes in which the job holder and his or her manager sit in front of a PC and are presented with a series of logically interrelated questions, the answers to which lead to a score for each of the built in factors in turn and a total score.

The case for computer-aided job evaluation

A computer-aided scheme can achieve greater consistency than when a panel of evaluators uses a paper scheme. With the help of the computer the same input information gives the same output result, which is not always the case with a panel. It can also increase the speed of evaluations, reduce the resources required and provide facilities for sorting, analysing, reporting on the input information and system outputs, and record keeping (database).

The case against computer-aided job evaluation

For some organizations the full approach is too expensive and elaborate a process. Others do not want to abandon the involvement of employees and their representatives in the traditional panel approach. There is also the problem of transparency in some applications. This is sometimes called 'the black box effect' – those concerned have difficulty in understanding the logic that converts the input information to a factor level score. Interactive systems such as those offered by Pilat Consultants (Gauge) and Watson Wyatt aim to overcome this difficulty.

It is perhaps for these reasons that fewer than half the respondents to the 2007 e-reward survey had computer-aided schemes, and over half of those used computers simply to maintain job evaluation records.

Choice of approach

The fundamental choice is between using formal or informal methods of valuing jobs. This may not be a conscious decision. A company may use informal methods simply because that's what it has always done and because it never occurs to its management that there is an alternative. But it may decide deliberately that an informal or semi-formal approach fits its circumstances best.

If it is decided that a formal or semi-formal approach is required, the advantages and disadvantages of each approach as summarized in Table 16.1 need to be considered, examined in the light of criteria for choice (such as those set out below) and compared with the objectives of the scheme and the context in which it will be used.

Table 16.1 Comparison of different job evaluation methods

Scheme	Characteristics	Advantages	Disadvantages
Point-factor rating	An analytical approach in which separate factors are scored and added together to produce a total score for the job that can be used for comparison and grading purposes.	As long as they are based on proper job analysis, point-factor schemes provide evaluators with defined yardsticks that help to increase the objectivity and consistency of judgements and reduce the over-simplified judgement made in non-analytical job evaluation. They provide a defence against equal value claims as long as they are not in themselves discriminatory.	Can be complex and give a spurious impression of scientific accuracy – judgement is still needed in scoring jobs. Not easy to amend the scheme as circumstances, priorities or values change.
Analytical matching	Grade profiles are produced that define the characteristics of jobs in each grade in a grade structure in terms of a selection of defined factors. Role profiles are produced for the jobs to be evaluated, set out on the basis of analysis under the same factor headings as the grade profiles. Role profiles are 'matched' with the range of grade profiles to establish the best fit and thus grade the job.	If the matching process is truly analytical and carried out with great care, this approach saves time by enabling the evaluation of a large number of jobs, especially generic ones, to be conducted quickly and in a way which should satisfy equal value requirements.	The matching process could be more superficial and therefore suspect than evaluation through a point-factor scheme. In the latter approach there are factor level definitions to guide judgements and the resulting scores provide a basis for ranking and grade design which is not the case with analytical matching. Although matching on this basis may be claimed to be analytical, it might be difficult to prove this in an equal value case.

Table 16.1 *continued*

Scheme	Characteristics	Advantages	Disadvantages
Job classification	Non-analytical – grades are defined in a structure in terms of the level of responsibilities involved in a hierarchy. Jobs are allocated to grades by matching the job description with the grade description (job slotting).	Simple to operate; standards of judgement when making comparisons are provided in the shape of the grade definitions.	Can be difficult to fit complex jobs into a grade without using over-elaborate grade definitions; the definitions tend to be so generalized that they are not much help in evaluating borderline cases or making comparisons between individual jobs; does not provide a defence in an equal value case.
Combined approach	Point-factor rating is used to evaluate benchmark posts and design the grade structure, and the remaining posts are graded either by analytical matching or job classification.	Combines the advantages of both methods.	Can be more complex to explain and administer. If job classification is used rather than analytical matching the disadvantages set out above apply so there may be more of a need to revert to the full point factor scheme in the event of disagreement.
Ranking	Non-analytical – whole job comparisons are made to place them in rank order.	Easy to apply and understand.	No defined standards of judgement; differences between jobs not measured; does not provide a defence in an equal value case.
Internal benchmarking	Jobs or roles are compared with benchmark jobs that have been allocated into grades on the basis of ranking or job classification, and placed in whatever grade provides the closest match of jobs. The job descriptions may be analytical in the sense that they cover a number of standard and defined elements.	Simple to operate; facilitates direct comparisons, especially when the jobs have been analysed in terms of a set of common criteria.	Relies on a considerable amount of judgement and may simply perpetuate existing relativities; dependent on accurate job/role analysis; may not provide a defence in an equal value case.

Criteria for choice

The following are the criteria to be used in making a choice:

- Thorough in analysis and capable of impartial application: the scheme should have been carefully constructed to ensure that its methodology is sound and appropriate in terms of all the jobs it has to cater for. It should also have been tested and trialled to check that it can be applied impartially to those jobs.

- Appropriate: it should cater for the particular demands made on all the jobs to be covered by the scheme.

- Comprehensive: the scheme should be applicable to all the jobs in the organization covering all categories of staff, and if factors are used they should be common to all those jobs. There should therefore be a single scheme that can be used to assess relativities across different occupations or job families and to enable benchmarking to take place as required.

- Transparent: the processes used in the scheme from the initial role analysis through to the grading decision should be clear to all concerned. If computers are used, information should not be perceived as being processed in a 'black box'.

- Non-discriminatory: the scheme should meet requirements relating to equal pay for work of equal value.

- Ease of administration: the scheme should not be too complex or time consuming to design or implement.

The decision may be to use one approach, for example point-factor rating or analytical matching. But an increasing number of organizations are combining the two: using point-factor rating to evaluate a representative sample of bench mark jobs (ie jobs that can be used as points of comparison for other jobs) and, to save time and trouble, evaluating the remaining jobs by means of analytical matching.

Making the choice

The overwhelming preference for analytical schemes shown by the e-reward 2007 survey suggests that the choice is fairly obvious. The advantages of using a recognized analytical approach that satisfies equal value requirements appear to be overwhelming. Point-factor schemes were used by 70 per cent of the respondents and others used analytical matching, often in conjunction with the points scheme.

There is much to be said for adopting point-factor methodology as the main scheme but using analytical matching in a supporting role to deal with large numbers of generic roles not covered in the original benchmarking exercise. Analytical matching can be used to allocate generic roles to grades as part of the normal job evaluation procedure to avoid having to resort to job evaluation in every case. The tendency in many organizations is to assign to job evaluation a supporting role of this nature rather than allowing it to dominate all grading decisions and thus involve the expenditure of much time and energy.

Developing a point-factor job evaluation scheme

Point-factor job evaluation schemes as described on page 238 are the most popular type of scheme. The sequence of activities required to develop one is shown in Figure 16.6.

Step 1: Set up the project

Establish project team

It is highly desirable to set up a project team to oversee and take part in the project. The team should include representatives of line management and staff. Technical support can be provided by HR, possibly with the help of outside consultants. The support will include the detailed work of job analysis and developing and testing factor plans.

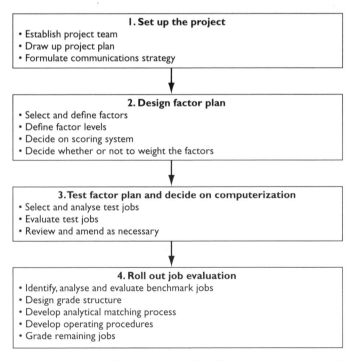

Figure 16.6   Developing and implementing a point-factor job evaluation scheme

Draw up project plan

A project plan should be prepared in as much detail as possible. This will provide the basis for managing the project. A plan set out as a bar chart is illustrated in Figure 16.7.

Formulate communications strategy

Job evaluation schemes can arouse intense suspicion, even fear. It is essential to have a strategy for communicating information about the scheme to allay these suspicions and fears. The strategy should be developed in consultation with the project team, who may well be involved in the communication process. The strategy should cover what should be communicated, who it should be communicated to and how it should be communicated. A checklist of the major points that might be included in the communications strategy is set out in Figure 16.8.

Step 2: Design factor plan

A factor plan is a matrix consisting of a number of factors (a factor is a criterion for judging the value of a job in one particular aspect or characteristic of the work involved), which are divided into a number of scored levels that can be used to determine the extent to which the factor is present in a job. The process of developing a basic factor plan involves the following steps:

1. Identify and define factors.

2. Decide on the number of levels for each factor and define them.

3. Decide on the scoring system to be used.

Activities	Months																							
	1	2	3	4	5	6	7	8	9	10	11	12	13	14	15	16	17	18	19	20	21	22	23	24
1 Agree deliverables																								
2 Design and test scheme																								
3 Evaulate benchmark jobs																								
4 Design grade structure																								
5 Evaluate remaining jobs																								
6 Conduct market survey																								
7 Design the pay structure																								
8 Implement																								

Figure 16.7 Project plan bar chart

Strategy area	Strategy contents
What	• The purpose of the exercise • The evaluation process • The outcomes, eg a new grade and pay structure • The fact that job evaluation is not concerned with individual performance • An undertaking that no one's pay will decrease when the new pay structure is increased but that no one should expect to get an increase • Assimilation and protection arrangements (it is best not to commit to a definite completion date – it often takes longer than you think)
Who	• Top management • Line managers • Staff • Trade unions
How	• Overall oral briefings by management • Team briefings • Written communications • The intranet • Special bulletins (attach to pay slips) • Informal question and answer sessions or 'town hall' meetings • Set up a network of 'champions' (not from HR) who can spread information about the project

Figure 16.8   Communications strategy

4.   Decide whether or not to have explicit weighting (this takes place when some factors are regarded as more important and are therefore allocated a higher range of points scores than others).

Select and define factors

A factor is a criterion for judging the value of a job in one particular aspect or characteristic of the work involved. The 2007 e-reward job evaluation survey established that the respondents' schemes had between 3 and 14 factors, the average number being five. Guidelines on the selection of factors are given in Table 16.2, and guidelines on defining factor levels are given in Table 16.3.

Decide on scoring system

The next step is to decide on the scoring system. Each level in the factor plan has to be allocated a points value so that there is a scoring progression from the lowest to the highest level. A decision needs to be made on how to set the scoring progression within each factor.

There are two methods. First, the arithmetic or linear approach assumes that there are consistent step differences between factor levels – for example, a five-level factor might be scored 10, 20, 30, 40 and 50. Alternatively, geometric scoring assumes that there are larger score differences at each

Table 16.2   Guidelines for selecting factors

1. The factors must be capable of identifying relevant and important differences between jobs that will support the creation of a rank order of the jobs to be covered by the scheme.

2. The factors should between them measure all significant job features and should be of broadly comparable scope.

3. The factors should reflect the values of the organization.

4. They should apply equally well to different types of work, including specialists and generalists, lower-level and higher-level jobs, and not be biased in favour of one gender or group.

5. The whole range of jobs to be evaluated at all levels should be covered without favouring men or women, people belonging to a particular racial group, different age groups or any particular job or occupation.

6. The scheme should fairly measure features of female-dominated jobs as well as male-dominated ones.

7. The choice should not lead to discrimination on the grounds of gender, race, disability, religion, age or any other reason. Experience should not be included as a factor because it could be discriminatory either on the grounds of gender or age. The same principle applies to education or qualifications as stand-alone factors.

8. Job features frequently found in jobs carried out mainly by one gender should not be omitted, for example, manual dexterity, interpersonal skills and 'caring' responsibilities. However, if such features are included, it is important that the scheme captures the range of skills across all jobs, including those that might be dominated by another gender.

9. Double counting should be avoided; in other words, each factor must be independent of every other factor – the more factors (or sub-factors) in the plan, the higher the probability that double counting will take place.

10. Elision or compression of more than one significant job feature under a single factor heading should be avoided. If important factors are compressed with others, it means that they could be undervalued.

11. The factor definitions should be clear, relevant and understandable, and written in a way that is meaningful to those who will use the scheme.

12. The factors should be acceptable to those who will be covered by the scheme.

Table 16.3   Guidelines on defining factor levels

1. Consider the number of levels (often four, five, six or seven) that may be needed to reflect the range of responsibilities and demands in the jobs covered by the scheme.

2. Analyse what would characterize the highest or lowest level for each factor and how these should be described.

3. Decide provisionally on the number of levels (say three) between the highest and lowest level so that the level structure reflects the graduation in responsibilities or demands. (This decision could be amended following the process of defining levels, which might reveal that more or fewer levels are required.)

4. Define each level as clearly as possible to help evaluators make 'best fit' decisions when they compare role data with level definitions.

5. Ensure that the levels should cover the whole range of demands in this factor that are likely to arise in the jobs with which the evaluation scheme is concerned.

6. Relate the content of level definitions to the definition of the factor concerned and ensure that it does not overlap with other factors.

7. Ensure that the factor levels represent clear and recognizable steps in demand.

8. Provide for uniform progression in the definitions level by level from the lowest to the highest level. There should be no gaps or undefined intermediate levels that might lead to evaluators finding it difficult to be confident about the allocation of a level of demand.

9. Define levels in absolute, not relative terms. So far as possible any dimensions should be defined. They should not rely upon a succession of undefined comparatives, eg small, medium, large.

10. Ensure that each level definition stands on its own. Level definitions should not be defined by reference to a lower or higher level; in other words, it is insufficient to define a level in words to the effect that it is a higher (or lower) version of an adjacent level.

successive level in the hierarchy to reflect progressive increases in responsibility. Thus the levels may be scored 10, 20, 35, 55 and 80. This increases the scoring differentiation between higher-level jobs. The e-reward 2007 job evaluation survey found that 73 per cent of respondents used the geometric model in their schemes. An example of a geometrically scored outline unweighted factor plan is given in Table 16.4.

Table 16.4 Outline unweighted factor plan

Knowledge and skills	15	40	70	110	160
Interpersonal skills	15	40	70	110	160
Planning and organizing	15	40	70	110	160
Judgement and decision making	15	40	70	110	160
Complexity	15	40	70	110	160
Responsibility for resources	15	40*	70	116	160

Decide whether or not to weight the factors

Weighting recognizes that there are differences in the importance of factors by allocating more or less points to them. The choice is first between weighting or not weighting factors. Only 19 per cent of the schemes of the e-reward 2007 survey respondents were unweighted. This reflects the view of the majority of people that some factors must be more important than others.

The most common but highly judgemental approach to decide on weighting is for the project team to discuss and agree subjective views on which factors are more important and arbitrarily allocate additional points or extra levels to them. A typical method of deciding on explicit weighting (ie extra points) is to get each member of the team to distribute 100 points amongst the factors; these are then revealed to the whole team, which reaches an agreement on the most acceptable distribution. This discussion may be expected to take account of guiding principles such as that no factor will have a weighting of less than 5 per cent or more than 30 per cent.

It is common practice to defer the final weighting decision until the unweighted factor plan has been tested. This test may reveal whether or not weighting is required.

The factor plan should not discriminate on the grounds of gender, race or disability. Guidelines on the factors to be considered are given in Chapter 17, Table 17.1.

Step 3: Test factor plan and decide on computerization

To test the factor plan it is necessary first to select, analyse and describe a representative sample of test jobs and then to evaluate the jobs, using the draft factor plan that may have been scored but is not yet weighted if it has been decided to defer a weighting decision. The aim of the test is to check on the extent to which:

- The factors are appropriate.
- Level definitions are worded clearly and graduated properly.

- Level definitions provide good guidance on the allocation of factor levels to evaluators and thus enable consistent evaluations to be made.

- As far as can be judged, the evaluation produces a valid result.

- Whether or not weighting is required (if a decision has been deferred).

Following the test, the factor plan can be revised and a decision on weighting made. This will produce the final 'paper' plan, but consideration at this stage can be given to the possibility of introducing computer-aided evaluation. (The two types of computer evaluation are described in the section on Methodology, page 249.)

The advantages and disadvantages of computer-aided evaluation are set out in Table 16.5.

Step 4: Roll out job evaluation

To roll out job evaluation it is necessary to:

- identify, analyse and evaluate benchmark jobs;

- design grade structure;

- develop analytical matching process;

- define operating procedures;

- grade remaining jobs.

Table 16.5   Advantages and disadvantages of computer-aided job evaluation

Advantages	Disadvantages
- Greater consistency can be achieved – the same input information gives the same output result. - The speed of evaluations can be increased. - Facilities are provided for sorting, analysing, reporting on the input information and system outputs and for record keeping on a database. - The resources required are reduced.	- Expensive. - Elaborate. - Lack of transparency. - Means abandoning the involvement of employees and their representatives in the traditional panel approach.

Identify, analyse and evaluate benchmark jobs

The final paper or computer-aided scheme is used to evaluate benchmark jobs. These are typical jobs that represent the different occupations and levels of work in an organization and are used as points of reference with which other jobs can be compared and evaluated. The evaluated benchmark jobs provide the basis for designing a grade structure and are used in analytical matching as described below. They will include the test jobs but it may be necessary to select additional ones to provide a sufficient number for designing a grade structure.

Design grade structure

The information on the benchmark job evaluation can be used to design a grade structure as described in the next section of this chapter. Grades may be defined in terms of a range of points scores. Additionally the grades may be defined descriptively in the form of grade profiles as a basis for using analytical matching to speed up the processes of grading the remaining jobs and of maintaining the grading system by grading or regrading new or changed jobs after the initial exercise.

Develop analytical matching process

Analytical matching involves matching jobs to be evaluated on a factor-by-factor basis either with analytical grade definitions (grade profiles) or analytical job descriptions for benchmark posts (role profiles). It will be necessary to ensure that the grade profiles are defined in terms of the job evaluation factors. It will also be necessary to define a protocol for analytical matching that specifies:

- what constitutes a perfect match, ie where all the elements in the role profile match all the elements in the grade or benchmark role profile;

- the number of matches of individual elements required to indicate that a profile match is justified, for example 6 out of 10; however, it is usual to restrict the mismatches allowed to fairly small variations – if there are any large ones, the match would be invalidated;

- any elements that must match for there to be a profile match (for example it may be decided that there must be a match for an element covering knowledge and skills);

- the procedure for grading if there has been a mismatch (this may specify a full evaluation of the role if the matching process is using the point-factor analytical scheme).

Define operating procedures

These will cover how jobs should be analysed and evaluated, including who is responsible, the basis upon which requests for re-evaluation can be made and the appeals procedure. The procedures should be set out and operated to ensure that there is no bias or discrimination on the grounds of gender, race or disability. Guidelines on avoiding discrimination are given in Chapter 17, Table 17.1.

Grade remaining jobs

The analytical matching procedure is used to grade the jobs not covered in the benchmark evaluation exercise.

Job evaluation: six tips

- Keep it simple: minimize paperwork and avoid bureaucracy.
- Involve managers, other employees and employee representatives in the choice of scheme and its design and operation.
- Use an analytical approach: analytical job matching underpinned by a point-factor scheme.
- Ensure it fits the context of the business: culture, type of work and people.
- Keep everyone informed on how it works and how it affects them.
- Ensure that the design of the scheme and the process of operating it does not involve any form of discrimination or bias.

References

Armstrong, M and Cummins, A (2008) *Valuing Roles*, Kogan Page, London

Dive, B (2004) *The Healthy Organization*, Kogan Page, London

Equal Opportunities Commission (2003) *Good Practice Guide: Job evaluation schemes free of sex bias*, Equal Opportunities Commission, Manchester

e-reward (2007) *Survey of Job Evaluation*, e-reward, Stockport

Gupta, N and Jenkins, G D (1991) Practical problems in using job evaluation to determine compensation, *Human Resource Management Review*, **1** (2), pp 133–44

Jaques, E (1956) *Measurement of Responsibility*, Harvard University Press, Cambridge Mass

Jaques, E (1961) *Equitable Payment*, Heinemann, London

Paterson, T T (1974) *Job Evaluation*, Business Books, London

Equal Pay

Introduction

In 1970 the difference between the earnings of men and women in the UK (the gender pay gap) was 37.9 per cent. Pay inequality between men and women in the UK is not so blatant now since the 1970 Equal Pay Act, the efforts of the Equal Opportunities Commission (now the Equality and Human Rights Commission) and a proliferation of reports – the 2001 Kingsmill *Review of Women's Employment and Pay*, the National Institute of Economic and Social Research (NIESR) (2001), the Task Force on Equal Pay (2001) and the Women and

Work Commission (2006). But in spite of all this effort there is still a significant gender gap. The government's 2008 *Annual Survey of Hours and Earnings* (ONS, 2008) revealed that the gap between the hourly earnings for full-time men and women was 17.1 per cent. This was the same as in 2005. So no recent progress has been made in reducing it, although it has declined a little from 21.2 per cent in 1998. One of the reasons for this slight narrowing of the gap has been the national minimum wage, which helped part-time women who had formerly been paid an hourly rate that was below that of their full-time male comparators.

As Robert Elliott (1991) commented: 'Discrimination arises when equals are treated unequally.' Historically, it has been generally accepted by men in a man's world that women's place was in the home, unless they were needed to carry out menial and therefore underpaid jobs. Women's work has been undervalued because of the low rates of pay. It has been a vicious circle. Prior to the Equal Pay Act, collective agreements tended to have only one rate of pay for women workers, with no differentiation between grades of work or levels of skill.

The entry of women into the professions in the 19th century and pressures for women's rights in the 20th heralded a very gradual change in this climate of discrimination. But it needed the Treaty of Rome (1957), Article 179 of which enshrined the principle of equal pay for equal work, to stimulate anti-discriminatory law in the United Kingdom. The first British legislation was the Equal Pay Act of 1970, amended by the Equal Pay Amendment Regulations in 1983.

The persistence of the gender pay gap in spite of this legislation is wrong in principle but also damaging in practice. As Denise Kingsmill wrote in her 2001 *Review of Women's Employment and Pay*:

> *I am convinced that the scale and persistence of the gender pay gap in Britain reflects a failure in human capital management that is neither good for the economy nor in the interests of the majority of employers or employees. The need to address issues of women's employment and pay is not just a matter of creating a society in which men and women have equal opportunities and are equally valued for the contribution they make, important though these are. It is also a matter of making the best use of the full range of human capital to promote economic growth.*

Any steps to tackle this problem must be based on an understanding of the causes of pay discrimination and these are analysed in the first section of this chapter. The major, but not hugely successful, instrument for dealing with it in the UK has been the UK legislation on equal pay, which is described in the second section of the chapter. The final sections cover the steps that can be taken to achieve equality, manage the risks of successful equal pay claims and defend claims.

Reasons for unequal pay

In an analysis of the economics of equal pay for work of equal value, Rubery (1992) suggested that the undervaluation of women's employment is caused by three interrelated factors: 1) gender discrimination in the ways in which jobs are graded and paid, 2) widespread occupational segregation by gender, and 3) differences in the labour supply and labour market conditions that allow the differences to be perpetuated. A further reason was given in the report of the Equal Pay Task Force (2001), namely, the unequal impact of women's family responsibilities.

Comprehensive research conducted by the NIESR (2001) into the causes of the gender pay gap identified the following five key factors:

- Human capital differences: differences in educational levels and work experience. Historical differences in the levels of qualifications held by men and women have contributed to the pay gap. Women are still more likely than men to have breaks from paid work to care for children and other dependents. These breaks impact on women's level of work experience, which in turn impacts on their pay rates.

- Part-time working: the pay gap between women's part-time hourly earnings and men's full-time hourly earnings is particularly large and, because so many women work part time, this is a major contributor to the gender pay gap. Some of this gap is due to part-time workers having lower levels of qualifications and less work experience. However, it is also due to part-time work being concentrated in less well-paid occupations.

- Occupational segregation: women's work is highly concentrated in certain occupations (60 per cent of working women work in just 10 occupations). And the occupations that are female-dominated are often the lowest paid. In addition, women are still underrepresented in the higher-paid jobs within occupations – the 'glass ceiling' effect.

- Workplace segregation: at the level of individual workplaces, high concentrations of female employees are associated with relatively low rates of pay. And higher levels of part-time working are associated with lower rates of pay, even after other factors have been taken into account.

- Travel patterns: on average women spend less time commuting than men. This may be because of time constraints due to balancing work and caring responsibilities. This can impact on women's work in two ways: a smaller range of jobs to choose from and/or lots of women wanting work in the same location (ie near to or where they live), which leads to lower wages for these jobs.

Other factors that affect the gender pay gap include: job grading practices, appraisal systems, reward systems, retention measures, career breaks, poor union representation and wage setting practices. In the latter case, wage levels set entirely on the basis of external comparisons (market rates) can lead to unequal pay for women within the organization simply because external rates reflect the pay inequities already existing in the labour market.

The design and operation of pay structures can contribute to maintaining or even enlarging the pay gap. For example, experienced men with skills that, because of unequal opportunities, women do not have to the same extent, may be started at higher rates of pay within a pay range for the job. It is said that men are better at negotiating higher rates of pay for themselves, although there is no supporting evidence for this.

Extended pay ranges, especially where progression is based on length of service, will favour men, who are much less likely than women to have career breaks and may therefore progress further and faster. The assimilation of men on their present higher rates of pay in the upper reaches of new pay ranges may leave women behind and they may take a long time to catch up, if they ever do. Broad-banded pay structures, as described in Chapter 19, can also lead to discrimination.

It is noteworthy that none of the key factors identified by the NIESR research refers specifically to pay inequities as a cause of the gender pay gap. Indeed, Diana Kingsmill (2001) commented that: 'Unlawful wage inequality – the occurrence of unequal pay... does not appear to be as commonplace as the 18 per cent headline gap would suggest.' This opinion seems to be backed up in part by the 2001 report of the Equal Pay Task Force, which stated that in their view, pay discrimination contributed to 25 per cent to 50 per cent of the pay gap – a wide range that seems to be matter of opinion rather than evidence.

The Kingsmill Review focused mainly on the other factors creating the pay gap and Diana Kingsmill commented that: 'Time and time again I have been confronted with data demonstrating that women are clustered towards the bottom of organizational hierarchies while men are clustered towards the top. This distribution clearly has a profound impact on the pay gap.'

The pay gap may have decreased slightly in recent years but it is still unacceptable. However, dealing with it is difficult. The equal pay legislation described below has had some effect, but it cannot deal with reasons for the pay gap that are not associated with unequal base rates of pay, such as part-time working, occupational segregation, workplace segregation or career breaks resulting in gaps in pay progression and starting rates for women.

These are complex issues and they are more difficult to cope with than relatively straightforward unequal base rates for like work. Increases in the National Minimum Wage have helped but are not enough. It will take radical changes in the ways that women are employed and their pay is managed (pay on starting a job or following promotion, and pay progression) to make a real difference. That will take time and a lot of effort that will not be forthcoming voluntarily in many organizations. But this does not detract from the need to deal with pay inequities. The next section of this chapter therefore concentrates on the equal pay legislation and how it affects pay policy and practice.

The equal pay legal framework

The equal pay for work of equal value legal framework is based on the provisions of European legislation, the 1970 Equal Pay Act as amended by the Equal Pay (Amendment) Regulations 1983, and case law. The legislation essentially provides that pay differences are allowable only if the reason for them is not related to the sex of the job holder. The Act and its amendment are implemented through employment tribunals. The Employment Act 2002 provided for the use of equal pay questionnaires.

The same principles of fairness and equity of course apply to other potential areas of discrimination, and although the rest of this chapter focuses on the equal pay legislation and its impact, it is also concerned with the conduct of equal pay reviews designed to identify any aspects of discrimination related to race, religion, disability or age that results in pay inequities.

European legislation

Article 119 of the EC founding Treaty of Rome of 1957 (now subsumed and expanded as Article 142 of the Treaty of Maastricht) stated that men and women should receive equal pay for equal work – in order to establish what is often described as a 'level playing field' in terms of wages. Article 119 was extended by the Equal Pay Directive of 1975, which stated that:

- Men and women should receive equal pay for work of equal value.

- Job classification systems (which is Euro-English for any formal grading systems and thus encompasses job evaluation schemes) should be fair and non-discriminatory.

- EC member states should take steps to implement the equal pay principle.

The Equal Pay Act 1970

The 1970 Equal Pay Act effectively outlawed separate women's rates of pay by introducing an implied equality clause into all contracts of employment. Under the Act, which came into force in 1975, an employee in the United Kingdom is entitled to claim pay equal to that of an employee of the opposite sex in the same employing organization in only two situations:

- where they are doing the same, or broadly similar work (often termed 'like work');

- where the work they do is rated equivalent under a job evaluation scheme.

The basis of the Act is that every contract of employment is deemed to contain an equality clause that is triggered in either situation. The equality clause modifies any terms in a woman's contract that are less favourable than those of the male comparator. Thus, if a woman is paid less than a man doing the same work, she is entitled to be upgraded to the same rate of pay. Although the Act refers to pay, it extends to all aspects of the employee benefits package.

The three important points to note about the original Act are that:

- Because it was confined to like work and work rated as equivalent, the scope of comparison was fairly narrow.

- It did not make job evaluation compulsory, but did establish the important point (or made the important assumption) that where job evaluation did exist and valued two jobs equally, there was a prima facie entitlement to equal pay.

- It recognized that a job evaluation scheme could be discriminatory if it set 'different values for men and women on the same demand under any heading'. It gave effort, skill and decision as examples of headings.

However, the European Commission's Equal Pay Directive of 1975 stated that the principle of equal pay should be applied to work of equal value. The Commission successfully argued before the European Court of Justice in 1982 that the United Kingdom had failed to implement the directive, because the Equal Pay Act enabled individuals to obtain equal pay for work of equal value only where their employer had implemented job evaluation. As a result the United Kingdom government had to introduce the 1983 Equal Pay (Amendment) Regulations of the Act, which came into force in 1984. These are often referred to as the equal value regulations.

The Equal Pay (Amendment) Regulations 1983

Under this equal value amendment women are entitled to the same pay as men (and vice versa) where the work is of equal value 'in terms of the demands made on a worker under various headings, for instance, effort, skill, decision'.

This removed the barrier built into the Act that had prevented women claiming equal pay where they were employed in women's jobs and no men were employed in the same work. Now any woman could claim equal pay with any man and vice versa, subject to the rules about being in the same employment. Equal value claims can be brought even if there are no job evaluation arrangements, although the existence of a non-discriminatory and analytical job evaluation scheme that has been applied properly to indicate that the jobs in question are not of equal value can be a defence in an equal value case.

The amendment also provided for the assignment of 'independent experts' by employment tribunals to assess equality of value between claimant and comparator under such headings as effort, skill and decision without regard to the cost or the industrial relations consequences of a successful claim.

Employment Act 2002

One of the biggest barriers to bringing equal pay claims has been a lack of access to information regarding other people's pay. The Equal Pay (Questions and Replies) Order 2003 of the Employment Act 2002 provided for an Equal Pay questionnaire that can be used by an employee to request information from their employer about whether their remuneration is equal to that of named colleagues. Unions may also lodge these forms on behalf of their members.

The questionnaire includes:

- A statement of why the individual (the complainant) thinks they are not receiving equal pay, followed by a statement of who they believe the comparators are. A comparator is the person the complainant is comparing themselves with. Complainants can compare themselves with a predecessor or successor in the job. The comparator must be in the same employment as the complainant.

- Factual questions to ascertain whether the complainant is receiving less pay than the comparator and, if so, the reason why.

- A question asking whether the employer (the respondent) agrees or disagrees (with reasons) that the complainant is being paid less than the comparator.

- A question asking whether the employer agrees or disagrees (with reasons) that the complainant and the comparator are doing equal work.

- Space for the complainant's own questions.

The employer is asked to respond within eight weeks but is not required to reply to the complainant's questions. However, if the employer fails without reasonable excuse to reply within eight weeks or replies in 'an evasive or ambiguous way', the Employment Tribunal may conclude that a respondent did not provide a proper explanation for a difference in pay because there was no genuine reason for the difference.

The Gender Equality Duty 2007

The Gender Equality Duty places a legal responsibility on public authorities in England, Scotland and Wales to promote gender equality, eliminate sex discrimination and demonstrate that they treat men and women fairly.

Case law

The following are some of the leading cases that provide guidance in a number of areas as indicated on how the equal pay legislation should be applied in a number of areas.

The basis of comparison

In the case of *Hayward* v. *Cammell Laird* (1988) the House of Lords ruled that the Act required a comparison of each term of the contract considered in isolation. The applicant was therefore entitled to the same rates of basic and overtime pay as the comparator even though the other terms of her contract were more favourable.

The definition of pay

In *Barber* v. *Guardian Royal Exchange Assurance Group* (1990) the European Court of Justice held that occupational pensions under a contracted-out pensions scheme constitute 'pay' under Article 119 and so must be offered to men and women on equal terms.

Extended pay scales

In *Crossley* v. *ACAS* (1999) the applicant claimed that she was doing work of equal value to the comparator but earned significantly less due to the fact that the ACAS pay scales required many years experience to reach the top of the pay band. This, it was argued, discriminated against women, who are more likely to have shorter periods of service. Although the Tribunal accepted that there was a period during which the job was being learnt, it agreed the period in this case was too long.

In *Cadman* v. *the Health and Safety Executive* (2006) The European Court ruled that pay could be related to service but might have to be objectively justified by demonstrating that longer service results in skills necessary to do a higher job. This means that employers can be challenged by women if the latter can provide evidence that longer service does not lead to better performance.

Market forces

In *Enderby* v. *Frenchay Health Authority* (1993) the European Court of Justice ruled that 'the state of the employment market, which may lead an employer to increase the pay of a particular job in order to attract candidates, may constitute an objectively justified ground' for a difference in pay. But tribunals will want clear evidence that a market forces material factor defence is based on 'objectively justified grounds', bearing in mind that the labour market generally discriminates against women. They may view with suspicion evidence gleaned only from published surveys that they may hold to be inherently discriminatory because they simply represent the status quo.

Red-circling

In *Snoxell* v. *Vauxhall Motors Ltd* (1977) it was held that if an employee's pay is not reduced, ie is 'protected', following a re-grading exercise when their pay falls above the maximum for their new grade (red-circling), the protection should not last indefinitely.

Transparency

In what is usually referred to in abbreviated form as the 'Danfoss' case, the European Court of Justice in 1989 ruled that:

> *The Equal Pay Directive must be interpreted as meaning that when an undertaking applies a pay system which is characterized by a total lack of transparency, the burden of proof is on the employer to show that his [sic] pay practice is not discriminating where a female worker has established, by comparison with a relatively large number of employees, that the average pay of female workers is lower than that of male workers.*

Use of job evaluation as a defence in an equal pay claim

In *Bromley* v. *Quick* (1988) the Court of Appeal ruled that a job evaluation system can provide a defence only if it is analytical in nature. The employer must demonstrate the absence of sex bias in the job evaluation scheme, and jobs will be held to be covered by a job evaluation scheme only if they have been fully evaluated using the scheme's factors.

Code of Practice on Equal Pay

This code was produced by the Equal Opportunities Commission in 2003. It is not legally binding but employment tribunals may take into account an employer's failure to act on its provisions.

Equal pay claims

Claims for equal pay, which may be supported by a completed equal pay questionnaire, can be made to an employment tribunal on any of the following three grounds:

- where the work is like work, meaning the same or very similar work;
- where the work is rated as equivalent under a job evaluation 'study';
- where the work is of equal value 'in terms of the demands made on a worker under various headings, for instance, effort, skill, decision'.

The person making the claim – the applicant – must find a comparator who is a person of the opposite gender doing like, equivalent or equal value work who is paid more or has more beneficial terms and conditions of employment than the applicant.

If a tribunal finds that the work is like, equivalent or of equal value it can invoke the equality clause in the legislation and rule that the man and the woman should be paid the same.

Achieving equal pay

The achievement of equal pay is a matter of eliminating discrimination or bias in fixing rates of pay. Bear in mind that discrimination can occur on grounds of race, disability, age, sexual orientation or religious belief as well as between men and women.

The following actions are required to ensure that equal pay is achieved:

- Use an analytical job evaluation scheme that is free of bias (see Table 17.1).

- Ensure that discrimination or bias does not occur in operating the job evaluation scheme (see Table 17.1).

- Design a grade and pay structure that is free of bias. This will cover such issues as discrimination in placing grade boundaries in the structure and over-extended pay scales (see Table 17.1).

- Ensure that the processes used for grading jobs in the structure are free of bias.

- Check the policy and practice on positioning employees within a pay range in a graded pay structure or on a pay point in a pay spine to ensure that bias does not occur (for example, if men are consistently placed at a higher point in the scale than women on appointment or promotion without justification in terms of qualifications or experience, or women returning from maternity leave are not re-entering their pay scale at the position they would have attained had they not been on leave).

- Check the policy and practice on assimilating staff into a new grade and pay structure to ensure that one category of staff is not favoured over another.

- Check the policy and practice on progressing the pay of staff within a pay structure to ensure that no category of staff is progressing faster up a grade or to higher points in a grade without good reason.

- Review policy and practice on upgradings and promotions to ensure that discrimination is not taking place, for example between white and Asian employees.

- Conduct an equal pay review to establish the extent to which there is inequality in rates of pay for work of equal value (eg part-time female workers paid less pro rata than full-time male workers carrying out like work or work of equal value) and identify the causes of the inequality, and take action as necessary to deal with any problem (see below).

- Ensure that line managers are aware of their responsibility for avoiding pay discrimination.

The Equality and Human Rights Commission (2009) in its guidance notes on equal pay also recommended that there should be only one pay system, which should be transparent and simple and that any change in the system should be evaluated to ensure that it will not be discriminatory.

Table 17.1 Avoiding bias in job evaluation and grade and pay structure design

Areas for avoiding bias		
Design of the analytical job evaluation scheme	**Operating the job evaluation scheme**	**Design of grade and pay structure**
<ul><li>The factors should not be biased in favour of one gender or group.</li><li>The whole range of jobs to be evaluated at all levels should be covered without favouring men or women, people belonging to a particular racial group, different age groups or any particular job or occupation.</li><li>The scheme should fairly measure features of female-dominated jobs as well as male-dominated jobs.</li><li>Experience should not be included as a factor because it could be discriminatory either on the grounds of gender or age. The same principle applies to education or qualifications as stand-alone factors.</li><li>Job features frequently found in jobs carried out mainly by one gender should not be omitted: for example, manual dexterity, interpersonal skills and 'caring' responsibilities.</li><li>Double counting should be avoided, ie each factor must be independent of every other factor – the more factors (or sub-factors) in the plan, the higher the probability that double counting will take place.</li><li>Elision or compression of more than one significant job feature under a single factor heading should be avoided. If important factors are compressed with others, it means that they could be undervalued.</li><li>The factor definitions should be clear, relevant and understandable, and written in a way that is meaningful to those who will use the scheme.</li></ul>	<ul><li>The scheme should be transparent; everyone concerned should know how it works (the basis upon which the evaluations are produced).</li><li>Appropriate proportions of women, those from ethnic minorities and people with disabilities should be involved in the process of applying job evaluation.</li><li>The quality of role analysis should be monitored to ensure that analyses produce accurate and relevant information that will inform the job evaluation process and will not be biased.</li><li>Consistency checks should be built into operating procedures.</li><li>The outcomes of evaluations should be examined to ensure that gender or any other form of bias has not occurred.</li><li>Particular care is necessary to ensure that the outcomes of job evaluation do not simply replicate the existing hierarchy – it is to be expected that a job evaluation exercise will challenge present relativities.</li><li>All those involved in role analysis and job evaluation should be thoroughly trained in the operation of the scheme and in how to avoid bias.</li></ul>	<ul><li>Grade boundaries should not be placed between jobs that have been evaluated as virtually indistinguishable, bearing in mind that the problem will be most acute if grade boundaries are placed between traditionally male and female jobs.</li><li>'Read-across' mechanisms should exist between different job families and occupational groups if they are not all covered by the same plan.</li><li>Market rate comparisons should be treated with caution to ensure that differentials arising from market forces can be objectively justified.</li><li>Male and female employees, those who are disabled or those from different ethnic groups should not be disadvantaged by the methods used to adjust their pay following regrading.</li><li>A non-discriminatory analytical job evaluation system should be used to define grade boundaries and grade jobs.</li><li>Discriminatory job descriptions should not be used as a basis for designing and managing the structure.</li><li>Women's or men's jobs should not cluster respectively at the higher and lower levels in the grade of the hierarchy.</li><li>Any variation between pay levels for men and women in similarly evaluated jobs (for example for market rate reasons) should be objectively justified.</li><li>Red-circling should be free of sex bias.</li><li>Objectively justifiable reasons should exist for any inconsistency in the relation of the grading of jobs in the structure to job evaluation results.</li></ul>

Risk assessment

Some organizations in low-risk situations may be convinced that they are doing enough about ensuring equal pay without introducing job evaluation. Others have decided that because their business imperatives are pressing they are prepared to accept a measure of risk in their policy on equal pay. Some, regrettably, may not care. But if there is medium or high risk then action needs to be taken to minimize it. Successful equal pay claims can be hugely expensive, especially in UK public sector organizations with powerful and active trade unions. Equal pay risk management may therefore involve using a non-discriminatory job evaluation scheme and following the prescriptions for achieving equal pay set out above.

The 2007 e-reward survey of job evaluation established that only 52 per cent of respondents had an analytical job evaluation scheme. The 2009 CIPD reward survey found that 52 per cent of respondents have already carried out or are planning an equal pay review. The remaining 48 per cent have not, nor do they have plans to do so. There are variations by sector, with manufacturing firms more resistant to reviews (60 per cent) and public sector organizations least resistant (20 per cent). A review had been completed by 2008 by 49 per cent of the public sector organizations and only 14 per cent of the manufacturing firms.

Clearly many organizations have decided that the risk of a claim is negligible. However, it is unwise simply to assume that there is little or no risk and it is advisable to carry out a risk assessment so that the organization is aware of the scale of the risk, if any. It can then decide whether or not to take steps to minimize the risk, such as introducing an analytical job evaluation scheme.

The best way to make this assessment is to carry out a formal equal pay review as described below. If an organization is unwilling or unable to take this step, it should at least carry out an analysis of the pay of men and women carrying out like work to identify the existence and cause of any unjustified differences.

Assessing the risk of a claim also means considering the possibility of individuals initiating action on their own or trade unions taking action on behalf of their members. Individual actions may come out of the blue but the person may have raised an equal pay grievance formally or informally, and line managers should understand that they must report this immediately to HR or senior management. A clear indication of trouble brewing in the UK is when an employee under the Employment Act 2002 submits an Equal Pay questionnaire to request information about whether his or her remuneration is equal to that of colleagues. Although trade unions are most likely to lodge questionnaires on behalf of their members, individuals can still do so independently by obtaining advice from the EOC (available on their website). The likelihood of trade union action will clearly be higher when there is a strong union with high penetration in the organization, which is often the case in the public sector. But any union member can seek help from her or his union. Even if the union is not recognized for negotiating purposes it can still provide support.

Equal pay review

The purpose of an equal pay review is to:

- establish whether any gender-related pay inequities have arisen;

- analyse the nature of any inequities and diagnose the cause or causes;

- determine what action is required to deal with any inequities that are revealed.

The three main stages to an equal pay review are:

1. Analysis: the collection and analysis of relevant data to identify any gender gaps.

2. Diagnosis: the process of reviewing gender gaps, understanding why they have occurred and what remedial action might be required if the differences can not be objectively justified.

3. Action: agreeing and enacting an action plan that eliminates any inequalities.

Defending an equal pay claim

The two most common grounds for defending a claim are: 1) that the work is not equal, and 2) that even if they are equal, there is a genuine material factor that justifies the difference in pay as long as the justification is objective. Objective justification has to demonstrate that:

- The purpose of the provision or practice is to meet a real business need.

- The provision or practice is appropriate and necessary as a means of meeting that need.

Employers cannot defend equal value cases on the grounds of the cost of implementation or the effect a decision could have on industrial relations, and part-time working per se cannot provide a defence to a claim. A tribunal can ask an independent expert to analyse the jobs and report on whether or not they are of equal value.

Note that it is not a defence to a claim to say that a lower hourly rate of pay for one person is compensated for by, for example, a better annual holiday entitlement. The contracts of the applicant and the comparator have to be compared clause by clause. The applicant can pick any part of the contract that provides more favourable terms to the comparator.

Proving that the work is not equal

The onus is on the employer to prove that the complainant is not carrying out like work, work rated as equivalent or work of equal value when compared with the comparator. If the employer invokes job evaluation to provide support to a claim that the jobs are not equal, the scheme must be analytical, unbiased and applied in a non-discriminatory way.

'Analytical' means that the scheme must analyse and compare jobs by reference to factors such as, in the words of the Equal Pay Regulations, 'effort, skill, decision'. Slotting jobs on a whole-job comparison basis is not acceptable as a defence. The legislation and case law do not specify that a point-factor or a scored factor comparison scheme should be used, but even if an 'analytical matching' process is followed (see Chapter 16) a tribunal may need to be convinced that this is analytical within the meaning of the Act and has not led to biased decisions.

Genuine material factor

The legislation provides for a case to be made by the employer that there is a 'genuine material factor' creating and justifying the difference between the pay of the applicant and the comparator. A genuine material factor could be the level of performance or length of service of the comparator, which means that s/he is paid at a higher level than the applicant in the pay range for a job. But this only applies if the basis for deciding on additions to pay and the process of doing so is not discriminatory. The Crossley case referred to above is an example of where a tribunal found that length of service criteria could be discriminatory if they meant that women are paid less than men and find it hard to catch up.

Pay differences because of market supplements can be treated as genuine material factors as long as they are 'objectively justified'. In the case of a claim that market pressures justify unequal pay, the tribunal will need to be convinced that this was not simply a matter of opinion and that adequate evidence from a number of sources was available when the decision was made. In such cases, the tribunal will also require proof that the recruitment and retention of the people required by the organization was difficult because pay levels were uncompetitive.

However, The Employment Appeals Tribunal in the case of *Sharp* v. *Caledonia Group Services* (2006) ruled that employers using the genuine material factor defence must 'objectively justify' it in all cases. This means showing that the pay disparity:

- is unrelated to sex;
- relates to a real need of the employer;
- is appropriate to achieving the objective pursued;
- is necessary to that end and is proportionate.

In other words, the difference must be sensible and necessary rather than merely due to a material factor.

Independent experts

If there is any doubt as to whether or not work is of equal value, employment tribunals will require an independent expert to prepare a report. The expert must:

- evaluate the jobs concerned analytically;

- take account of all information supplied and representations that have a bearing on the question;

- before reporting, send the parties a written summary of the information and invite representations;

- include the representations in the report, together with the conclusion reached on the case and the reason for that conclusion;

- take no account of the difference in sex, and at all times act fairly.

The independent expert's task differs in a number of ways from that of someone carrying out a conventional job evaluation within an organization. This is because the aim in the latter case is to establish relative value by ranking a number of jobs, while an independent expert will be concerned with comparative value – comparing the value of a fairly narrow range of jobs.

Equal pay: six tips

- Conduct an equal pay review.

- Develop and apply a non-discriminatory analytical job evaluation scheme.

- Ensure that the grade and pay structure is non-discriminatory.

- Ensure that pay system policies and practices in the form of grading jobs, procedures for fixing rates of pay and pay progression systems are non-discriminatory.

- Conduct an assessment of the risk of a successful equal pay claim.

- Ensure that line managers are aware of their responsibility to avoid pay discrimination.

References

CIPD (2009) *Reward Management Annual Survey Report*, CIPD, London

Elliott, R F (1991) *Labor Economics*, McGraw-Hill, Maidenhead

Equality and Human Rights Commission (2009) [accessed 4 September 2009] *Equal Pay in Practice: Guidance notes* [online] www.equalityhumanrights.com

Just Pay (2001) *Report of the Equal Pay Task Force to the Equal Opportunities Commission*, EOC, Manchester

Kingsmill, D (2001) *Review of Women's Employment and Pay*, Department of Trade and Industry, London

National Institute of Economic and Social Research (NIESR) (2001) *The Gender Pay Gap*, Women and Equality Unit, Department of Trade and Industry

Office for National Statistics (ONS) (2008) *Annual Survey of Hours and Earnings*, ONS, London

Rubery, J (1992) *The Economics of Equal Value*, Equal Opportunities Commission, London

Women and Work Commission (2006) *Shaping a Better Future*, Communities and Local Government, London

18

Market Rate Analysis

- Arithmetic mean or average
- Benchmark jobs
- Capsule job description
- Derived market rate
- Inter-quartile range
- Job matching

- Lower quartile
- Market rate
- Market rate survey
- Market stance
- Median
- Upper quartile

Learning outcomes

On completing this chapter you should be able to define these key concepts. You should also know about:

- The aims of market rate analysis
- The concept of a market rate
- Factors affecting the validity and reliability of market rate data
- Job matching

- Uses of benchmark jobs
- Sources of data
- Interpreting and presenting market rate data
- Using survey data

Introduction

Market rate analysis is conducted through surveys that produce data on the levels of pay and benefits for similar jobs in comparable organizations. It is the basis either for extreme market pricing, as defined in Chapter 16, or for maintaining competitive rates of pay and benefits by deciding on rates of pay for specific jobs or pay ranges in a grade and pay structure.

Aims of market analysis

- Obtain relevant, accurate and representative data on market rates.
- Compare like with like, in terms of data, regional and organizational variations and, importantly, type and size of job or role.
- Obtain information that is as up to date as possible.
- Interpret data in a way that clearly indicates the action required.

Decisions on levels of pay following market rate analysis will be guided by the pay policy of the organization or its 'market stance' – that is, how it wants its pay levels to relate to market levels.

Effective market rate analysis depends on understanding the concept of a market rate and the factors affecting the validity and reliability of market rate data, as considered in the first two parts of this chapter. The rest of the chapter deals with selecting the benchmark jobs used for comparison, the sources of market rate data and how it should be used.

The concept of a market rate

People often refer to the 'market rate', but this is a much more elusive concept than it seems. There is no such thing as a definitive market rate for any job, even when comparing identically sized organizations in the same industry and location. There are local markets and there are national markets, and none of them is perfect in the economists' sense. Different market information sources for the same types of jobs produce different results because of variations in the sample, the difficulty of obtaining precise matches between jobs in the organization and jobs elsewhere (job matching), and timing (the dates on which the data is collected may differ).

This means that market rate analysis is most unlikely to produce information on the rate for the job. The possibly incomplete data from a number of sources, some more reliable than others, have to be interpreted to indicate what the organization should do about them. The result of a market rate survey is often what is called a 'derived rate', which is a judgement on what appears to be a reasonable rate made on the basis of an analysis of the data obtained from a number of sources.

Factors determining the validity and reliability of market rate data

- Job matching: the extent to which the external jobs with which the internal jobs are being compared are similar; in other words, like is being compared with like.

- Sample frame: the degree to which the sample of organizations from which the data have been collected is fully representative of the organizations with which comparisons need to be made in such terms as sector, technology or type of business, size and location.

- Timing: the extent to which the information is up to date or can be updated reliably. By their very nature, published surveys, upon which many people rely, can soon become out of date. This can happen even at the moment they are published – pay levels may have changed and people may have moved in or out since the date of the original survey. Whilst it is not possible to overcome this completely, as data must be gathered and analysed, surveys that aim to have as short a time as possible between data collection and the publication of results are likely to be of more use than those with longer lead times. Estimates can be made of likely movements since the survey took place, but they are mainly guesswork.

Job matching

Inadequate job matching is a major cause of inaccuracies in the data collected by market analysis. So far as possible, the aim is to match the jobs within the organization and those outside (the comparators) so that like is being compared with like. It is essential to avoid crude and misleading comparisons based on job titles alone or vague descriptions of job content. It is first necessary to ensure that a broad match is achieved between the organization concerned and the types of organizations used as comparators in terms of sector, industry classification, size and location.

The next step is to match jobs within the organizations concerned. The various methods in ascending order of accuracy are:

1. Job title: this can be misleading. Job titles by themselves give no indication of the range of duties or the level of responsibility, and are sometimes used to convey additional status to employees or their customers regardless of the real level of work done.

2. Brief description of duties and level or zone of responsibility: national surveys frequently restrict their job-matching definitions to a two or three-line description of duties and an indication of levels of responsibility in rank order. The latter is often limited to a one-line

definition for each level or zone in a hierarchy. This approach provides some guidance on job matching, which reduces major discrepancies, but it still leaves considerable scope for discretion and can therefore provide only generalized comparisons.

3. Capsule job descriptions: club or specialist 'bespoke' surveys frequently use capsule job descriptions that define main responsibilities and duties in about 100 to 200 words. To increase the refinement of comparisons, modifying statements may be made indicating where responsibilities are higher or lower than the norm. Capsule job descriptions considerably increase the accuracy of comparisons as long as they are based on a careful analysis of actual jobs and include modifying statements. But they are not always capable of dealing with specialist jobs and the accuracy of comparisons in relation to levels of responsibility may be limited, even when modifiers are used.

4. Full role profiles, including a factor analysis of the levels of responsibility involved, may be used in special surveys when direct comparisons are made between jobs in different organizations. They can be more accurate on a one-for-one basis but their use is limited because of the time and labour involved in preparing them. A further limitation is that comparator organizations may not have available, or not be prepared to make available, their own full role profiles for comparison.

5. Job evaluation: can be used in support of a capsule job description or a role profile to provide a more accurate measure of relative job size. A common method of evaluation is necessary. An increasing number of international and UK consultancies now claim to be able to make this link, either through a point-factor scheme or a matching approach. However, they do not necessarily restrict survey participation only to those organizations that are prepared to conduct a full evaluation process. This approach will further increase the accuracy of comparisons but the degree of accuracy will depend on the quality of the job evaluation process.

Use of benchmark jobs

A market rate survey should aim to collect data on a representative sample of benchmark jobs, which will be used to provide guidance on the design of a pay structure or as a basis for market pricing. The jobs selected should be ones for which it is likely that market data will be available. There are usually some jobs that are unique to the organization and for which comparisons cannot be made. When conducting a market pricing exercise, it is necessary to make a judgement on the positioning of these jobs in the structure on the basis of comparisons with the benchmark jobs. A point-factor evaluation scheme, if available, helps to make these comparisons more accurate.

Sources of market data

There is a wide variety of sources of varying quality. They include published surveys, special surveys conducted by organizations, 'pay clubs' (groups of organizations that exchange information on pay and benefits) and advertisements. It is not advisable to rely on only one possibly unreliable source.

Should improvements in the quality of job matching be desirable, an individual survey can be conducted or a salary club can be joined if there is room. If several sources are used, an objective justification can be produced for any market supplement or premium (an addition to the normal rate for the job to reflect the market value of a job) that might create unequal pay.

In choosing data sources it is important to take account of how easily replicable the analysis will be in future years. Trends can only be identified if a consistent set of sources is used, and if those sources are reasonably stable.

Published surveys

Published surveys are readily accessible and are usually based on a large sample. If the information can be obtained online, so much the better. But the sources have to be relevant to the needs of the organization and particular attention should always be paid to the range of data and the quality of job matching. Published surveys are of widely varying content, presentation and quality and are sometimes expensive. They can be national, local, sector, industrial or occupational.

When selecting a published survey the following questions should be considered:

- Does it cover relevant jobs in similar organizations?
- Does it provide the required information on the relevant pay and benefits?
- Are there enough participants to provide acceptable comparisons?
- So far as can be judged, is the survey conducted properly in terms of its sampling techniques and the quality of job matching?
- Is it reasonably up to date?
- Are the results well presented?
- Does it provide value for money?

As a starting point to identifying a relevant survey, look at the regular reviews included in publications from Incomes Data Services (IDS) and the Industrial Relations Services (IRS). Pay analysts IDS also publishes a directory that brings together information on virtually every available survey of salaries and benefits produced in the UK, providing an unmatched guide to data sources. It currently lists some 290 surveys of salaries and benefits from 76 UK survey producers, covering national surveys, local surveys, benefit surveys and international surveys, and gives details of employee groups and jobs covered by each survey, sample size, date of the survey data and the length and price of the report. Subscribers to the directory can also access it online and search for data by job title, type of benefit, sector, UK region or overseas region. Contact www.salarysurveys.info.

Consultants' databases

Many consultancies concerned with reward management have databases of market rates produced by their own surveys and contacts and often linked to their proprietary job evaluation scheme.

Special surveys

Special surveys can be 'do it yourself' affairs or they can be conducted for companies by management consultants. The latter method costs more but it saves a lot of time and trouble, and some organizations may be more willing to respond to an enquiry from a reputable consultant.

Conducting a special survey

1. Decide what information is wanted.

2. Identify the 'benchmark' jobs for which comparative pay data is required. This could have been done as part of a job evaluation exercise as described in Chapter 16.

3. Produce capsule job descriptions for those jobs.

4. Identify the organizations that are likely to have similar jobs.

5. Contact those organizations and invite them to participate. It is usual to say that the survey findings will be distributed to participants (this is the quid pro quo) and that individual organizations will not be identified.

6. Provide participants with a form to complete, together with notes for guidance and capsule job descriptions. This includes provision for participants to indicate by a + or – whether the size or scope of the job is larger or smaller than the capsule job description indicates. Give them a reasonable amount of time to complete and return the form, say two to three weeks.

7. Analyse the returned forms and distribute a summary of the results to participants.

Special surveys can justify the time and trouble, or expense, by producing usefully comparable data. It may, however, be difficult to get a suitable number of participants to take part, either because organizations cannot be bothered or because they are already members of a survey club or take part in a published survey.

Club surveys

Club surveys (pay clubs) are conducted by a number of organizations that agree to exchange information on pay in accordance with a standard format and on a regular basis. They have all the advantages of special surveys plus the additional benefits of saving a considerable amount of time and providing regular information. It is well worth joining one if you can. If a suitable club does not exist you could always try to start one, but this takes considerable effort.

Advertisements

Many organizations rely on the salary levels published in recruitment advertisements. But these can be very misleading as you will not necessarily achieve a good match and the quoted salary may not be the same as what is finally paid. However, although it is highly suspect, data from advertisements can be used to supplement other more reliable sources.

Other market intelligence

Other market intelligence can be obtained from the publications of IDS and the IRS. This may include useful information on trends in the 'going rate' for general, across-the-board pay increases that can be used when deciding on what sort of uplift, if any, is required to pay scales.

The features of the main sources and their advantages and disadvantages are listed in Table 18.1.

Interpreting and presenting market rate data

Market rate data need to be interpreted by reference to the details provided from each source and by assessments of their reliability, accuracy and relevance.

Data can be presented as measures of central tendency or measures of dispersion. Measures of central tendency consist of the arithmetic mean (average) and the median – the middle item in a distribution of individual items. The latter is the most commonly used measure because it avoids the distortions to which arithmetic averages are prone.

Table 18.1 Analysis of market rate data sources

Source	Brief description	Advantages	Disadvantages
Online data	Access data from general surveys.	Quick, easy, can be tailored.	May not provide all the information required.
General national published surveys	Available for purchase – provide an overall picture of pay levels for different occupations in national and regional labour markets.	Wide coverage, readily available, continuity allows trend analyses over time, expert providers.	Risk of imprecise job matching, insufficiently specific, quickly out of date.
Local published surveys	Available for purchase – provide an overall picture of pay levels for different occupations in the local labour market.	Focus on local labour market, especially for administrative staff and manual workers.	Risk of imprecise job matching, insufficiently specific, quickly out of date; providers may not have expertise in pay surveys.
Sector surveys	Available for purchase – provide data on a sector such as charities.	Focus on a sector where pay levels may differ from national rates; deal with particular categories in depth.	Risk of imprecise job matching, insufficiently specific, quickly out of date.
Industrial/occupational surveys	Surveys, often conducted by employer and trade associations on jobs in an industry or specific jobs.	Focus on an industry; deal with particular categories in depth; quality of job matching may be better than general or sector surveys.	Job matching may still not be entirely precise; quickly out of date.
Management consultants' databases	Pay data obtained from the databases maintained by management consultants.	Based on well-researched and matched data. Often highly tailored to specific market segments.	Only obtainable from specific consultants and often confidential to participants. Can be expensive.

Table 18.1 *continued*

Source	Brief description	Advantages	Disadvantages
Special surveys	Surveys specially conducted by an organization.	Focused, reasonably good job matching, control of participants, control of analysis methodology.	Takes time and trouble; may be difficult to get participation; sample size may therefore be inadequate. May not be repeated, therefore difficult to use for ongoing pay management.
Pay clubs	Groups of employers who regularly exchange data on pay levels.	Focused, precise job matching, control of participants, control of analysis methodology; regular data, trends data, more information may be available on benefits and pay policies.	Sample size may be too small; involve a considerable amount of administration; may be difficult to maintain enthusiasm of participants.
Published data in journals	Data on settlements and pay levels available from IDS or IRS, and on national trends in earnings from the New Earnings Survey.	Readily accessible.	Mainly about settlements and trends; little specific well-matched information on pay levels for individual jobs.
Analysis of recruitment data	Pay data derived from analysis of pay levels required to recruit staff.	Immediate data.	Data random and can be misleading because of small sample. Can be distorted if applicants inflate their salary history or if data geared to recruitment salaries.
Job advertisements	Pay data obtained from job advertisements.	Readily accessible, highly visible (to employees as well as employers), up to date. Data can be quite specific for public and voluntary sector roles.	Job matching very imprecise; pay information may be misleading.
Other market intelligence	Pay data obtained from informal contacts or networks.	Provide good background.	Imprecise, not regularly available.

Measures of dispersion consist of:

- The upper quartile: the value above which 25 per cent of the individual values fall (this term is often used more loosely to indicate any value within the top 25 per cent.

- The lower quartile: the value below which 25 per cent of the individual values fall.

- The inter-quartile range: the difference between the upper and lower quartiles.

Using survey data

The use of market survey data as a guide on pay levels is a process based on judgement and compromise. Different sources may produce different indications of market rate levels. As a result it is often necessary to produce a 'derived' market rate based on an assessment of the relative reliability of the data. This would strike a reasonable balance between the competing merits of the different sources used. It is an intuitive process.

Once all the data available have been collected and presented in the most accessible manner possible (ie job by job for all the areas the structure is to cover), reference points can be determined for each pay range in a graded pay structure, as described in Chapter 19. This process will take account of the place in the market the business wishes to occupy: that is, its market 'stance' or 'posture'.

Market rate analysis: six tips

- Select benchmark jobs for which external market data is available.

- Identify all the sources of market rate information available, including pay clubs, published data, consultancies and agencies and other sources of market rate intelligence.

- Evaluate the sources to assess the likelihood of their producing valid and reliable information.

- Use more than one source to collect as much comparative data as possible.

- Make every attempt to match internal benchmark jobs with jobs covered in the data sources in order to compare like with like.

- Analyse the data from each source and if variable results are obtained (which is likely) use judgement to produce a 'derived market rate' using the most reliable results.

19

Grade and Pay Structures

Key concepts and terms

- Base pay management
- Broad-banded structure
- Broad-graded structure
- Career-family structures
- Compa-ratio
- Differential
- Grade and pay structure
- Grade boundary
- Grade drift
- Grade structure
- Increment
- Individual job grades
- Job family
- Job-family structure
- Market anchor
- Market group
- Mid-point
- Mid-point management
- Multi-graded structure
- Pay spine
- Pay structure
- Reference point
- Span
- Zone (in a broad band)

Learning outcomes

On completing this chapter you should be able to define these key concepts. You should also know about:

- The nature of grade and pay structures
- Choice of grade and pay structure
- Guiding principles for grade and pay structures
- Developing a grade and pay structure
- Types of grade and pay structures

Introduction

Grade and pay structures provide a framework within which an organization's base pay management policies are implemented. Base pay management can involve the design and operation of formal grade and pay structures that define where jobs should be placed in a hierarchy, what people should be paid for them and the scope for pay progression. Base pay management enables pay practices to be monitored and controlled, facilitates the management of relativities, and helps to communicate the pay and sometimes the career opportunities available to employees. Alternatively, it may be concerned with the administration of unstructured arrangements consisting of spot rates or individual job grades.

This chapter is mainly concerned with formal grade and pay structures; reference will be made to the other less formal pay arrangements of spot rates and individual job grades, which, while not strictly structures, are frequently used by organizations to indicate how much a job or a person should be paid.

The chapter starts with definitions of grade and pay structures and the other pay arrangements. This is followed by a list of guiding principles for grade and pay structures and descriptions of each type of structure or arrangement, namely: narrow-graded, broad-graded and broad-banded structures, career and job families, pay spines, spot rates and individual job grades.

Grade structures

A grade structure consists of a sequence or hierarchy of grades, bands or levels into which groups of jobs that are broadly comparable in size are placed. There may be a single structure that is defined by the number of grades or bands it contains; alternatively the structure may be divided into a number of career or job families consisting of groups of jobs where the essential nature and purpose of the work are similar but the work is carried out at different levels.

The main types of graded structures described in this chapter are:

- Narrow-graded structures, which consist of a sequence of narrow grades (generally 10 or more). They are sometimes called multi-graded structures.

- Broad-graded structures, which have fewer grades (generally six to nine).

- Broad-banded structures, which consist of a limited number of grades or bands (often four or five). Structures with six or seven grades are sometimes described as broad-banded even when their characteristics are typical of broad grades.

- Career-family structures, which consist of a number of families (groups of jobs with similar characteristics) each divided typically into six to eight levels. The levels are described in terms of key responsibilities and knowledge, skill and competence requirements, and therefore define career progression routes within and between career families. There is a common grade and pay structure across all the career families.

- Job-family structures, which are similar to career families except that pay levels in each family may differ to reflect market rate considerations (this is sometimes referred to as market grouping). The structure is therefore more concerned with market rate relativities than mapping careers. The number of levels in families may also vary.

- Combined structures, in which broad bands are superimposed on career/job families or broad bands are divided into families.

- Pay spines, consisting of a series of incremental 'pay points' extending from the lowest to the highest-paid jobs covered by the structure.

Pay structures

A grade structure becomes a pay structure when pay ranges, brackets or scales are attached to each grade, band or level. In some broad-banded structures, as described later in this chapter, reference points and pay zones may be placed within the bands and these define the range of pay for jobs allocated to each band.

Pay structures are defined by the number of grades they contain and, especially in narrow or broad-graded structures, the span or width of the pay ranges attached to each grade. They define the different levels of pay for jobs or groups of jobs by reference to their relative internal value as determined by job evaluation, to external relativities as established by market rate surveys, and sometimes to negotiated rates for jobs. They provide scope for pay progression in accordance with performance, competence, contribution or service.

There may be a single pay structure covering the whole organization or there may be one structure for staff and another for manual workers, but this is becoming less common. There has in recent years been a trend towards 'harmonizing' terms and conditions between different groups of staff as part of a move towards single status. This has been particularly evident in many public sector organizations in the UK, supported by national agreements on 'single status'. Executive directors are sometimes treated separately.

The CIPD 2009 reward survey found that 35 per cent of respondents had individual pay rates/ranges/spot salaries, 24 per cent had broad-banded structures (this includes broad-graded structures), 19 per cent had pay spines, 15 per cent had job or career-family structures and 19 per cent had narrow-graded structures.

Guiding principles for grade and pay structures

Grade and pay structures should:

- be appropriate to the culture, characteristics and needs of the organization and its employees;

- facilitate the management of relativities and the achievement of equity, fairness, consistency and transparency in managing gradings and pay;

- enable jobs to be graded appropriately and not be subject to grade drift;

- be flexible enough to adapt to pressures arising from market rate changes and skill shortages;

- facilitate operational flexibility and continuous development;

- provide scope as required for rewarding performance, contribution and increases in skill and competence;

- clarify reward, lateral development and career opportunities;

- be constructed logically and clearly so that the basis upon which they operate can readily be communicated to employees;

- enable the organization to exercise control over the implementation of pay policies and budgets.

Narrow-graded structures

Until fairly recently the typical type of structure was the narrow, multi-graded pay structure illustrated in Figure 19.1.

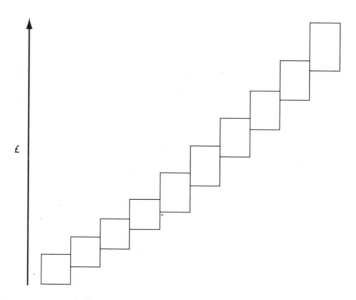

Figure 19.1   A narrow-graded structure

However, this type of structure is being replaced in many organizations by structures that have fewer grades (broad-grade structures) or with broad-banded, career-family or job-family structures.

Grades in a narrow-graded structure

A narrow-graded structure consists of a sequence of job grades into which jobs of broadly equivalent value are placed. There may be 10 or more grades, and long-established structures, especially in the public sector, may have as many as 18. Grades may be defined by a bracket of job evaluation points so that any job for which the job evaluation score falls with the points bracket for a grade would be allocated to that grade. Alternatively, grades may be defined by grade definitions or profiles that, if analytical factor comparison is used as described in Chapter 16, provide the information required to match jobs set out under job demand factor headings. This information can be supplemented by reference to benchmark jobs that have been already graded as part of the structure design exercise.

Pay ranges

A pay range is attached to each grade. This allows scope for pay progression related to performance, contribution or competence. In a narrow-graded pay spine, progression is through fixed increments based on length of service in the job. The four characteristics of pay ranges as described below are span, reference points or target rates, differentials and overlap.

Span

Pay ranges may be described in terms of their span (the percentage by which the highest point exceeds the lowest point). This is usually between 20 per cent and 50 per cent (30 to 40 per cent is typical). A span of 40 per cent would be £20,000 to £28,000. The centre of the range is called the mid-point.

Alternatively, ranges are described as a percentage of the mid-point, for example, 80 per cent to 120 per cent. In this case, the mid-point of 100 per cent could be £25,000 and the minimum and maximum would be £20,000 (80 per cent) and £30,000 (120 per cent) respectively. This span is on the high side at 50 per cent.

Mid-point management techniques, as described in Chapter 28, can help to control the structure. They use compa-ratios that express the actual rate of pay as a percentage of the mid-point when the latter is regarded as the policy rate of pay or the reference point.

Reference point

A reference point or target rate is often defined in each grade, which is the rate for a fully competent individual who is completely qualified to carry out the job. This is sometimes called the policy rate because it is usually aligned to market rates in accordance with company policies on the relationship between its pay levels and market rates for similar jobs (its 'market stance'). The reference point is commonly the mid-point of the pay range for a grade. It may be called a target rate when it is regarded as the consolidated rate to which individuals should aspire when they are fully competent and experienced in their roles. In some schemes people who reach this rate are then only entitled to non-consolidated cash bonuses for exceptional achievement, although this may be consolidated (ie incorporated in the base rate) if the level of achievement is sustained over two or three years.

Differentials

Differentials between pay ranges – the percentage by which the mid-point of a range is higher than the mid-point of the range below – are typically between 15 per cent and 20 per cent but they can be as high as 25 per cent. Too low a differential means that the scope for pay progression on upgrading is limited. Too high a differential means that a decision to upgrade may mean that the increase in pay is disproportionate to the increase in responsibility.

Overlap

There is usually an overlap between ranges. Thus if a pay range for a grade is £20,000 to £24,000 and the range for the grade above is £22,000 to £26,000, the overlap is £2,000 (£24,000 minus £22,000. This is illustrated in Figure 19.2.

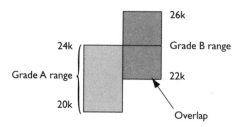

Figure 19.2 Example of overlap

This can be expressed as the difference between the highest point of the range below and the lowest point of the range above as a percentage of the difference between the lowest and highest point in the range below by means of the following formula:

$$\frac{24,000 - 22,000}{24,000 - 20,000} \times 100 = 50\%$$

In this example the differential between the mid-points of the adjacent grades is fairly low at 9 per cent. Increasing the differential to about 15 per cent and adjusting the higher range to £23,000–£28,000 would decrease the overlap to 25 per cent. The degree of overlap can be manipulated at the design stage by varying differentials and ranges. An overlap provides more flexibility. It enables recognition to be given to the fact that a highly experienced individual at the top of a range may be contributing more than someone who is still in the learning curve portion of the next higher grade.

Advantages and disadvantages of narrow-graded structures

Narrow-graded structures provide a framework for managing relativities and for ensuring that jobs of equal value are paid equally. In theory they are easy to manage because the large number of grades enables fine distinctions to be made between different levels of responsibility. They define career ladders, and staff may favour them because they appear to offer plenty of opportunities for increasing pay by upgrading.

The main problem with narrow, multi-graded structures is that if there are too many grades, there will be constant pressure for upgrading, leading to grade drift (unjustified upgradings). They can be aligned to a traditional extended hierarchy that may no longer exist, and can function rigidly, which is at odds with the requirement of flexibility in new team and process-based organizations. They also reinforce the importance of promotion as a means of progression, which may run counter to the need for organizations to be more flexible and grow capability by moving people within grades to broaden their experience and competencies.

Example: Lands' End

Salaried staff at Lands' End are on a 10-grade pay structure, with the bottom two grades overlapping with hourly rates of pay and the top grade covering directors. Each grade has a range, divided into thirds:

- Bottom third of the range: for those who have moved into the job, and are developing their skills; staff generally stay in it for about 18 months.

- Middle third of the grade: for effective and experienced staff; many will stay in this third.

- Top third: for the best performers, those who are pushing at the limits of the job and who are regularly appraised as highly effective.

Broad-graded structures

Broad-graded structures generally have six to nine grades rather than the 10 or more grades contained in narrow-graded structures. More and more organizations are adopting them because they represent the realities of hierarchies in today's 'flatter' structures, are easier to manage, can be used more flexibly and can reduce grade drift.

The grades and pay ranges are defined and managed in the same way as narrow-graded structures except that wider pay spans mean that organizations sometimes introduce mechanisms to control progression in the grade so that staff do not inevitably reach its upper pay limit. The mechanisms available consist of:

- Reference point control: scope is provided for progression according to competence by increments to the reference point. Thereafter, individuals may earn cash bonuses for high achievement, which may be consolidated up to the maximum pay for the grade if high achievement levels are sustained.

- Threshold control: a point is defined in the pay range beyond which pay cannot increase unless individuals achieve a defined level of competence and achievement.

- Segment or zone control: an extension of threshold control that involves dividing the grade into, usually, three segments or zones.

All these mechanisms require the use of some form of contingent pay, as described in Chapter 10.

Broad-graded structures are used to overcome or at least alleviate the grade drift problem endemic in narrow-graded structures. If the grades are defined, it is easier to differentiate them, and matching (comparing role profiles with grade definitions or profiles to find the best fit) becomes more accurate. But it may be difficult to control progression and this would increase the costs of operating such systems, although these costs could be offset by better control of grade drift.

Example of broad-grading at Bristol-Myers Squibb

Pay is determined in relation to the market, and is pitched at the median, though the total reward package is upper quartile. There are eight overlapping bands, each with a span of between 80 per cent and 100 per cent, covering everyone apart from the UK's dozen or so senior executives. The bands are:

D 1   Basic clerical, factory semi-skilled.

D 2   Clerical and factory semi-skilled.

D 3   Clerical and factory supervisor.

D 4   Senior supervisor, entry level for professionals (eg scientists), customer-facing sales staff.

D 5   Customer-facing sales staff.

D 6   First level manager, head of department.

D 7   Function heads.

D 8   Business heads, eg oncology, finance.

These eight bands are used in all the countries in which Bristol-Myers Squibb operates, though the salaries attached to them are locally determined. But the bands are seen as more of a safety net than anything else and something that the US parent is keen to retain, although the market is more important in the UK. The company says the bands are helpful if there is an intention to recruit someone at a salary way over or under the band, which signals that the job may need to be re-graded.

Example of broad-grading at Camelot

The broad-graded structure at Camelot is market driven – its focus is on paying the market rate for each job. Every salary is benchmarked against the market to ensure that jobholders are being 'paid fairly for the job that they do', with base pay set at the median market rate. The following six-level banding structure, covering everyone except the chief executive, is used:

- Bands A and B cover administrative support and IT roles.

- Band C includes supervisors, professionals and specialists.

- Band D is for middle management.

- Band E is for heads of department.

- Band F covers functional directors.

Bands have some overlap, and each job has its own pay range within a band. The range is 85 per cent to 115 per cent, with 100 per cent being the rate for the job. The ranges are benchmarked against the market twice a year.

Example of broad-grading at COLT Telecom

There are nine job levels or grades at COLT Telecom. They were introduced as a way of:

- providing transparency in the organizational structure;
- providing an equitable reward framework for base pay, variable pay and long-term incentives;
- ensuring consistency and fairness across functions and countries;
- allowing cross-function and country comparison;
- beginning to clarify career development and progression;
- supporting the 'One COLT' culture and values of open and honest communication;
- aiding internal and external benchmarking of remuneration.

COLT levels seek to aid succession planning and promotion. An advantage of having a formal job level structure is that managers will be able to communicate how and when their team members can progress. As the levels are fairly broad, not all promotions or role changes will result in a level change. However, if a role changes or a move is made within the organization to a different department, the job level can be reviewed and adjusted as appropriate.

Example of broad-grading at Friends Provident

At Friends Provident there are eight bands, five for non-management staff, to replace the nine previous grades, and three additional bands to cover everyone below executive director level. Generic skills and competency levels have been established to describe the broad requirements for each band. Each of the career bands is broad, and although there is a mid-point the company tells staff that they should not believe that the rate for the job is the mid-point or control point. Staff who are developing their role should be in the lower quartile of the range, staff who are fully performing are at the median, while those who are regularly exceeding all requirements should be being paid at the upper quartile. A normal distribution would be 25 per cent developing, 50 per cent fully performing and 25 per cent exceeding requirements.

Example of broad-grading at Lloyds TSB

Every role in Lloyds TSB has a market reference point that indicates the normal rate of pay for a fully effective performer. There is a published salary range for each grade (in other words, a minimum and maximum salary) based on pay rates within the market. Each grade has three zones:

- Primary zone: for people new to the role and still developing in that role. Typically – but not in every case – Lloyds TSB expects an employee to be performing to a 'fully effective' level after two or three years in the role and to move to the next zone. If an employee's salary is currently below the bottom zone and his or her work is judged satisfactory, pay will automatically be adjusted upwards.

- Market zone: if an employee is fully effective in a role, his or her pay should be managed towards or in the 'market' zone (if an employee moves to a new role, pay will start in the market zone as long as he or she has the necessary knowledge, competencies and skills to be fully effective from the outset). Broadly speaking, the market zone reflects the rate that other employers would pay for a particular job. These rates are set with data provided by independent pay consultants.

- High-performance zone: if an employee consistently makes a superior contribution to the business, his or her pay is managed towards or in the high-performance zone.

Work levels at Unilever

Unilever rejected the notion of broad-banding and introduced its 'work level' structure in the mid-1990s. This is a variation of broad-grading using different nomenclature and a special approach to defining levels. There are six work levels, each subdivided into a number of pay grades. The levels were determined according to the idea of the time-span of discretion developed by Eliot Jaques (1961) and also measure the strategic importance of particular jobs. The three principles underlying levels are:

- The major tasks of any job fall into a single work level. This is the case despite the fact that a job may include a mixture of tasks, with an executive making strategic decisions also undertaking less demanding administrative tasks.

- At each successive higher work level, decisions of a broader nature are taken in an increasingly complex environment. Discretion and the authority required to do the job also increase, and more time is required to assess the impact of these decisions. Assigning jobs to work levels involves identifying the decisions that are unique to a job. This helps to highlight differences in management decision making and accountability, which in turn allows the management structure to be more clearly delineated.

- Each work level above the first requires one and only one layer of management. A layer of management is necessary only where a manager makes decisions that could not be taken by subordinates, who may be more than one level below their boss. The company's work levels approach ensures that job holders take decisions that cannot be taken at a lower level.

Broad-banded structures

Broad-banded structures have up to six 'bands' as distinct from the 10 or more grades in a narrow-graded structure and the six to nine grades in a broad-graded structure, as illustrated in Figure 19.3. The term broad-banded is often used to describe a structure with over six bands or grades but it is useful to make the distinction between broad-graded structures, which are managed in the same way as narrow-graded structures, and broad-banded structures, which are managed quite differently as described below. The process of developing broad-banded structures is called 'broad-banding'.

Genesis of the concept

The notion of broad-banding crossed the Atlantic in the early 1990s, although it was referred to, briefly, by Armstrong and Murlis in 1988. An article by Leblanc (1992) produced one of the earliest definitions of broad-banding: 'Fewer pay grades for all types of jobs and more horizontal (lateral) movement'. Broad-banding really came to the fore in the mid-1990s when Gilbert and Abosch (1996) wrote about how it had been developed in General Electric in support of the Jack Welch philosophy of boundaryless (and de-layered) organizations. Since then it has burgeoned.

The difference between a broad-graded structure and a broad-banded structure is important. It was originally made by Gilbert and Abosch in 1996. They referred to broad-grade structures with seven or eight grades in which a fairly conventional approach to pay management is often adopted using mid-point management, compa-ratio analysis and pay matrix techniques. They contrasted these with what they called 'career band' structures with four to five bands where the emphasis is on individual career development, flexible roles and competence growth.

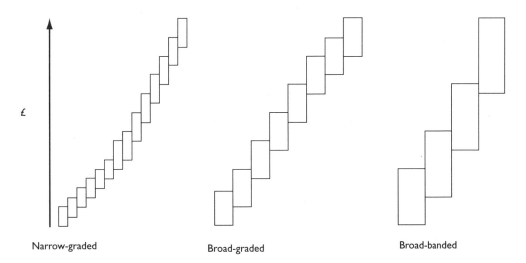

Figure 19.3 Narrow, broad-graded and broad-banded structures

The original concept of broad-banding

In its original version, a broad-banded structure contained no more than five bands, each with, typically, a span of 70 per cent to 100 per cent. Bands were unstructured and pay was managed much more flexibly than in a conventional graded structure (no limits may be defined for progression) and much more attention was paid to market rates, which governed what were in effect the spot rates for jobs within bands. Progression in bands depended on competency and the assumption of wider role responsibilities. Bands were described verbally, not by reference to the results of analytical job evaluation. More authority was devolved to line managers to make pay decisions within a looser framework.

Research conducted by Armstrong and Ryden (1997) found that in the 10 organizations they studied the median number of bands was five. There were no fixed limits to bands in three of them and the others typically had limits of up to 100 per cent.

Later research by Armstrong and Brown (2001) established that in organizations with broad bands, 62 per cent had bands with widths between 50 per cent and 75 per cent, while the rest had bands with widths between 75 per cent and 100 per cent. Typically, there were between four and six bands in such structures. The band boundaries were often, but not always, defined by job evaluation. Jobs were placed in the bands purely by reference to market rates or by a combination of job evaluation and market rate analysis. Bands were described by an overall description of the jobs allocated to them (senior management etc) or by reference to the generic roles they contained, for instance technical support.

This concept was, and still is, beguiling. Broad-banded structures are simpler and therefore easier to design. They satisfy the desire for more flexibility, and Armstrong and Brown's (2001) research established that this was by far the most important reason for introducing broad-bands. Flexibility is achieved by catering for broader roles rather than tightly defined jobs, by adopting less rigid approaches to the allocation of roles to bands and how people progress within them, and by being able to respond more quickly to market rate pressures. In the United States the advantages of doing without formal job evaluation and using market pricing were originally the most powerful arguments in favour of broad-banding. This remains the case there, but in the UK the use of job evaluation rather than market pricing is still common and the original concept of broad-banded structures has never been taken up as enthusiastically as in the United States. An aspect of flexibility that is seldom discussed in public is that when introducing broad-bands the wider span of pay means that fewer anomalies are created and the cost of implementation is reduced.

Moreover, broad-banding was in accord with the drive for de-layering. The reduction in the number of grades meant that the pressure for upgrading was reduced, there was less likelihood of grade drift and it was thought that grades would be easier to manage.

Further developments in the concept

The original notion of unstructured broad bands is now no longer general practice in the UK. It created expectations of the scope for progression that could not be met. Progression had to stop somewhere if costs were going to be controlled, and no rationale was available for deciding when and why to stop. Line managers felt adrift without adequate guidance and staff missed the structure they were used to. Questions were asked about the point of having broad bands at all when in effect all they consisted of was spot rates determined mainly by market relativities. Why, people asked, should organizations not be honest with themselves and their staff and revert to the complete freedom and therefore flexibility that spot rates provide?

Inevitably, therefore, structure crept in. It started with reference points aligned to market rates around which similar roles could be clustered. These were then extended into zones for individual jobs or groups of jobs, as illustrated in Figure 19.4 (based on a structure in a financial services company). Reference points are frequently placed in zones so that they increasingly resemble conventional structure grades. Armstrong and Brown (2001) established that 80 per cent of organizations had introduced some controls in the form of zones (43 per cent) and zones with reference points (37 per cent). Job evaluation was used not only to define the boundaries of the band but to size jobs as a basis for deciding where reference points should be placed in conjunction with market pricing. Progressively, therefore, the original concept of broad-banding was eroded as more structure was introduced and job evaluation became more prominent to define the structure and meet equal pay requirements. Zones within broad bands began to look very like conventional grades. An example of a broad-banded structure linked to job evaluation is given in Figure 19.5 (based on a structure developed for Notting Hill Housing Association).

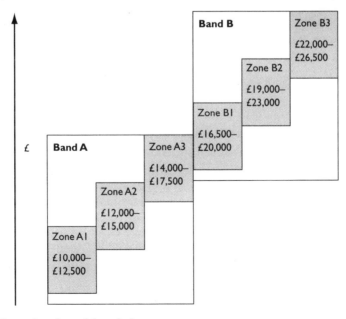

Figure 19.4   Zones in a broad-banded structure

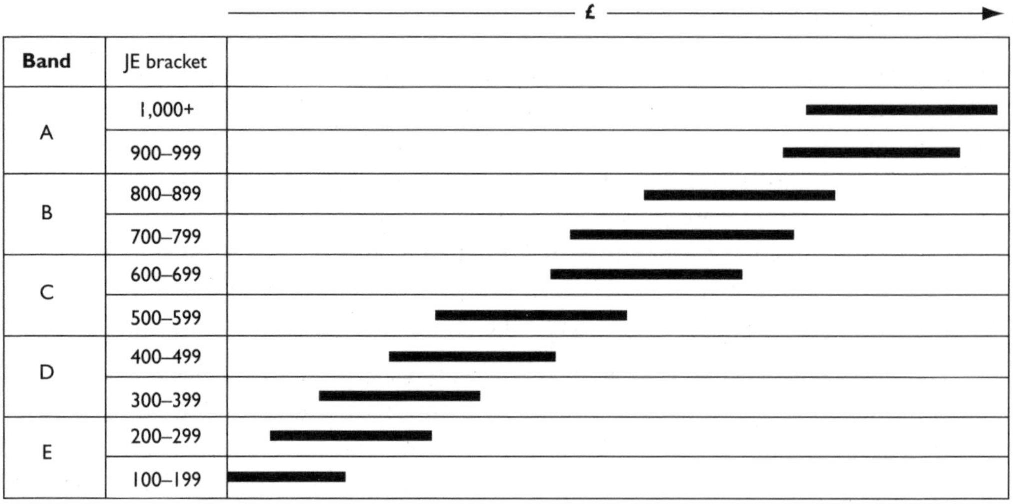

Band	JE bracket	£ →—————————————————————————————
A	1,000+	
A	900–999	
B	800–899	
B	700–799	
C	600–699	
C	500–599	
D	400–499	
D	300–399	
E	200–299	
E	100–199	

Figure 19.5 A broad-banded structure with zones defined by job evaluation score brackets

Band definitions

There are five ways of defining bands, as set out below. The first four are descriptive in increasing degrees of complexity. They simplify the process of allocating roles to bands although judgement is required. However, this may not matter too much if there is a considerable amount of overlap in pay spans or opportunities between adjacent bands. The fifth method is the use of job evaluation.

1. Descriptive labels: these refer to the generic roles that have been allocated to bands – for example, senior managers, managers, team leaders, individual contributors (technical and professional) and individual contributors (administration and support).

2. Outline generic descriptions of jobs in band: these briefly expand descriptive labels, eg:

   – Senior managers: executives in charge of a major function or department.

   – Managers: of a sub-division of a major function or department, or a small department.

   – Team leaders: in charge of a small team of individual contributors.

   – Individual contributors (technical and professional): junior technical or professional specialists working as members of a team.

   – Individual contributors (administration and support): members of teams carrying out basic administrative or support roles.

3. Summary analytical description of bands: a brief analysis of the characteristics of roles in the band as illustrated in Figure 19.6.

1. Administrators and support workers	• Provide basic administrative and support services. • Work largely prescribed, freedom to act fairly limited. • Role requirements clearly defined.
2. Senior administrators and support workers	• Provide fairly complex administrative and support services. • Work generally standardized. • Limited freedom to decide on methods and priorities.
3. Team leaders and specialists	• Lead a small team of administrators or support workers, or provide specialist/basic professional services. • Some diversity in role requirements. • Act within specified policy and procedural guidelines.
4. Middle managers	• Manage a function or department within an operational or technical area, or provide professional advice and services in an important aspect of the organization's activities. • The work is diverse. • Freedom to act within broad policy frameworks.
5. Senior managers	• Head of a major function or department, making a major and strategic impact on the performance of the organization, or is the main provider of professional advice and services in a key aspect of the organization's activities. • The work is complex and involves making a broad range of highly diverse decisions. • A considerable amount of independent action is required within the framework of organizational strategies and plans and subject only to general guidance.

Figure 19.6   Brief analytical band definitions

4. Extended analytical description of bands: a full analysis of the generic characteristics of jobs in the bands is illustrated in Figure 19.7.

5. Use of job evaluation: bands can be defined in terms of a range of job evaluation points, as illustrated in Figure 19.5. Jobs are traditionally graded in conventional pay structures through analytical job evaluation – points brackets are attached to each grade and individual roles are 'sized' and allocated into grades by comparing scores with the points brackets attached to them. The difference when developing a broad-banded structure is that an a priori decision may have been made on the number of bands and how they should be described and defined. In these circumstances, job evaluation is simply used to determine points dimensions for the bands as a guide to where roles should be allocated.

Allocation of jobs to bands

When bands are defined descriptively, a job slotting or analytical matching approach can be used to allocate jobs to them. Slotting is the process of placing a job in a band by reference to grade definitions that have not been analysed into factors. It is essentially the non-analytical job evaluation technique of job classification, but it is easier to make decisions if broad generic definitions exist for a small number of bands than in a multi-graded structure. Analytical matching means allocating benchmark roles to bands by comparing their characteristics as expressed in a role profile with the previously prepared band definitions or profiles that have

- Occasional supervision of staff temporarily assigned or shared supervision or permanent staff.
- Creativity is a feature of the job but exercised within the general framework of recognized procedures.
- Contacts which are generally not contentious but where the need or potential outcome may not be straightforward, or where the circumstances call for an element of tact or sensitivity. Contacts at this level would include interviewing to establish details or service needs, the supply of straightforward advice, and initiating action to provide assistance. Contacts within the organization would require the provision of advice or guidance on matters that are less well established.
- Work is carried out within policies and objectives where there is a wide range of choices and where advice is not normally available.
- Decisions that have significant implications for the organization or significant effects on employees or other individuals or other organizations.
- Ability to undertake work concerning more involved tasks confined to one function or area of activity that requires a good standard or practical knowledge and skills in that area of activity.
- Work subject to changing problems or circumstances or demand.

Figure 19.7   Analytical definition of a band in a charity

been analysed into factors. Valid allocations can be made quickly if a good analytical framework exists. Analytical matching is a form of job evaluation, but it is much simpler and less time-consuming than point-factor job evaluation because detailed measurement is not required.

Where bands are described in terms of job evaluation scores, the allocation can be made by reference to an evaluation using a point-factor scheme. However, analytical matching is being increasingly used for broad bands and, indeed, in conventional graded structures.

Reservations about broad-banding

The two reservations that emerged from the experience of developing broad bands in the 1990s and early 2000s were: 1) What's the point of unstructured broad bands if they simply consist of spot rates? and 2) What's the difference between, say, a four-banded structure with three zones in each band and a 12-graded structure? The answer given by broad band devotees to the first question was that at least there was some overall structure within which spot rates could be managed. In reply to the second question, the usual answer was that as roles develop, movements between zones within bands could be dealt with more flexibly. Neither of these responses is particularly convincing.

Objections to broad-banding

Apart from these fundamental reservations, there are a number of other objections to broad-banding. In general, it has been found that broad-banded structures are harder to manage than narrower graded structures in spite of the original claim that they would be easier – they make considerable demands on line managers as well as HR. It was noted by Armstrong (2000) that broad-banding was not an easy option. Pay can spin out of control unless steps are taken to prevent that happening. As a reward manager in an engineering company told him: 'Broad bands offer huge scope for flexibility, but equally huge scope for getting it wrong.'

Broad-banding can build employee expectations of significant pay opportunities, which are doomed in many cases if proper control of the system is maintained. It can be difficult to explain to people how broad-banding works and how they will be affected, and they may be concerned by the apparent lack of structure and precision. Decisions on movements within bands can be harder to justify objectively than in other types of grade and pay structures.

Broad-banded structures may be more costly than more conventional structures because there is less control over pay progression. Research conducted by Fay *et al* (2004) in the United States found that both base pay and total cash compensation was significantly higher in the companies with broad-banded structures than in those with more conventional structures. They estimated that broad-banding increased pay roll costs by 7 per cent plus.

Another major objection to broad-banding is that it can create the following equal pay problems:

- Reliance on external relativities (market rates) to place jobs in bands can reproduce existing inequalities in the labour market.

- The broader pay ranges within bands mean that they include jobs of widely different values or sizes, which may result in gender discrimination.

- Women may be assimilated at their present rates in the lower regions of bands and find it impossible, or at least very difficult, to catch up with their male colleagues who, because of their existing higher rates of pay, are assimilated in the upper reaches of bands.

Broad-banding in its original sense is therefore not the panacea it was once thought to be. More organizations are settling for a broad-graded structure with six to nine grades, with the possibility of restricting the number to five but recognizing that they have to contain control mechanisms that might take the form of a series of zones.

Examples

Britannia Building Society

The Britannia Building Society has a six-band structure, although within these there are 38 separate role profiles. The pay ranges for the bands are based on external market comparisons. Mapping individual staff to the role profiles involved a process of job evaluation and validation by management teams.

GlaxoSmithKline

GlaxoSmithKline has five bands: A and B for are for top executives, band C is for directors and managers, band D covers professional and technical staff and band E comprises administrative staff. These bands determine benefit entitlements. Pay for manufacturing staff is negotiated with the trade unions; these job grades are subject to local agreement and are not included in the grading structure.

Each band is divided into a number of zones for pay purposes. For example, band D is divided into six zones, and band E has five zones. The combination of band and zone produces the grade, and there are 29 grades in total. These grades are also important for determining bonus entitlement. The pay for each grade ranges approximately 25 per cent either side of the range mid-point.

Tesco

The broad-banded structure consists of six 'work levels' that cover all staff from the shopfloor to the main board, replacing the previous 22 grades:

- Work level 1 covers all clerical jobs.

- Work levels 2, 3 and 4 cover all staff other than those in clerical jobs and directors. The maximum of each of the bands in these levels is at least 100 per cent above the minimum.

- Work levels 5 and 6 are for main board and senior directors, whose pay is determined on an individual basis.

Career-family structures

Career or job families consist of jobs in a function or occupation such as marketing, operations, finance, IT, HR, administration or support services that are related through the activities carried out and the basic knowledge and skills required, but in which the levels of responsibility, knowledge, skill or competency needed differ. In a career-family structure as illustrated in Figure 19.8, the different career families are identified and the successive levels in each family are defined by reference to the key activities carried out and the knowledge and skills or competencies required to perform them effectively. They therefore define career paths – what people have to know and be able to do to advance their career within a family and to develop career opportunities in other families. These career paths are the distinguishing characteristic of career-family structures, which are as much about defining career progression routes as they are about defining a pay structure. Typically, career families have between six and eight levels, as in broad-graded structures. Some families may have more levels than others.

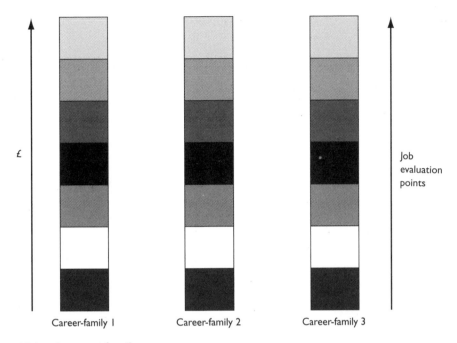

Figure 19.8 A career-family structure

In effect, a career structure is a single graded structure in which each grade has been divided into families. The difference between a conventional graded structure and a career-family structure is that in the former the grade definitions are all the same. In a career-family structure, although the levels may be defined generally for all families, separate definitions expressed as competency requirements exist for levels in each of the career families.

Competency-defined grades or bands in a career-family structure

Defining grades or bands in terms of competencies results in what Risher (2002) describes as a 'career ladder' structure. He reports the practice of three companies – Dow, IBM and Marriott Hotels – which have defined a set of brief competency factors or criteria that provide a simple and transparent framework based on levels in a career ladder. The criteria consist of the competencies such as knowledge, skills and abilities required at each level.

An example of a UK approach to career ladders is provided by the NHS as part of its 'Agenda for Change' project. Its skills ladder is illustrated in Figure 19.9.

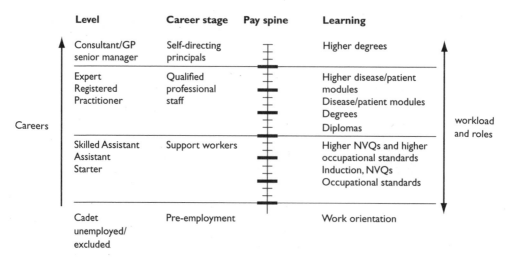

Figure 19.9 The NHS skills ladder

Advantages and disadvantages

Career-family structures provide the foundation for personal development planning by defining the knowledge, skills and competencies required at higher levels or in different functions, and describing what needs to be learnt through experience, education or training. Level definitions in a family can be more accurate than in a conventional structure because they concentrate on roles within the family with common characteristics and do not attempt to cover a wide and in some ways unconnected set of skills across the whole organization. Furthermore, the existence of a common grading system when it is supported by job evaluation facilitates the achievement of equal pay for work of equal value. Finally, linking pay and grade management with career development is in accordance with good practice human resource management in the shape of 'bundling' – the belief, supported by extensive research, that HR practices will be more effective if they are interrelated and therefore complement and reinforce one another.

But career structures can be more difficult to develop, explain and manage than single grade structures. A considerable amount of work is required to produce clear analytical level definitions that are properly graded and provide good career guidelines. A broad-graded structure, for example, is a simple and straightforward concept, and splitting it into families may increase the complexity without providing commensurate benefits. Maintaining the accuracy of the level definitions also demands much care and attention. It is these problems that are perhaps the main reason why career structures have not yet caught on.

Furthermore, whatever emphasis is placed on career development between as well as within families, they could be perceived as being divisive and in conflict with the principle of identical treatment for all enshrined in a single grade structure. It may be inferred that progression can only take place in an occupational 'silo'. This has meant that career-family approaches have been abandoned where the silos have been narrowly drawn and managed rigidly – the simpler they are the better.

Examples

Career families at Aegon UK

The range of different roles within the business has been organized into four career families, which are defined as groups of jobs where the technical knowledge and behavioural skills are similar and recognizable by the external labour market. The families are operations delivery, team leader and technical, junior management, professional and senior technical, and management and senior professional.

The aim is to provide information on development opportunities and career paths that, as part of a performance management process, can contribute to performance development and training. Within each career family there are defined career paths for progressing to higher levels by clarifying what skills individuals have to demonstrate if they wish to move to a new career path. The career families can therefore provide the foundation for personal development planning by defining the knowledge and skills required at higher levels or in different functions and what needs to be learnt through experience, education or training. Employees are able to understand not only how they can develop their skills and competence within their current role, but also how they can move through their career path to specialist roles. Routes are also shown into career paths in other parts of the organization.

Career bands at Friends Provident

The pay structure at Friends Provident has eight overlapping career bands below executive director level. Bands A to E cover non-management staff, as shown in Table 19.1 and the three additional bands are manager, head of department and director. Career bands reflect each of the significant steps in an individual's career. Movement from one band to another is earned when individuals demonstrate real potential for working to the higher level of skills and knowledge and when there is a requirement for someone at this level within the business unit.

Each band is broadly defined in terms of the minimum expected level of competence required for entry. This aims to encourage a focus on the requirements at either end of the band, and therefore highlight the range of salary potential between the two.

In bands A and B, staff are carrying out generalist administrative support functions, so the differentials between job families tend to be insignificant. Salary ranges apply to all staff across the company and are not related to job family (though the impact of location is recognized).

Table 19.1 Career bands at Friends Provident

Career band	Job example
A	Junior clerical and administrative staff
B	Customer services consultant
C	Customer services team leader
D	Customer services team manager
E	Assistant customer services manager (responsible for 30–40 staff)

In career bands C, D and E, however, staff will often be following a specific career path and will be developing specialist skills and knowledge and possibly studying for additional qualifications. The market rates of pay reflect this with noticeable differences in the rates of pay for different job families.

Career-family structure at Norwich Union Insurance

There are 19 career families, defined as a cluster of jobs with similar skill requirements and activities. Levels of responsibility vary within the family. The career framework helps staff to understand how their jobs fit within their business unit and the organization as a whole and supports movement across the organization, since individuals can identify jobs at a similar level in other families that they might like to join. The skills, knowledge and behaviours profile for each role is published to facilitate this. Each family contains between four and seven levels, each with a pay range with an 80 per cent minimum, a market salary guide for competent performance and no maximum. Career families also aim to facilitate the payment of market rates, since jobs can be benchmarked more directly with comparable jobs elsewhere.

Each of the career bands is broad, and although there is clearly a mid-point the company tells staff that they should not believe that the rate for the job is the mid-point or control point. Broadly speaking, staff who are developing their role should be in the lower quartile of the range, staff who are fully performing are at the median while those who are regularly exceeding all requirements should be being paid at the upper quartile. A normal distribution would be 25 per cent developing, 50 per cent fully performing and 25 per cent exceeding requirements.

A career-family structure in a university

In this university's career-family structure, illustrated in Table 19.2, the range of pay for all staff in a level is the same. Each of the generic roles has a role profile that is used for job matching purposes. There are only three families and the structure is presented to demonstrate that while teaching, learning and research are the reasons the university exists, managerial and learning support are essential for this purpose to be achieved. This arrangement also facilitates the definition of career paths between families, especially from learning support roles to teaching and research roles.

Table 19.2 University career-family structure

Levels	Career families		
	Managerial, professional administrative and support	Teaching, learning and research	Learning and research support
1	Support worker		Learning support assistant
2	Administrator/ Senior support worker		Learning support worker
3	Senior Administrator/ Section head/Craft worker		Senior learning support worker
4	Specialist or professional/ Activity leader	Associate lecturer/ Research associate	Advancer learning support worker
5	Senior specialist or professional Head of small/medium-sized department	Lecturer/researcher	Learning support expert/ Team leader
6	Leading specialist or professional, Head of large operational department	Senior lecturer/Research fellow/Reader	Leading learning support expert/ Departmental manager
7	Head of major department	Professor/Head of department	Head of major department
8	Head of major function		

Career families at NSPCC

There are seven career families in the NSPCC covering the different job functions such as Work with children, Fundraising, IT and Finance. The families were developed by evaluating all jobs using a new and tailor-made system of analytical job matching. Detailed role profiles were written and then jobs were slotted into the new structure of seven grades by matching them with the most appropriate grade description.

Career-family structure at XANSA

The categorization of career families, jobs, jobs map and skills profiles for each job at XANSA is known as the career framework. It is a tool that provides a common approach to people development and performance management and is designed to help employees and line managers to:

- identify career options;
- prepare for performance review and personal development discussions;
- assess suitability for job moves;
- identify training and development needs;
- assist in recruitment and selection interviews;
- position new employees into appropriate roles.

The career families fall into four groups:

- Delivery: design, build/integrate, run and support, management, business services and training.
- Consultancy.
- Business development: general management, sales and strategic development, and client development.
- Professional support: business support, finance human resources and marketing/communications.

Job-family structures

Job-family structures as illustrated in Figure 19.10 resemble career structures, in that separate families are identified and levels of knowledge, skills and competency requirements defined for each level, thus indicating career paths and providing the basis for grading jobs by matching role profiles to level definitions. Like career families, job families may have different numbers of levels depending on the range of responsibility they cover.

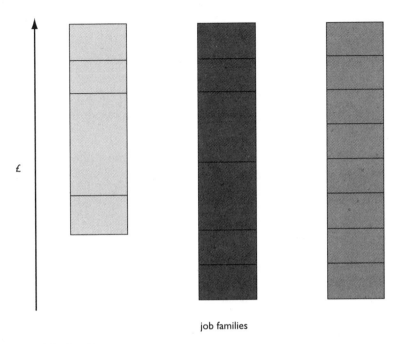

job families

Figure 19.10   A job-family structure

The difference between a career-family structure and a job-family structure is that in the former there is a common grade and pay structure. Jobs in the same level in each career family are deemed to be the same size as assessed by job evaluation, and the pay ranges in corresponding levels across the career families are the same. In contrast, the families in a job-family structure have in effect their own pay structures that take account of different levels of market rates between families (this is sometimes called 'market grouping'). The size of jobs and rates of pay can vary between the same levels in different job families, which means that there may be no read-across between them unless they are underpinned by job evaluation. Because they may cover a number of market groups, there are often more families in a job-family structure than in a career-family structure.

Advantages and disadvantages

Job-family structures can help organizations to flex rates of pay for different occupations to reflect variations in market rates and therefore provide for competitive pay to attract and retain people with essential skills. They can also indicate career paths within and, to a certain extent, between families.

But they can result in unequal pay for work of equal value between job families. This can arise if jobs of the same size are paid differently when pay levels vary between families to cater for market rate pressures. Such variations may be difficult to justify objectively because the market pay differentials in job-family structures are common to a whole family. In other structures, including career-family structures, the alternative and preferable approach is to use market supplements, which are easier to justify on an individual basis. Pay inequities in job-family structures can also arise because of read-across difficulties when trying to assess the relative size of jobs in different families. In theory this problem can be solved by the use of job evaluation but in practice this is difficult when there are considerable differences in the structure and definition of family levels.

In addition, like career-family structures, job families can be more difficult to develop, explain and manage than single grade structures.

Examples

Job-family structure at BT

The overall objective of setting up the new grade and pay structure in BT was to be simple and complete, avoiding over-complicated structures. More specifically, the company decided to opt for a system of job families in order to:

- achieve internal consistency of reward in alignment with external market rates;

- ensure that status, rank and relative position within hierarchies will become less important than what an individual achieves;

- help to clarify the roles and potential career paths available to individuals, particularly within a job family and, to a certain extent, between families;

- offer visibility of roles and salary ranges across other job families;

- achieve more flexibility in managing reward for different occupations to reflect differences in market rates and therefore provide for competitive pay to attract and retain people with essential skills.

The job-family structure was developed to replace a traditional graded structure containing eight core grades together with a separate sales structure. Ranges were 'quite broad' with significant overlap. According to the Connect trade union, there were 'deep-rooted problems' with the system. In what was once a typical multi-graded pay structure the emphasis was very much on hierarchy: the only way ahead was upward, through promotion or re-grading. The focus is now on flexible roles and the individual's contribution in the role, and more priority is given to external competitiveness. A salary range provides BT line managers with flexibility in managing reward within their teams. Gone are the days when pay progression and career development at BT were simply a matter of getting promotion to a higher grade.

A job-family structure in the Financial Services Authority (FSA)

The FSA has 12 job families that vary in size from the 38 people in economics and research to 900 in regulatory. Within each job family there are a number of broad levels, ranging from four to six according to the family. The levels reflect the different contributions that individuals make according to their skills, knowledge and experience, and the roles they perform.

Each level has an associated indicative pay range that has been determined by comparing levels in the markets in which the FSA competes for staff. Pay ranges are used rather than a specific rate for the job, to reflect that there is no single market rate of pay for a given job. Instead, there is a range of pay in the market related to the specific backgrounds, experience and delivery of individuals performing the roles. The broad overlapping ranges are designed to give management the flexibility to reflect the differences in contribution that individuals are making.

A job-family structure at IMS Health

An example of a job-family approach is provided by IMS Health, a global business providing information for pharmaceutical companies that employs a large proportion of scientists. The aim of the development programme was 'to evolve a system which could be flexible enough to cope with the ever-changing business environment we were in'. The reason for going down the job-family route was that it would give IMS Health the flexibility needed, bearing in mind the different functions operating in the organization. Defining career paths was an important consideration affecting the decision to develop job families, as was the need to focus on establishing appropriate pay levels in each job family that were related to market rates. The progression policy is for a personal development plan to be prepared for individuals who were recruited to a role below the reference point that would enable them to reach the level of competence required. A salary development plan would also be prepared to bring up the individual's rate of pay to the reference point. Progression to the reference point (in effect competence-related pay) is determined by managers within their budgets. Individuals were briefed during induction both on the career opportunities available to them and the reward associated with their progress.

A job-family structure at Kent County Council

Jobs are allocated to one of 35 generic job profiles organized into seven job families. They were evaluated using the Hay system and then placed into one of six pay grades. Summary band descriptions of these grades have been written to provide staff with a better understanding of why their job falls in a particular grade, and the analytical points factor system ensures that staff are all evaluated on a fair and equal basis.

A job-family structure at Nationwide

Nationwide decided to opt for a system of job families because they:

- offer the flexibility to respond to occupational and labour market pressures, in contrast to more rigid systems where market rates may fall outside the grading structure;

- encourage flexible working practices and multiskilling;

- encourage people to move jobs and build up a broad base of skills in different areas while still remaining in the same job family, although there must be flexibility in the pay ranges to reward people for this;

- clarify routes to career progression;

- flatten the organizational structure, driving accountability down to the lowest possible level so that the person dealing with the customers is empowered to solve their problems.

The job-family structure was developed following a detailed analysis of work. Jobs across the whole organization were found to fall into three broad areas – customer service, support services and specialist advice – providing the basis on which to group roles into job families. The project considered whether to construct families on the basis of function or on the basis of similarities in the nature of people's work. The latter was chosen as it was believed that this would help to keep the number of families to a minimum. It was subsequently decided to base the new structure on 11 job families, each with five levels reflecting the extent of employees' decision-making responsibilities, which range from level 1, where decision making extends over a few days or weeks to level 5, director level, where strategic decision making involves tasks with a time span of between one and five years.

Combined career/job-family and broad-banded structures

It is possible to combine career or job-family structures with broad-banded structures. This can be done by superimposing a broad-banded structure on career/job families, as illustrated in Figure 19.11. In effect this means that in each job or career family the levels are restricted to four or five rather than the more typical seven or eight.

Another approach to the combination of family and broad-banded structures is to divide each band in a broad-banded structure into job families, as illustrated in Figure 19.12. This enables internal and external relativities to be dealt with individually for each family and also identifies career paths within families.

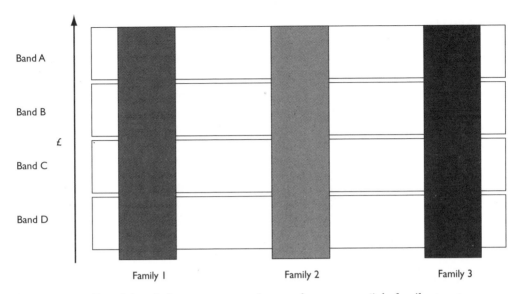

Figure 19.11   Broad-banded structure superimposed on a career/job-family structure

Figure 19.12   Broad bands divided into career families

Pay spines

Pay spines are found in the public sector or in agencies and charities that have adopted a public sector approach to reward management. They consist of a series of incremental 'pay points' extending from the lowest to the highest-paid jobs covered by the structure, as illustrated in Figure 19.13. Typically, pay spine increments are between 2.5 per cent and 3 per cent. They may be standardized from the top to the bottom of the spine, or the increments may vary at different levels, sometimes widening towards the top. Job grades are aligned to the pay spine, and the pay ranges for the grades are defined by the relevant scale of pay points. The width of grades can vary and job families may have different pay spines. Progression through a grade is based on service, although an increasing number of organizations provide scope for accelerating increments or providing additional increments above the top of the scale for the grade to reward contribution or merit.

Advantages and disadvantages of pay spines

The advantages of pay spines are first that they just about manage themselves. Either no decisions on pay progression have to be made by management and line managers, or decisions on extra increments, if they are provided for, are made within an explicit framework. Additionally, because the need for managers to make possibly biased or inconsistent judgements on pay increases does not exist or is severely limited, they give the impression of being fairer than structures where progression is governed by managerial decisions on performance or contribution. For this reason they are favoured by trade unions and many managements in the public sector.

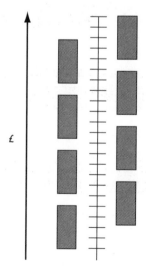

Figure 19.13 A pay spine

The disadvantages are that: 1) relating pay almost entirely to service means that people are rewarded for 'being there' and not for the value of their contribution, 2) pay spines can be costly in organizations with low staff turnover where everyone drifts to the top of the scale, and 3) where there are a large number of incremental points in the scale, equal value complications can arise as men progress to the top while the progress of women is delayed because of career breaks. For this reason the Local Government Pay Commission recommended a move away from service-related increments to pay for contribution, restricting increments to the first few years in a job.

Spot rates

Some organizations do not have a graded structure at all for any jobs, or for certain jobs such as directors. Instead they use 'spot rates'. These may also be called the 'rate for the job', more typically for manual jobs where there is a defined skilled or semi-skilled market rate, which may be negotiated with a trade union. Spot rates are quite often used in retail firms such as B&Q for customer service staff (see Chapter 21).

Spot rates are sometimes attached to a person rather than a job. Unless they are negotiated, rates of pay and therefore relativities are governed by market rates and managerial judgement. Spot rates are not located within grades and there is no defined scope for progression while on the spot rate. There may, however, be scope for moving on to higher spot rates as skill, competence or contribution increases. Job holders may be eligible for incentive bonuses on top of the spot rate.

Spot rates can be used where there is a very simple hierarchy of jobs, as in some manufacturing and retailing companies. They may be adopted by organizations that want the maximum amount of scope to pay what they like. They often exist in small or start-up organizations that do not want to be constrained by a formal grade structure and prefer to retain the maximum amount of flexibility. But they can result in serious inequities that may be difficult to justify.

Individual job grades

Individual job grades are, in effect, spot rates to which a defined pay range of, say, 20 per cent on either side of the rate has been attached to provide scope for pay progression based on performance, competence or contribution. Again, the mid-point of the range is fixed by reference to job evaluation and market rate comparisons.

Individual grades are attached to jobs not persons but there may be more flexibility for movement between grades than in a conventional grade structure. This can arise when people have expanded their role and it is considered that this growth in the level of responsibility needs to be recognized without having to upgrade the job. Individual job grades may be restricted to certain jobs, for example more senior managers, where flexibility in fixing and increasing rates of pay is felt to be desirable. They provide for greater flexibility than more conventional structures but can be difficult to manage and justify and can result in pay inequities. As described earlier in this chapter, the 'zones' that are often established in broad-banded structures have some of the characteristics of individual job grades.

Choice of grade and pay structures

There is a choice among the different types of structures. Their advantages and disadvantages are summarized in Table 19.3 and this is followed in Table 19.4 by an assessment of the criteria for choice of structure.

Table 19.3 Summary description of different grade and pay structures

Type of structure	Features	Advantages	Disadvantages
Narrow-graded	• A sequence of job grades – 10 or more. • Narrow pay ranges eg 20%–40%. • Progression usually linked to performance.	• Clearly indicate pay relativities. • Facilitate control. • Easy to understand.	• Create hierarchical rigidity. • Prone to grade drift. • Inappropriate in a delayered organization.
Broad-graded	• A sequence of between 6 and 9 grades. • Fairly broad pay ranges, eg 40%–50%. • Progression linked to contribution and may be controlled by thresholds or zones.	As for narrow graded structures but in addition: • the broader grades can be defined more clearly; • better control can be exercised over grade drift.	• Too much scope for pay progression. • Control mechanisms can be provided but they can be difficult to manage. • May be costly.

Table 19.3 *continued*

Type of structure	Features	Advantages	Disadvantages
Broad-banded	• A series of, often, 5 or 6 'broad' bands. • Wide pay bands – typically between 50% and 80%. • Progression linked to contribution and competence.	• More flexible. • Reward lateral development and growth in competence. • Fit new style organizations.	• Create unrealistic expectations of scope for pay rises. • Seem to restrict scope for promotion. • Difficult to understand. • Equal pay problems.
Career family	• Career families identified and defined. • Career paths defined for each family in terms of key activities and competence requirements. • Same grade and pay structure for each family.	• Clarify career paths within and between families. • Facilitate the achievement of equity between families and therefore equal pay. • Facilitate level definitions.	• Could be difficult to manage. • May *appear* to be divisive if 'silos' emerge.
Job family	• Separate grade and pay structures for job families containing similar jobs. • Progression linked to competence and/or contribution.	• Can appear to be divisive. • May inhibit lateral career development. • May be difficult to maintain internal equity between job families unless underpinned by job evaluation.	• Facilitate pay differentiation between market groups. • Define career paths against clear criteria.
Pay spine	• A series of incremental pay points covering all jobs. • Grades may be superimposed. • Progression linked to service.	• Easy to manage. • Pay progression not based on managerial judgement.	• No scope for differentiating rewards according to performance. • May be costly as staff drift up the spine.

Table 19.4   Grade and pay structures: criteria for choice

Type of structure	Criteria for choice – the structure may be considered more appropriate when:
Narrow-graded	• The organization is large and bureaucratic with well defined and extended hierarchies. • Pay progression is expected to occur in small but relatively frequent steps. • The culture is one in which much significance is attached to status as indicated by gradings. • Some but not too much scope for pay progression is wanted.
Broad-graded	• It is believed that if there is a relatively limited number of grades it will be possible to define and therefore differentiate them more accurately as an aid to better precision when grading jobs. • An existing narrow-graded structure is the main cause of grade drift. • It is considered that pay progression through grades can be related to contribution and that it is possible to introduce effective control mechanisms.
Broad-banded	• Greater flexibility in pay determination and management is required. • It is believed that job evaluation should no longer drive grading decisions. • The focus is on rewarding people for lateral development. • The organization has been de-layered.
Career family	• There are distinct families, and different career paths within and between families can be identified and defined. • There is a strong emphasis on career development in the organization. • Robust methods of defining competencies exist.
Job family	• There are distinct market groups that need to be rewarded differently. • The range of responsibility and the basis upon which levels exist vary between families. • It is believed that career paths need to be defined in terms of competence requirements.
Pay spine	• This is the traditional approach in a public or voluntary sector organization and it fits the culture. • It is believed to be impossible to measure different levels of contribution fairly and consistently. • Ease of administration is an important consideration.

Approaches to the design of the most popular types of structure, namely broad-graded and career family, are described below.

Developing a grade and pay structure

This section describes how two of the most popular types of structure – broad-graded and career family – can be developed. Whichever structure is selected, there will be a number of design options. These comprise the number of grades, bands or levels, the width of the grades (the span of pay ranges), the differentials between grades, the degree to which there should be overlap between grades, if any, and the method of pay progression within grades. In career-family structures there are options concerning the number of families, the composition of families and the basis upon which levels should be defined. The options are summarized in Table 19.5.

Table 19.5   Grade and pay structure design options

Design feature	Design considerations
Number of grades, levels or bands	• The range and types of roles to be covered by the structure. • The range of pay and job evaluation points scores to be accommodated. • The number of levels in the organizational hierarchy (this will be an important factor in a broad-banded structure). • Decisions on where grade boundaries should be placed following a job evaluation exercise that has produced a ranked order of jobs – this might identify the existence of clearly defined clusters of jobs at the various levels in the hierarchy between which there are significant differences in job size. • The problem of 'grade drift' (unjustified upgradings in response to pressure, lack of promotion opportunities or because job evaluation has been applied laxly), which can be increased if there are too many narrow grades.
Pay range spans	• Views on the scope that should be allowed for performance, contribution or career progression within grade. • Equal pay considerations – wide spans, especially extended incremental scales, are a major cause of pay gaps between men and women because women, who are more likely to have career breaks than men, may not have the same opportunity as men to progress to the upper regions of the range. • In a broad-banded structure, the range of market rates and job evaluation scores covering the jobs allocated to the band.

Table 19.5 *continued*

Design feature	Design considerations
Differentials between pay ranges	• Differentials between pay ranges should provide scope to recognize increases in job size between successive grades. • If differentials are too close – less than 10 per cent – many jobs become borderline cases, which can result in a proliferation of appeals and arguments about grading. • Large differentials below senior management level of more than 25 per cent can create problems for marginal or borderline cases because of the amount at stake. • In most organizations with conventional grade structures a differential of between 15 and 20 per cent is appropriate except, perhaps, at the highest levels.
Pay range overlap	• There is a choice on whether or not pay ranges should overlap and, if so, by how much. • Large overlaps of more than 10 per cent can create equal pay problems where, as is quite common, men are clustered at the top of their grades and women are more likely to be found at the lower end.
Pay progression	• There is a choice of methods of pay progression between the various forms of contingent pay, namely performance, contribution or competence-related as described in Chapter 10, and the fixed service-related increments common in the public sector.

The steps required to design graded and career-family pay structures are described below.

Graded pay structure design

Graded pay structure involves first designing the grade structure and then deciding on the pay ranges that should be attached to it.

The two approaches to designing the grade structure are: 1) the derived method in which decisions on the grade structure are led by point-factor job evaluation; and 2) the pre-emptive method in which the number of grades is determined first and each grade is then defined as a basis for analytical matching or market pricing.

The derived method (use of point-factor job evaluation)

The derived method consists of the following steps:

1. Use point-factor job evaluation to produce a rank order of jobs according to their job evaluation scores.

2. Either (a) take a preliminary view on the preferred number of grades or (b) analyse the rank order to establish by inspection where jobs might be grouped into grades and how many grades emerge from this procedure.

3. Decide where the boundaries that will define grades should be placed in the rank order (guidelines on defining boundaries are given in Figure 19.14).

4. Remember that, so far as possible, the grade boundaries in the rank order should divide groups or clusters of jobs that are significantly different in size, so that all the jobs placed in a grade are clearly smaller than the jobs in the next higher grade and larger than the jobs placed in the next lower grade.

Table 19.6 Method of deciding on grade boundaries

Analyse the rank order to identify any significant gaps in the points scores between adjacent jobs. These natural breaks in points scores will then constitute the boundaries between clusters of jobs which can be allocated to adjacent grades. This is the preferred approach but in many cases there will be no significant gaps. If so, the following method can be used:

● Jobs with common features as indicated by the job evaluation factors are grouped together so that a distinction can be made between the characteristics of the jobs in different grades – it should be possible to demonstrate that the jobs grouped into one grade resemble each other more than they resemble jobs placed in adjacent grades.

● The grade hierarchy should take account of the organizational hierarchy, ie jobs in which the job holder reports to a higher level job holder should be placed in a lower grade although this principle should not be followed slavishly when an organization is over-hierarchical with, perhaps, a series of one-over-one reporting relationships.

● The boundaries should not be placed between jobs mainly carried out by men and jobs mainly carried out by women.

● The boundaries should ideally not be placed immediately above jobs in which large numbers of people are employed because this will result in a large number of appeals against the grading.

● The grade width in terms of job evaluation points should represent a significant step in demands on job holders as indicated by the job evaluation scheme.

The grades in a structure established in this manner can be defined in the form of grade profiles using the job evaluation factors as the headings for each profile. These can form the basis for analytical matching.

Pre-emptive method

The pre-emptive method takes place in the following steps:

1. Assume number of grades. The assumption on how many grades are required is based on an analysis of the existing hierarchy of jobs and a judgement on how many levels are needed to produce a logical grouping of those jobs, level by level. A logical grouping is one in which each grade contains jobs whose levels are broadly comparable and there is a step difference in the degree of responsibility between each level.

2. Define grades. There is a choice between a simple non-analytical or semi-analytical job classification approach and a full analytical approach. The job classification approach involves preparing an overall definition of the grade to enable 'job slotting' to take place. This means slotting 'whole jobs', ie ones that have not been analysed under job evaluation factor headings, to grades by comparing the whole-job description with grade. A full analytical approach involves the preparation of grade profiles. These use job evaluation factors as the headings for the profile of each grade, which can be compared with role profiles set out under the same headings so that analytical matching can take place.

3. Revise initial assumption as necessary. The process of definition may reveal that the number of grades assumed to be required initially was either too many (the distinctions between them cannot be made with sufficient clarity) or too few (it becomes apparent that the range of jobs to be fitted into the structure is too great to be accommodated into the number of grades available). If this is the case, the number of grades would have to be adjusted iteratively until a satisfactory result is obtained.

4. Match benchmark jobs. The benchmark jobs are matched to grades in accordance with a pre-determined analytical matching protocol, as described in the job evaluation toolkit. When matched, the information on the benchmark roles may suggest changes to the grade profiles, which would thus become even more realistic.

5. Match remaining roles. The remaining roles can be matched to the grade profiles using the protocol. A confirmation of the match can be obtained by comparing them with the graded benchmark roles.

Pay range design

The steps required to determine pay ranges are:

1. Obtain information on the market rates for benchmark jobs where available. If possible this should indicate the median rate and the upper and lower quartiles. Remember that there may be some key jobs for which market rate data is not available.

2. List the jobs within each grade on the basis of job evaluation (these might be limited to benchmark jobs that have been evaluated but there must be an adequate number of them if a proper basis for the design is to be provided).

3. Establish the actual rates of pay of the job holders.

4. For each grade set out the range of pay for job holders and calculate their average or median rate of pay (the pay practice point). It is helpful to plot this pay practice data as illustrated in Figure 19.14, which shows pay in each grade against job evaluation scores and includes a pay practice trend line.

5. Agree policy on how the organization's pay levels should relate to market rates – its 'market stance'. This could be at the median, or above the median if it is believed that pay levels should be more competitive.

6. Calculate the average market rates for the benchmark jobs in each grade according to pay stance policy, eg the median rates. This produces the range market reference point.

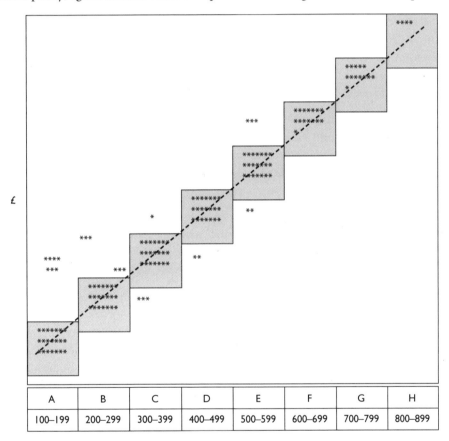

A	B	C	D	E	F	G	H
100–199	200–299	300–399	400–499	500–599	600–699	700–799	800–899

Pay practice trend line - - - - - - - -

Figure 19.14 Scattergram of evaluations and pay

7. Compare the practice and market reference points in each range and decide on the range reference point. This usually becomes the mid-point of the pay range for the grade and is regarded as the competitive rate for a fully competent job holder in that grade. This is a judgemental process that takes into account the difference between the practice and policy points, the perceived need to be more competitive if policy rates are higher, and the likely costs of increasing rates.

8. Examine the pay differentials between reference points in adjacent grades. These should provide scope to recognize increases in job size, and, so far as possible, variations between differentials should be kept to a minimum. If differentials are too close – less than 10 per cent – many jobs become borderline cases, which can result in a proliferation of appeals and arguments about grading. Large differentials below senior management level of more than 25 per cent can create problems for marginal or borderline cases because of the amount at stake. Experience has shown that in most organizations with conventional grade structures a differential of between 15 and 20 per cent is appropriate except, perhaps, at the highest levels.

9. Decide on the range of pay around the reference point. This might be 20 per cent on either side of the reference point; thus if that point is 100 per cent, the range is from 80 per cent to 120 per cent. The range can, however, vary in accordance with policy on the scope for progression and, if a given range of pay has to be covered by the structure, the fewer the grades the wider the ranges.

10. Decide on the extent, if any, to which pay ranges should overlap. Overlap recognizes that an experienced job holder at the top of a range may be making a greater contribution than an inexperienced job holder at the lower end of the range above. Large overlaps of more than 10 per cent can create equal pay problems where men are at the top of their grades and women are likely to be found at the lower end.

11. Review the impact of the above pay range decisions on the pay of existing staff in order to calculate implementation costs. Establish the number of staff whose present rate of pay is above or below the pay range for the grade into which their jobs have been placed, and the extent of the difference between the rate of pay of those below the minimum and the lowest point of that pay range. Calculate the costs of bringing them up to the minimum. Software such as the pay modellers produced by Link and Pilat or locally tailored Excel spreadsheets can be used for this purpose.

When the above steps have been completed, it may be necessary to review the decisions made on the grade structure and pay reference points and ranges, especially when the costs calculated in Stage 11 are too high. Iteration is almost always necessary to obtain a satisfactory result that conforms to the criteria for grade and pay structures mentioned earlier and minimizes the cost of implementation. Alternatives can be modelled using the software mentioned above.

Career-family structure design

The steps required to design a career-family structure are:

1. Select and define career families.

    Decide on what career families are required. Typically, not more than four or five families are identified. The choice of families is between functions, such as marketing or finance, and activities, such as administration and support staff, or a combination of functions and activities.

2. Decide on the number of levels in the career-family structure and define them with level profiles.

    Level profiles are required that apply to all the families in the structure, bearing in mind that the defining characteristic of a career family is that the levels and the pay ranges attached to them are common to all the families in the structure (as distinct from job-family structures in which levels and ranges differ between some or all of the families).

3. Identify, define and match benchmark roles.

    A representative sample of benchmark roles are identified, defined as role profiles and matched with the level profiles as described above for a graded structure.

4. Conduct analytical matching.

    Analytical matching procedures are used to allocate the remaining roles to levels. It is advisable to test the process first in one family; this will not only test the procedure but will also enable model career-family structures to be used when dealing with the other career families.

5. Attach pay ranges to levels.

    Pay ranges are established for each level, as described above for graded structures.

6. Validate relativities between career families.

    The allocation of jobs to levels through matching across the career families is validated by reference to job evaluation scores to ensure that the relativities between them look reasonable. Some adjustment may need to be made as a result of this cross-check if it exposes inequities between families.

Developing a grade and pay structure: six tips

- Involve stakeholders (top management, line managers and staff) in drawing up guiding principles on the design and operation of the structure.

- Analyse the options available and select one that meets the guiding principles and fits the values and methods of work in the business.

- Keep it as simple as possible.

- Ensure that good data are available on which to base the design (job evaluation and market rates).

- Obtain the buy-in of stakeholders.

- Communicate very widely and very often what is being done and why.

References

Armstrong, M (2000) Feel the width, *People Management*, 3 February, pp 34–38

Armstrong, M and Brown, D (2001) *New Dimensions in Pay Management*, CIPD, London

Armstrong, M and Murlis, H (1988) *Reward Management*, 1st edn, Kogan Page, London

Armstrong, M and Ryden, O (1997) *The IPD Guide on Broadbanding*, IPD, London

Chartered Institute of Personnel and Development (CIPD) (2009) *Reward Management 2009: A survey of policy and practice*, CIPD, London

e-reward (2004) *Survey of Grade and Pay Structures*, e-reward.co.uk, Stockport

Fay, C H, Schulz, E, Gross, S E and Van De Voort, D (2004) Broadbanding, pay ranges and labour costs: an empirical test, *WorldatWork Journal*, **19** (2), pp 21–29

Gilbert, D and Abosch, K S (1996) *Improving Organizational Effectiveness Through Broad-banding*, American Compensation Association, Scottdale, Ariz

Jaques, E (1961) *Equitable Payment*, Heinemann, London

Leblanc, P V (1992) Banding: the new pay structure for the transformed organization, *Journal of Compensation and Benefits*, January–February, pp 34–38

Risher, H (2002) Planning a 'next generation' salary system, *Compensation & Benefits Review*, November/December, pp 19–23

Part IV
Rewarding Special Groups

20

Rewarding Directors and Senior Executives

Key concepts and terms

- Agency theory
- Bonus scheme
- Clearing mechanism
- Combined Code
- Corporate governance
- Deferred bonus
- Earnings per share
- Executive restricted share scheme
- Incentive alignment
- Long-term bonus

- Market forces
- Moral hazard
- Non-executive director
- Performance share scheme
- Remuneration committee
- Share option scheme
- Shareholder return
- Shareholder value
- Stewardship theory
- Tournament theory

Learning outcomes

On completing this chapter you should be able to define these key concepts. You should also know about:

- The problem with executive pay levels
- The factors affecting the level and nature of executive rewards
- The role of remuneration committees
- The meaning and significance of corporate governance
- The combined code on corporate governance

- The Turner Review proposals on executive remuneration and risk
- The components of executives' remuneration – base pay, bonuses and share schemes
- Executive benefits
- Directors' contracts

Introduction

Probably no aspect of remuneration has attracted as much attention recently as that of the pay of directors and senior executives, especially since the 2008/09 banking crisis. Searching questions are being asked frequently about the level of remuneration, the basis upon which pay decisions are made, the conditions for earning bonuses, and pension arrangements.

This chapter starts with a review of the issues surrounding executive pay: What is the problem? What are the factors affecting executive pay? Why has it grown so much? Decisions on the pay of directors and, to a degree, senior executives are influenced by corporate governance considerations and the associated codes, as described in the next part of the chapter. The final section examines the different aspects of remuneration packages for directors and senior executives, namely base pay, incentives, benefits and service contracts.

Executive pay levels

According to Duncan Brown (2009), executive pay is out of control. As reported by Seager and Finch in *The Guardian* in September 2009, the think tank Compass has established that the average ratio of chief executive-to-employee pay has risen from 47 to 128 over the past 10 years. A non-executive director interviewed by Perkins and Hendry (2005) during their research on top pay remarked: 'There is neither a moral nor a market argument to justify the explosion in pay, but once started, it is hard to stop. You cannot be seen to be left out.'

It has been established by research (Conyon and Leech, 1994; Gomez-Mejia and Balkin, 1992; Gregg *et al* 1993) that there is no evidence that the huge increases in pay have resulted in improved company performance. Timothy Garton Ash (2009) commented that:

The conduct of the bankers who pitched us into the slurry pit – not all bankers of course, but quite a few of them – may not have been illegal but it was selfish, irresponsible and immoral. Year after year they took huge personal gains for themselves on the basis of assets whose real nature and prospects they either did not understand or cynically ignored. Their pay and bonuses, out of all proportion to the sums almost everyone else was earning in the societies around them, were justified as 'performance-related', but 'performance' was measured by inadequate indicators over too short a time-frame. Remuneration at the top was based on competitive benchmarking against rivals, and big shots were heard to complain that it was 'unfair' that someone else was earning £5m a year while they were only earning £4 million a year.

Factors affecting the level and nature of executive rewards

The five factors are agency theory, tournament theory, market forces, the perceived inherent value of chief executives and the operation of remuneration committees.

Agency theory

The basic proposition of agency theory is that the only way in which owners (principals) can get loyalty from their managers (agents) is by paying them more. This is because owners do not have complete control over their managers and the latter may act in their own interests and not those of the owners. It is therefore desirable to operate a system of financial incentives to motivate behaviour and generate results that are in the interests of the owners. This is called 'incentive alignment'.

Gomez-Mejia *et al* (2005) suggested that agency theory does not assume opportunism on the part of the agent, but simply that the agent has self-interest, which can manifest as opportunism under certain conditions. Opportunism is defined as: 'The adaptation of one's actions to circumstances in order to further one's immediate interests, without regard for basic principles or consequences'.

According to Perkins and Hendry (2005):

Agency problems arise for investors in assessing whether they are getting the best return from the executives to whom the firm's management is delegated [who can in effect act as the dominant stakeholder]. If it were easy to assure alignment between payments (inputs) to executives and performance (outputs), shareholders could simply pay their executives a fixed salary (in effect, a form of insurance payment), and then assess whether that agent is supplying optimal effort in the shareholder's interest. That not being the case, they resort (according to the theory) to forms of variable performance-related pay.

It has been suggested by Bruce *et al* (2005) that this provides rewards for risk-taking.

Tournament theory

Tournament theory explains that the remuneration of a chief executive is in effect a prize and executives expend effort to increase the likelihood of winning it. As Conyon *et al* (2001) note, the theory explains that: 'Analogous to a sports game, what matters for winning is not the absolute level of performance, but how well one does in relation to the other competitors.' The effect is that the relationship between organizational and pay levels is convex, with a considerably greater gap between the next-to-highest and the highest levels.

Market forces

The way market forces work in executive pay tends to be through 'comparisons with other executives in relevant industry labour markets' (Stiles and Taylor, 2002). Thus, the Hampel Report (1998) stated that British boardroom remuneration will be 'largely determined by the market', although the earlier Greenbury Report (1995) argued that the market was imperfect and only set a broad framework.

Data collected by Perkins and Hendry (2005) over 10 years for 81 of the FTSE 100 companies tended to show a relative lack of intra-company movement among executive directors, in particular internationally. This, they commented, undermines the presumption of a market in executives and hence in executive pay. They went on to point out that: 'While the evidence for a market with price as a clearing mechanism remains questionable, therefore, there is certainly no widespread subjective sense of such a market among those who are closest to it. Rather, there are a series of localized bargains.' They quoted a remuneration committee member they interviewed who categorically denied the existence of a recognizable market for executives, 'certainly not like that for beef or shares'. Instead, he said, there are 'just key people in unique positions at a given moment in time, who are not readily interchangeable'.

The perceived inherent value of chief executives

The price of chief executives may be influenced by beliefs in their value to the business as the generators of shareholder value. But as Perkins and Hendry (2005) wrote presciently: 'There is more spectacular evidence that misjudged CEO and board decisions contribute far more to destroying value than creating it (for example, GEC/Marconi, to name but one case).' Later events, notably crises in a number of banks largely due to the activities of their chief executives, have proved them right.

Remuneration committees

The Committee on Corporate Governance (2000) of the Stock Exchange and other reports recommended the establishment of remuneration committees to provide an independent basis for setting the salary levels and the rules covering incentives, share options, benefit entitlements and contract provisions for executive directors. Such committees were to be accountable to shareholders for the decisions they take and the non-executive directors who sat on them would have no personal financial interests at stake. They would be constituted as sub-committees of company boards, and boards should elect both the chairman and the members. Their essential role would be to set broad policy for executive remuneration as a whole as well as the remuneration packages of executive directors and, sometimes, other senior executives. They should consist exclusively of non-executive directors and should determine remuneration policy and the reward packages of individual executive directors, which should appear as a section in the annual report. This report should include statements on remuneration policy and the methods used to form that policy and disclose details of the remuneration of individual directors. The Combined Code of Practice (see later in this chapter) laid down the principles they should take into account when considering pay levels.

Remuneration committees are now well established as bodies for making recommendations on directors' pay, often with the advice of remuneration consultants. The Combined Code states that they should avoid paying more than is necessary, and should also be sensitive to pay and employment conditions elsewhere in the group, especially when determining annual salary increases. But the extent to which they follow either of these precepts is often questionable. So is the degree to which they are independent; after all, members of the remuneration committee are also colleagues of the board members on whose remuneration they deliberate.

As Perkins and Hendry (2005) observed following their discussions with remuneration committee members, consultants engaged by managements to 'advise' committees were felt to be encouraging a 'pernicious process of choosing comparators' that 'just leads to the ratcheting up of top pay… The problem becomes particularly acute when companies all strive to achieve the statistically impossible feat of setting reward levels to locate themselves in the upper quartile of their benchmark group.' They also noted the ambiguities and weaknesses of the non-executive directors and commented that: 'The workings of a market in executive pay are fatally undermined by the social realities.'

Why has executive pay grown so much?

The reasons for the growth in executive rewards as explained by Dymond and Murlis (2009) are:

- Agency theory: shareholders must structure the CEO's compensation arrangements to reward behaviours that increase shareholder wealth (this is the most important reason).

- Tournament theory: the high rewards received by CEOs have little to do with what they deserve. Rather the main purpose of such rewards is to send signals to senior managers to motivate them to compete for the number one spot.

- The changing nature of companies and the increasing demands made on chief executives.

- Star culture: the creation of the celebrity CEO.

- The talent shortage.

- Pay disclosure in annual reports lead to demands from CEOs to achieve parity. Hampel (1998) noted that a perverse outcome of the requirements for greater disclosure of directors' pay and the administration of salary surveys was to help 'ratchet up' pay levels among full-time board members.

To which could be added the ways in which remuneration committees can sometimes function as conduits for pay increases, aided and abetted by remuneration consultants.

Corporate governance and executive remuneration

Corporate governance is the internal set of processes and policies that determine the way a corporation is directed and controlled, and serve the needs of shareholders and other stakeholders. It involves the board of a company and includes how members of that board are remunerated.

It is usually assumed that a company is owned by its shareholders and that the prime, if not the only responsibility, of its management (ie the board) is to increase the value of the shares owned by shareholders – shareholder value. But, as Simon Caulkin (2009) noted: 'Contrary to common assumptions, shareholders do not own companies (how could they and benefit from limited liability at the same time?), and directors owing their duty to the company can't be "agents" of shareholders – indeed they are charged with acting fairly as between all company members.' As reported by Caulkin, Professor Bob Garret recently told a meeting of the Human Capital Forum that the first duty of directors was not to shareholders but to the company itself: 'Organizations have to move from agency theory to stewardship theory.' The latter is the theory that managers, left on their own, will act as responsible stewards of the assets they control on behalf of all stakeholders. This may not necessarily happen in reality, but as an aspiration has more to offer than agency theory.

It follows that focusing only on increasing shareholder value is a questionable approach. Caulkin quotes Jack Welch, formerly head of GE and the foremost management icon of the age, as saying that shareholder value 'is the dumbest idea in the world – a result not a strategy – your main constituents are your employees, customers and products'.

The Combined Code on Corporate Governance

Corporations may or may not pursue shareholder value at the expense of good corporate governance or stewardship, but their role in general and their specific role in deciding on remuneration arrangements for directors has been questioned regularly since 1992 when the Cadbury committee reported. This was followed by a report from the Greenbury Committee (1995) and the Hampel Report (1998). These led to The Combined Code on Corporate Governance produced by the Financial Reporting Council in 2008, which lays down general principles of governance and a number of specific principles relating to the remuneration of directors. These are:

- Levels of remuneration should be sufficient to attract, retain and motivate directors of the quality required to run the company successfully, but a company should avoid paying more than is necessary for this purpose. A significant proportion of executive directors' remuneration should be structured so as to link rewards to corporate and individual performance.

- The remuneration committee should judge where to position their company relative to other companies. But they should use such comparisons with caution, in view of the risk of an upward ratchet of remuneration levels with no corresponding improvement in performance. They should also be sensitive to pay and employment conditions elsewhere in the group, especially when determining annual salary increases.

- The performance-related elements of remuneration should form a significant proportion of the total remuneration package of executive directors and should be designed to align their interests with those of shareholders and to give these directors keen incentives to perform at the highest levels.

- The remuneration committee should consider whether the directors should be eligible for annual bonuses. If so, performance conditions should be relevant, stretching and designed to enhance shareholder value. Upper limits should be set and disclosed. There may be a case for part payment in shares to be held for a significant period.

- Payouts or grants under all incentive schemes, including new grants under existing share option schemes, should be subject to challenging performance criteria that reflect the company's objectives. The total rewards potentially available should not be excessive.

- The remuneration committee should consider the pension consequences and associated costs to the company of basic salary increases and any other changes in pensionable remuneration, especially for directors close to retirement.

But it seems that these principles are frequently more honoured in the breach than in the observance.

The Turner Review

The banking crisis of 2008 prompted the Turner Review, which proposed the following code of good practice:

- Firms must ensure that their remuneration policies are consistent with effective risk management.

- Remuneration should reflect an individual's record of compliance with risk management procedures, rules and appropriate culture, as well as financial measures of performance.

- Financial measures used in remuneration policies should entail the adjustment of profit measures to reflect the relative riskiness of different activities.

- The predominant share (two-thirds or more) of bonuses that exceed a significant level, should be paid in a deferred form (deferred cash or shares), with a deferral period that is appropriate to the nature of the business and its risks.

- Payment of deferred bonuses should be linked to financial performance during the deferral period.

Directors' and senior executives' remuneration

The main elements of directors' and senior executives' remuneration are basic pay, short and long-term bonus or incentive schemes, share option and share ownership schemes, benefits and service contracts. The salary is usually a one-off, negotiated rate and commonly incorporates a golden hello or pay-off deal. It should be set through a remuneration committee that meets good practice guidelines.

Basic pay

Decisions on the base salary of directors and senior executives are usually founded on views about the market worth of the individuals concerned. Remuneration on joining the company is commonly settled by negotiation, often subject to the approval of a remuneration committee. Reviews of base salaries are then undertaken by reference to market movements and success as measured by company performance. Decisions on base salary are important not only in themselves but also because the level may influence decisions on the pay of both senior and middle managers. Bonuses are expressed as a percentage of base salary, share options may be allocated as a declared multiple of basic pay and, commonly, pension will be a generous proportion of final salary.

Bonus schemes

Virtually all major employers in the UK (90 per cent according to recent surveys by organizations such as Monks and Hay) have annual incentive (bonus) schemes for senior executives. Bonus schemes provide directors and executives with cash sums based on the measures of company and, frequently, individual performance.

Typically, bonus payments are linked to achievement of profit and/or other financial targets and they are sometimes 'capped'; that is, a restriction is placed on the maximum amount payable. There may also be elements related to achieving specific goals and to individual performance. Bonuses tend to be high – 70 per cent of base salary or more. They are ostensibly intended to motivate directors to achieve performance improvements for the business. A more common although not always disclosed reason for bonuses is to ensure that what is believed to be a competitive remuneration package is available: 'Everyone else is doing it so we must too.'

One of the problems with high bonus expectations is that of the 'moral hazard' involved. For example, directors might be tempted to manipulate reported profits to drive up the share price, frequently an important determinant of bonuses. Or they may go for high returns in risky short-term projects, ignoring the possible downside of longer-term losses.

Long-term bonuses

Cash bonus schemes can be extended over periods of more than one year on the grounds that annual bonuses focus too much on short-term results. The most common approach to providing longer-term rewards is through share ownership schemes as described later.

Deferred bonus schemes

Some companies have adopted deferred bonus schemes under which part of the executive's annual bonus is deferred for, say, two years. The deferred element is converted into shares, each of which is matched with an extra, free share on condition the executive remains employed by the company at the end of the deferral period. Such a scheme is designed to reward performance and loyalty to the company.

Scheme effectiveness

In an effective bonus scheme:

- Targets will be tough but achievable.

- The reward should be commensurate with the achievement.

- The targets will be quantified and agreed.

- The measures used will refer to the key factors that affect company performance, and these performance areas will be those that can be directly affected by the efforts of those eligible for bonus payments.

- The formula will be simple and clear.

On the evidence of recent bonus pay-outs to failing company directors, it does not seem that these criteria are being applied successfully.

Share option schemes

Many companies have share option schemes that give directors and executives the right to buy a block of shares on some future date at the share price ruling when the option was granted. They are a form of long-term incentive on the assumption that executives will be motivated to perform more effectively if they can anticipate a substantial capital gain when they sell their shares at a price above that prevailing when they took up the option.

Conditions may be laid down to the effect that the company's earnings per share (EPS) growth should exceed inflation by a set amount over a number of years (often three) and that the executive remains employed by the company at the exercise date.

The arguments advanced in favour of executive share options are that, first, it is right for executives to share in the success of their company to which, it is assumed, they have contributed and, second, they encourage executives to align their interests (incentive alignment) more closely in the longer term with those of the shareholders as a whole (the latter argument is based on agency theory although it is quite possible that those who advance it are unaware that such a thing as agency theory exists). The first point is valid as long as the reward for exercising share options is commensurate with the contribution of the executive to the improved performance of the business. The second point is dubious. The vast majority of shares acquired in this way are sold almost immediately and the gain is pocketed as extra income.

Share options have been severely criticized recently because of the enormous gains made by some executives. There is a strong feeling among the major investment institutions that share options do not achieve community of interest between executives and shareholders and are in effect no more than a form of cash bonus in which the pay-out has little or nothing to do with the executive's performance, and indeed can become a reward for failure.

Performance share schemes

Some companies have performance share schemes under which executives are provisionally awarded shares. The release of the shares is subject to the company's performance, typically determined on a sliding scale by reference to the company's total shareholder return (a combination of share price growth and dividend yield) ranking against its chosen peer companies over a three-year period. Release is also conditional on the executive remaining employed by the company at the vesting date. Such a scheme rewards loyalty to the company and the value delivered to shareholders in the form of share price performance and dividends but does not link directly to business performance.

Executive restricted share schemes

Under such schemes free shares are provisionally awarded to participants. These shares do not belong to the executive until they are released or vested; hence they are 'restricted'. The number of shares actually released to the executive at the end of a defined period (usually three or, less commonly, five years) will depend on performance over that period against specific targets. Thereafter there may be a further retention period when the shares must be held although no further performance conditions apply.

Benefits

Employee benefits for executives may amount to over 20 per cent of the total reward package. The most important element is the pension scheme, and directors may be provided with a much higher accrual rate than in a typical final salary scheme. This means that, typically, the maximum two-thirds pension can be achieved after 20 years' service or even less, rather than the 40 years it takes in a typical one-sixtieth scheme. Pensions are easily inflated, as in a recent notorious case, by presenting the departing director with a last-minute substantial increase in pensionable salary.

Service contracts

Long-term service contracts for directors have been fairly typical, but they are disliked in the City because of the high severance payments to departing chief executives and directors that are made if the contract is two or three years, even when it was suspected or actually the case that they had been voted off the board because of inadequate performance. Rolling contracts for directors are now more likely to be restricted to one year.

Rewarding directors: six tips

- Follow the principles of corporate governance laid down by the Combined Code.

- Make decisions on levels of remuneration by reference to objective evidence, not hearsay or assumptions.

- Justify rates of pay on the basis of the performance of the chief executive or director, as demonstrated by the performance of the business.

- Ensure that members of the remuneration committee are properly briefed and supported in making their recommendations.

- Subject all bonus plans to careful scrutiny to ensure that they conform to good practice.

- Subject proposed bonus payments to rigorous scrutiny to ensure that they genuinely reflect the level of performance achieved and do not reward failure.

References

Ash, T G (2009) This epochal crisis requires us to resolve the paradox of capitalism, *Guardian*, 7 May, p 28

Brown, D (2009) Executive pay remains out of control [online] www.e-reward.co.uk/blog

Bruce, A, Buck, T and Main, B G (2005) Top executive remuneration: a view from Europe, *Journal of Management Studies*, **42** (7), pp 1493–1506

Cadbury, A (1992) *Report of the Committee on the Financial Aspects of Corporate Governance*, Gee Publishing, London

Caulkin, S (2009) It's time to explode the myth of the shareholder, *Observer*, 29 March

The Combined Code on Corporate Governance (2008) The Financial Reporting Council, London

Committee on Corporate Governance (2000) *The Combined Code: Principles of good governance and code of best practice*, London Stock Exchange, London

Conyon, M J and Leech, D (1994) Top pay, company performance and corporate performance, *Oxford Bulletin of Economics and Statistics*, **56** (3), August, pp 229–47

Conyon, M J, Beck, S I and Sadler, G V (2001) Corporate tournaments and executive compensation: evidence from the UK, *Strategic Management Journal*, **22** (8), pp 805–15

Dymond, J and Murlis, H (2009) Executive rewards: 'don't you just give them loads of money?' in *Rethinking Reward*, ed S Corby, S Palmer and E Lindop, Palgrave Macmillan, Basingstoke

Gomez-Mejia, L R and Balkin, D B (1992) *Compensation, Organizational Strategy, and Firm Performance*, South Western, Cincinnati OH

Gomez-Mejia, L, Wiseman, R M and Dyke, B J (2005) Agency problems in diverse contexts: a global perspective, *Journal of Management Studies*, **42** (7), pp 1507–17

Greenbury, R (1995) Report of the Study Group on Directors' Remuneration, Gee Publishing, London

Gregg, P, Machin, S and Szymanski, S (1993) The disappearing relationship between directors' pay and corporate performance, *British Journal of Industrial Relations*, **3** (1), pp 1–9

Hampel, R (1998) *Committee on Corporate Governance: Final report*, Gee Publishing, London

Perkins, S and Hendry, P (2005) Ordering top pay: interpreting the signals, *Journal of Management Studies*, **42** (7), pp 1443–68

Seager, A and Finch, J (2009) Salary gap widens between workers and their directors, *The Guardian*, 16 September, p 20

Stiles, P and Taylor, B (2002) *Boards at Work: How directors view their roles and responsibilities*, Oxford University Press, Oxford

Turner, A (2009) *The Turner Review: A regulatory response to the banking crisis*, Financial Services Authority, London

21

Rewarding Sales and Customer Service Staff

Learning outcomes

On completing this chapter you should know about:

- Methods of rewarding sales staff
- Methods of rewarding customer service staff

Introduction

Sales and customer service staff make a strong and immediate impact on business results. This has led to an emphasis on financial incentives, especially for sales representatives and sales staff in retailers, who are often treated quite differently from other people. The reward system for sales and service staff also has to take account of the fact that they are the people who are in direct contact with customers, and this also applies to people in call centres.

Rewarding sales representatives

Sales representatives are more likely to be eligible for commission payments or bonuses than other staff on the grounds that their sales performance will depend on or at least be improved by financial incentives. Many companies believe that the special nature of selling and the type of person they need to attract to their sales force requires some form of additional bonus or commission to be paid. The nature of the work of sales representatives means that it is usually easy to specify targets and measure performance against them, and sales incentive schemes are therefore more likely to meet the line of sight requirement (ie that there should be a clear link between effort and performance) than schemes for other staff such as managers and administrators. Sales staff, including those in retail establishments, are often paid spot rates with a commission on sales.

Financial methods of rewarding sales staff

The approaches to rewarding sales staff described below are:

- salary only;
- basic salary plus commission;
- basic salary plus bonus;
- commission only.

Table 21.1 summarizes the different schemes, their advantages and disadvantages and when they may be appropriate.

Salary only

Companies may adopt a salary only (no commission or bonus) approach when sales staff have little influence over sales volume, when representing the company and generally promoting its products or services is more important than direct selling, and when the company wants to encourage sales staff to build up good and long-term relationships with their customers, the emphasis being on customer service rather than on high-pressure selling.

Basic salary only may also be paid to sales staff who work in highly seasonal industries where sales fluctuate considerably, and businesses where regular orders for food and other consumer goods give little opportunity for creative selling.

However, companies that do not pay commission or bonus may have a pay-for-contribution scheme that provides for consolidated increases based on an assessment of performance and competence in such areas as teamwork, customer relations, interpersonal skills and communications. Where sales staff have to work together to achieve results or where it is difficult to apportion a successful sale to individuals, a team pay approach may be adopted. Additionally, salary-only sales representatives may be eligible for incentives in the form of prizes as described later.

If no commission or bonus is offered, it is necessary for companies to ensure that the salaries paid to their sales staff are competitive. They have to take account of the total earnings of sales staff in markets from which they recruit people or where their own staff move. If they cannot or do not want to at least match these earnings they may have to offer other inducements to join or stay with the company. These can include opportunities for promotion, learning new skills, more stable pay and greater security.

Table 21.1 Summary of payment and incentive arrangements for sales staff

Method	Features	Advantages	Disadvantages	When appropriate
Salary only	Straight salary, no commission or bonus.	Encourages customer service rather than high pressure selling; deals with the problem of staff who are working in a new or unproductive sales territory; protects income when sales fluctuate for reasons beyond the individual's control.	No direct motivation through money; may attract under-achieving people who are subsidized by high achievers; increases fixed costs of sales because pay costs are not flexed with sales results.	When representing the company is more important than direct selling; staff have little influence on sales volume (they may simply be 'order takers'); customer service is all-important.
Salary plus commission	Basic salary plus cash commission calculated as a percentage of sales volume or value.	Direct financial motivation is provided related to what sales staff are there to do, ie generate sales; but they are not entirely dependent on commission – they are cushioned by their base salary.	Relating pay to the volume or value of sales is too crude an approach and may result in staff going for volume by concentrating on the easier-to-sell products not those generating high margins; may encourage high-pressure selling as in some financial services firms in the 1980s and 1990s.	When it is believed that the way to get more sales is to link extra money to results but a base salary is still needed to attract the many people who want to be assured of a reasonable basic salary which will not fluctuate but who still aspire to increase that salary by their own efforts.

Table 21.1 *continued*

Method	Features	Advantages	Disadvantages	When appropriate
Salary plus bonus	Basic salary plus cash bonus based on achieving and exceeding sales targets or quotas and meeting other selling objectives.	Provides financial motivation but targets or objectives can be flexed to ensure that particular sales goals are achieved, eg high margin sales, customer service.	Does not have a clear line of sight between effort and reward; may be complex to administer; sales representative may find the system hard to understand and resent the use of subjective judgements on performance other than sales.	When flexibility in providing rewards is important; it is felt that sales staff need to be motivated to focus on aspects of their work other than simply maximizing sales volume.
Commission only	Only commission based on a percentage of sales volume or value is paid, there is no basic salary.	Provides a direct financial incentive; attracts high performing sales staff; ensures that selling costs vary directly with sales; little direct supervision required.	Leads to high-pressure selling; may attract the wrong sort of people who are interested only in money and not customer service; focuses attention on high volume rather than profitability.	When sales performance depends mainly on selling ability and can be measured by immediate sales results; staff are not involved in non-selling activities; continuing relationships with customers are relatively unimportant.
Additional non-cash rewards	Incentives, prizes, cars, recognition, opportunities to grow.	Utilizes powerful non-financial motivators.	May be difficult to administer; does not provide a direct incentive.	When it is believed that other methods of payment need to be enhanced by providing additional motivators.

Basic salary plus commission

Salary plus commission plans provide for a proportion of total earnings to be paid in commission, while the rest is paid in the form of a fixed salary. The commission is calculated as a percentage of the value of sales. The proportion of commission varies widely. As a general rule it is higher when results depend on the ability and effort of individuals or when there is less emphasis on non-selling activities. As a rule of thumb, most sales managers believe that the commission element will not motivate their staff unless they have a reasonable opportunity to earn at least 20 per cent of base pay.

The commission may be a fixed percentage of all sales, possibly with a 'cap' or upper limit on earnings. Alternatively the commission rate can increase at higher levels of sales on a rising scale to encourage sales representatives to make even greater efforts.

Basic salary plus bonus

Cash bonuses may be paid on top of basic salary. They are based on the achievement of targets or quotas for sales volume, profit or sales 'contribution' (sales revenue minus variable expenses). They differ from commission payments in that the latter are based simply on a percentage of whatever sales have been attained. In a bonus scheme, targets or objectives may be set just for sales volume but they can also focus on particular aspects of the results that can be achieved by sales staff that it is felt should be stimulated. These may include the sales of high-margin or more profitable products or services in order to encourage staff to concentrate on them rather than simply aiming to achieve sales volume with low-margin products that are easier to sell. They may also cover reviving moribund accounts, promoting new products and minimizing bad debt. Other criteria may include the level of customer service, the volume of repeat business, the number of productive calls made, product knowledge, teamwork and quality of administration.

There are many ways in which bonuses can be determined. The method used will take into account the following considerations:

- The formula for relating bonuses to sales: a bonus may be triggered when a sales threshold is reached, with additions related to increased sales directly or on an accelerated basis.

- The size of bonus payments available at different levels of performance.

- The maximum bonus that will be paid out.

- The bonus criteria: sales revenue is often used, but some companies use profit or contribution to encourage sales representatives to focus on selling high-margin products rather than going for volume.

- Any other factors to be included in the bonus plan such as those mentioned above.

Commission only

Sales staff who are at the 'hard' end of selling (eg double glazing) may only receive a straight commission based on a percentage of the value of their sales. No basic salary is paid.

Additional non-cash rewards

While it is possible that the prime motivator for a typical sales representative is cash, there are a number of other effective non-cash ways of providing motivation as described below.

Other means of rewarding sales representatives

Financial rewards are usually important for members of the sales force but there are other valuable means of recognizing achievement. These include prizes and non-financial forms of recognition ('sales representative of the month' etc) and other items in the total reward package such as opportunities for growth. As pointed out by Gundy (2002):

> In assessing how to motivate the sales force, leading companies view commissions and bonuses as just one tool in the motivational toolbox... Performance management, career pathing and recognition programmes can be powerful ways of producing and managing sales results. Companies that consider the impact of all these programmes in the design process are generally more successful in driving both short- and long-term results.

Other forms of reward are described below.

Gifts and vouchers

Gifts and vouchers provide a tangible means of recognizing achievements. They may be linked to the achievement of specified targets but should not be restricted too much to the 'super sales representatives'; the solid dependable salesperson also needs motivating through the recognition that such incentives provide. Gifts are subject to income tax.

Competitions

Prizes can be awarded to individuals or teams for notable sales achievements, such as bringing in new business. However, competitions can demotivate those who do not win prizes and they should be designed to ensure that all those who are doing well feel that they have a good chance of getting a prize.

Cars as perks

Sales representatives can be motivated by the opportunity to get a bigger and better car if they are particularly successful. The car may be retained for a defined period and made available again if the high performance is maintained.

Recognition schemes

Recognition schemes, as described in Chapter 14, are particularly appropriate for sales staff. Public applause and private thanks are both important.

Effectiveness and use of sales incentives

A survey of the effectiveness of incentive plans by Mercer Human Resource Consulting (2004) established that: 'Many organizations feel their plans do not encourage or reward the right performance. Of equal concern is that many staff do not understand the plan.' The survey found that:

- 17 per cent of respondents had between five and eight separate reward criteria.

- 3 per cent used nine or more performance measures.

- Volume production targets such as sales revenue, gross profit or units sold were the most used.

- 72 per cent used profit targets for sales directors, along with revenue measures in 64 per cent of organizations and individual objectives in 60 per cent.

- For sales representatives the most widely used measure was sales volume (72 per cent of schemes).

Rewarding customer service staff

Customer service staff work mainly in retail establishments and in call or customer contact centres. Their rewards need to reflect the nature of their duties, ie enhancing levels of customer service as well as selling.

Reward practices

The CIPD in conjunction with the Institute of Customer Service commissioned Professor Michael West and a team from Aston University to investigate how customer service staff were employed and rewarded (West *et al*, 2005).

The 580 staff covered by the research illustrated that front-line customer service workers do not all conform to the young/female/fleeting image. While 70 per cent were women, their average age was 34 years and average length of service six years. Eighty per cent were employed on a full-time basis and just 9 per cent on temporary contracts.

Nor did their typical working environment and conditions reflect the stereotypical 'sweat-shop' image. While the HR and reward practices varied, working conditions were generally good and staff rated their supervisors' skills, as well as their colleagues and the level of team-working. Staff benefits such as company pension plans and sick pay schemes were the norm, as were various training courses.

The pattern of pay practices used by these 15 organizations for front-line staff and their first-line managers is shown in Table 21.2. Base pay levels were generally competitive for the location and sector, and a number mentioned the effect of the national minimum wage.

Table 21.2   The pattern of pay practices for customer service staff in the Aston research organizations

Pay structure	Managers	Customer service staff
Grades	6	6
Broad bands	3	3
Individual ranges	4	4
Pay spine	2	2
Pay progression and bonus		
Individual performance-related pay	4	5
Skills/competency pay	2	2
Contribution pay	3	3
Individual bonus	5	6
Team bonus	4	6
Commission	0	1
Profit sharing	2	2

Most employees in the researched organizations had the opportunity to progress their base pay on the basis of their performance or competence, either through a range or up a pay spine, or between grades/levels of job. Such arrangements have generally supplanted 'spot' rate pay rates for service roles in call centres and retail shops.

At Boots the Chemists, for example, shop staff can progress up through a number of pay points according to their level of performance and skill – from entry level, to experienced, to advanced, to expert/specialist. At B&Q, customer advisors are paid on one of six different spot rates. Pay progression is based on the acquisition – and application on the shopfloor – of skills and knowledge. There are four additional spot rates beyond the established rate designed to reward 'excellence in the role'. Each additional level represents an hourly increase up to a maximum rate. At House of Fraser, employees are allocated to one of four competency bands – training, bronze, silver and gold – with staff assessed for a 'promotion' every six months. At Lands' End, there is a six-grade pay structure for hourly-paid staff, with spot rates for starters.

Low base pay/high commission arrangements were rare amongst the 15 organizations, but most of them operated variable performance-related pay schemes of some type, which again has become the norm for service staff today in these contexts, at least in the private sector. Tesco and John Lewis staff, for example, received company-wide profit sharing payments. British Gas uses a company-wide balanced scorecard bonus scheme, while Homebase, Asda and Marks and Spencer use team, store-based schemes. A number of the organizations used multiple plans.

All forms of performance-related pay and recognition schemes were used more frequently and more extensively by the highest-performing organizations in the research than amongst the other participants or amongst UK organizations as a whole. They were twice as likely as other UK organizations to use individual performance-related pay and various forms of individual and team non-financial recognition schemes, and five times as likely to use some form of team/collective bonus scheme as the remaining organizations in the study.

Reward policies in the research study organizations did not by themselves create high customer service performance. They operated through the medium of staff perceptions and in a general work and management context that encouraged positive perceptions and high levels of staff commitment – see Figure 21.1. The best organizations recognize that when it comes to delivering outstanding service, staff perceptions and management practice, rather than fancy reward and HR strategy statements, plans and policies are what make the difference.

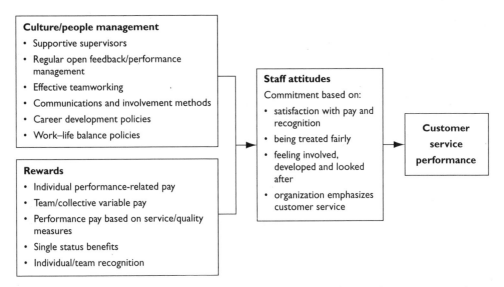

Figure 21.1 A summary of the relationships between HR and reward practices, employee attitudes and customer service performance

(Source: West et al, 2005)

Rewarding sales and service staff: six tips

- Analyse the business in terms of what is being sold or what customer services are provided to establish what types of people are required.

- Select the approach to reward that is most likely to motivate the different types of people to deliver results in accordance with the business model.

- Identify critical selling and customer service behaviours and capabilities and reinforce them through the reward package.

- Determine the optimum mix of base pay and incentive pay based on selling or service requirements. An emphasis on customer relations may suggest more base pay and less incentive pay (even no incentive at all and a competitive base salary), while an emphasis on hard selling may suggest less base pay and more incentive.

- Ensure that incentives and goals are consistent with the business plan. For example, the focus in the plan, and therefore the criteria for sales commission, could be more about getting new customers and retaining existing ones than just sales volume goals.

- Segment the reward package as necessary to reflect the different demands made on members of the sales or customer service teams.

References

Gundy, P (2002) Sales compensation programmes: built to last, *Compensation & Benefits Review*, September/October, pp 21–28

Mercer Human Resource Consulting (2004) *Sales Effectiveness Report*, Mercer, London

West, M, Fisher, G, Carter, M, Gould, V and Scully, J (2005) *Rewarding Customer Service? Using reward and recognition to deliver your customer service strategy*, CIPD, London

Rewarding Knowledge Workers

Introduction

A knowledge worker was originally defined by Peter Drucker (1988) as someone 'who knows more about his or her work than anyone else in the organization'. Today, knowledge workers are generally regarded as people whose work requires a marked degree of expertise. Their work is defined by the knowledge they need to do it. The term therefore embraces such diverse groups as academics, accountants, HR professionals, IT specialists, lawyers, media workers and researchers.

Knowledge workers play a steadily increasing part in organizations. According to the government's Occupational Employment Trends and Projections, UK 1982–2012, by 2012 knowledge workers will have increased from roughly a quarter of all jobs 20 years ago to almost a half.

The importance of the contribution made by knowledge workers means that attention has to be given to how reward policies and practices can be developed to attract, retain and motivate them having taken account of their particular needs. This is an area of reward management where segmentation may be appropriate. For example, the fluid grading system used in the scientific civil service allows for much more flexibility in rewarding scientists in line with their levels of competence rather than by the levels of responsibility that characterize traditional narrow-graded structures. The requirement to consider how knowledge workers should be rewarded is studied in this chapter, which starts with an analysis of what motivates them and then examines the approaches that can be adopted to their rewards.

What motivates knowledge workers?

In the words of Reeves and Knell (2001), it can be said of all knowledge workers that: 'The brightest and the best want an intellectual challenge and the chance to keep learning.' And Coyle (2001) explains that: 'Skilled programmers don't seem to fret about getting enough money. The more highly valued reward, because it is so much harder to come by, is the esteem in which they are held by their peer group.'

A study by Tampoe (1993) identified four key motivators for knowledge workers:

- Personal growth: the opportunity for individuals to fully realize their potential.

- Occupational autonomy: a work environment in which knowledge workers can achieve the task assigned to them.

- Task achievement: a sense of accomplishment from producing work that is of high quality and relevance to the organization.

- Money rewards: an income that is a just reward for their contribution to corporate success and that symbolizes their contribution to that success.

To which could be added, especially for scientific or research and development workers, the facilities required to carry out their work and the opportunity to gain recognition and prestige from their achievements. These may be more significant than financial rewards relating pay to performance.

Approaches to rewarding knowledge workers

Approaches to rewarding knowledge workers are described below under the headings of total reward, pay flexibility, pay related to competency, and career and job-family structures.

Total reward policies

Taking into account the factors that motivate knowledge workers mentioned above, there is an overwhelming case for adopting a total reward policy. As explained in Chapter 3, this would mean focusing on non-financial rewards such as recognition, opportunity to grow and achieve, and learning and development opportunities as well as financial rewards.

The following are examples of the approach used by two firms employing large numbers of knowledge workers.

Bristol-Myers Squibb

The pharmaceutical company states that 'reward is much wider than just paying its staff a competitive salary.' It has designed its total reward package knowing that everyone works for the company for different reasons and that everyone places a different emphasis on the importance of each of the elements of total reward – there is no one-size-fits-all. It has also set out to use total reward to 'elevate and differentiate' Bristol-Myers Squibb from other companies, both in the same industry and beyond.

The three elements of total reward are:

- Compensation: salary, performance-based bonus and stock options.

- Benefits: non-contributory pension, life cover, private health care, perks and cars.

- Work experience: defined as: 'All the elements which contribute to providing you with an environment that enables you to optimize your contribution to the company and achieve your full potential, whilst maintaining a balance between your personal and professional life'. These include:

  - acknowledgement, appreciation and recognition;

  - balance of work and life;

  - culture of Bristol-Myers Squibb;

  - employee development;

  - the working environment.

The total reward approach at Bristol-Myers Squibb embraces what they call the 'work experience', described above. This, says the company, to its staff 'recognizes that you are an individual with unique needs and offers something for everyone'. Work experience comprises acknowledgement, appreciation and recognition, balance of work and life, organizational culture, employee development and the working environment.

Elan Computers

The company's approach to total reward stresses investment in people, recognition, the quality of life and fair and competitive reward. It is part of Elan's people strategy, the stated aims of which are to:

> *Support the group vision, to invest in talented people, and to maintain a people-focused environment that is fun, challenging and rewarding. Starting with our comprehensive induction programme, we aim to secure long term commitment and inspire enthusiasm from day one. And we never stop listening to people. People are given the opportunity every year to take part in a survey to give feedback on every aspect of their life at Elan, and there are open question and answer sessions with board members. And to ensure that we are doing what we can to keep the best people, we study the reasons why people leave, and what retains our most talented people. This strategy allows us to continually improve our position as an employer and as a market force.*

The complete package, the concept of which is based on employees understanding the total value of all the rewards they receive, not just the individual elements, is designed to attract, retain, motivate and develop the best talent. The proposition for employees is that 'TotalReward' gives them the opportunity to share in the company's success, makes it easier to balance home and working life, and helps them to take care of themselves and their families.

Pay flexibility

The overall approach to rewarding knowledge workers should be flexibility within a framework. This means that a common framework of reward policies exists across the organization but within that framework some segmentation, as described in Chapter 28, can take place. This would involve tailoring arrangements to suit the specific needs of particular groups of knowledge and professional workers and the individuals within those groups. Pay flexibility could include market rate supplements to attract and retain specific categories of staff and the use of selected 'market groups' (separate pay structures for certain types of staff). This is in accord with the view expressed by Lawler (2002) that there should be a move away from job-based pay to person-based pay related to the market value of a person's skills and knowledge. On a wider scale, career or job families can be installed as described in Chapter 19.

Pay related to competency

If knowledge workers exist to apply their expertise then it seems reasonable to reward them according to the level of expertise (competency) they possess and apply. There are three ways of doing this, as described below: 1) by competency-related pay, 2) through structures in which grades or bands are defined in competency terms, and 3) the incorporation of skills and competencies into job evaluation factor plans.

Competency-related pay

In a competency-related pay scheme, people receive financial rewards in the shape of increases to their base pay by reference to the level of competence they demonstrate in carrying out their roles. It is a method of paying people for the ability to perform now and in the future. This seems to be a highly relevant approach for knowledge workers but there are measurement problems that have restricted its use.

Competency defined grade and pay structures

Job or career family structures typically define levels in terms of competencies.

Use of competencies in job evaluation

Traditional job evaluation schemes have always incorporated competencies in their factor plans, although they called them knowledge, skill or know-how. Factor plans have recently been developed that deliberately include competencies. This has applied in sectors or organizations such as higher education (the HERA scheme), the senior civil service (the JESP system) and the NHS, where there are 16 measurement factors but the knowledge, skills and experience factor accounts for almost a quarter of the total points weighting. This scheme acknowledges the explicit bias towards knowledge in an organization with huge numbers of professional workers.

Job and career families

Job and career-family structures as described in Chapter 19 consist of separate families of jobs with similar characteristics. Within each family the successive levels of competency required to carry out typical activities are defined, thus indicating career paths. In a job-family structure such as that at Canon UK or Norwich Union Insurance, each job family has its own pay structure, which takes account of different levels of market rates between families (this is sometimes called 'market grouping'). In a career-family structure as at Southampton University, the ranges of pay for each family are the same and the emphasis is on defining career progression rather than market pricing, although market supplements may be paid.

Job and career families are particularly appropriate for knowledge workers because they spell out the career ladders that apply specifically to the different categories employed in an organization.

Rewarding knowledge workers: six tips

- Adopt total reward policies emphasizing scope for achievement, recognition and growth.
- Consider segmenting the reward package for specified groups of knowledge workers.
- Introduce competency-based pay.
- Create a career-family structure with levels defined in competency terms.
- Define career ladders and the rewards associated with career progression.
- Develop a work environment that ensures that knowledge workers have the resources they need, the scope to use and develop their knowledge and skills and the recognition they deserve.

References

Coyle, D (2001) Power to the people, in *The Future of Reward*, ed N Page, CIPD, London

Drucker, P (1988) The coming of the new organization, *Harvard Business Review*, January–February, pp 45–53

Lawler, E E (2002) Pay strategies for the next economy: lessons from the dot-com era, *World at Work Journal*, **11** (1), pp 6–10

Occupational Employment Trends and Projections, UK 1982–2012, Office for National Statistics, London

Reeves, R and Knell, J (2001) All of these futures are yours, in *The Future of Reward*, ed N Page, CIPD, London

Tampoe, M (1993) Motivating knowledge workers: the challenge for the 1990s, *Long-range Planning*, **26** (2), pp 37–44

23

Rewarding Manual Workers

Key concepts and terms

- Base rate
- Effort bargain
- Effort rating
- Harmonization
- High day rate
- Incentive scheme
- Measured day work
- Payment-by-results
- Pay/work bargain

- Performance-related pay
- Piece work
- Single status
- Skill-based pay
- Spot rate
- Taylorism
- Time rate
- Wage drift

Learning outcomes

On completing this chapter you should be able to define these key concepts. You should also know about:

- The factors affecting the pay of manual workers
- The use of time rates
- The use of pay structures

- Types of shopfloor incentive schemes
- Considerations affecting the use of incentive schemes
- The meaning of single status and harmonization

Introduction

Manual worker pay systems that have not been 'harmonized' – that is, brought into line with the reward system for staff – frequently differ from the systems described elsewhere in this book in three ways. First, the use of a time-rate basis of payment, second the use of spot rates, and third the use of individual payment-by-results schemes.

Factors affecting the pay of manual workers

The three main factors affecting the pay of manual workers are: first, bargaining arrangements; second, local labour market pressures; and third, trends in the use of technology on the shopfloor.

Bargaining arrangements

The pay of manual workers is often influenced strongly by national and local agreements with trade unions, which will determine rates for particular jobs or skill levels. This constitutes an aspect of the effort bargain. The objectives of workers and their trade union officials and representatives is to strike a bargain with management about what they consider to be a reasonable amount of pay that should be provided by their employer in return for their contribution. It is, in effect, an agreement between workers and management – the pay/work bargain – that lays down the amount of work to be done for an agreed wage, not just the hours to be worked. Explicitly or implicitly, all employers are in a bargaining situation with regard to payment systems. This applies whether or not workers are unionized. Negotiated wage settlements can also affect non-unionized companies.

Local labour market pressures

Manual workers are usually recruited from the local labour market, where the laws of supply and demand can have a marked effect on the rates of pay for particular occupations if there is a skills shortage or surplus, or reluctance on the part of workers to carry out certain jobs. The local labour market is a fairly perfect market in one of the senses used by economists, namely that there is widespread and easily available knowledge of rates of pay (the price of labour) and there may also exist, although not for every occupation, a fair degree of choice by both buyers and sellers of where they obtain labour or where they provide it.

Technology

The increased use of technology on the shopfloor, for example, in the form of computer-aided manufacture, has meant that the demand for a number of the traditional skills has diminished while the demand for new ones has increased. Computer-controlled machines are more likely to be operated by technicians than by members of the old skilled trades. This is one of the factors that has led to pressures to harmonize shopfloor and office or laboratory payment systems.

Time rates

Time rates, also known as day rates, day work, flat rates or hourly rates, provide workers with a predetermined rate for the actual hours they work. The rate is fixed by formal or informal negotiations, on the basis of local rates or, less often, by reference to a hierarchy produced by job evaluation. The rate only varies with time, never with performance or output. However, additional payments are made on top of base rates for overtime, shift working, night work, call outs, adverse working conditions and, sometimes, location.

The situation where time rates are most commonly used is where it is thought impossible or undesirable to use a payment-by-results system, for example in maintenance work. From the viewpoint of employees, the advantage of time rates is that their earnings are predictable and steady and they do not have to engage in endless arguments with rate fixers and supervisors about piece rate or time allowances. The argument against them is that they do not provide a direct incentive relating the reward to the effort or the results. Two ways of modifying the basic time-rate approach are to adopt high day rates as described below or measured day work as covered later in this chapter.

Time rates may take the form of what are often called high day rates. These are higher than the minimum time rate and may contain a consolidated bonus rate element. The underlying assumption is that higher base rates will encourage greater effort without the problems created when operating an incentive scheme. This is in line with the theory of the economy of high wages mentioned in Chapter 15. High day rates are usually above the local market rates to attract and retain high-quality workers.

Pay structures

Pay systems for manual workers are seldom graded in the ways described in Chapter 19 unless their conditions have been harmonized (see later in this chapter). Time rates are usually paid in the form of spot rates: that is, a fixed rate for a job or an individual. However, spot rates may be designated for different levels of skill. Traditionally, a person-based pay system was adopted with three basic rates of pay attached to people – unskilled, semi-skilled and skilled – above which there might be special rates for highly skilled occupations such as toolmakers. Earnings from payment-by-result schemes were added to these rates. Another arrangement is to have a more discerning hierarchy of rates linked to skill levels: a form of skill-based pay. Yet another arrangement is to have a job-based pay system with different rates for different jobs; in a distribution centre for example: picker, packer and forklift-truck driver.

Incentive schemes for manual workers

Incentive schemes for manual workers consist of:

- Payment-by–results (PBR) schemes, which pay for output and include piecework, work-measured schemes and measured day work. Payments are added to base rate although, rarely, payment is entirely related to output.

- Contingent pay schemes, which relate pay to performance or skill (performance-related pay and skill-based pay). Increases may be consolidated or paid as lump sum bonuses.

- Collective schemes, which pay bonuses related to either team or plant performance.

Each of these methods is described below. First, however, it is necessary to deal with the considerations affecting the use of incentive schemes.

Considerations affecting the use of incentive schemes

The considerations to be taken into account in developing and maintaining incentive schemes are the criteria of effectiveness and their advantages and disadvantages.

Criteria of effectiveness

Incentive schemes aim to motivate employees to exert greater effort. They will do so effectively only if:

- The link between effort and reward is obvious and easily understood, ie there is a clear line-of-sight.

- The value of the reward is worthwhile in relation to the effort.

- Individuals are able to influence their level of effort or behaviour in order to earn a reward.

- Rewards closely follow the effort.

- The integrity of the scheme is preserved – it is not allowed to degenerate and cannot be manipulated so that individuals are over-rewarded.

The rationale for incentive schemes

The basic rationale of incentive schemes is the simple proposition that people are motivated by money. It is believed that they will work harder if rewards are tied directly to the results they achieve. This is essentially 'Taylorism' – FW Taylor's concept of scientific management, meaning the use of systematic observation and measurement, task specialism and, in effect, the reduction of workers to the level of efficiently functioning machines who will only work harder if they are paid more.

Certainly, the experience of most people who have installed a PBR scheme in a workplace where it did not previously exist is that productivity increases substantially when the scheme is new, although the level of increase is not always maintained. Studies in the United States by Binder (1990), Guzzo, Jette and Katsell (1985), Lawler (1971) and Nalbantian (1987) have shown productivity increases of between 15 per cent and 35 per cent when incentive schemes have been put into place.

Incentive schemes are used in the belief that they yield increased output, lower the cost of production and provide higher earnings for the workers concerned. It is also commonly believed that less supervision is needed to keep output up. Indeed, when direct supervision is difficult, PBR is often advocated as the only practicable form of payment.

Disadvantages of incentive schemes

The argument that people work harder only when they are paid more is regarded by some people as overwhelming. They do not accept the proposition that intrinsic and non-financial motivators can have an equally, if not more, powerful and longer-lasting impact.

The disadvantages of shopfloor incentive schemes are that they can:

- Be unfair: earnings may fluctuate through no fault of the individual because of lack of work, shortage of materials, design modifications or the need to learn new skills. It may also be felt that the method of altering rates is unfair.

- Be ineffective: workers may have their own ideas about how much they want to earn or how hard they want to work, and regulate their output accordingly.

- Penalize skill: the more skilled workers may be given the more difficult and often less remunerative jobs.

- Cause wage drift: the difficulty of conforming to criteria such as clearly relating pay to effort and the lax approach of some organizations to the management of incentive schemes contribute to increases in earnings at a higher rate than productivity. Degeneration and wage drift are a particular problem with work-measured schemes as discussed later in this chapter.

- Lead to management escaping its responsibilities: team leaders and supervisors may rely on the incentive scheme to control output. Instead of taking poor performers to one side and informing them that their work is not up to standard, they are tempted to take the soft option and simply point to the figures.

- Be costly to maintain: extra work-study engineers, rate fixers and inspectors are often needed to maintain the scheme and exercise quality control.

- Produce strife in the workplace: arguments about rates and accusations of unjustified rate-cutting are common in workshops where incentive schemes are used.

- Create reluctance to exert the expected level of effort: workers may believe that management will progressively increase the performance targets required to trigger the same bonus payment. They may therefore be reluctant to carry on at the incentivized level of performance they have achieved, on the grounds that this will only result in higher targets that will make the bonus more difficult to obtain.

- Result in poor-quality work: concentration on output can lead to neglect of quality.

- Lead to poor teamwork: individual incentive schemes by definition encourage individual rather than team effort.

- Result in accidents and health hazards: workers may be tempted to cut corners and ignore safety precautions to achieve output targets; repetitive strain injury (RSI) may result if they work too hard on tasks requiring repeated small movements.

These are powerful arguments but shopfloor incentive schemes persist. The number of workers paid on this basis may have diminished, but this is because of structural (the reduction in manufacturing) and technological reasons rather than because managements have turned against it.

Payment by results schemes

Piecework

Piecework is the oldest and simplest form of incentive scheme for manual workers. Operators are paid at a specific rate according to their output or the number of 'pieces' they produce. Pay is directly proportional to output, although most piecework schemes provide a fallback rate at minimum earnings level. The proportion of the minimum rate to average earnings varies. It is typically set at 70 or 80 per cent, although it can be as low as 30 per cent.

Work-measured schemes

Work-measured schemes are the most popular form of incentive plan for shopfloor workers. They use work-measurement techniques to determine standard output levels over a period or standard times for tasks. The incentive pay is then linked with the output achieved relative to the standard, or to the time saved in performing each task.

The form of work measurement used is time study. Jobs are broken down into their constituent parts or tasks and the time taken by workers to complete each part is measured with a stopwatch by a work-study or industrial engineer. A number of measurements will be made of the time taken by different workers on the same task or the same worker carrying out the task at different times of the day and night. Time study is based on objective measurements, but account has to be taken of the fact that there will probably be significant differences between the rates at which operators work – the effort they put into the job. Work-study engineers have therefore to assess what that rate is, a process known as effort rating.

Individual effort is rated in terms of 'standard performance'. This is the performance that a qualified and motivated worker should be able to achieve without over-exertion. The effort needed to achieve standard performance is sometimes represented as equivalent to walking at four miles an hour (ie quite briskly). All the operators studied are given an effort rating relative to this standard. The raw times observed in the work study are then adjusted by the work-study engineer to produce a basic time that represents a rating of 100 to indicate the performance of an average operator working conscientiously without financial motivation. This involves a large element of subjectivity, although experienced and well-trained engineers should be capable of making reasonably accurate and consistent assessments.

The basic time will be further adjusted to incorporate allowances for relaxation, personal needs, fatigue and any time regularly taken up by other aspects of the work such as cleaning or resetting machines. The result is the standard time for the task, usually expressed as 'standard minutes'.

Work-measured schemes can use performance ratings that are calculated by a formula as in the following example:

$$\frac{\text{Number of units produced per day (132)} \times \text{standard minutes per unit (4)}}{\text{Actual time taken in minutes per day (48)}} = \frac{528}{480} \times 100 = 110\%$$

In the most common proportionate system of payment, the performance rating is applied directly to the base rate, so that in the above example the incentive payment would be an additional 10 per cent.

The problem with time study is that, although it is based on objective measurements, the standard time that is ultimately obtained is the product of a number of additional subjective judgements. Employees who are being timed may deliberately restrict their performance in order to achieve low standard times and therefore higher bonuses with less effort. It is up to the work-study engineer's skill and judgement to detect such restrictions, and this can lead to arguments and even strife. In organizations with trade unions it is common practice to train some representatives in work-measurement techniques to promote the achievement of acceptable judgements on standard times.

Alternatively, PBR payments can be based on the time-saved principle. The amount of the bonus depends on the difference between the actual time taken to perform the task and the standard time allowed. If a task is done in less than the standard time, then the percentage of time saved is applied to the base rate to calculate the bonus. The standard times may be determined by work measurement, although traditionally 'rate fixers' were employed to make more subjective and therefore often more controversial judgements.

Measured day work

Measured day work schemes were originally developed for large batch or mass-production factories in the 1950s and 1960s, when it became evident that, despite all efforts, it was impossible to control wage drift. They are, however, much less common now. Manufacturing firms often prefer to pay a high day rate.

When they exist, measured day work schemes provide for the pay of employees to be fixed on the understanding that they will maintain a specified level of performance, but in the short term pay does not fluctuate with their performance. The arrangement depends on work measurement to define the required level of performance and to monitor the actual level. The fundamental principles of measured day work are that there is an incentive level of performance and that the incentive payment is guaranteed in advance, putting employees under the obligation to perform at the effort level required. In contrast, a conventional work-measured incentive scheme allows employees discretion as to their effort level but relates their pay directly to the results they achieve. Between these two extremes there are a variety of alternatives, including banded incentives, stepped schemes and various forms of high day rate.

Contingent pay schemes

Performance-related pay

Performance-related pay systems such as those described in Chapter 10 can be used for manual workers. Employees receive a high base rate and an additional performance-related payment, which is either a lump sum bonus or consolidated into basic pay. The award is governed by assessments of skill and performance ratings under headings such as quality, flexibility, contribution to teamworking and ability to hit targets. The percentage award is usually small – up to 5 per cent.

Performance-related pay is sometimes introduced for manual workers as part of a programme for harmonizing their conditions of employment with those of salaried staff. It can be appropriate in circumstances where work measurement is difficult or impossible to use, in high-technology manufacturing where operations are computer-controlled or automated and teamwork and multiskilling are important, in organizations where the emphasis is on quality, and in those where just-in-time systems are used. But it is difficult to operate and trade unions tend to be hostile, and it is therefore uncommon.

Skill-based pay

Skill-based pay, as described in detail in Chapter 10, rewards people with extra pay for acquiring and using additional skills. It can be paid as a supplement to a base rate or it can result in workers being placed on a higher spot rate.

Collective schemes

Group or team incentive schemes

Group or team incentive schemes provide for the payment of a bonus to members of a group or team related to the output achieved by the group in relation to defined targets or to work-measured standards.

Factory or plant-wide schemes

Factory or plant-wide schemes pay a bonus to individuals that is related to the performance of the factory as a whole, which may be measured in terms of added value as in a gain-sharing scheme (see Chapter 13) or some other index of productivity (eg units produced, cost per unit of output). The bonus may be added to individual incentive payments.

Assessment of schemes

Table 23.1 contains an assessment of the advantages and disadvantages of each type of scheme from the viewpoint of employers and employees and a review of the circumstances when the scheme is more likely to be appropriate.

Table 23.1 Comparison of shopfloor incentive schemes

Scheme	Main features	For employers		For employees		When appropriate
		Advantages	Disadvantages	Advantages	Disadvantages	
Piecework	Bonus directly related to output.	Direct motivation; simple, easy to operate.	Lose control over output; quality problems.	Predict and control earnings in the short-term; regulate pace of work themselves.	More difficult to predict and control earnings in the longer term; work may be stressful and produce RSI.	Fairly limited application to work involving unit production controlled by the person, eg agriculture, garment manufacture.
Work-measured schemes	Work measurement used to determine standard output levels over a period or standard times for job/tasks; bonus based by reference to performance ratings compared with actual performance or time saved.	Provides what appears to be a 'scientific' method of relating reward to performance; can produce significant increases in productivity, at least in the short term.	Schemes are expensive, time-consuming and difficult to run, and can too easily degenerate and cause wage drift because of loose rates.	Appear to provide a more objective method of relating pay to performance; employees can be involved in the rating process to ensure fairness.	Ratings are still prone to subjective judgement and earnings can fluctuate because of changes in work requirements outside the control of employees.	For short-cycle repetitive work where changes in the work mix or design changes are infrequent, down time is restricted, and management and supervision are capable of managing and maintaining the scheme.

Table 23.1 *continued*

Scheme	Main features	For employers		For employees		When appropriate
		Advantages	Disadvantages	Advantages	Disadvantages	
Measured day work	Pay fixed at a high rate on the understanding that a high level of performance against work-measured standards will be maintained.	Employees are under an obligation to work at the specified level of performance.	Performance targets can become easily attained norms and may be difficult to change.	High predictable earnings are provided.	No opportunities for individuals to be rewarded in line with their own efforts.	Everyone must be totally committed to making it work; high standards of work measurement are essential, with good control systems to identify shortfalls on targets.
Performance-related pay	Payments on top of base rate are made related to individual assessments of performance.	Reward individual contribution without resource to work measurement; relevant in high-technology manufacturing.	Measuring performance can be difficult; no direct incentive provided.	Opportunity to be rewarded for own efforts without having to submit to a pressured PBR system.	Assessment informing performance pay decisions may be biased, inconsistent or unsupported by evidence.	As part of a reward harmonization (shop-floor and staff) programme; as an alternative to work-measured schemes or an enhancement of a high day rate system.

Table 23.1 *continued*

Scheme	Main features	For employers		For employees		When appropriate
		Advantages	Disadvantages	Advantages	Disadvantages	
Skill-based pay	Payments for acquiring and using new skills.	Encourage skills acquisition.	May pay for skills not used.	Scope to develop.	Proper training may not be available.	Where skills requirements are exacting.
Group or team basis	Groups or teams are paid bonuses on the basis of their perform-ance as indicated by work meas-urement ratings or the achieve-ment of targets.	Encourage team cooperation and effort; not too individualized.	Direct incentive may be limited; depends on good work measurement or the availability of clear group output or productivity targets.	Bonuses can be related clearly to the joint efforts of the group; fluctuations in earnings minimized.	Depend on effective work measurement, which is not always available; individual effort and contribution not recognized.	When team-working is important and team efforts can be accurately measured and assessed; as an alternative to individual PBR if this is not effective.
Factory wide bonuses	Bonuses related to plant per-formance – added value or productivity.	Increase com-mitment by sharing success.	No direct motivation.	Earnings increased without individual pressure.	Bonuses often small and unpredictable.	As an addition to other forms of incentive when increasing commitment is important.

Single status and harmonization

Single status means that manual or shopfloor workers on wages are on salaried terms and conditions and are entitled to the same conditions of employment, such as sick pay, as other members of staff. Harmonization means the reduction of differences in the pay structure and other employment conditions between categories of employee, usually manual and staff employees. It involves the adoption of a common approach and criteria to pay and benefits for all employees.

The pressure for harmonization has occurred because of the belief that status differentials between people in the same employment cannot be justified. Harmonization facilitates the more flexible use of labour, and the impact of technology has enhanced the skills of shopfloor workers and made differential treatment harder to defend. Equal pay legislation has been a major challenge to differentiation between staff and manual workers.

ACAS (1982) suggested that organizations, before pursuing a programme of harmonization, should seek answers to the following questions:

- What differences in the treatment of groups of employees are a rational result of differences in the work or the job requirements?

- Is it possible to estimate the direct costs of removing these differences?

- What differences in status are explicitly recognized as part of the 'reward package' for different groups in the labour force?

- What would be the possible repercussive effects of harmonization?

- How do the existing differences affect industrial relations in the organization?

Rewarding manual workers: six tips

- Consider scope for single status or harmonization.

- Ensure that rates of pay for jobs and people are linked to the level of skill or the degree of multiskilling required.

- If planning to introduce new payment-by-results schemes or amend existing ones, involve employees and their representatives in discussions on what needs to be done and reach agreement on how the changes should be introduced.

- Consider introducing team pay or gain-sharing.

- Ensure that payment-by-results schemes are based on work measurement and provide a clear line of sight between effort and reward.

- Review all existing payment-by-results schemes to ensure that they are functioning properly and are not encouraging wage drift.

References

ACAS (1982) *Developments in Harmonization: Discussion Paper No 1*, ACAS, London

Binder, A S (1990) *Paying for Productivity*, Brookings Institution, Washington, DC

Guzzo, R A, Jette, R D and Katsell, R A (1985) The effect of psychological-based intervention programmes on worker productivity: a meta analysis, *Personnel Psychology*, **38**, pp 275–91

Lawler, E E (1971) *Pay and Organizational Effectiveness*, McGraw-Hill, New York

Nalbantian, H (1987) *Incentives, Cooperation and Risk Sharing*, Rowman & Littlefield, Totowa, NJ

Part V

Employee Benefit
and Pension Schemes

24

Employee Benefits

Introduction

Employee benefits consist of arrangements made by employers for their employees that enhance the latter's well-being. They are provided in addition to pay and form important parts of the total reward package. As part of total remuneration, they may be deferred or contingent, like a pension scheme (see Chapter 26), insurance cover or sick pay, or they may be immediate, like a company car or a loan. Employee benefits also include holidays and leave arrangements, which are not strictly remuneration. Benefits are sometimes referred to dismissively as 'perks' (perquisites) or 'fringe benefits', but when they cater for personal security or personal needs they could hardly be described as 'fringe'.

Employee benefits are a costly part of the remuneration package. They can amount to a third or more of basic pay costs and therefore have to be planned and managed with care.

Note that many benefits such as company cars, interest-free loans, private medical insurance, and prizes, gifts and vouchers can be taxed quite heavily. It is worth seeking advice from a tax specialist if in any doubt.

Rationale for employee benefits

Employee benefits provide for the personal needs of employees and they are a means of increasing their commitment to the organization and demonstrating that their employers care for their well-being. Not all employers care but, like the ones that do, they still provide benefits to ensure that the total remuneration package is competitive. And some benefits, such as maternity leave, have to be provided by law in the UK.

Employee benefit strategies and policies

Employee benefit strategies will be concerned in general terms with the direction the organization wants to go with regard to the range and scale of benefits it wants to provide and the costs it is prepared to incur. The strategy forms the foundation for the formulation of employee benefit policies.

Employee benefit policies are concerned with:

- the types of benefits to be provided, taking into account their value to employees, their cost and the need to make the benefit package competitive;
- the size of the benefits;
- the need to harmonize benefits;
- the total costs of benefits provision in relation to the costs of basic pay;
- the use of flexible benefits, as described in Chapter 25.

Types of benefit

The main benefits deal with personal security, financial assistance, personal needs, holidays, company cars, other benefits, voluntary benefits and concierge services as described below.

Personal security

Personal security benefits include:

- Health care: the provision through medical insurance of private health care to cover the cost of private hospital treatment (permanent health insurance), making periodic health screening available and, sometimes, dental insurance.

- Insurance cover: for death in service (if not already provided in a pension scheme), personal accident and business travel.

- Sick pay: providing full pay for a given period of sickness and a proportion of pay (typically half-pay for a further period). Sick pay entitlement is usually service-related. Sick pay can be costly unless attendance management and control practices are introduced.

- Redundancy pay: additions can be made to the statutory redundancy pay, including extra notice compensation, extra service-related payments (eg one month per year of service) and ex gratia payments to directors and executives in compensation for loss of office (sometimes called golden handshakes).

- Career counselling (outplacement advice) can be provided by specialist consultants to employees who have been made redundant.

Financial assistance

Financial assistance can take the following forms:

- Company loans: interest-free modest loans, or low interest on more substantial loans, which are usually earmarked for specific purposes such as home improvements.

- Season ticket loans: interest-free loans for annual season tickets.

- Mortgage assistance: subsidized interest payments on mortgages up to a given price threshold. This benefit is most likely to be provided by financial services companies.

- Relocation packages: for staff who are being relocated by the organization or recruited from elsewhere, the costs of removal and legal/estate agents' fees may be refunded.

- Fees to professional bodies: eg the CIPD.

Personal needs

Employee benefits satisfying personal needs include:

- maternity and paternity leave and pay above the statutory minimum;
- leave for personal reasons;
- childcare through workplace nurseries or vouchers;
- pre-retirement counselling;
- personal counselling through employee assistance programmes;
- sports and social facilities;
- company discounts, whereby employees can buy the products or services offered by the company at a reduced price;
- retail vouchers to buy goods at chain stores.

Holidays

Before the European Working Time Directive in 1998, there was no statutory obligation to offer any paid holiday except for the standard 'bank' holidays. Employers are now obliged to offer a minimum of 20 days' paid holiday per year, including bank holidays.

In practice, most organizations have always offered annual leave well in excess of this minimum, with few UK companies giving less than four weeks to employees at any level. Basic holiday entitlements are typically five weeks plus bank holidays, with some organizations offering up to six weeks for senior executives (who in practice may rarely have time to take full advantage of the provision) or on a service-related basis to more junior staff. The entitlement for holiday begins to accrue on the first day at work.

Organizations are obliged by statute to provide paid maternal and paternal leave and unpaid family leave.

Company cars

Although the tax liability for individuals with company 'status' cars has increased steadily over the last decade, they still remain one of the most valued perks, perhaps because people do not have to make a capital outlay, do not lose money through depreciation and are spared the worry and expense of maintenance.

Other benefits

Other benefits include free car parking, Christmas parties and tea/coffee/cold drinks.

Voluntary ('affinity') benefits

Voluntary benefit schemes provide opportunities for employees to buy goods or services at discounted prices. The employers negotiate deals with the providers but the scheme does not cost them anything.

Popular voluntary benefits include:

- Health: private medical insurance, dental insurance, health screening.

- Protection: critical illness insurance, life insurance, income protection insurance, personal accident insurance.

- Leisure: holidays, days out, travel insurance, computer leasing, bicycle leasing, pet insurance, gym membership.

- Home: household goods, online shopping.

Concierge services

Concierge services can include dealing with home and car repair and maintenance, financial services, buying presents, restaurant reservations, theatre tickets and travel arrangements. They originated in the United States in response to the long-hours culture that limited personal time away from the workplace. Businesses benefit from providing these services because they enable staff to concentrate on their jobs by freeing them from mundane personal tasks such as waiting at home for deliveries or getting their cars serviced.

At PricewaterhouseCoopers staff can pay a fixed sum a month for requests. These can be for anything from shopping, theatre tickets, travel arrangements or arranging a plumber, to event planning – 'so long as it's legal'.

Incidence of benefits

The proportion of respondents to the 2009 CIPD reward management survey providing six key benefits were:

- 25 days paid leave: 67 per cent.
- Free car parking: 60 per cent.
- Childcare vouchers: 56 per cent.
- Life insurance: 51 per cent.
- Enhanced maternity/paternity leave: 43 per cent.
- An employee assistance programme: 42 per cent.

Choice of benefits

Some benefits, such as holidays, maternity leave and redundancy pay, have to be provided by statute – there is no choice except on the extent to which statutory provisions may by enhanced. Neither, for a responsible employer, is there any real choice over the provision of pensions, life insurance or sick pay. Company cars for executives are still popular in spite of the tax penalties because of the felt need to be competitive.

Some optional benefits such as health insurance, childcare and low-interest loans may be selected because they will be appreciated and because they help to make the reward package competitive.

The factors affecting the choice of or provision or scale will be:

- what employees want, as established by opinion surveys;
- what other employers are providing, as established by market surveys;
- what the organization can afford.

Flexible benefit schemes give employees a choice within limits of the type or scale of benefits offered to them by their employers.

Administering employee benefits

Employee benefits can be expensive and it is necessary to monitor the costs of providing them and the extent to which a cost–benefit comparison justifies continuing with them on the present scale or at all. There should be a budget for employee benefit costs and expenditure should be monitored against it. Regular surveys should be undertaken of the attitude of employees to the benefits package. They may suggest where benefit expenditure could be redirected to areas where it would be more appreciated. They may also suggest that there is a need to adopt a flexible benefit policy, as described in the next chapter.

Total reward statements

Total reward statements communicate to employees the value of the employee benefits such as pensions, holidays, company cars, free car parking and subsidized meals they receive in addition to their pay. They also describe any other rewards they get, such as learning and development opportunities. The aim is to ensure that they appreciate the total value of their reward package. Too often, people are unaware of what they obtain in addition to their pay. Table 24.1 shows how a total reward statement can be set out.

Table 24.1 Example of total reward statement

Total reward statement		
Pay	Basic annual salary	£30,000
	Bonus	£3,000
	Total	£33,000
Employee benefits	Retirement, life insurance and ill-health	£5,000
	Holidays	£1,000
	Other fringe benefits (subsidized meals, employee assistance programme, concierge service, voluntary benefits, staff discount, free car parking)	£2,000
	Total	£8,000
Total remuneration		£41,000
Other rewards/benefits	Learning and development programmes Further education assistance Flexible hours Additional maternity/paternity leave	

Employee benefits: six tips

- Review the benefit package regularly to establish that the benefits provided are desirable and cost-effective, that they are appreciated and that they are administered efficiently.
- Survey employees to find out what they think of the benefits package and what they think it should look like.
- Ensure that the benefits package reflects good practice as established by benchmarking.
- Ensure that the benefits package is competitive and enhances the reputation of the business as a good employer.
- Ensure that employees appreciate the value of the benefits they receive by issuing total reward statements.
- Consider giving employees the opportunity to choose their benefits through a flexible benefits scheme.

Reference

CIPD (2009) *Survey of Reward Management*, CIPD, London

Flexible Benefits

Introduction

Flexible benefit schemes give employees a choice within limits of the type or scale of benefits offered to them by their employers. A wide variety of approaches is available.

Interest in such schemes has been generated because employee benefits are not all equally wanted or appreciated by the staff that receive them and, from the employer's point of view, some benefits will not therefore provide value for money. However, the number that have introduced formal flexible schemes is relatively small – only 13 per cent of the respondents to the CIPD 2008 Reward Management Survey had them. In this chapter the reasons for introducing flexible benefits are set out, the different types of flexible benefit schemes are defined and the steps required to introduce a scheme are explained.

Reasons for introducing flexible benefits

Flexible benefit schemes may be introduced in order to:

- meet the diverse needs of employees and increase the perceived value of the package to them – enabling them, to a degree, to decide for themselves what benefits they want and the size of particular benefits to suit their own life style rather than being forced to accept what their employers think is good for them;

- enable employers to get better value for money from their benefits expenditure because it meets the needs and wants of employees;

- control costs by providing employees with a fund to spend rather than promising a particular level of benefits;

- aid recruitment and retention – as flexible benefits are generally preferred by employees to fixed benefits of equivalent value;

- help to harmonize terms and conditions in a merger.

Types of flexible benefits schemes

The main types of schemes are described below.

Flex individual benefits

Employees are given the opportunity to vary the size of individual benefits, paying extra if they want more or, in effect, being paid cash if they want less. A typical example is a flexible car scheme that enables people to pay more for a better model or, if they decide to downsize, receive the reduction in cost to the company in cash. Choices are made on recruitment or when the car is replaced.

Another common arrangement is to provide scope, within limits, to buy or sell holiday time over the holiday year; for example, so many extra days could be 'bought' at the daily rate of the employee or so many could be 'sold' and the amount at the daily rate added to pay.

This is a simple approach that is easy to introduce and administer and is therefore the most common method of flexing benefits. The disadvantage is that the impact may be limited.

Flex existing entitlement

Employees may choose to increase, decrease or end their current benefits and select new benefits from the menu provided. The value of the benefits bought and sold is then aggregated and the net amount added to or deducted from pay. An example of how this might look for an employee whose salary is £30,000 per annum is shown in Table 25.1.

Table 25.1 Example of variation around existing entitlement

Benefit	Standard entitlement	Selected entitlement	Monthly cost saving (or extra cost)
Holidays	25 days	22 days	£35
Car	Lease cost £300 per month	£240 per month	£60
Company pension contribution	10% of salary	10% of salary	Nil
Private medical insurance	Cover for self	Cover for self, partner and child	(£45)
Dental insurance	Nil	Nil	Nil
Childcare vouchers	Nil	£200 per month	(£200)
Total monthly adjustment			(£150)

This arrangement can be simplified by making only two or three benefits flexible. The rules often stipulate that such essential core benefits as pensions and life insurance cannot be reduced, and limits may be placed on the scope for flexing other benefits, for example holidays.

Flex fund

Employees are allocated a fund of money to 'spend' on benefits from a menu. This is therefore sometimes described as the 'cafeteria' approach. Certain 'core' compulsory benefits such as pensions and life insurance have to be maintained. The value of the flex fund is big enough to enable individual employees to 'buy' their existing benefits and thus retain them without additional cost.

A simplified example of a flex fund benefits-choice menu for someone with a salary of £30,000 with a flex fund of £12,000 is shown in Table 25.2.

The impact of the choices made is shown in Table 25.3.

Any overspend would be funded by salary sacrifice. In this example, where less than £12,000 has been spent, the unspent flex fund would be paid as a monthly, non-consolidated cash sum.

Table 25.2   Example of flex fund benefits-choice menu

Benefit	Minimum choice	Maximum choice	Price
Holidays	20 days	30 days	0.4% of salary per day
Lease car	£300 per month (£3,600 per annum)	£500 per month (£6,000 per annum)	Annual lease times 1.25 (to allow for insurance and maintenance)
Company pension contribution	5% of salary	15% of salary	Face value less 10%*
Private medical insurance	Cover for self only	Cover for self, partner and children	£500 each per adult. £200 for one or more children
Dental insurance	n/a	Level 3 cover for self, partner and children	£40, £100, £180 per individual for Level 1, 2 or 3 cover, respectively
Childcare vouchers	n/a	20% of salary	Face value less 5%*

* The adjustment reflects the fact that Employer NICs are not payable on these benefits. The adjustment for childcare vouchers is lower to allow for the charge payable to the provider.

Table 25.3   Example of impact of flex fund choices made (shown in Table 25.2)

Benefit	Choice	Cost
Holidays	25 days	£3,000
Lease car	£350 per month	£5,250
Company pension contribution	10% of salary	£3,000
Private medical insurance	Cover for self and partner	£1,000
Dental insurance	Level 2 cover for self and partner	£200
Childcare vouchers	Nil	Nil
Total		**£11,400**
Flex fund		£12,000
Under (over) spend		£600

Introducing flexible benefits

The steps required to introduce flexible benefits are described below:

1. Define business need: the benefits in terms of meeting the diverse needs of employees, helping recruitment and retention and getting better value for money from expenditure on employee benefits.

2. Seek views: conduct an opinion survey of employees on what they think of present benefit arrangements, what they think about flexible benefits and what benefits they would like to be eligible for flex (this could be accompanied by information about how flexible benefits might work, and would therefore be the first shot in a communications campaign – communicating about flexible benefits is important).

3. Decide objectives and essential elements: the objectives of the scheme should be determined and its essential elements defined. This will include broadly the extent to which it is believed that the approach should be to go for a full scheme based either on flexing existing benefits or a flex fund, or whether the approach should be to flex individual benefits. There may be something to be said for starting with the latter, simpler approach (which will be cheaper to install) with the possibility of extending it at a later stage when experience has shown that it is working well. The strategy should also explore the need for outside advice and, on the basis of initial discussions with potential advisors, how much would need to be spent on developing and maintaining the scheme. One of the common objections to flexible benefits is the costs involved, especially when the proposed scheme is a fairly complex one and outside professional advice and support is required. Preliminary decisions need to be made at this stage on the likelihood that such advice will be required so that the costs involved can be estimated. It is also necessary to decide on the need for a project team with employee involvement.

4. Set up project team: this could be a joint management/employee team (involvement is very desirable) with the responsibility of planning and overseeing the development programme.

5. Decide who is going to carry out the development work: someone from within the organization should be in charge of the project, with help as required and available from flexible benefit, finance, tax and pensions specialists. The development of a scheme requires considerable expertise in these areas in developing and costing schemes, exploring tax considerations and setting up the administration.

6. Design scheme: this involves deciding on core benefits, which will have to be maintained, identifying benefits that can be flexed and any limits on the extent to which these benefits can be flexed, costing the benefits as necessary to enable menus to be produced and flex funds set up, if appropriate, and considering how the scheme should be administered. Simple schemes can be administered on paper but there is software available to administer

more elaborate ones. An intranet can be used to help with administration – employees can make their choice of benefits from the screen and calculate the financial implications.

7. Communicate details of the scheme: employees need to be given detailed but easily understood information about the proposed scheme – how it will work, how it will affect them, its advantages, and how and when it will be introduced.

8. Pilot test: there is much to be said for piloting the scheme in a part of the organization to test reactions and administrative arrangements.

9. Introduce scheme: the earlier communications need to be reinforced generally at this stage and arrangements must be made to provide individual employees with advice through personal contact, a help line or a help screen on the intranet.

10. Evaluate scheme: monitor and measure impact.

Flexible benefits: six tips

- Define business need for flexible benefits.
- Obtain views of employees about their benefits and the degree to which they would like them to be flexed.
- Decide on essential elements of the scheme: core benefits which have to be maintained, benefits that can be flexed and limits on the extent to which these benefits can be flexed, and costing the benefits as necessary to enable menus to be produced and flex funds set up, if appropriate.
- Decide how the scheme should be administered and develop administrative systems.
- Communicate to staff how the flexible benefits scheme works and its advantages for them.
- Provide for advice to employees as required.

Reference

CIPD (2008) *Reward Management Survey*, CIPD, London

26
Pension Schemes

Key concepts and terms

- Accrual rate
- Defined contribution scheme
- Defined benefit scheme
- Occupational pension
- Pension scheme

Learning outcomes

On completing this chapter you should be able to define these key concepts. You should also know about:

- The nature of occupational pensions
- Why they are provided
- The two main types of occupational schemes – defined benefit and defined contribution
- Other types of pension schemes
- The legal limits on providing pensions advice
- Communicating to staff about pensions

Introduction

Pensions provide an income to employees when they retire and to their surviving dependants on the death of the employee, and deferred benefits to employees who leave. Occupational schemes offered by organizations, as distinct from state pensions, are funded by contributions from the organization and usually, but not always, the employee. Occupational pensions are the most significant employee benefit and are a valuable part of the total reward package. But they are perhaps the most complex part.

The so-called 'pensions crisis' has arisen because many occupational schemes are underfunded and suffering the strain of having to cope with more pensioners who are living longer. But to put it in perspective it should be remembered that a huge amount of money in the UK (£1,300 billion) is invested in pension funds, more than in the rest of the EU put together.

The aim of this chapter is to present an outline of why pensions are provided, what they provide and the main types of schemes. The reasons for the shift in occupational schemes from defined benefits (final salary) schemes to defined contribution (money purchase schemes) are discussed, and the chapter continues with a summary of the law relating to providing pensions advice and a discussion of approaches to communicating about pensions.

Why occupational pensions are provided

Pensions are provided because they demonstrate that the organization is a good employer concerned about the long-term interests of its employees who want the security provided by a reasonable pension when they retire. Good pension schemes help to attract and retain high-quality people by maintaining competitive levels of total remuneration.

What occupational pension schemes provide

The range and level of benefits from pension schemes depend on the type of scheme and the level of contributions. In general, schemes provide:

- Benefits on retirement: these are related to the final salary of individuals when they retire or the amount that has been paid into a defined contribution scheme while the individuals were members.

- Benefits on death: the pensions of widows or widowers and children are normally related to the member's anticipated pension; the most common fraction is half.

- Benefits on leaving an employer: individuals leaving an employer can elect to take one of the following options: a deferred pension from the occupational scheme they are leaving, the transfer of the pension entitlement from the present employer to the new employer (though this is not always possible), or a refund of their contributions (but only if they have completed less than two years' membership of the pension scheme).

The two main types of occupational schemes

The two main types of occupational schemes are described below. Other types are covered in the next section.

Defined benefit (final salary) schemes

The main features of a defined benefit scheme are outlined below.

Pension entitlement on retirement

- On retiring the employee is entitled to a pension that is calculated as a fraction of their final salary (on retirement or an average of the last two or three years) multiplied by the length of pensionable service.

- The maximum proportion of salary allowed by the Inland Revenue is two-thirds of final salary after 40 years service.

- The amount of the pension depends on the final salary, the value of the annuity that provides the pension and the accrual rate. The accrual rate refers to the fraction of final salary that can be earned per year of service. When a pension is described as 1/60th it means that 40 years service would produce a two-thirds of final salary pension, and 30 years would produce a pension of half the final salary. This is a fairly typical fraction in private sector firms.

Employer and employee contributions

- Employer contributions can be a fixed percentage of salary. Alternatively the percentage increases with service or is a multiple of the employee's contribution (eg the employer contributes 15 per cent if the employee contributes 5 per cent). The level of employer contribution is typically around 16 per cent.

- Employee contribution rates vary considerably, ranging from 3 per cent to 15 per cent with a median of around 8 per cent.

Pension fund

- Employee and employer contributions are paid into a combined fund and there is no direct link between fund size and the pensions paid.

- The money remaining in the fund after any lump sums have been taken out is invested in an annuity to provide a regular income, the amount of which may be revised upwards periodically to compensate for inflation.

Dependants

Dependants are entitled to a percentage of the employee's pension entitlement if he or she dies during retirement or in service with the company.

Lump sum

Part of the pension may be exchanged for a tax-free lump sum, up to a maximum under Inland Revenue rules of 1/80th per year for up to 40 years service.

Defined contribution (money purchase) schemes

The main features of a defined contribution scheme are discussed below.

Pension entitlement

The employee receives a pension on retirement that is related to the size of the fund accumulated by the combined contributions of the employee and employer. The amount of the pension depends on the size of contributions, the rate of return on the investment of the accumulated fund and the rate of return on an annuity purchased by the employer. It is not related to the employee's final salary.

Contributions

The employer contributes a defined percentage of earnings, which may be fixed, age-related or linked to what the employee pays. The level of employer contribution is typically around 6 per cent. The employee also contributes a fixed percentage of salary.

Pension fund

The contributions are invested and the money used at retirement to purchase a regular income, usually via an annuity contract from an insurance company. The retirement pension is therefore whatever annual payment can be purchased with the money accumulated in the fund for a member.

Members have individual shares of the fund, which represent their personal entitlements and which will directly determine the pensions they receive.

Dependants

Dependants receive death in service and death in retirement pensions.

Lump sum

One-quarter of the pension can be taken as a tax-free lump sum on retirement.

Comparison of defined benefits and defined contribution schemes

The main differences are that a defined benefits (final salary) scheme provides a guaranteed pension to the employee but the employer is unable to predict the costs, which can fluctuate unfavourably. Conversely, a defined contribution (money purchase) scheme provides an uncertain pension and the cost to the employer is predictable. The differences are summarized in Table 26.1.

Defined benefit or defined contribution?

Defined benefit scheme costs and risks

Defined benefit schemes are more costly to employers (16 per cent average contribution) than defined contribution schemes (6 per cent average contribution). They are also more risky for employers because the pension is based on a guaranteed formula and the cost of providing this guaranteed benefit may be higher than expected. Typically, employee contributions are fixed and those of the employer vary on the basis of specialist advice from the scheme actuary. Hence, the risk of higher than expected costs falls on the employer. Costs

Table 26.1   Comparison of defined benefit and defined contribution schemes

Defined benefit (final salary)	Defined contribution (money purchase)
Benefits defined as a fraction of final pensionable pay.	Benefits purchased as an annuity by an accumulation of contributions invested.
Benefits do not depend on investment returns or annuity rates.	Benefits dependent on investment returns, contributions, and cost of annuities at retirement.
Employer contributes necessary costs in excess of employee contributions.	Employer contributions are fixed.
Employer takes financial risk.	Member takes financial risk.
Not easily portable to other employers.	Easily portable to other employers.
Benefits appropriate for long-serving employees with progressive increases in pensionable pay.	Benefits appropriate for short-serving employees or those whose pensionable pay fluctuates.

might exceed expectations for a number of reasons, for example pensioners are living longer (an important factor in putting up costs), the fund investments may perform less well than expected (another important factor recently) or salaries may grow faster than expected. Costs have in fact increased significantly in many schemes and as a result some large pension funds are in deficit.

Defined contribution scheme costs and risks

In a defined contribution scheme the cost of employer contributions is predictable and generally lower than in defined benefit schemes. However, there is a risk that the resulting pension falls short of expectations because the fund investments perform poorly or because the annuity rate (ie the conversion rate from lump sum to regular pension) is unfavourable. This risk falls on the employee.

The move towards defined contribution schemes

Many leading companies have questioned the financial wisdom of final salary provision. Defined benefit schemes provide much more value to older and longer-serving employees but greater labour mobility has led many employers to question this emphasis, particularly in newer industries with young, high-turnover workforces.

The CIPD 2009 Reward Management Survey established that 52 per cent of employers had defined benefit schemes but these were much more common in the public sector (91 per cent). Private sector companies have mainly closed their defined benefit schemes to new entrants and a number are switching existing employees into defined contribution schemes.

Defined benefit schemes are liked by employees and trade unions because they produce a guaranteed income. Trade unions are therefore always hostile to any move towards defined contribution schemes. Such a move will appear to threaten personal security and be detrimental. Even if the change is restricted to new staff, existing employees may well believe, with some reason, that it will be applied to them some time.

Rather than change to a defined contribution scheme, some companies have taken steps to reduce final salary scheme costs. This means retaining final salary provision but with some benefits scaled back. For example, employers have reduced the accrual rate from 1/60th per year of service to 1/80th or, more commonly, have increased employee contributions. Employees and unions are likely to resist such changes but may eventually be persuaded that they are better than a move towards defined contribution provision.

Other types of pension schemes

Hybrid schemes

Hybrid occupational pension schemes aim to split the risk between both parties, although only 2 per cent of the CIPD respondents had them. For example, a defined benefit scheme might be provided for staff who meet an age and/or service qualification, with defined contribution provision applying to other staff.

Personal pensions

Employers cannot compel their employees to join their scheme. As an alternative, employees can take out their own personal pension plan from an approved provider, either as an alternative to an occupational scheme provided by the employer or because there is no occupational scheme available. Personal pension schemes can be contracted out of the State pension scheme and may take contributions from an employer. They are defined contribution (ie money purchase) schemes, which means that the pension is based on what has been paid into the scheme and not on final salary.

Group schemes

Group schemes are in effect a bundle of individual personal pensions for which the employer carries out a payroll function by remitting contributions to a pensions provider.

Stakeholder pension

A stakeholder pension is a government-sponsored scheme, primarily designed for lower-paid employees. It is a low-cost personal pension scheme regulated by the government and provided through pension companies. Employers who employ five or more staff and do not provide a suitable occupational pension scheme for their employees are required by law to offer access to a stakeholder scheme and deduct and pass on employee contributions to the scheme. But employers do not have to make contributions themselves.

A stakeholder pension is a defined contribution arrangement that satisfies certain conditions, designed to ensure that it provides good value for money and that members' interests are protected. These conditions are:

- Flexible contributions: members must be free to pay whatever contributions they like.

- Charges: the maximum charge is 1.5 per cent of the fund.

- Transfers: the scheme is required to accept transfer payments.

- FSA regulation: all stakeholder schemes are regulated by the Financial Services Agency.

- Investments: the scheme must offer a default investment scheme for members who are unwilling to choose between different funds.

Executive pensions

In the private sector, executive pensions are typically provided for by a defined benefit scheme with an accelerated accrual compared with that for other staff. Instead of providing a maximum two-thirds pension after 40 years of service (an accrual rate of 1/60th per year of service), a full pension may be earned after only 20 or 30 years' service (equivalent to an accrual rate of 1/30th or 1/45th). The two-thirds pension provided is normally inclusive of any pensions from previous employments.

The state pension scheme

State pension arrangements are subject to change, and this section is based on the current (2010) arrangements. The State Pension Scheme has two parts, as described below.

The Basic State Pension

The basic state pension is paid at a standard rate, which may be increased each year as long as the required number of National Insurance contributions have been paid.

The State Second Pension

The State Second Pension (also known as the State Additional Pension) pays a pension on earnings for which Class 1 National Insurance contributions have been paid over the years that fall between the lower and the upper earnings limit. The lower earnings limit corresponds roughly with the flat-rate pension for a single person while the upper limit is currently about eight times the lower earning limit. Both limits are adjusted from time to time.

Employers and individuals with a personal pension plan can contract out of the State Second Pension. Occupational pension schemes can contract out if they meet an overall quality test. When a scheme is contracted out, both the employer and the employee pay National Insurance contributions at a lower rate.

Advising employees on pensions

The Financial Services Act 1986 and the Pensions Act 1995 place restrictions on the provision of financial advice to employees. Only those who are directly authorized by one of the regulatory organizations or professional bodies are permitted to give detailed financial advice on investments. Specific advice on the merits or otherwise of a particular personal pension plan – personal pensions are classed as investments by the Financial Services Act – can, however, be given to employees:

- On the company's occupational pension scheme, since it is not classed as an investment.

- About the general principles to be borne in mind when comparing an occupational pension scheme with a personal pension; these could include spelling out the benefits of the company's scheme, thus leaving employees in a better position to compare the benefits with whatever an authorized adviser may indicate are the benefits from a personal plan. What should not be done is to tell people categorically that they will be better off with the company's scheme or to advise them to look elsewhere.

- On their rights, for staff who are leaving, to preserve their pension and the advisability of finding out from their prospective employer whether existing rights can be transferred to their scheme and, if so, what the outcome will be in terms of pension rights at the new company.

- On the general advantages of making additional voluntary contributions.

HR specialists should restrict themselves to giving factual information. They should never suggest what people should do. If in any doubt as to how to respond to a request for information or advice, it is best to refer the matter to the company's own pension specialist or adviser or, if none is available, suggest that the employee should talk to an authorized adviser, for example the individual's own insurance company or bank.

Developing and communicating pensions policies

The pension benefits provided by employers should be developed as an important part of a coherent total reward package. Good schemes demonstrate that employers care about the future security and well-being of their employees, and pensions are a valuable means of gaining and keeping employee commitment to the organization. Younger and more mobile employees are often indifferent to pensions, but the older they get the more they are concerned, and these mature employees contribute largely to organizational success.

Careful consideration needs to be given to telling employees about the scheme. They need to know how it works and how it benefits them – it is too easy for employees to take pensions for granted. It is particularly important to communicate the reasons for any changes and how they will affect staff. This is a demanding situation if a defined benefit scheme is to be replaced by a defined contribution scheme. HR professionals have a key role to play in being honest about the real picture and its alternatives, and informing employees of all the implications.

Pension schemes: six tips

- If you have a defined benefit (final salary) scheme, evaluate the pros and cons of replacing it with a defined contribution (money purchase) scheme for all employees or only for newly recruited employees.

- If you believe it is necessary to switch to a defined contribution scheme, evaluate the pros and cons of leaving existing employees in their defined benefit scheme or transferring them into a defined contribution scheme.

- When examining the pros and cons, consider the possible effects on the morale of existing employees and the impact it might have on attracting new employees.

- Prepare the case for replacing a defined benefits scheme with great care. It is essential to provide convincing reasons for a change that will adversely affect the terms and conditions of employees.

- Communicate the decision through all the channels available. Be prepared for a hostile reception.

- Consider the possibility of alleviating the negative response by offering improvements to other terms and conditions.

Reference

CIPD (2009) *Survey of Reward Management*, CIPD, London

Part VI

The Practice of
Reward Management

Developing Reward Systems

Introduction

The critical and most demanding task that anyone concerned with reward will have to undertake is that of developing and implementing new or revised reward systems that are mainly concerned with total rewards, job evaluation, grade and pay structure design, contingent pay and employee benefits. This is an exacting process of change management and it is where all the knowledge and experience acquired in the different aspects of reward management as covered in this book are put into practice to respond to new demands and circumstances.

It is not enough to know what to do; it is just as necessary to know how to do it and even more necessary to ensure that it has been done as it was supposed to have been done. This means being absolutely clear about the objectives of the change, planning the change on the basis of an analysis of the situation and a diagnosis of the causes of any problems, involving people – managers and staff alike – in the change process, communicating to them about what is happening and why. It also means ensuring that everyone acquires the skills needed to manage the new processes and play a part in them. Finally it involves planning the implementation, managing the implementation process effectively, and monitoring and evaluating outcomes to ensure that the objectives of the exercise have been achieved.

This chapter is mainly concerned with the overall process of developing reward systems, but it includes examples of the specific approaches that can be used in two main areas for development, namely job evaluation and the design of grade and pay structures. The development of other aspects of the reward system is dealt with in the following chapters: total rewards Chapter 3, contingent pay schemes Chapter 10, point-factor evaluation schemes Chapter 16, grade and pay structures Chapter 19, and flexible benefits Chapter 25.

The task of developing and implementing reward systems

The task of development and implementation is a critical one because of the fast-moving nature of the reward scene. It is necessary constantly to review the system to ensure that it is meeting business needs and this frequently means innovating new or fundamentally revised processes. Business and HR strategies change and the reward strategy must change accordingly. This applies to all the main areas of reward management, namely: job evaluation, pay structures, contingent pay and pensions and benefits. Job evaluation schemes decay in use and do not fit new organizational arrangements, pay structures are no longer appropriate, contingent pay schemes do not deliver what was expected from them and pension and benefit schemes have to be changed to meet new legal and fiscal requirements, to cater for different employee needs or to make them more affordable. The task starts with objective setting and continues with processes of analysis, diagnosis, evaluation of alternatives and selection of the most appropriate one, design or development, implementation and evaluation.

Objective setting

It is important at an early stage to be clear about the objectives of any initiative, to clarify what is to be achieved and, after implementation, serve as a basis for evaluation. Broad objectives may be formed at the beginning of the exercise but these are likely to be modified during the project as more information on requirements is obtained and processed. The following are some examples of reward development project objectives.

BT

At BT their objectives were expressed as follows:

Use the full range of rewards (salary, bonus, benefits and recognition) to recruit and retain the best people, and to encourage and reward achievement where actions and behaviours are consistent with the BT values.

Diageo

The objectives at Diageo were to:

- support and enable the talent agenda;
- provide clear principles to enable reward decision making in the business;
- align the reward approach with Diageo business strategy;
- enable every employee to understand why they get paid what they get paid;
- have a customer service ethic that results in great execution.

A finance sector company

The objectives for their 'fresh approach to reward' produced by a finance sector company were:

Change the emphasis from measuring the job and its accountabilities to recognizing the person and the contribution they make to the business; reflect the way the organization is changing by encouraging us to be more responsive to customers; improve reward for excellent performance by freeing up salary ranges.

Friends Provident

The objectives at Friends Provident were to:

- match salaries directly to the market;
- give line managers greater accountability for staff salaries and career progression;
- increase the flexibility of pay arrangements at business unit level;
- facilitate a real and fundamental top-down change in corporate culture;
- reward the best performers by paying salaries above the market rate;
- manage salary costs;
- encourage greater accountability by staff for development of their own competencies.

Tesco

At Tesco the objectives of introducing a broad-banded structure were to:

- achieve more flexibility in determining pay;

- develop a flatter, more flexible organization;

- reward staff for their contribution;

- link remuneration to responsibility and contribution;

- simplify career planning and job classification.

The approach to development and implementation

No initiative should be planned without making a business case for it. The extent to which it will add value rather than create work should be assessed. A value-added approach means that processes and schemes will not be introduced or updated without assessing the effect they are expected to have on the engagement and performance of people, on the ability of the organization to recruit and keep the right sort of employees and, ultimately, on the results achieved by the organization.

Bearing this in mind, and against the background of a preliminary statement of objectives, the approach to the development and implementation of reward systems should be evidence-based, realistic about risks, costs and what can be achieved, focused on how it will be put into effect, and positive about involving stakeholders and communicating information to them on proposals and plans and how they will be affected by them.

Evidence-based development

Evidence-based development means considering what needs to be done by reference to an analysis of the internal and external context and the strengths and weaknesses of the present reward arrangements, benchmarking good practice elsewhere and consulting relevant research. This leads to an assessment of requirements that means addressing questions such as:

- What are the aims of our reward practices? What do we want to achieve with them?

- What would successful reward practices look like? How would we know? What criteria and measures can we use to assess their effectiveness?

- What evidence do we have to assess the current level of effectiveness and to highlight the strongest and weakest aspects of the current rewards package?

- What information can we gather to inform that review and how do we relate financial and non-financial information in making any assessment?

- What should we do in response to these findings?

- What level and type of change is appropriate?

- What are the objectives of the change in such terms as higher levels of engagement, and how will we know they have been achieved?

- How do we pilot, test and implement any changes to maximize their chances of success?

- How do we ensure continuing success in the future, and how should rewards respond to further internal and external changes and developments?

Issues and risk assessment

A major overhaul of a reward system will raise a number of issues involving risks. These need to be analysed, as in the example from a private sector company given in Table 27.1.

Costs

A new or substantially revised reward system is an investment. But the costs of that investment need to be assessed to answer the question 'is it affordable?' and thus provide the basis for deciding whether or not the investment is worthwhile and indicate what can be done to contain costs, and how costs will be controlled during the project.

Table 27.1   Analysing and addressing the issues and risks when changing a reward system

Issues and risks	How we address them
New arrangements not communicated or managed as intended.	<ul><li>Extensive preparation.</li><li>Investment in communications and management training.</li></ul>
Plethora and over-complexity of different reward schemes and practices emerge, damaging cohesion and mobility.	<ul><li>Common principles and frameworks for all aspects of reward.</li></ul>
Hostile employee/trade union reaction.	<ul><li>Effective design and implementation.</li><li>Phased approach to implementation.</li></ul>
Availability and quality of relevant market data.	Source from a variety of quality providers.
Timing and cost overruns.	Effective project management and phasing.

Introducing a new grade structure will almost inevitably incur costs. This is because while the pay of those who are over-graded (red-circled) will not be reduced, at least in the short term, the pay of those who are under-graded (green-circled) will have to be increased immediately or over two or at most three years. Respondents to the e-reward 2007 survey of grade and pay structures who had introduced new structures indicated that the average proportion of employees who were red-circled was 4.9 per cent and the proportion of those green-circled (ie underpaid) was 13.2 per cent. Their costs of dealing with green-circled staff were as high as 8 per cent of pay roll, with an average of just over 2 per cent. It is prudent to assume a cost of 3–4 per cent.

A reality check

Any proposals or plans should be subjected to a reality check:

- Is it worth doing? – What return will we get on our investment? What's the business case in terms of added value? What contribution will it make to supporting the achievement of the organization's strategic goals?

- Can it be done?

- Who does it?

- Have we the resources to do it?

- How do we manage the change?

Planning for implementation

It is normally assumed that the processes of development and implementation are sequential: you develop something and then you implement it. This is a mistake. If constant thought is not given during and throughout the development of a reward system on how it will work and how it will be made to work, then the implementation will fail. The two go together. Implementation plans have to take account of the barriers to reward changes revealed in the research conducted by Brown and Purcell (2007) as shown in Figure 27.1, especially those concerned with the attitudes of line managers and staff, communications and line managers' skills.

The plan for implementation should cover:

- the use of pilot tests to identify any operational problems;

- the possibility of phasing the introduction of the changed system so that each step is manageable in the time available;

- setting up a projects team with an experienced project manager;

- developing an involvement strategy – deciding who should be involved in the development programme and how they should be involved;

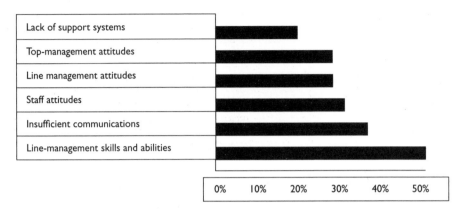

Figure 27.1 Barriers to the implementation of reward changes

- preparing a detailed project plan setting out objectives, timings and cost budgets for each phase and indicating how the project will be controlled;

- formulating a communications strategy;

- preparing a plan for briefing and training line managers.

Involvement

Involve stakeholders from the word go – bottom up as well as top down. It is vital to get the contribution of line managers, staff and employee representatives as well as senior management at all stages of the project. Use attitude surveys, focus groups and workshops to obtain views, explore issues and exchange ideas. The aim is to achieve ownership and acceptance of the outcome of the project.

Communication

Effective communications are important because reward systems can be complex and difficult to understand and therefore need to be explained carefully. Rewards are an emotive issue. So many personal needs are tied up in them – for security, recognition, status and so on – that changes to them almost inevitably generate emotional and often hostile responses from at least some employees. People can be suspicious about the reasons for change and feel that it will affect them adversely. It may be difficult to overcome these fears but a sustained attempt must be made to do so.

The development and implementation programme

The stages of a development and implementation programme are illustrated in Figure 27.2.

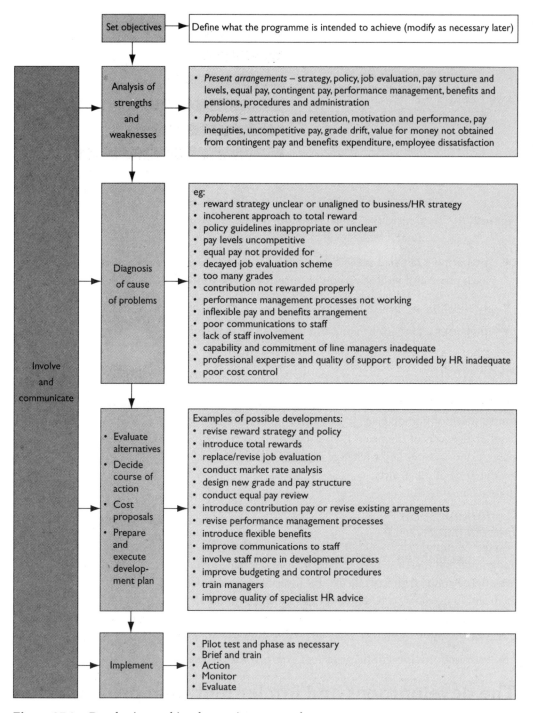

Figure 27.2   Developing and implementing a reward system

Advice from practitioners

The practical advice given below originates from e-reward research interviews (2003 to 2009).

B&Q

B&Q carried out a thorough investigation into the context of the organization – its internal and external environment – and the characteristics of the existing reward system and the views of all the relevant stakeholders. The aim was to get, via an in-depth research exercise, a full understanding of the present arrangements, changing employment situation and future requirements. The company gathered and marshalled data from two perspectives:

External perspective

The analysis of the external environment included:

- examination of the changing labour market;
- literature review of employers' responses to emerging employment trends and how competitors reward staff;
- an analysis of the HR and reward strategies typically adopted by high-performing organizations;
- a survey of 50 high-performing people in a sample of 20 high-performing organizations, examining what these staff need in the reward package;
- two commissioned surveys of 200 people each to examine 'external' perceptions of B&Q as an employer;
- a benchmarking exercise using retail industry salary.

Internal perspective

The analysis of the internal environment included:

- a full audit of the current reward investment and its focus;
- consideration of existing use of bonus schemes;
- examination of pay for performance arrangements;
- current provision of financial and non-financial rewards;
- findings of 20 focus groups comprising people from different levels of B&Q and different divisions.

To gain an understanding of employee needs and the rewards that motivate its people to deliver results, B&Q consulted its stakeholders. It canvassed the opinions of middle managers, team leaders, line managers and store employees generally through a series of focus groups. The company commissioned a total of 20 focus groups, each consisting of at least 10 people to facilitate discussion. Their members were representative of the different activities and occupations in the organization.

Will Astill, B&Q's reward manager, recommends these guiding principles:

- Without cooperation change strategies are likely to fail.

- Secure directors' 'buy-in' right away.

- Never underestimate the value of in-depth employee consultation.

- Remember that strategy formulation is an evolutionary process.

- Look at how well you communicate your reward package.

- No initiative should be implemented without examining the return on investment.

- Evaluate the effectiveness of programmes and take action as required.

- Budget well in advance.

A final word from Will Astill:

An overriding theme running through our review was on the desirability of adopting a strategic approach. It wasn't a case of 'let's follow best practice', nor were we lured into adopting the latest 'fads' and 'fashions'. Applying a bespoke system – taking what someone has done before and adapting it to your organization – will not push you ahead of rivals. Our emphasis throughout the two-year process was on what's right for the business.

Implement and review – the BT approach

Kevin Brady, HR Director, Reward and Employee Relations at BT made the following suggestions:

- Business sponsorship and ownership is key

  Secure 'sponsorship and ownership' amongst senior people – a feeling that the change is something that they are happy to live with because they have been involved in its planning and introduction – it has become their change.

- Don't underestimate resistance

  The level of resistance that may arise when reorganizing reward systems should never be underestimated, hence the importance of sponsorship, communication and training.

- Project management skills are critical

  The project must be carefully planned and managed under a skilled project manager.

- Engage, engage, engage!

  Ownership and acceptance are much more likely if the maximum degree of engagement of all concerned is built into the entire change programme.

- Clear, consistent communications

  It is imperative to communicate clearly and consistently to staff at every stage of the process.

Centrica

Centrica's nine success criteria for developing reward systems are:

- partnership;
- preparation;
- business engagement;
- employee engagement;
- union engagement;
- financial modelling;
- communications;
- project administration;
- business-as-usual administration.

GlaxoSmithKline

'Don't expect people to change overnight and don't try to force change. It is better to reinforce desirable behaviour than to attempt to enforce a particular way of doing things' (Paul Craven, Compensation Director, R&D).

Lloyds TSB

When developing new reward systems Tim Fevyer, then Senior Manager, Compensation and Benefits, recommended these guiding principles:

- The success of new reward systems depends heavily on talking to people, and asking what they would like to see.

- It is imperative to communicate to staff at every stage of the process – even in advance of launch – explaining the planned changes, the rationale behind them, and how it affects the workforce. You then need to continue to give progress reports to employees and obtain their input on an ongoing basis.

- The success of any total reward programme will hinge on the degree to which employees feel a sense of ownership – a feeling amongst people that the change is something that they are happy to live with because they have been involved in its planning and introduction – it has become their change.

- It's vital that you get pay right – otherwise much damage can be done. But once it is, don't treat it like a sophisticated lever to influence motivation and empowerment. Pay is no longer the great differentiator. The only way we are going to keep people is by engaging them.

- Remember that reward processes can indeed underpin structural and cultural change and support the achievement of business goals. But not on their own, and they do not lead change.

- Although a fundamentally simple concept, nobody should pretend that total reward is not a difficult and time-consuming process to put into practice.

- All reward initiatives should be prioritized – only those processes and schemes that are expected to generate the greatest value should be introduced.

A final word from Tim Fevyer:

> *You cannot succeed without focusing on business goals and understanding what these mean for your core people goals. Shareholder value was our ultimate objective. But we unbundled this objective and examined how we would generate shareholder value through our reward strategy. We wanted to recruit, retain and engage good people. You might do that in the short term by throwing more money at people but we wanted a long-term solution that really focused on the individual and their contribution within the business. Meeting individual needs by providing flexibility within a framework has enabled us to generate significant value for both employees and the company.*

Tesco

Richard Sullivan, Tesco's group reward manager, recommends that managers should keep in mind these guiding principles:

- Don't underestimate the old culture – it will take time to change it.

- Be prepared to challenge any return to the old ways.

- Management capability is key to communicating issues.

- Employee communication is key to having the new system understood.

- Obtain managers' input when designing the new process; this will help them explain it to others and will increase their commitment to it.

Duncan Brown

Interviews conducted in 2009 by Duncan Brown, Director of the Institute for Employment Studies (Armstrong, Brown and Reilly, forthcoming), produced the following comments:

You can't adopt a market-based, 'must be' approach. Pay attention to the organization, its culture and its needs, gather information and evidence for (reward) change, but help managers to understand, support and make those changes (a Head of Reward and Development in a software company).

In a service-driven organization like ours, with lots of professional people, if you come up with a grand master-plan, people will find 53 reasons why they can't do it. You have to change more subtly, helping them to see the connections and support it, introducing change 'under and up' rather than down from the top. People now totally buy into the behaviours and indicators we have developed (Liz Booth, Director of Human Resources, NSPCC).

Reward symposium

A symposium of reward specialists as reported by Sandringham (2000) produced the following suggestions on developing reward systems that work:

- Align your system with the culture of the organization.

- Be careful about generalizations: segmenting staff in the way you segment customers may allow you to target your reward system better.

- Look at the whole bundle of reward, not just pay; people leave because the job is not satisfying or interesting, or because they feel their boss is treating them badly.

Developing reward systems: six tips

- Be clear on what has to be achieved and why.
- Ensure that what you do fits the strategy, culture and circumstances of the organization.
- Don't follow fashion – do your own thing.
- Keep it simple – over-complexity is a common reason for failure.
- Don't rush – it takes longer than you think.
- Communicate, involve and train.

References

Armstrong, M, Brown, D and Reilly, P (forthcoming) *Evidence-Based Reward Management*, Kogan Page, London

Brown, D and Purcell, J (2007) Reward management: on the line, *Compensation and Benefits Review*, **39**, pp 28–34

e-reward (2003–2009) Research reports, e-reward, Stockport

e-reward (2007) *Survey of Job Evaluation*, e-reward, Stockport

Sandringham, St J (2000) Pay per view, *People Management*, 3 February, pp 41–43

Managing Reward Systems

Learning outcomes

On completing this chapter you should be able to define these key concepts. You should also know about:

- Reward policies
- Reward forecasting
- Reward budgets
- Compa-ratio analysis
- Attrition analysis
- Assessing added value

- Conducting general pay reviews
- Conducting individual pay reviews
- Reward procedures
- Computer-assisted reward
- Communicating to employees

Introduction

Reward management involves the management of complex systems. This is a demanding task requiring the formulation and implementation of policies, control, monitoring and evaluation, pay reviews, procedures, using computers and communicating to employees as explained in this chapter. The starting point is a clear set of policies.

Reward policies

Reward policies set specific guidelines for decision making and action and therefore provide the framework for managing a reward system. They indicate what the organization and its management are expected to do about managing reward and how they will behave in given circumstances when dealing with reward issues. They can be distinguished from guiding principles, which usually express a more generalized philosophy. The key reward policy areas are described below.

Level of rewards

The policy on the level of rewards indicates whether the company is a high payer, is content to pay median or average rates of pay or even, exceptionally, accepts that it has to pay below the average. Pay policy, which is sometimes referred to as the 'pay stance' or 'pay posture' of a company, will depend on a number of factors. These include the extent to which the company demands high levels of performance from its employees, the degree to which there is competition for good-quality people, the traditional stance of the company, the organization culture, and whether or not it can or should afford to be a high payer. A firm may say that, 'We will pay upper quartile salaries because we want our staff to be upper quartile performers.'

Policies on pay levels will also refer to differentials and the number of steps or grades that should exist in the pay hierarchy. This will be influenced by the structure of the company. In today's flatter organizations an extended or complex pay hierarchy may not be required on the grounds that it does not reflect the way in which work is organized and will constrain flexibility.

Policies on the level of rewards also cover employee benefits – pensions, sick pay, health care, holidays and perks such as company cars.

External competitiveness versus internal equity

A policy needs to be formulated on the extent to which rewards are market driven rather than equitable. This policy will be influenced by the culture and reward philosophies of the organization and the pressures on the business to obtain and keep high-quality staff. Any organizations that have to attract and retain staff who are much in demand and where market rates are therefore high, may, to a degree, have to sacrifice their ideals (if they have them) of internal equity to the realism of the market place. They will provide 'market pay'; in other words, they will be 'market driven'.

The pay management process must cope as best it can when the irresistible force of market pressures meets the immovable object of internal equity. There will always be some degree of tension in these circumstances, and while no solution will ever be simple or entirely satisfactory, there is one basic principle that can enhance the likelihood of success. That principle is to make explicit and fully identifiable the compromises with internal equity that are made and have to be made in response to market pressures.

The policy may indicate that market considerations will drive levels of pay in the organization. It may, however, allow for the use of market supplements – a payment that reflects market rates in addition to the rate for a job as determined by internal equity . The policy may lay down that these payments should be reviewed regularly and no longer offered if they are unnecessary. Market supplements for those who have them may not be withdrawn (the people concerned would not lose pay), but adjustments may be made to pay progression to bring their rates more into line with those for comparable jobs. Market pay and market supplements can lead to gender inequalities if, as is often the case, men in comparable jobs are paid more generally or more men get market supplements than women. Equal pay case law has ruled that market pay and market supplements should be 'objectively justified', and the requirement to do this should be included in the pay policy.

The 2007 e-reward survey of grade and pay structures revealed that respondents with market supplements adopted the following policies when such supplements were no longer required:

- remove immediately – 33 per cent;

- retain until upgraded – 30 per cent;

- reduce progressively – 19 per cent;

- protect in line with policy – 18 per cent.

Segmentation

Segmentation involves varying the reward package for different jobs or to reflect the types and levels of contribution people make, or providing rewards that are tailored to meet individual needs.

A policy on segmentation will recognize that parts of the workforce and individuals in the successive stages of their career may be motivated by different combinations of rewards. A total rewards package can be tailored to meet these needs. Rewards may be segmented to take account of key employee differences. This could mean individual performance-related pay for some, team reward for others, and other forms of pay progression and recognition rather than incentives for a third group. This is a flexible approach to reward management although it should be flexibility within a framework, the framework being provided by guiding principles that apply to all aspects of reward.

Assimilation policies

The introduction of a new or considerably revised pay structure means that policies have to be developed on how existing employees should be assimilated into it. These policies cover where people should be placed in their new grades and what happens to them if their new grade and pay range means that their existing rate is above or below the new scale for their job. The policy should therefore cover 'red-circling' (identifying and dealing with overpaid people) and 'green-circling' (identifying and dealing with underpaid people). In the case of red-circled staff, 'protection' policies may have to be formulated to safeguard their existing rates of pay. In the case of green-circled staff, the policy may have to determine when (not if) their pay should be increased to fit into the new scale. It is sometimes necessary to save costs by phasing the increase, and this should be included as a possible policy.

Protection policies

Protection (sometimes called safeguarding) is the process of dealing with the situation when, following the introduction of a new pay structure, the existing pay of some employees may be above the maximum for their new grade and they are therefore 'red-circled'. In these circumstances the general rule is that no one should suffer a reduction in their present rate of pay. Beyond this, the issues are what exactly is to be protected and whether or not the protection should be for a limited period, and if so, for how long.

The usual approach is to allow staff to continue to earn any increments to which they are entitled under existing arrangements up to the maximum of their present scale. They are also entitled to receive any across-the-board (cost of living) increases awarded to staff generally for the protection period, if it is limited, or for as long as they remain in their present job if there is no limit (in the latter case they are on what is sometimes called a 'personal to job holder' scale). If the period is limited, they will no longer be entitled to general increases after the limit has been reached until their rate of pay falls within the new scale for their job. They will then be entitled to the same increases as any other staff in their grade. When the individual concerned leaves the job, the scale of pay for the job reverts to the standard range as set up following job evaluation.

The argument for limiting the protection period is that, unless this is done, equal pay problems may arise because an inequitable differential will have been perpetuated. The Equal Opportunities Commission (EOC) in its Good Practice Guide on Job Evaluation Schemes Free of Sex Bias, stated that red-circling 'should not be used on such a scale that it amounts to sex discrimination'. And as suggested by the Equal Pay Task Force: 'The use of red or green circling which maintains a difference in pay between men and women over more than a phase-in period of time will be difficult to justify.'

The respondents to the 2007 e-reward survey of grade and pay structures adopted the following protection periods:

- unlimited – 53 per cent;
- one year – 12 per cent;
- two years – 10 per cent;
- three years – 6 per cent;
- four years – 15 per cent;
- five to ten years – 4 per cent.

The role of line managers

The extent to which the responsibility for rewards should be devolved to line managers is a policy decision. The aim may be to devolve it as far as possible, bearing in mind the need to ensure that other reward policy guidelines are followed and that consistent decisions are made across the organization by line managers. The policy may cover the level of decisions managers can make, the guidance that should be made available to them and how consistency will be achieved.

Transparency

Traditionally, organizations in the private sector have kept information about pay policies secret. This is no longer a tenable position. Without transparency, people will believe that the organization has something to hide, often with reason. There is no chance of building a satisfactory psychological contract unless the organization spells out its reward policies and practices. Transparency is achieved through involvement and communication.

Controlling reward

The implementation of reward policies and procedures should be monitored and controlled to ensure that value for money is obtained. Control is easier if the grade and pay structure is well defined and clear guidelines exist on how it and the benefits arrangements should be managed. Control should be based on forecasts, budgets and costings, as described below, and by monitoring and evaluating the implementation of reward policies as discussed in the next part of this chapter.

Reward forecasts

It is necessary to forecast future payroll costs taking into account the number of people employed and the impact of pay reviews and contingent pay awards. The cost implications of developments such as a revised job evaluation scheme, a new grade and pay structure or a flexible benefits scheme also have to be forecast.

Reward budgets

Pay review budgets set out the increase in payroll costs that will result for either general or individual pay reviews and are used for cost forecasts generally and as the basis for the guidelines issued to line managers on conducting individual reviews.

Total payroll budgets are based on the number of people employed in different jobs and their present and forecast rates of pay. In a budgetary control system they are aggregated from the budgets prepared by departmental managers but HR provides guidance on the allowances that should be made for pay increases. The aim is to maintain control over payroll costs and restrain managers from the temptation to overpay their staff.

Costing reward processes

Proposed changes to the reward system need to be costed for approval by senior management. The costs would include development costs such as consultants' fees, software, literature, additional staff and, possibly, the opportunity costs arising when staff are seconded to a development project.

Implementation costs also have to be projected. A new grade and pay structure, for example, can easily result in an increase to the payroll of 3–4 per cent. New contingent pay schemes may also cost more, although the aim should be to make them self-financing.

Monitoring and evaluating reward policies and practices

The effectiveness of reward policies and practices should be monitored and evaluated against the requirements of the organization. Monitoring is carried out through compa-ratio analysis, attrition analysis, assessing added value and the use of attitude surveys. Evaluation, as described in more detail in Chapter 29, should compare outcomes with the objectives set for the new practice (this is why setting objectives for reward initiatives is so important).

Compa-ratio analysis

A compa-ratio (short for 'comparative ratio') measures the relationship in a graded pay structure between actual and policy rates of pay as a percentage. The policy value used is the mid-point or reference point in a pay range, which represents the 'target rate' for a fully competent individual in any job in the grade. This point is aligned with market rates in accordance with the organization's market stance (its policy on the relationship between its levels of pay and market rates).

Compa-ratios can be used to define the extent to which pay policy is achieved (the relationship between the policy and actual rates of pay). The analysis of compa-ratios indicates what action may have to be taken to slow down or accelerate increases if compa-ratios are too high or too low compared with the policy level. This is sometimes called 'mid-point management'. Compa-ratios can also be used to measure where an individual is placed in a pay range, and therefore provide information on the size of pay increases when a pay matrix is used, as described later in this chapter.

Compa-ratios are calculated as follows:

$$\frac{\text{actual rate of pay}}{\text{mid or reference point of range}} \times 100$$

A compa-ratio of 100 per cent means that actual pay and policy pay are the same. Compa-ratios that are higher or lower than 100 per cent mean that, respectively, pay is above or below the policy target rate. For example, if the target (policy) rate in a range were £20,000 and the average pay of all the individuals in the grade were £18,000, the compa-ratio would be 90 per cent. Compa-ratios establish differences between policy and practice. The reasons for such differences need to be established.

Analysing attrition

Attrition or slippage takes place when employees enter jobs at lower rates of pay than the previous incumbents. If this happens payroll costs will go down, given an even flow of starters and leavers and a consistent approach to the determination of rates of pay. In theory attrition can help to finance pay increases within a range. It has been claimed that fixed incremental systems can be entirely self-financing because of attrition, but the conditions under which this can happen are so exceptional that it probably never happens.

Attrition can be calculated by the formula: total percentage increase to payroll arising from general or individual pay increases minus total percentage increase in average rates of pay. If it can be proved that attrition is going to take place, the amount involved can be taken into account as a means of at least partly financing individual pay increases. Attrition in a pay system with regular progression through ranges and a fairly even flow of starters and leavers is typically between 2 per cent and 3 per cent, but this should not be regarded as a norm.

Assessing added value

Assessing the added value or value for money provided by existing practices, or by new practices when they are implemented, is a major consideration when monitoring and evaluating reward management processes. Evaluating the cost of innovations may lead to the reconsideration of proposals in order to ensure that they will provide added value. Evaluating the value for money obtained from existing reward practices leads to the identification of areas for improvement.

Affordability should be a major issue when reviewing reward management developments and existing practices. Added value is achieved when the benefits of a reward practice either exceed its cost or at least justify the cost. At the development stage it is therefore necessary to carry out cost–benefit assessments. The two fundamental questions to be answered are: 1) 'What business needs will this proposal meet?' and 2) 'How will the proposal meet the needs?' The costs and benefits of existing practices should also be assessed on the same basis.

Attitude surveys

An attitude survey is a valuable means of evaluating and monitoring reward practices by assessing the views of those at the receiving end of pay policies as a basis for taking action. An example of a reward attitude survey is given in Appendix A.

Conducting pay reviews

Pay reviews are general or 'across-the-board' reviews in response to movements in the cost of living or market rates, or following pay negotiations with trade unions or individual reviews that determine the pay progression of individuals in relation to their performance or contribution. They are one of the most visible aspects of reward management (the other is job grading) and are an important means of implementing the organization's reward policies and demonstrating to employees how these policies operate.

Employees expect that general reviews will maintain the purchasing power of their pay by compensating for increases in the cost of living. They will want their levels of pay to be competitive with what they could earn elsewhere. And they will want to be rewarded fairly and equitably for the contribution they make.

General reviews

General reviews take place when employees are given an increase in response to general market rate movements, increases in the cost of living, or union negotiations. General reviews are often combined with individual reviews but employees are usually informed of both the general and individual components of any increase they receive. Alternatively the general review may be conducted separately to enable better control to be achieved over costs and to focus employees' attention on the performance-related aspect of their remuneration.

Some organizations have completely abandoned the use of across-the-board reviews. They argue that the decision on what people should be paid should be an individual matter, taking into account the personal contribution people are making and their 'market worth' – how they as individuals are valued in the market place. This enables the organization to adopt a more flexible approach to allocating pay increases in accordance with the perceived value of individuals to the organization.

The steps required to conduct a general review

1. Decide on the budget.

2. Analyse data on pay settlements made by comparable organizations and rates of inflation.

3. Conduct negotiations with trade unions as required.

4. Calculate costs.

5. Adjust the pay structure – by either increasing the pay brackets of each grade by the percentage general increase, or by increasing pay reference points by the overall percentage and applying different increases to the upper or lower limits of the bracket, thus altering the shape of the structure.

6. Inform employees.

Individual reviews

Individual pay reviews determine contingent pay increases or bonuses. The e-reward 2004 survey of contribution pay found that the average size of the contingent pay awards made by respondents was 3.5 per cent (it was 3.3 per cent in 2004). Individual awards may be based on ratings; an overall assessment that does not depend on ratings or ranking as discussed below.

Individual pay reviews based on ratings

Managers propose increases on the basis of their performance management ratings within a given pay review budget and in accordance with pay review guidelines. Eighty per cent of the respondents to the e-reward 2009 survey of contingent pay used ratings to inform contingent pay decisions.

There is a choice of methods. The simplest way is to have a direct link between the rating and the pay increase; for example:

Rating	Increase (%)
A	6
B	4
C	3
D	2
E	0

This approach was used by 36 per cent of the respondents to the e-reward 2009 survey.

A more sophisticated approach is to use a pay matrix, as illustrated in Table 28.1. This indicates the percentage increase payable for different performance ratings according to the position of the individual's pay in the pay range. This is sometimes referred to as an 'individual compa-ratio' and expresses pay as a percentage of the mid-point in a range. A compa-ratio of 100 per cent means that the salary would be at the mid-point.

This approach was used by 41 per cent of the respondents to the e-reward 2009 survey.

Linking pay reviews to performance reviews

Many people argue that linking performance management too explicitly to pay prejudices the essential developmental nature of performance management. However, realistically, it is accepted that decisions on performance-related or contribution-related increases have to be based on some form of assessment. One solution is to 'decouple' performance management and the pay review by holding them several months apart, and 47 per cent of the respondents to the e-reward 2009 survey did this. There is still a read-across but it is not so immediate. Some try to do without formulaic approaches (ratings and pay matrices) altogether, although it is impossible to dissociate contingent pay completely from some form of assessment.

Table 28.1 A pay matrix

	Percentage pay increase according to performance rating and position in pay range (compa-ratio)			
Rating	Position in pay range			
	80%–90%	91%–100%	101%–110%	111%–120%
Excellent	12%	10%	8%	6%
Very effective	10%	8%	6%	4%
Effective	6%	4%	3%	0
Developing	4%	3%	0	0
Ineligible	0	0	0	0

Doing without ratings

Twenty per cent of the respondents to the 2009 e-reward survey of contingent pay did without ratings. One respondent to the e-reward survey explained that in the absence of ratings, the approach used was 'informed subjectivity', which meant considering ongoing performance in the form of overall contribution.

Some companies adopt what might be called a holistic approach. Managers propose where people should be placed in the pay range for their grade, taking into account their contribution and pay relative to others in similar jobs, their potential and the relationship of their current pay to market rates. The decision may be expressed in the form of a statement that an individual is now worth £30,000 rather than £28,000. The increase is 7 per cent, but what counts is the overall view about the value of a person to the organization, not the percentage increase to that person's pay.

Ranking

Ranking is carried out by managers who place staff in a rank order according to an overall assessment of relative contribution or merit and then distribute performance ratings through the rank order. The top 10 per cent could get an A rating, the next 15 per cent a B rating and so on. The ratings determine the size of the reward. A forced ranking or 'vitality curve' system may be used to compel managers to conform to predetermined proportions of staff in each grade. But ranking depends on fair, consistent and equitable assessments, which cannot be guaranteed, and assumes that there is some sort of standard distribution of ability across the organization, which may not be the case.

Guidelines to managers on conducting individual pay reviews

Whichever approach is adopted, guidelines have to be issued to managers on how they should conduct reviews. These guidelines will stipulate that they must keep within their budgets and may indicate the maximum and minimum increases that can be awarded with an indication of how awards could be distributed. For example, when the budget is 4 per cent overall, it might be suggested that a 3 per cent increase should be given to the majority of staff and the others given higher or lower increases as long as the total percentage increase does not exceed the budget. Managers in some companies are instructed that they must follow a forced pattern of distribution (a forced choice system) but only 8 per cent of the respondents to the 2003 CIPD survey (Armstrong and Baron, 2004) used this method. To help them to explore alternatives, managers may be provided with a spreadsheet facility in which the spreadsheets contain details of the existing rates of staff and can be used to model alternative distributions on a 'what if' basis. Managers may also be encouraged to 'fine tune' their pay recommendations to ensure that individuals are on the right track within their grade according to their level of performance, competence and time in the job compared with their peers. To do this, they need guidelines on typical rates of progression in relation to performance, skill or competence, and specific guidance on what they can and should do. They also need information on the relative positions of their staff in the pay structure in relation to the policy guidelines.

Conducting individual pay reviews

Steps required to conduct individual pay reviews

1. Agree budget.

2. Prepare and issue guidelines on the size, range and distribution of awards and on methods of conducting the review.

3. Provide advice and support.

4. Review proposals against budget and guidelines and agree modifications to them if necessary.

5. Summarize and cost proposals and obtain approval.

6. Update payroll.

7. Inform employees.

A description of how a company makes individual pay decisions is given below.

Making pay decisions in a finance sector company

We look at a number of things when making a decision on an individual's pay. One will be the size of the role as determined by job evaluation, and we also consider market data and location to determine the average salary that you would expect to pay for that role. We then look at how the individual has performed over the last 12 months: Have they contributed what was expected of them? Have they contributed above and beyond their peers? Have they underperformed in respect of what was required of them? These are not ratings, they are just guidelines given to managers as to whether the individual should be given an average, above-average or below-average increase. We have a devolved budget and managers have to make decisions as to what percentage they should give to different people. We suggest that if, for example, a manager has six people carrying out the same roles then, from an equal pay point of view, if they are delivering at the same level and are all competent, they should be getting similar salaries. Individuals paid below the market rate who are performing effectively may get a bigger pay rise to bring them nearer the market rate for the role.

It is essential to provide advice, guidance and training to line managers as required. Some managers will be confident and capable from the start. Others will have a lot to learn.

Reward procedures

Reward procedures deal with grading jobs, fixing rates of pay and handling appeals.

Grading jobs

The procedures for grading jobs set out how job evaluation should be used to grade a new job or re-grade an existing one. A point-factor evaluation scheme that has defined grades may be used for all new jobs and to deal with requests for re-grading. However, an analytical matching process (see Chapter 16) may be used to compare the role profiles of the jobs to be graded with grade or level profiles or profiles of benchmark jobs. This is likely to be the case in large organizations and for broad-banded structures.

Fixing rates of pay on appointment

The procedure should indicate how much freedom line managers and HR have to pay above the minimum rate for the job. The freedom may be limited to, say, 10 per cent above the minimum or two or three pay points on an incremental scale. More scope is sometimes allowed to respond to market rate pressures or to attract particularly well-qualified staff by paying up to the reference point or target salary in a pay range, subject to HR approval and bearing in mind the need to provide scope for contingent pay increases. If recruitment supplements or premia are used the rules for offering them to candidates must be clearly defined.

Promotion increases

The procedure will indicate what is regarded as a meaningful increase on promotion, often 10 per cent or more. To avoid creating anomalies, the level of pay has to take account of what other people are paid who are carrying out work at a similar level, and it is usual to lay down a maximum level that does not take the pay of the promoted employee above the reference point for the new range.

Appeals

It is customary to include the right to appeal against gradings as part of a job evaluation procedure. Appeals against pay decisions are usually made through the organization's grievance procedure.

The use of computers in reward management

The ever-evolving world of IT and electronic communications has changed the way salary data are reviewed and managed quite radically in the last decade. Applications and data can now be accessed and assessed from almost anywhere in the world; organizations are making increasing use of the internet, data on market rates and pay settlements is published on the internet and users can communicate at speed through e-mail. Computers and the software are becoming more and more powerful and sophisticated. HR or reward specialists can analyse the implications of new grade structures, cost pay review matrices and plan salary reviews, and options can rapidly be costed through simple changes on a spreadsheet. 'Self-serve' systems enable line management to carry out a number of reward tasks, such as pay reviews. Increasing use is being made of computers to support reward administration and decision making in the areas of:

- providing a reward database;
- job evaluation;
- grade and pay structure modelling;
- pay review modelling;
- equal pay reviews.

The reward database

The reward database stores data on employees' pay, earnings and benefits so that it can be updated, processed and communicated as information to users. It consists of systematically organized and interrelated sets of files (collections of records serving as the basic unit of data storage) and allows for combinations of data to be selected as required by different users. The database contains information imported from the payroll or personnel information system. This information may include personal and job details, job grade, basic pay, position in the pay range (compa-ratio), earnings through variable pay, pay history (progression, and general and individual pay increases), performance management ratings, details of employee benefits, pension contributions, contributions to Save as You Earn schemes and the choices made under a flexible benefits system, including pension contributions.

The database can be used, for example, to:

- Produce listings of employees by job category, job grade, rate of pay, position in range and size in actual or percentage terms of the last increase and, if required, previous individual performance pay increases.

- Generate reports analysing distributions of pay by grade, including compa-ratios for each grade and the organization as a whole. Extracts from these reports can be downloaded to the personal computers of managers responsible for pay decisions to assist them in conducting pay reviews.

- Initiate and print notifications of pay increases and update the payroll database.

- Use electronic mail facilities to transmit data.

In using the database it is necessary that the provisions of the Data Protection Act 1998 are met. Among other things, this requires that personal data held for any purpose should not be used or disclosed in any manner incompatible with that purpose, and appropriate security measures must be taken against unauthorized access to or disclosure of those data. If data are going to be downloaded it will be essential to control who gets what. The importance of data protection will also have to be spelt out to managers.

Computer-aided job evaluation

Computers can be used to help directly with job evaluation processes, as described in Chapter 16.

Software packages

Micro-based software packages have been developed to carry out the various processes referred to above. Proprietary software is usually designed as a standard software shell within which there are a number of functions that allow users to customize the system to meet their own needs.

Grade and pay structure modelling

Software packages available from firms such as Link Consultants and Pilat UK use the output from a computerized job evaluation exercise contained in the database to model alternative grade structures by reference to the distribution of points scores against the existing pay rates for the jobs covered by job evaluation. The computer produces a scattergram and a trend line showing the relationship between pay and the job evaluation scores. The programme will then enable a proposed grade structure to be superimposed on the scattergram, identifying those jobs above or below the new grade boundaries. The cost of bringing the pay of those below the new boundaries to the minimum rate for their new grades is then calculated by the computer.

Alternative grade configurations can then be superimposed on the scattergram to find out if the number of jobs below the lower limits of their new grades will be reduced. The computer then calculates the lower costs of bringing the fewer jobs which are now below the minimum up to the minimum. This modelling process can continue until the optimum configuration of grades from the point of view of costs is achieved. A decision can then be made about whether this grade structure or one of the others should be selected. The lowest-cost option would not necessarily be chosen as it might produce an unmanageable grade structure, for example having too few grades with too much scope for pay progression within them.

Pay review modelling

General reviews

The computer can use the database to provide information on the total cost of a proposed general pay review and the effect this will have on other costs, for example pensions. The program can then model alternative levels. Computers can model the effect on costs of alternative increases.

Individual reviews

It is now increasingly typical to manage pay reviews for an organization on a spreadsheet, through which a number of alternative options can be tested. Spreadsheets provide line managers with a worksheet, divided into cells, into which can be inserted text, numbers or formulae. This allows the user to carry out complex 'what if' analyses of the impact on the pay review budget of alternative distributions of awards to staff. Analyses can be saved as a separate file for future recall when the proposals are approved. Spreadsheets can be printed out in report or graphical form. In some organizations, line managers carry out the modelling themselves using a spreadsheet with data provided by HR, and their conclusions can be reviewed and approved and aggregated into an overall cost of the review analysed by departments. In others, HR and reward specialists carry out salary reviews for each function or department with the relevant line managers on-site, using a laptop.

The problem with spreadsheets is that they can be quite complex and do not always work well in larger applications. Software such as the Pay Modeller marketed by Link Consultants may be the answer to these problems.

Equal pay reviews

Software is available to support equal pay reviews and analyses. These range from database tools that enable data to be imported from a range of sources to generate pay gap analyses, such as the e-Review Equal Pay toolkit, to more sophisticated tools that allow for a broader range of analysis possibilities using different data cuts, including the tool developed by Link.

Communicating to employees

Transparency is important. Employees need to know how reward policies will affect them and how pay and grading decisions have been made. They need to be convinced that the system is fair. They should also be given information on the value of their total reward package. But bear in mind that as Erickson (2004) pointed out: 'Employees won't hear unless they feel they're being listened to – no matter how professionally you handle top-down communications.'

Communicating to employees collectively

Employees and their representatives should be informed about the guiding principles and policies that underpin the reward system and the reward strategies that drive it. They should understand the grade and pay structure, how grading decisions are made, including the job evaluation system, how their pay can progress within the structure, the basis upon which contingent pay increases are determined and policies on the provision of benefits, including details of a flexible benefits scheme if one is available.

Communicating to individual employees

Individual employees should understand how their grade, present rate of pay and pay increases have been determined, and the pay opportunities available to them – the scope for pay progression and how their contribution will be assessed through performance management. They should be informed of the value of the benefits they receive so that they are aware of their total remuneration and, if appropriate, how they can exercise choice over the range or scale of their benefits through a flexible benefits scheme.

As many means as possible should be used to communicate to employees. Possible methods include:

- individual briefings;
- team briefings;
- road shows and open days;
- intranet, including bulletin boards;
- CD-ROMs;
- newsletters;
- individual letters to employees' home addresses;
- meetings, Q&A sessions, focus groups;
- demonstrations with computer modelling;
- telephone and e-mail helplines;
- one-to-one consultations.

Conducting individual pay reviews: six tips

- Agree budget.
- Prepare and issue guidelines on the size, range and distribution of awards and on methods of conducting the review.
- Provide advice and support.
- Review proposals against budget and guidelines and agree modifications to them if necessary.
- Summarize and cost proposals and obtain approval.
- Inform employees.

References

Armstrong, M and Baron, A (2004) *Performance Management: Action and impact*, CIPD, London

e-reward (2004) *Survey of Contingent Pay*, e-reward, Stockport

e-reward (2007) *Survey of Grade and Pay Structures*, e-reward, Stockport

e-reward (2009) *Survey of Contingent Pay*, e-reward, Stockport

Erickson, W (2004) Connecting engagement with reward, address at the Society for Human Resource Management's Annual Conference, New York

Evaluating Reward Management

Introduction

A cold economic climate makes it more essential than ever to obtain value for money from investment in any HR activity. This particularly applies to reward, which is the most expensive of them all. The best-performing firms, as established by Watson Wyatt (2002), make greater efforts than others to measure reward plan effectiveness.

The CIPD 2009 reward management survey found that only 32 per cent of the respondents assess the impact of their reward practices and no more than 54 per cent could calculate the size of their total remuneration spend (pay, benefits and other financial rewards plus National Insurance Contributions). Just 12 per cent of respondents to the e-reward 2009 survey of contingent pay evaluate the effectiveness of their individual performance-related pay schemes, a remarkably low proportion considering the cost of such schemes and the problems of making them work well.

In their research on the evaluation of changes in pay structures, amongst 15 large employers Corby *et al* (2003) found that only one organization made any real attempt systematically to evaluate the effectiveness of the changes, and most managers were cynical about the value of attempting to do so. The researchers established that 'significant decisions are the outcomes of a social and political process only partly shaped by the evidence.' Rather than spending time and incurring the cost of carrying out detailed monitoring, which would not provide conclusive results, the research indicated that managers often relied on anecdotal evidence. They used an approach to evaluation categorized by Kearns (1995) as 'we think it worked.'

In his classic 1995 article 'On the folly of rewarding A, while hoping for B', Steven Kerr commented that: 'Managers who complain about lack of motivation in their workers might do well to consider the possibility that the reward systems they have installed are paying off for behaviours other than what they are seeking.'

Other researchers and commentators have come to broadly similar conclusions:

> *The study found that few, if any, employers, built in a monitoring and evaluation process as part of the introduction of an individual performance-related pay scheme. This was because most employers did not have clearly articulated objectives for introducing such schemes against which they could measure subsequent success or failure. Furthermore, little thought appeared to [be given to] the indicators that could be used to measure the effectiveness of the scheme and the type of information that should be collected. (Thompson, 1992)*

> *Little evidence demonstrates the efficacy of rewards, although much evidence indicates that rewards and their design loom large in management attention. (Pfeffer, 1998)*

> *Compensation is a complex and often confusing topic. Although compensation costs comprise, on average, 65 per cent to 70 per cent of total costs in the US economy and are likewise substantial elsewhere, most managers are not sure of the likely consequences of spending either more, or less on employees or of paying employees in different ways. (Gerhart and Rynes, 2003)*

> *There are no less than six substitutes that managers often use for the best evidence; 'obsolete knowledge, personal experience, specialist skills, hype, dogma and mindless mimicry of top performers'. (Pfeffer and Sutton, 2006)*

Why evaluate?

Vast amounts of money are being wasted on pay and benefits but organizations are not getting added value from this expenditure because they are not measuring the effectiveness of their reward practices. While the literature and practice in the area of, for example, learning and development, is replete with models and debates regarding the best methodology to apply to judge 'the ROI on training', the reward literature is remarkably silent on this issue.

The reasons for evaluating the effectiveness of reward policies and practices are:

- to establish whether reward innovations are functioning as planned and achieving the objectives set for them;

- to find out how well the established reward practices are working and identify any problems;

- to ensure that value for money is obtained from the different parts of the reward system;

- to provide an evidence-based approach to improving reward practices.

Why don't people evaluate?

Possible reasons for the lack of interest in evaluation include:

- The problem of isolating pay and rewards to assess their effects. A wide range of variables, often intangible, are generally involved. For example, performance management, communications and other factors as well as the plan design will impact on the success of performance-related pay initiatives. Changes in pay are also typically accompanied by changes in associated HR processes, with job evaluation exercises, for example, often accompanied by changes in job content and organization design.

- The difficulty of carrying out controlled research studies and comparative experiments with different approaches to pay and rewards.

- Perceived lack of time and resources to evaluate (even though stronger evidence of effectiveness might lead to more resources being allocated to the reward management function).

- A bewildering array of sources is used to generate management advice. Pfeffer and Sutton (2006) cite references to Shakespeare, Billy Graham, Jack Welch, Tony Soprano, fighter pilots, Santa Claus and Attila the Hun.

- Lack of training and skills in statistics, finance, quantitative methods, research and other relevant disciplines amongst the HR community (although it might be thought that this would be less true about reward practitioners than other HR professionals given the requirement for numeracy and, frequently, their finance background).

- Sheer laziness, especially when practitioners are not being pushed by others to do it (though HR functions are coming under more pressure to justify their existence).

Steven Kerr (1995) commented on this as follows:

One major reason [for failure to evaluate] is that the individuals (in human resources, or organization development) who would normally be responsible for conducting such evaluations are the same ones often charged with introducing the change effort in the first place. Having convinced top management to spend money, say, on outside consultants, they usually are quite animated afterwards in collecting rigorous vignettes and anecdotes about how successful the program was. The last thing many desire is a formal, revealing evaluation. Although members of top management may actually hope for such systematic evaluation, their reward systems continue to reward ignorance in this area. And if the HR department abdicates its responsibility, who is to step into the breach? The consultants themselves? Hardly! They are likely to be too busy collecting anecdotal 'evidence' of their own, for use on their next client.

What can be done about it?

Interesting suggestions on how to evaluate reward have been made by researchers Corby *et al* (2003) Heneman (2002), Kanungo and Mendonca (1988) and Scott, McMullen and Sperling (2006).

Corby *et al* (2003) advise that practitioners should have a realistic view of what is achievable, focus on evaluation in only a few key areas rather than compiling a wish-list, use existing mechanisms such as employee attitude surveys and human capital reports as far as possible, and consider perceptions and qualitative criteria, not just 'hard' cost and business figures.

Heneman remarks that the evaluation of the effectiveness of a strategic reward system is often overlooked among many organizations, but it is an indispensable final step in the process of implementing a compensation programme. Indeed, assessing the effectiveness of any procedure is just as important, if not more so, as its design and execution. Since it is often complicated to evaluate the effectiveness of a reward programme in terms of financial performance, so-called 'soft factors' such as employee behavioural reactions to the programme are sometimes an acceptable replacement.

Kanungo and Mendonca (1988) advocate a final review stage in introducing new reward systems. This consists of reformulating the reward package objectives or redesigning the reward system or both, based upon the diagnosis of the present reward system. At this stage, a great deal of learning takes place, as management reflects on the perceptions and expectations of its employees and their impact on organizational goals. It is also a time for important decisions – not merely to respond in a reactive mode, but more in a proactive stance that considers how best the reward system can be creatively employed to cope with the new challenges that constantly confront a dynamic organization. Therefore, although review is the final step, it is an ongoing process that enables management to keep on top of the situation at all times.

Research into assessing reward effectiveness conducted by e-reward (2009b) found that respondents used the following methods to measure the effectiveness of rewards:

- external market survey: 113 respondents;

- staff attitude survey: 99 respondents;

- benchmarking: 71 respondents;

- internal data analysis: 66 respondents;

- equal pay reviews: 41 respondents.

As one respondent commented: 'Do it! Why would anyone spend £xxm pa and not try and understand each element's effectiveness (and leverage it more)?' Another remarked: 'Build review and continuous improvement practices into all of your reward programmes, but recognize that it is not an activity that will happen overnight. It will require a fundamental shift in your management information and project practices.'

Evaluating reward management involves two activities, as described below: 1) conducting regular reviews to assess the effectiveness of the existing reward system, and 2) establishing the extent to which the objectives of a reward innovation have been achieved.

Reward effectiveness reviews

As recommended by Armstrong *et al* (2010) a reward effectiveness review requires the following seven steps:

1. Identify reward goals and success criteria.

2. Research and collect both quantitative and qualitative information and evidence on existing reward policies and practices from inside the organization. This will include conducting a reward attitude survey (an example is given in Appendix A).

3. Gather information on external reward practices, levels and trends; this can be used to assess the competitiveness and distinctiveness of rewards in the organization, as well as drawing out learning from relevant organizations externally, and from external research on specific reward practices.

4. Use this information to make assessments of the effectiveness of the delivery of reward goals and of the various pay and reward practices.

5. Determine key reward issues to address.

6. Consider possible options and changes to improve the delivery of the reward goals, and assess their strengths and weaknesses relative to the current reward practices.

7. Agree the improvements required to increase effectiveness and plan their implementation.

This logical sequence may look like a good structure for a review but the actual process will depend on the circumstances and needs of the organization. As Mabey *et al* (1998) point out, such approaches provide 'a model of management which is more rational than is achievable in practice'. Cultural and political factors influence perceptions and judgements, and the extent to which people behave rationally is limited by their capacity to understand the complexities of the situation they are in and by their emotional reactions to it – the concept of bounded rationality as expressed by Simon (1957).

However, there are three basic requirements that exist in any survey: 1) an understanding of goals, 2) means of assessing outcomes and impacts related to those goals, and 3) a reasonably systematic approach to interpreting the results of an assessment and drawing conclusions on the issues involved and how they should be addressed.

Reward goals

Reward goals can be expressed in guiding principles (see Chapter 4) or the objectives defined for reward initiatives. Here are some examples:

- Aegon UK: Motivate staff sufficiently so that they will ensure the company remains successful, thereby allowing for continued competitive levels of reward for superior performance.

- British Airways: Support a performance culture.

- BT: Use the full range of rewards (salary, bonus, benefits and recognition) to recruit and retain the best people.

- Colt Telecom: Promote a performance culture that underpins the company business strategy.

- Diageo: Support and enable the talent agenda.

- Financial services company: Reflect the way the organization is changing by encouraging us to be more responsive to customers.

- Friends Provident: Facilitate a real and fundamental top-down change in corporate culture.

- KPMG: Market-leading rewards for market-leading performance.

- Tesco: Develop a more flexible organization.

These goals can be classified broadly under the four headings suggested by Corby *et al* (2003):

- Resourcing: recruitment, retention and employee turnover.

- Behaviour: engagement, motivation and commitment.

- Working practices: flexibility.

- Performance: productivity, profitability.

But none of the objectives listed above sets out any specific quantitative targets against which performance can be measured. The field work carried out by Corby *et al* (2003) found that only 2 of the 15 organizations sought to evaluate the impact of their new pay system on performance, and both were in the public sector. They reported that Customs & Excise, when evaluating its trial of team bonuses, measured financial performance by first establishing a baseline for the six trial sites and three 'blind' control sites, and then carrying out a further review after a year. In addition, one of the trial sites carried out a customer satisfaction survey. Partly because of the limited timescale (one year) and partly because there was 'a lot of noise in the system', to quote the HR manager (ie restructuring and new appraisal and promotion systems), the results were not conclusive. An NHS trust asked staff about the impact of the new pay system on patient care and a small majority thought that the impact was positive.

There is a reason why people don't set quantitative targets – it is rarely if ever possible to be confident about the extent to which reward can impact on performance, and targets therefore look like hostages to fortune. Post hoc measurements of the impact can also be problematic because of the amount of work involved and the difficulty of establishing causation. Corby *et al* (2003) found that managers were sceptical about the process of pay system evaluation, holding the view that the link between a pay system and a given outcome – eg staff attitudes or service/product delivery – was well nigh impossible to prove.

Measures

Ideally, the measurement of the impact of reward would compare actuals and trends with targets, but if it is difficult to set quantified targets this is unlikely to happen. Organizations that do assess reward practices use a wide variety of measures, as established by the CIPD 2009 reward survey and shown in Table 29.1. Resignation rates, staff surveys and performance management data are the most popular measures. Profit and productivity measures are used to a much smaller extent in the private sector.

The possible measures suggested by Armstrong *et al* (2010) are shown in Table 29.2.

Table 29.1   Common measures used to assess reward practices, by sector

Manufacturing and production	Private sector services	Voluntary sector	Public services
• Employee resignation rates (83%) • Staff surveys (71%) • Performance management and appraisal data (64%) • Employee absence/well-being (61%) • Time taken to fill vacancies (55%) • Profit (50%) • Job offer refusal rate (36%) • Length of service distribution (36%) • Percentage of staff participating in staff benefits (33%) • Productivity per employee (33%)	• Employee resignation rates (74%) • Staff surveys (70%) • Performance management and appraisal data (58%) • Percentage of staff participating in staff benefits (51%) • Employee absence/well-being (41%) • Time taken to fill vacancies (40%) • Profit (39%) • Vacancy rate (37%) • Reward budget costs (33%) • Productivity per employee (33%)	• Staff surveys (75%) • Employee resignation rates (67%) • Performance management and appraisal data (67%) • Percentage of staff participating in staff benefits (58%) • Length of service distribution (50%) • Workforce demographics (50%) • Employee absence/well-being (50%) • Vacancy rate (42%) • Time taken to fill vacancies (42%) • Competency/staff skill level (42%)	• Staff surveys (88%) • Employee resignation rates (83%) • Vacancy rate (71%) • Employee absence/well-being (71%) • Performance management and appraisal data (54%) • Customer satisfaction (54%) • Time taken to fill vacancies (50%) • Workforce demographics (50%) • Length of service distribution (46%) • Competency/staff skill level (38%)

Note: Percentage of respondents in brackets.

(Source: CIPD annual Survey of Reward Management, 2009)

Table 29.2 Possible reward evaluation measures

Reward strategy	• Clear reward strategy and annual plan in support of business strategy and plans.
Productivity and reward costs	• Overall staff productivity and return on staff costs versus competition. • Profit, value added or sales per employee. • Total pay and reward costs compared to competition.
Financial and non-financial rewards	• Financial and non-financial recognition for behaviours in line with strategy and values. • Appropriate forms of rewarding performance and contribution in place – individual/team, short/long-term etc. • Proportion of staff covered by methods of rewarding performance and contribution. • Rewards effectively integrated with performance management process. • Risk assessment of bonus plan design – fixed/variable mix, range of performance measures etc. • Clear demonstration of return on costs of bonus.
Employment	• Ratio of job offers/acceptances. • Staff involuntary turnover/resignation rates, and retention of high performance/key skill staff. • Staff turnover and absence levels.
Reward management general	• Actual market position compared to desired. • Take-up and level of activity in flexible rewards. • Equal pay reviews carried out and acted upon. • Quantity, quality and frequency of reward communications – clarity, range of media etc. • Training and evidence of line manager capability.
Engagement and satisfaction with rewards	• Surveyed overall employee engagement levels. • Employee overall satisfaction with pay and rewards. • Employee opinions that rewards are competitive. • Employee opinions that performance is rewarded and managed effectively. • Employee opinions on level of understanding of rewards. • Managers feel reward arrangements are flexible and meet their needs.

Evaluating the impact of reward innovations

The objectives of a reward innovation should be expressed from the outset as part of a business case: 'This is what we propose to do.' 'This is why we propose to do it.' 'This is how much it will cost.' 'This is how the organization and its people will benefit.' Success criteria should be defined for each objective. These could be quantitative – eg a reduction in employee turnover, an increase in employee engagement or reward opinion survey scores. They might often have to be qualitative, in effect completing the statement: 'This innovation will have been successful when… happens'. Examples of possible objectives and associated success criteria are given in Table 29.3 and of an engagement survey in Appendix B.

A model of evaluation as a continuous process is illustrated in Figure 29.1. The final step is to review the whole process by answering the following questions:

- How well have the reward changes been implemented, and to what extent are they delivering on the reward objectives?

- Given what we have learnt, will any changes in design and/or process improve their effectiveness?

- How are we going to review and assess their effectiveness on an ongoing basis and perhaps in some detail after a sufficient time has elapsed to witness the full impact of the changes?

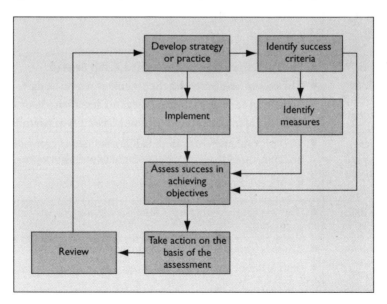

Figure 29.1   A model for evaluation

Table 29.3 Reward objectives and success criteria

Reward innovation objective	Success criteria: This objective will have been successfully achieved when:
Develop perform-ance culture	• Reports of performance reviews show that performance has improved. • There is evidence of improvement from other performance indicators.
Enhance engagement	• Scores in the engagement survey have increased by x%.
Increase overall employee satisfaction with rewards	• Scores in the rewards survey have increased by x%.
Increase key staff retention levels	• Employee turnover for key categories of staff has reduced by x%.
Attract high-quality applicants	• Surveys of new starters reveal that x% of them were attracted by the employee value proposition offered by the firm.
Develop employee value proposition	• There is evidence that attraction and retention rates have improved.
Enhance pay competitiveness	• Survey data show that pay levels are competitive in line with market stance policy.
Increase employee satisfaction with contingent pay decisions	• Scores in the contingent pay section of the rewards survey have increased by x%.
Replace decayed job evaluation scheme and use to develop new grade structure	• The evaluation scheme is accepted as fair by staff. • The cost of administering the scheme is within budget. • Successful appeals against gradings are less than x% of staff. • The cost of implantation does not exceed x% of payroll.
Introduce career-family structure to support career planning	• There is evidence that career ladders defined as competency levels are being used to guide career planning and development.
Reduce grade drift	• There is evidence that upgradings are being properly justified by job evaluation.
Introduce contribu-tion-related pay scheme	• There is evidence that it has improved performance. • Staff feel that the scheme fairly recognizes their contribution.
Conduct an equal pay review and act on it	• Equal pay review is conducted as planned. • Action is taken which reduces the pay gap by x%.
Introduce flexible benefits	• Take-up of scheme. • Level of satisfaction in reward attitude survey.

Evaluating reward systems: six tips

- Ensure that objectives are set for each key element of the reward system.
- Identify evaluation criteria.
- Select an evaluation methodology – data analysis, surveys etc.
- Collect and analyse data.
- Interpret findings.
- Develop and implement programme improvements.

References

Armstrong, M, Brown, D and Reilly, P (2010) *Evidence-based Reward Management*, Kogan Page, London

CIPD (2009) *Survey of Reward Management*, CIPD, London

Corby, S, White, G, Dennison, P and Douglas, F (2003) *Does it work? Evaluating a new pay system*, University of Greenwich, London

e-reward (2009a) *Survey of Contingent Pay*, e-reward, Stockport

e-reward (2009b) *Assessing Reward Effectiveness Survey*, e-reward, Stockport

Gerhart, B and Rynes, S L (2003) *Compensation: Theory, evidence and strategic implications*, Sage, Thousand Oaks, CA

Heneman, R L (2002) *Strategic Reward Management: Design, implementation, and evaluation*, Information Age Publishers, Greenwich, Conn

Kanungo, R N and Mendonca, M (1988) Evaluating employee compensation, *Californian Management Review*, **31** (1), pp 23–39

Kearns, P (1995) *Measuring Human Resources and the Impact on Bottom Line Improvements*, Technical Communications Publishing, Hitchin

Kerr, S (1995) On the folly of rewarding A, while hoping for B, *Academy of Management Executive*, **9** (1), pp 7–16

Kerr, S (1999) Organizational rewards: practical, cost-neutral alternatives that you may know but don't practice, *Organizational Dynamics*, **28** (1), pp 61–70

Mabey, C, Salaman, G and Storey, J (1998) *Human Resource Management: A strategic introduction*, Blackwell, Oxford

Pfeffer, J (1998) *The Human Equation: Building profits by putting people first*, Harvard Business School, Boston, MA

Pfeffer, J and Sutton, R I (2006) Evidence-based management, *Harvard Business Review*, **84** (1), 62–74

Scott, D, McMullen, T D and Sperling, R S (2006) Evaluating pay program effectiveness: a national survey of compensation professionals, *WorldatWork*, **15** (3), pp 47–53

Simon, H (1957) *Administrative Behavior*, Free Press, New York

Thompson, M (1992) *Pay and Performance: The employer experience*, IMS, Brighton

Watson Wyatt (2002) *Strategic Reward Survey*, Watson Wyatt, New York

Responsibility for Reward

Learning outcomes

On completing this chapter you should know about:

- The role of the reward professional
- The reward role of line managers
- How to use reward consultants

Introduction

Reward strategy is formulated and actioned by people. Top management is in charge but HR professionals, especially reward specialists, are actively involved. Increasingly, however, it is line managers who have the responsibility for implementing reward policies and practices. This chapter deals with the roles of the reward professional and line managers. The chapter concludes with a brief note on the use of management consultants.

The role of the reward professional

HR and reward specialists develop and implement reward strategies, policies and processes, administer and audit existing systems, and provide advice and guidance to line managers. They deal with employee relations issues such as involvement, communications, negotiations, appeals and grievances.

The key roles for 'high value-adding' reward professionals as described by Brown and Christie (2005) are:

- keeping up with leading-edge thinking and approaches and staying ahead of the game on environmental trends;

- tailoring approaches and arrangements to suit the unique goals, character and culture of the organization, and measuring and demonstrating the value added by them, always .in the context of business and organizational knowledge and understanding;

- developing and applying administrative expertise to deliver highly efficient and well-serviced reward processes;

- assessing and influencing the culture of the organization, with responsibility for reward communications;

- operating as an integral part of the HR and business team and providing a reward strategy framework that coordinates all the policies and practices designed to engage and motivate staff to deliver the organization's strategy.

Perhaps the most valuable contribution reward professionals make is to develop reward arrangements that support the business strategy, working with line managers as consultants to assist in this – as one head of reward put it to Brown and Christie: 'Shifting our culture to a more performance-oriented business and aligning reward policies accordingly'. Yet research conducted by the CIPD in 2005 found that significant portions of the function's time are still being absorbed in routine administrative activities and responding to immediate queries and crises.

At Citigroup the role of reward specialists is to bring parties together to facilitate and make sustainable and effective decisions, share experiences, transfer successes and encourage a focus on long-term sustainability and future development.

The role of reward in Diageo comprises five key elements:

- align the reward approach with the business strategy;

- support and enable the talent agenda;

- provide clear principles to enable decision making in the business;

- enable every employee to understand why they get paid what they get paid;

- have a customer service ethic that results in great execution.

Qualities required

Reward specialists need the skills and expertise to design and manage complex systems that meet the needs of users. Strategic thinking is necessary but this is not enough; service delivery is equally important. Reward innovations can affect people deeply and they will resist or at least resent changes that they perceive to be detrimental. It is therefore essential for reward specialists to have change management skills.

The 150 respondents to the 2007 e-reward census of reward professionals stated that the top four qualities required were: 1) business awareness, 2) numeracy and analytical ability, 3) technical reward skills and 4) influencing skills.

The CIPD performance and reward profession map highlights the following competencies required by senior reward professionals:

- understand the organization's strategy, performance goals and drivers;

- speak the language of the business and understand how reward can drive performance;

- know how to translate organization strategy into performance and reward strategies and operating plans;

- consider constituent parts of the reward and recognition package for the organization, ensuring that there is coherence in the overall offer and that it is aligned with and will drive the organization's strategy and plans;

- manage the delivery of planned reward programmes;

- challenge executive leadership to adopt a performance-driven culture underpinned by a strong performance management capability.

Organization of the reward function

The e-reward 2007 census found that 78 per cent of the respondents' organizations had a reward centre of expertise and 40 per cent had a shared service centre.

The role of a reward centre of expertise is to develop and contribute to the implementation of reward strategy, formulate reward policies, provide professional support to business policy for corporate HR, and deal with complex issues raised by the shared service centre if one exists. Its members act as consultants in assessing and designing reward solutions.

The role of a reward shared service centre is to handle some or all day-to-day administrative (transactional) processes. Its activities are centralized into one common unit, often using call centre technology and/or intranet systems for online self-service.

The following are three examples drawn from e-reward 2008 case studies of organizations with centres of expertise and shared service centres:

- Lloyds TSB has two centres of expertise, a service delivery function and four dedicated HR sections The head of pay policy and employee benefits is responsible for external benchmarking, flexible benefits, pay reviews, pay reporting, total reward statements, bonus schemes and reward communications. In addition, there are four reward business partners for each of the main divisions.

- National Australia Bank Group adopts the Ulrich 'three-legged stool' model with a reward centre of expertise and – dealing with all HR matters, including reward – a shared services centre and seven business partners.

- PricewaterhouseCoopers operates a centralized human capital shared services centre alongside a number of centres of expertise, including one dedicated to reward. The role of the three senior managers in the centre is to act as business partners and provide advisory and consultancy services.

Role of line managers

The trend is to devolve more authority to line managers for decisions on pay increases awarded in periodical individual pay reviews and, less commonly, fixing rates of pay on appointment or promotion. This process reflects the general tendency to devolve more decision-making authority to line managers on the grounds that, if managers are to be held accountable for the management of their resources and the performance of their teams, they ought to be given scope within guidelines to determine how their team members should be rewarded. It is also argued that line managers are close to individual employees and are in the best position to know how they should be valued.

The arguments for devolving more authority to line managers for pay decisions are powerful but it is still necessary to ensure that reward policies are followed, pay decisions are consistent and fair, and pay costs are controlled. Policy guidelines as described in Chapter 28 are required to spell out the basis upon which rates of pay are fixed and reviewed. Managers should be expected to keep within their pay budgets.

There is also the issue of the capacity of line managers to carry out their devolved role effectively. As Brown and Purcell (2007) commented: 'How can your reward arrangements ever be effective if your managers can't manage and communicate them?' They described a vicious circle of:

- line managers being given increasing responsibility to manage ever-more complex pay processes, with reduced levels of HR function support;

- managers lacking the skills to cope with these increased demands;

- HR therefore not trusting line managers and restricting their discretion in these processes, which leads to managers feeling disempowered and employees not understanding and trusting them either.

Line managers should not be expected to make crucial pay decisions without training in the processes involved and briefing on the policy guidelines. Reward or HR specialists have a crucial role not only in monitoring the implementation of pay policies but also in providing advice and guidance, always with the aim of developing the skills and confidence of the line managers with whom they are involved.

The major difficulties presented by devolving more responsibility to line managers are that:

- They may not have the knowledge or skills to carry out their responsibilities.

- They may be unenthusiastic about this aspect of their role, which they would see as a diversion from their real job – 'What's the HR department there for?' they might say.

- It might be difficult to achieve acceptable standards of fairness, equity and consistency without policing managers so closely that devolution becomes a farce.

The answers to these problems are to develop clear guidelines for managers on the factors they should take into account in making pay decisions, brief and train managers on how to interpret and apply the guidelines, provide continuing but not oppressive support from HR when required and monitor pay decisions to ensure that guidelines are being followed but, again, not oppressively.

Respondents to the 2007 e-reward survey made the following comments on the line manager's role in managing contingent pay schemes:

- ensure managers have bought-in to the scheme and are trained and fully understand its operation;

- make sure managers are willing and able to differentiate high performers from the rest;

- ensure managers can also manage poor performance;

- make certain the messages coming from management and more senior levels are the same and that, overall, decisions made are consistent.

Using reward consultants

Reward consultants are frequently engaged to help with major development projects by providing expertise and additional resources (an extra pair of hands). They can conduct diagnostic reviews and employee attitude surveys, and provide disinterested advice. Effective consultants add credibility and value because they have the knowledge of good practice and project management that may not be available in the organization. The e-reward 2007 survey found that 72 per cent of the respondents had employed them.

To make good use of consultants it is necessary to:

- spell out terms of reference, deliverables and the timetable;

- take great care when selecting them, to ensure that they have the expertise and experience required and will 'fit' into the organization, and that they produce realistic and acceptable indications of the cost of their fees and expenses;

- meet and vet the consultant who is going to carry out the work, not just the senior consultant who presents the proposal;

- agree up front how they will work alongside line management, HR and trade unions, and the basis upon which the project will be monitored and controlled;

- ask for regular reports and hold 'milestone' meetings in order to review progress and costs.

It seems that reward specialists are good at applying these precepts – 97 per cent of the respondents to the e-reward 2007 survey who had used consultants were satisfied with them.

Line managers' responsibility for reward: six tips

- Devolve as much responsibility for reward decisions to line managers as possible consistent with the need to ensure that reward policy guidelines are followed and reward decisions are fair and reasonably consistent.

- Ensure that reward policies and guidelines are clear and unequivocal.

- Brief managers thoroughly on the policies and guidelines.

- Train newly appointed managers (and retrain existing managers as necessary) in their reward management responsibilities.

- Provide guidance and help from HR or reward specialists whenever it is needed.

- Monitor reward decisions and advise line managers on alternative approaches as necessary.

References

Brown, D and Christie, P (2005) From octopus to sharks: the current and future roles of the rewards professional, *WorldatWork Journal*, second quarter, pp 6–14

Brown, D and Purcell, J (2007) Reward management: on the line, *Compensation and Benefits Review*, **39**, pp 28–34

CIPD (2005) *Reward Management* Survey, CIPD, London

e-reward (2007) *Reward Census*, e-reward, Stockport

e-reward (2008) *Reward Census Case Studies*, e-reward, Stockport

Appendix A: Reward Attitude Survey

Please state the extent to which you agree or disagree with the following statements by placing a circle around the number that most closely matches your opinion.

		Strongly agree	Agree	Disagree	Strongly disagree
1	My contribution is adequately rewarded	1	2	3	4
2	Pay increases are handled fairly	1	2	3	4
3	I feel that my pay does not reflect my performance	1	2	3	4
4	My pay compares favourably with what I could get elsewhere	1	2	3	4
5	I am not paid fairly in comparison with other people doing similar work in the organization	1	2	3	4
6	I think the organization's pay policy is overdue for a review	1	2	3	4
7	Grading decisions are made fairly	1	2	3	4
8	I am not clear how decisions about my pay are made	1	2	3	4
9	I understand how my job has been graded	1	2	3	4
10	I get good feedback on my performance	1	2	3	4

		Strongly agree	Agree	Disagree	Strongly disagree
11	I am clear about what I am expected to achieve	1	2	3	4
12	I like my job	1	2	3	4
13	The performance pay scheme encourages better performance	1	2	3	4
14	I am proud to work for the organization	1	2	3	4
15	I understand how my pay can progress	1	2	3	4
16	The job evaluation scheme works fairly	1	2	3	4
17	The benefits package compares well with those in other organizations	1	2	3	4
18	I would like more choice about the benefits I receive	1	2	3	4
19	I feel motivated after my performance review meeting	1	2	3	4
20	I do not understand the pay policies of the organization	1	2	3	4

Appendix B: Employee Engagement Survey

Please circle the number that most closely matches your opinion.

	Strongly agree	Agree	Disagree	Strongly disagree
I am very satisfied with the work I do	1	2	3	4
My job is interesting	1	2	3	4
I know exactly what I am expected to do	1	2	3	4
I am prepared to put myself out to do my work	1	2	3	4
My job is not very challenging	1	2	3	4
I am given plenty of freedom to decide how to do my work	1	2	3	4
I get plenty of opportunities to learn and develop	1	2	3	4
The facilities/equipment/tools provided are excellent	1	2	3	4
I do not get adequate support from my boss	1	2	3	4
My contribution is fully recognized	1	2	3	4
I am treated fairly at work	1	2	3	4
I find it difficult to keep up with the demands of my job	1	2	3	4

	Strongly agree	Agree	Disagree	Strongly disagree
I have no problems in achieving a balance between my work and my private life	1	2	3	4
I like working for my boss	1	2	3	4
I get on well with my work colleagues	1	2	3	4
I think this organization is a great place in which to work	1	2	3	4
I believe I have a good future in this organization	1	2	3	4
I intend to go on working for this organization	1	2	3	4
I am not happy about the values of this organization – the ways in which it conducts its business	1	2	3	4
I believe that the products/services provided by this organization are excellent	1	2	3	4

Index